GW01276076

INCORPORATING THE NOTES OF THE LATE COMMANDER
OF THE WIKING DIVISION, SS-OBERGRUPPENFÜHRER AND
GENERAL OF THE WAFFEN-SS FELIX STEINER

EUROPEAN VOLUNTEERS

by Peter Strassner
Translated by David Johnston

J.J. Fedorowicz Publishing

EUROPEAN VOLUNTEERS

By Peter Strassner
An English translation by David Johnston

Copyright 1988 by
J.J. Fedorowicz Publishing

Originally Published in German
As EUROPAISCHE FREIWILLIGE, by
Munin Verlag, Osnabruck

Published by
J.J. Fedorowicz Publishing
267 Whitegates Cr.
Winnipeg Manitoba
Canada R3K 1L2

Printed in Canada
ISBN 0-921991-04-5

Typesetting - Designtype

Printed and Bound by -
Hignell Printing

EDITOR'S ACKNOWLEDGEMENTS

I wish to thank the following individuals who have contributed to the publishing of this book:

David Johnston - Translation
Miles Krogfus - Proofreading
Michael Horetsky - WIKING cuffband
Roger Bender - Support and valuable advice

I also wish to thank you the reader for purchasing this volume. The first book, THE LEIBSTANDARTE I, has met with tremendous enthusiasm and so I have intensified my efforts to bring you more quality translations of the best German books which up to now have been denied to those who do not read German. Many more books are being either translated or planned and will be published in the coming years. Suggestions for further titles are always welcome.

John Fedorowicz

Books published by J.J. Fedorowicz Publishing
    THE LEIBSTANDARTE I (1 SS Panzer Division)
    THE LEIBSTANDARTE II
    EUROPEAN VOLUNTEERS (5 SS Panzer Division)
    OTTO WEIDINGER (Waffen-SS Knight's Cross Recipient)

In Preparation:
    THE LEIBSTANDARTE III
    DAS REICH I (2 SS Panzer Division)
    TIGER (History of a Legendary Weapon)
    OTTO KUMM (Waffen-SS Knight's Cross Recipient)

CONTENTS

Author's Foreword		1
The Division's Commanders		3
Introduction		3
I.	**ESTABLISHMENT AND DEPLOYMENT**	6
	The Division's Origins	6
	The Commanders	7
	Experiences With the European Volunteers	9
	Drill and Training Grounds	10
	Transfer to Silesia	10
	The March into the Polish Assembly Areas	11
II.	**ACTION IN THE EAST**	12
	Lemberg—Tarnopol—Proskurov—Shitomir	12
	The Situation at the Beginning	12
	First Test Against the Enemy	13
	Tarnopol—Satanov—Husyatin—Proskurov	16
	The *NORDLAND* Rgt. Stops a Soviet Army Corps	18
	GERMANIA Rgt.'s Defensive Success	21
	Combat in the Battle for Uman	22
III.	**THROUGH SMELA—KORSUN TO THE DNEPR**	26
	The Battle near Smela	26
	Crossing the Dnepr—Establishing the Bridgehead	29
	The Capture of Kamenka and Enlarging the Bridgehead	33
	Kremenchug—Opening the Dnepropetrovsk Bridgehead	35
	A Destructive Battle of Encirclement	41
IV.	**THE WINTER BATTLE OF ROSTOV**	42
	A Daredevil Dane	43
	Advance Against Stiffening Resistance	44
	Ghostlike Soviet Cavalry	46
	In Combat With Superior Enemy Forces	47
	First Retreat	50
	In the Winter Position on the Mius	52
	A High Ranking Visitor from Finland	57
	Change of Command	58
	Turn of the Year 1941/42	59
	With *I./WESTLAND* in the *"Felsennest"*	61
	Bringing Men and Material up to Strength	62
	Attack on Rostov	64
V.	**FORWARD TO THE CAUCASUS!**	69
	In Giant Steps across the Steppe	70
	Crossing the Kuban	72
	The Battle for Krapotkin	75
	The Laba Sector and Belaja	78
	The *"Brandenburger"*'s Coup de Main	78
	Conquest of the Maikop Oil Region	79
VI.	**BATTLE IN THE CAUCASUS**	80
	Transition to Defence	80
	From the Caucasian Forests to the East Caucasus	85
	A Difficult Operation	87

	The Capture of Malgobek	92
	The Finns Take Hill 701	94
	Defence between Fiagdon and Alagir	96
	Battles in the Tschikola Valley	100
VII.	**RETURN TO THE DONEZ**	102
	Departure from the Caucasus	102
	Change of the Year 1942/43—The Race to Rostov	103
	In Combat with Armoured Group Popoff	110
	The End of Armoured Group Popoff	112
	In the Suchoj-Torez Sector	114
	Departure of the *NORDLAND* Rgt. and the Finnish Battalion	116
	Arrival of the Estonian Battalion	117
VIII.	**DEFENSIVE BATTLE FOR KHARKOV AND ISJUM**	119
	The Estonian's Baptism of Fire	121
	The Battle for Golaja-Dolina	122
	The Defensive Battle for Kharkov and the Dnepr	123
	"Gruschki Grave"	125
	In Combat with Partisans and Enemy Paratroops	127
IX.	**DEFENSIVE BATTLE ON THE DNEPR**	130
	Battles on "Foxtail Island"	131
	Sturmbrigade *WALLONIEN* Reaches the WIKING Division	132
	Battle at the Irdyn Marsh	133
X.	**THE TCHERKASSY POCKET**	135
	The Pocket Wanders to the West	137
	The Wait for Relief	138
	The Last Act	142
	Breakout to Freedom	146
XI.	**"FORTRESS KOVEL"**	156
	Gille Flies to Kovel	156
	Ostuf. Nicolussi-Leck's Success	158
	The Freeing of Kovel	163
	The Tank Battle of Maciejow	165
XII.	**FROM BIALYSTOK TO WARSAW**	170
	The Division's "Toughest Assignment"	171
	Formation of IV. SS-Panzerkorps	173
	The First Defensive Battle for Warsaw	174
	The Second Defensive Battle	176
	The Third Defensive Battle	179
	The Battles in the "Wet Triangle"	183
XIII.	**BATTLE IN HUNGARY**	191
	"Dorpmüllern to Julischka"	191
	The Encirclement of Budapest	192
	The First Relief Attempt	194
	The Second Relief Attempt	199
	The Third Relief Attempt	200
	Irresistable Retreat	202
	The Arrival of 6. SS-Panzer-Armee	206
	The Evacuation of Stuhlweißenburg	206
XIV.	**SURRENDER AND IMPRISONMENT**	210
XV.	**DOCUMENT APPENDIX**	215

XVI.	LIST OF COMMANDERS	272
XVII.	DECORATIONS	279
XVIII.	*WIKING* DIVISION STRENGTH REPORTS	291
XIX.	OFFICIAL LIST OF ENGAGEMENTS	293
XX.	*WEHRMACHT* BULLETINS	295
XXI.	TABLE OF FIELD POST NUMBERS	297
XXII.	*WAFFEN-SS* SERVICE RANKS	300
XXIII.	GERMAN TERMS AND ABBREVIATIONS	301
XXIV.	FOOTNOTES	304
XXV.	SOURCES	314

Foreword to the First Edition

Should American professor George H.Stein's supposition (*Geschichte der Waffen-SS*, Düsseldorf 1967,S.259) that the *Waffen-SS* was, "the largest multinational army ever to fight under one flag", prove to be correct, then certainly the multinational division WIKING, named in retrospect by its founder and first commander, is due recognition. The WIKING Division represented the model for this type of unit within the Waffen-SS. Through it all the theories required for the operation of an integrated unit on this large scale were worked out and tested, enabling the Division to operate effectively in victory and defeat. That the *Waffen-SS* Division WIKING, in whose ranks fought volunteers from eight European nations, distinguished itself in the course of the war in the east, does not need to proved by this history.

The main difficulty in preparing this work was that no complete war diary for the Division is available. The number of documents which survived the war's end and the post-war period and which were made available by ex-members of the Division is unfortunately modest and thus the documents appendix must remain limited in certain areas. Additional sources which proved useful were the memoirs of General Steiner, which were written following the war, the notes of General Gille and the personal diaries of former officers Phleps and Dorr. Special thanks go to their families for providing these valuable documents. No small thanks are due the Division's last commander, Ullrich, as well as the *Truppenkameradschaft WIKING e.V.*, which provided the author with assistance and placed its small archive at my disposal.

Although they came from all parts of Europe, the Division's volunteers were united by a strong bond of comradeship which survived the capitulation and without which this unit's successes would not have been thinkable. It is these men therefore, wherever they may live, in spite of persecution, defamation and constant neglect, who are still proud to have been "*Wikinger*".

Munich,fall 1968
Peter Strassner

Foreword to the Second Edition

Earlier than expected the release of an improved second edition has been made necessary. The presentation of a previously unknown original order by former war correspondent Hans Ulrich Frhr. von Wangenheim sets right the facts and units involved in the battle for Rostov in 1942.

At this time I wish to express my thanks to all readers who contributed to this history by word or deed. Thanks also go to those former members who contacted me by letter or spoke with me.

To those critics who took offence at the book's title, let it be said that the phenomenon of the *Waffen-SS*, and especially that of the European volunteers who provided a model for integration in a "multinational division", as the WIKING was designated by General Felix Steiner, is now beginning to be examined more closely, above all by the American government and military.

It must be stated again at this point that the former volunteers from the European nations—the largest number coming from the Netherlands with 55,000 men—made their fateful decision out of the most noble of motives. Those who like the author saw them fight and die, have the duty to testify on their behalf and to stand in their defence.

Munich, February 1971
The author

Foreword to the Third Edition

The fact that a third edition of "*Europäische Freiwillige*" has become necessary, confirms the fact that the attempt to form and test a European volunteer movement in the 5. *SS-Pz.-Division WIKING* has lost none of its interest, nor even fascination. Naturally that attempt cannot be a guide in the completely changed present day situation for achieving the old and new goal, namely a united Europe. But one should consider for a moment that these men, frequently misjudged by their countrymen, who decided to join in Germany's fight against bolshevism and out of their yearning for a united Europe volunteered willingly, had anything but material interests in mind. They, who were prepared to make the highest sacrifices, may serve today as examples of decisive action toward the realization of an ideal for those responsible Europeans who are determined not to allow it to fall to ruin.

Munich, June 1977
Peter Strassner

Commanders of the *WIKING* Division

1.12.1940 to 5.1943
Steiner, Felix
SS-Obergruppenführer and General of the Waffen SS, holder of The Knights Cross of The Iron Cross with Oak Leaves and Swords, last Commanmander in Chief of the 11.Panzer Army. Died on 12.May 1966.

5.1943 to 6.8.1944
Gille, Herbert, O.
SS-Obergruppenführer and General of the Waffen SS, holder of The Knights Cross of The Iron Cross with Oak Leaves, Swords and Diamonds, was last Commanding General of IV. SS-Panzerkorps. Died on 26.December 1966.

6.8.1944 to 9.10.1944
Mühlenkamp, Johannes
SS-Standartenführer, holder of The Knights Cross of The Iron Cross with Oak Leaves,last Inspector of Panzer Troops Waffen-SS.

9.10.1944 to end of war
Ullrich, Karl
SS-Oberführer, holder of The Knights Cross of The Iron Cross with Oak Leaves, last commander of 5.SS-Panzerdivision WIKING.

Introduction

The 5. SS-Panzerdivision, which comprised soldiers from different nations, was by virtue of its structure and character one of the most interesting divisions of the Waffen-SS. Under predominantly German leadership and orders, Danish, Estonian, Finnish, Flemish, Wallonian, Dutch, Norwegian and Swiss volunteers fought shoulder to shoulder with their German comrades from within the Reich as well as Volksdeutsche from Hungary, Rumania, Poland, Yugoslavia, and the Soviet Union. What significance the common battle experiences of members of different European nations in combat during World War Two might have for modern integrated national and international armed forces is left to the judgement of the experts.

There are of course numerous examples in the history of warfare of military units comprising members from different nations serving under a unified command. These historical examples do not, however, serve as comparisons for the *WIKING* Division which was unique in several respects. In the first place, the Division contained Europeans who had decided to volunteer for service in a war with which their own countries did not identify. In the case of the Dutch or Norwegian volunteers, they were confronted by the fact that the Wehrmacht in which they served was the same one which occupied their homelands. Their voluntary entry into the German armed forces was, for the most part, condemned by their fellow countrymen. Following defeat, most of the volunteers were forced to suffer extraordinarily as a result of their undoubtedly courageous decision as they encountered the many pitfalls placed before them by the governments of their own nations.[1] Another reason why comparisons between past integrated combat units and *WIKING* are not valid is that the European volunteers served only in the war against bolshevism. The non-German members of the *WIKING* Division refused to bear arms against the English, French or Americans. They acted from the conviction that through their service they were defending, above all, their own countries but also their vision of a united Europe, from the threat of bolshevism. That this concept was problematical and controversial did not alter the fact that it guided the foreign volunteers of the *WIKING* Division. Many of them, especially the Estonians and Finns, had seen the danger of bolshevism and were prepared to offer themselves in defence against it. Former commander Felix Steiner has commented extensively on the diversity of reasons which brought volunteers from eight nations to this "multinational division".[2]

Thus the responsible commanders and officers, but also the noncommissioned officers, saw themselves assigned a completely new task which they approached with great enthusiasm. "Create a high grade operational division of comparable quality!"; this was the sole command given to the Division's first commander, SS-Brigadeführer and Generalmajor der Waffen-SS Felix Steiner. So little had his superiors recognized the problems involved in such a task, that they failed to make Steiner aware of its related political objectives. Therefore the solution of all unit related problems was left solely to him. It is not surprising that in the beginning mistakes were made and that only gradually did things get in stride and a closely knit unit emerged from the initial conglomeration. Within the Division, because of its composition, no substantial problems arose with the command or the unit's employment. Naturally problems were not to be solved using the conventional methods of the Prussian-German tradition in which the commanders of the Waffen-SS, including Felix Steiner, had been brought up. New untried methods had to be found in order to bring up and train the young troops. Thus the commission held a great risk for the new division's commanders; fortunately they were young and unbiased. Certainly they lacked the experience of longstanding peacetime officers, but in the previous years they had learned to approach the most difficult situations with confidence, were full of spirit, intelligent and open minded. After completion of their service in the Reichsarbeitsdienst (Reich labor service), they had undergone the hard training of the SS-Verfügungstruppe and in the early campaigns had shared good and bad times, hardship and fear with their comrades. They then passed through the Junkerschule, the SS equivalent of the Wehrmacht's Kriegsschule, which provided the Waffen-SS with future officers for the force.[3] In combat, however, they learned that leadership was determined more by fulfillment of duty then by rank. This concept contributed to the fact that every member of the division always felt himself to be a part of the whole.

Many young officers and NCO's were all too inclined to pay little heed to the indispensible need in modern warfare to preserve one's own life. They were continuing to emulate the old Prussian soldier's maxim which Walter Flex once formulated as:

"To serve as a lieutenant means to live as an example for your men.

Dying as an example is thus a part of it.

The *WIKING* divisional command demanded categorically that every battle be fought with sufficient forces and that lives not be sacrificed through disregard or excessive daring.

Certainly the rule of example and duty demanded a higher degree of readiness for action and performance of duty of the officers and NCO's than from the rank and file. But at the same time no less important was the responsibility of the commander for the lives of his men. This realization in particular was always taken seriously. Nevertheless, after the war was lost, numerous reproaches were raised against the Waffen-SS denouncing the force for alleged self-destructive fanaticism or lack of regard for losses, because of a conscious or unconscious misinterpretation of the facts that the regiments and divisions of the Waffen-SS retained their composure in battle and were often enough thrown into desperate situations as welcome support for the front. It is not objective to reproach them for the resulting heavy casualties.

The strong inner unity of the force was based directly on the conviction of the volunteers that they were being led by officers who were militarily competent as well as conscientious. Without this constant firm responsibility of command, it would not have been possible to create an elite unit, which WIKING admittedly was, from a collection of young individuals of different nationalities in so short a time and to maintain its quality throughout the entire war up to the bitter end. Indeed, since the war the foreign members of the Division themselves have never, despite the condemnation they have received, reproached their German comrades and superiors but have testified in moving fashion to their membership in the unit.

This piece cannot be ended without remembering the fallen of the Division. Which frontline soldier does not remember a good comrade who gave up his life for an ideal that appeared to give his life meaning? For this reason his death and all the other deaths have not been senseless. In memory to them, the fallen of the WIKING Division, a piece by the poet Florian Seidl:

> And sometimes they call me from the table
> and stand demandingly before the doors outside,
> and stand demandingly in the middle of the room;
> there is stillness and at the same time a roar.
>
> They ask sternly, as never a man has asked,
> asking too about my last journey:
> "What no more then dared hope for,
> you returned home, how do you bear this mercy?
>
> You stood with us for years in the ranks,
> have not been sacrificed and not surrendered;
> answer yourself: do you preserve the consecration?
> Yes or no?"—They ask and drift away.
>
> Yes or no? It burns like an old scar.
> Do you live as tall and free, as those who died?

I. ESTABLISHMENT AND DEPLOYMENT

The Division's Origins

With the cancellation of operation "Sealion", the planned invasion of England, on 12. October 1940 the 3. Motorized Infantry Regiment *"Germania"* and the reserve units of the SS-Verfügungsdivision were released. Included in the new Wehrmacht formations ordered by the "Oberste Befehlshaber" (Hitler) in early 1941 was the creation of an SS-Division (mot) utilizing manpower from the racially related nations (Norway, Denmark and Holland[1]). The new division was formed from the units released from "Sealion": the young *WESTLAND* Regiment in Munich and the *NORDLAND* Regiment in Vienna and Klagenfurt. On 9. November 1940, the former commander of the SS-Inf.Regiment (mot) - *DEUTSCHLAND*, SS-Brigadeführer Felix Steiner, was assigned the task of setting up the new division.

At Munich, the site of the divisional staff, the first preparations were already underway. SS-Sturmbannführer Ecke, until now Waffen-SS liason officer in the Führer's headquarters, had begun the setting up of the divisional staff and the assignment of accomodation and assembly areas for the units. Accomodations for the divisional staff and the artillery were in the area between Augsburg and Munich, while the remaining units were scattered all over the Reich.

Effective from 1. 12. 1940, SS-Brigadeführer Steiner was named Division Commander of 5. SS-Inf.Div.(mot) *GERMANIA*, in whose formation were combined the designated units.[2] In addition came SS-Artl.Rgt. 5 from Dachau, the Div.Pi.Btl. setting up in Dresden, the Nachrichtenabteilung stationed in Nuremberg, A.A. 5 setting up in Munich-Freimann, and the Nachschubtruppe located in Berlin-Lichterfelde. Thus for the present time two thirds of the new division was not under the direct control of the divisional command.

The constant confusion of the names of the *GERMANIA* Division with its regiment of the same name resulted in requests that the Division be renamed. Based on a unit recommendation, the Division was renamed by the Führerbefehl of 21. 12. 1940 (diary nr. 518 secret from 29. 1. 1941) as 5.SS-Inf.Div.(mot) *WIKING*.

The order read:

Berlin, 21. 12. 1940

The Führer and Supreme Commander

I decree that the former SS-Division of the SS-Verfügstruppe carry the name

SS-Division *"Reich"*,

the newly created nordic SS-Division carry the name

SS-Division *"Wiking."*

signed Adolph Hitler

The 5. SS-Division (mot) thus acquired its ultimate title which was to be spoken with respect by friend and foe alike. In August 1942, it would be presented with a sleeve band with the inscription *WIKING*, which was put on by all the Division's units, while the Grenadier regiments wore their own sleevebands bearing the name of the particular regiment.[3] From 9. November 1942, the Division was reformed into 5. SS.Panzergrenadier-Division *WIKING*.[4] In February 1944 with its designation as 5. SS-Panzer-Division, *WIKING* became a new Panzer Division thus attaining its ultimate form. Troop inspections, officer briefings and wargames took place in the presence of the divisional commanders in the first weeks and months of the Division's formation, in Munich, Vienna, Klagenfurt, Dresden, Berlin and Nuremberg. The regimental commanders constantly shuttled back and forth between the command posts of their battalions. During the setting up period, training was not permitted to be neglected. Equipment still left something to be desired, however, with the exception of the *GERMANIA* Regiment and II. Abt.Artl.Rgt. taken from the *REICH* Division, weapons and vehicles were still lacking. Only gradually did these arrive after energetic efforts by the Division, while the arrival of young troops was at the same time almost complete. Consequently a systematic training program could not be implemented until January 1941.

"It is always the initial form that a young unit receives, which directly determines its future development and which is decisive for its success in war and peace. Experience shows that mistakes in the formative stages are extremely difficult to correct and most appear only in a serious crisis"; so wrote General Steiner in his personal memoirs. This Division's initial form was stamped with the mark of its commanders, who could scarcely have been better. All of these men acquired the highest decorations during the course of the war and became generals.

The Commanders

The Division's first commander was SS-Brigadeführer and Generalmajor of the Waffen-SS Felix Steiner. He was inducted in March 1914 as a seventeen year old officer cadet into the 5th East Prussian Inf.Rgt. and during the First World War fought on the eastern and western fronts. During the war he was wounded and awarded the Iron Cross, First Class. In the Reichswehr he had already successfully passed the General Staff examinations by 1922. After his retirement in 1934, Steiner became an advisor to the head ot the training organization and a short time later chief of that department. After the establishment of the new Wehrmacht he took command of III./SS-Rgt 1. In June 1936, he was named as commander of the SS-Regiment *DEUTSCHLAND* in Munich. He took part in the Polish and western campaigns as commander of a regimental battlegroup and was awarded the Knight's Cross on 22. 8. 1940. Later he earned the Oak Leaves and Swords as well. Even so critical a historian as Gerald Reitlinger was forced to admit that Steiner could "almost pass as a Wehrmacht general".[1] And George H. Stein maintained that,"of far greater importance was the influence of former officers of the regular army such as Paul Hausser, Felix Steiner, Herbert Gille, Wilhelm Bittrich and Georg Keppler. If the divisions of the SS sometimes could not be told from those of the Wehrmacht, then it was thanks in no small part to the efforts of these men."[2]

The SS-Inf.Regiment *GERMANIA*, a veteran regiment of the Verfügungstruppe which had received thorough peacetime training and education, stood under the command of SS-Standartenführer Reichsritter von Oberkamp. Already a proven leader in the western campaign, von Oberkamp had been an Hussar officer in the First World War and a company commander in a Gebirgsdivision in the Reichswehr.

The SS-Inf.Regiment *WESTLAND* had developed into a good combat unit under the firm hand of its commander, SS-Standartenführer Hilmar Wäckerle. A volunteer Bavarian cadet in 1917, Wäckerle later fought with the Freikorps. Commander of 1. Company of the "Württemberg Political Squad" in 1934, Wäckerle later led I. Btl. SS-Reg. *GERMANIA* in Hamburg. With a cadre from this unit Wäckerle was transferred to the newly-created III./SS-Rgt. *DER FÜHRER* in Klagenfurt, which he led in May 1940 in the assault on and breakthrough of the Grebbe position. He was assigned as Regimental Commander in the formation of SS-Rgt. *WESTLAND* where he worked with dedication to form the cadre of German personnel and the Dutch volunteers into a closely-knit unit. His idealism provided the foundation for the attitudes and later proving of this Regiment which he did not survive; during the first battle on 2. July 1941, he was shot dead by a straggling Russian soldier while inspecting captured enemy weapons.

The training and upbringing of the SS-Regiment *NORDLAND* was left solely to its commander, SS-Standartenführer Fritz von Scholz. This splendid officer, who was extremely popular with his troops, had retired from the army in 1918 as an Oberleutnant in the artillery with the highest Austrian medal for bravery, the Goldenem Tapferkeitsmedaille. Several days after he died a hero's death at Narwa in 1944, this brave soldier was awarded the Swords.

Another trusted officer was the commander of Artillery Regiment 5., Herbert O. Gille, formerly an active artillery officer in the Imperial German Army. In the VT, Gille, as company commander, battalion commander and Abteilung commander, had proven himself to be a shrewd leader and organizer. He later relieved Steiner as commander of the *WIKING* Division.

Each one of these regimental commanders was an individualist with a strong personality and left his mark on the new units. Their influence remained with the regiments they had created throughout the entire war.

In the case of the *GERMANIA* Infantry Regiment though, a new commander took over after barely a year. Reichsritter von Oberkamp was named Inspector of Infantry (Pz.Gren.) In2 and was replaced by SS-Standartenführer Jürgen Wagner. Wagner had won his spurs as a batallion commander with the - *DEUTSCHLAND* Regiment in two campaigns. Wagner came from an old Prussian officer family and had been a cadet in his youth. Like his father, the former commanding general of the XVII. Prussian Army Corps, his pronounced originality, known throughout the army, could at the same time be a virtue and a disadvantage. It proved advantageous for his regiment, however, which was the nucleus of the Division and remained so until the end of the war.

The *WESTLAND* Regiment also bore the unmistakeable traits of its first commander, who was killed at the outset of the Eastern Campaign. It was strictly disciplined, correctly brought up and carefully trained. Its second commander was the former Imperial Rumanian General of Mountain Troops, Phleps a.k.a. Stolz, who had reported to the Division as a volunteer. After a successful career as a general staff officer in the Imperial Army, Phleps, a resident of Siebenburg and son of a prominent Kronstadt family, entered the Rumanian army when his homeland was incorporated into the Rumanian state. He reached a position of prominence and influence as creator of the Rumanian mountain troops, commander of the War

College and temporary adjutant to the King. In spite of his former high service positions he was not hesitant to take over the WESTLAND Regiment, which he led with the skill of a seasoned commander. Phleps fell on 21. 9. 1944 as a General directing the defence of his homeland.

Of the divisional units, SS-Hauptsturmführer Freiherr von Reitzenstein led Aufklärungsabteilung 5. He was in every respect suited for his position. Commanding SS-Panzerjäger- Abteilung 5 was SS-Sturmbannführer Maack. A former First World War officer, he left a high civilian political position to become a career soldier.

SS-Hauptsturmführer Stoffers, commanding SS-Flakabteilung 5, came from the SS-Inf.Reg. *GERMANIA*. An excellent company chief, he now became acquainted with the duties of a Flak commander. His conscientious attitude ensured that his troops received sound military and technical leadership.

Where SS-Pionierbtl. 5 was concerned, the formative hand of its commander SS-Sturmbannführer Klein was apparent in the unit's operations until war's end. The commanders of these auxiliary units, including the Divisionsnachshubführer, were initially beyond the direct control of the Division command. However, they were experienced World War and Reichswehr veterans and were able to handle the extra responsibility which fell to them.

The Nachrichtenabteilung, which included European volunteers but consisted mainly of Germans, had found an able officer and comrade in its commander SS-Sturmbannführer Kemper, as had Sanitätsabteilung 5 in SS-Sturmbannführer Dr. Unbehaun, who was at the same time Divisionsarzt. The accomplishments of the doctors and first aid personnel during the war had to be seen to be appreciated.

Experiences with the European Volunteers

One of the new and difficult problems faced by the commanders and their officers and NCO's was the handling of the Germanic volunteers. The Division IIb's strength report of 18. 8. 1941 made on 22. June showed a total of 1,143 Germanic volunteers comprising 631 Dutch, 294 Norwegians, 216 Danes, 1 Swede and 1 Swiss. Notwithstanding losses of 121 killed and wounded, (the losses of the *WESTLAND* Rgt. are not included), three months later on 19. 9. 1941 the Division counted 1,416 Germanic volunteers including 821 Dutch, 291 Norwegians, 251 Danes, 45 Flemish and 8 Swedes.[1] Despite overcoming the initial communications problems, things began to become more difficult. Certainly the young men from abroad were very openminded. Everything they saw and experienced was new to them. The young Norwegians who mostly came from the small towns and villages of their large country and who had grown up in a comparatively close family circle, saw the old imperial city of Vienna as the manifestation of western history. The young Danes in Klagenfurt experienced the beauty of mountain country for the first time and soon felt right at home in the easy cheerfulness of their training garrison. The Norwegians and Danes found the military training more difficult than their German comrades who had the advantage of premilitary training and service in the Reichsarbeitsdienst. As men these young people were a varied group. The Danes were more robust and less sensitive than the Norwegians, loved good food and drink, but now and then were obstinate and tended to be strongly critical. Encouragingly though, they were approachable and had a strong sense of fairness and comradely spirit. The Norwegians on the other hand worked harder and were more serious and contemplative. They were quieter and of an often youthful carefree nature, but once they placed their trust it remained firm. In their military achievements they developed a nearly totally instinctive awareness which led them to be somewhat careless with regard to their own safety.

The Dutch serving with the *WESTLAND* Regiment in Munich were perhaps of a stronger individuality. In the beginning these recruits were a source of trouble for their German instructors, who considered them of use only for barrackgrounds duty. After the humiliation of defeat and because of national sensitivity they required of their German instructors a particularly sympathetic understanding. Many of the latter may not have realized until having seen them in action what excellent soldiers these Dutch volunteers really were. In January the political circle around Mussert and other related organizations pulled out.[2] About 120 volunteers were granted discharges from the service. The remainder, however, worked themselves month by month into an excellent unit which soon stood comparison with its sister regiment *GERMANIA*.

Drill and Training Grounds

In April 1941, the Division was assembled around the Heuberg training grounds in the area of Balingen—Ebingen—Sigmaringen. At this same time it was incorporated into the army.[1] Day and night exercises in battalion, regiment and division strength combined with battle-ready motorized deployments and target shooting with all weapons followed the completion of small unit training in the training areas. After eight weeks of basic training, the Division had become a dependable operational unit whose usability in the field, as Steiner remembered, was attested to by the commanding general of the XXXX. Panzerkorps, General der Panzertruppen Frhr. Geyr von Schweppenburg, whose 25. Infanteriedivision was stationed at the Münsingen training grounds in Württemberg. This recognition was double in that the subtle training which would have been provided in peacetime had to be dispensed with. Well-prepared despite a comparatively short training period, its units getting into their stride welded together by comradeship, the Division looked forward to its coming assignments with confidence.

Transfer to Silesia

And they did not have long to wait. The first rumors started to circulate while they were still at the training grounds. When handbooks about the Soviet Union were given out several weeks after the transfer of the Division to Silesia, there were no more doubts. With great seriousness the Division's units had to acquaint themselves with the particulars of the Russian method of conducting war and as far as possible, gain an understanding of the Russian mentality.

This was the situation at the beginning of June 1941. The Division was transported by rail from the Württemberg training grounds through Czechoslovakia to Silesia and assembled in the area north and northeast of Breslau between Oels, Militisch and Wohlau. There it came under the command of 1. Panzerarmee of Generaloberst von Kleist, who had previously commanded the VT- Division in the west. The Division was under the Corps Headquarters of General der Infanterie Gustav von Wietersheim, who knew the Waffen-SS from the western campaign and had accompanied several division commanders and their battle groups during the surprise attacks on Poitiers and Angoléme.

The brief sojourn in the Silesian area was used to review and ensure supplies of vehicles, weapons and clothing as well as the establishment of liason with the higher commands. Instruction on the political situation, the Geneva convention, conduct in enemy territory and the combat methods, mentality and organization of the Red Army supplemented the daily program. Time was used as available to become familiar with the Silesian country and people. Short and long-range driving practice in the surrounding areas combined the driving-in of vehicles with sightseeing. The limited time available did not permit a comprehensive training program, however there was enough time for some additional weapons training.

The March into the Polish Assembly Areas

The assembly of powerful motorized units in Silesia left no more doubts as to where their dangerous journey was taking them. The radiators of their vehicles pointed clearly to the east and it was rumored that the bulk of the infantry forces of the German Reich were already assembled in Poland and East Prussia. It came as no surprise, therefore, when the Division crossed the border of the Reich near Gross-Wartenberg on 18. June 1941 with orders to march to Wielun. The motorized march to the actual assembly areas took place in burning heat over endless sandy roads. They crossed Poland via Konskie and Baranow in three days. From Passow on they travelled only by night without lights. On the night of 20/21. June, the Division reached its assembly area west of the German-Soviet demarcation line and immediately disappeared in the villages and forests near Lublin. No one was permitted to move outside his rest area without permission, so as to give no indication to enemy aerial reconaissance of the assembly of large German forces. But the march had been interrupted only for à brief rest.

The first impression that the young German soldiers and their foreign comrades received of the east was not encouraging. Not only was the countryside foreign and the roads in terrible condition, but the people and their villages were miserable and run down. Much was different than in the homes they had left behind and which they now carried with them as fond memories.

II. ACTION IN THE EAST

Lemberg—Tarnopol—Proskurov—Shitomir

"Now look at this map for yourself, Steiner.", said the Commander in Chief to the Waffen-SS General, who had just reported at the headquarters of Panzergruppe. 1. Referring to the map which lay spread out before them he pointed out a powerful Soviet armored concentration east of the demarcation line. "Look at the strong Russian tank forces concentrated near Berdichev and to the south, and answer my question if that doesn't look like the preparations for an offensive whose two motorized spearheads north and south of the Pripet marshes are already visible here!" The commander of the *WIKING* Division nodded his head. In fact, the Russians had planned their deployment exactly as had the Germans. Their armoured forces were sited far to the rear but would quickly be available after a day's march and were massed in two powerful groups as Generaloberst von Kleist had pointed out. Their appearance in the first days of the fighting could be counted on.

It is crystal clear to the writers of today when they cite "the surprise attack of Nazi Germany against the peace loving Soviet Union"; however this is in no way clear. Military historians like von Tippelskirch[1] and Fabry[2] point out that the Soviet deployments were superior in strength to those of the Germans. On the first day of the war, 140 German divisions met 184 large Russian formations deployed in depth. It should be mentioned that the concentration of such significant forces on Russia's western borders and the order for these units to alert status on 10. April 1941, preceeded by a considerable period of time the movement of German offensive forces into the eastern areas of the Reich. Therefore, the Russian preparations could not have been in response to a recognized buildup of German offensive forces, since this did not begin until several weeks later. Generalfeldmarschall von Manstein[3] also referred to the existence of a threat to the Reich by demonstrable Russian military preparations and the chief of the Wehrmacht High Command, Generalfeldmarschall Keitel[4], commented in a similar vein in his memoirs written shortly before his death. For the opinion from the political viewpoint one can refer to the memoirs of von Ribbentrop.[5] Questions concerning the reasons for the German attack on the Soviet Union will always be asked, but to this time the answers are in no way clear cut or convincing.

The Situation at the Beginning

On 22. June, the German armed forces launched an attack against the Soviet Union between the Carpathians and the Baltic and met an enemy massed in depth. In its assembly areas on the demarcation line, Army Group South, comprising 17. Armee northwest of Lemberg, Panzergruppe 1 in the center of the front east of Zamosc and 6. Armee as the northern group east of Cholm, faced the Soviet 5th and 6th Armies with a total of 16 rifle divisions, 3 cavalry divisions, 3 motorised divisions and a tank brigade. South of Lemberg was the 16th army with 14 rifle divisions, 2 cavalry divisions, a motorised division and two tank brigades. Its appearance opposite 7. Armee had been reckoned with, since it was not tied down to the area at the edge of Carpathians. Deep in Soviet territory were strong mobile forces gathered in two groups, a northern group to the north of Proskurov with 2 cavalry divisions, a motorized division and 3 tank brigades and a southern group between Czernowitz and Proskurov with 3 cavalry divisions, a tank division, 2 motorized divisions and a tank brigade. Opposite the Rumanians were two Soviet armies with powerful tank and motorized forces.

Army Group South's operations sector was separated from those of the two northern Army Groups by the impassable Pripet marshes and in Soviet territory divided by two large through roads, the southern through Lemberg—Tarnopol—Proskurov—Vinnitza and the northern through Cholm—Rovno—Novo Volinsk—Shitomir—Kiev, which offered the main line of movement for the intended advance to the east, especially for the Panzers.

By the evening of 22. June, powerful elements of 6. Armee had broken through enemy positions east of Cholm, paving the way for a thrust into the heart of the Ukraine towards the Dnjepr by the combined Panzerkorps of Panzergruppe 1., while 17. Armee southeast of Zamosc had to fight desparately to make any noticeable headway in its attack against part of the Soviet 16th Army. But after the breakthrough in the Proskurov area by 6. Armee, Soviet tank forces were set in motion and moved up through Rovno towards Luck where they ran headlong into the advancing XXXXVII. Panzerkorps under General Kempf and III. AK (mot) under General der Kav. von Mackensen, resulting in the first large tank battle of the Eastern Campaign.

The fighting was hard but the Soviets were no match for the mobile Panzer tactics of the Germans and their KV-1 tanks were too unwieldy compared to the German Panzers III and IV. So the Germans emerged victorious and were able to make gains followed closely by infantry units of 6. Armee in the direction of Kiev—Berdischev to the east.

First Test Against the Enemy

Of Panzergruppe 1.'s units gathered in the rear, only the divisional artillery of 9. Panzerdivision and the SS-Division *WIKING* had been moved up to provide preparatory fire for the assault on the Bug on 22. June. The reinforced - *GERMANIA* Regiment was detached from the Division and assigned to clear the wooded country west of Luck through which both of the leading Panzerkorps were advancing. The Regiment quickly completed the assignment and returned to the Division. XIV. Panzerkorps was ordered by Heeresgruppe to swing south in the direction of Lemberg to assist the hard pressed 17. Armee and regain the initiative. So on Sunday, 25. June, the *WIKING* Division finally marched out of its assembly area 25km east of Cholm towards Zamosc to the south in order to reach the south road. On the morning of the following day, the Division passed through Zamosc and the march continued to Rava-Ruska where XIV. Panzerkorps deployed in two columns with 9. Panzerdivision as the northern, moving from Rava-Ruska toward Tarnopol, and *WIKING* the southern through Lemberg toward Tarnopol. After 17. Armee had gained some breathing room by beating off attacks by enemy reserves thrown into the fighting, and as the enemy had decided to break off the border battle, the way east across the Soviet frontier appeared to be open. While the vanguard of the Division, Gefechtsgruppe Wäckerle, had passed through Lemberg in the direction of Tarnopol, it was the Gebirgsjägern of 1. Geb.Div. who succeeded in clearing the heights to the east and opening the way for the fast units to drive eastwards and lead the way deep into enemy territory for the following infantry.

It was at this time that Artl.Rgt. 5 saw its first action. The unit's 8. Battery had received orders to turn off the main road with the vanguard of the NORDLAND Regiment after Tarnopol and proceed north through Zlotschov and Zbaracz, securing the Division's northern flank against enemy tank attack. Wedged in halted columns, the Btl. Adjutant finally reached the battery and delivered the operational orders: "Advance with one gun and sufficient ammunition to assist the infantry antitank weapons and the Aufklärungsabteilung in combatting enemy tanks." Immediately the unit's number one gun, named "Peter" after their home regiment's commander, SS-Standartenführer Peter Hansen, the chief's vehicle and the munitions carrier were made ready to go. Then they were on their way, following behind the Battery Chief. Finally they sighted the column of vehicles. The personnel carriers and motorcycles were camouflaged behind bushes and trees. Drivers and gunners had dismounted and were covering the terrain to the east. Machine gun and cannon fire from the Panzerspähwagen could be clearly heard. The Division's eight wheeled Spähwagen was likewise directing its fire to the east. The NORDLAND Regiment's commander, SS-Staf. von Scholz, was standing with the battalion commander in the shadow of the trees at the side of the road briefing the adjutant. Numerous enemy tanks and vehicles could be seen through the glasses, and then also with the naked eye. The Platoon Leader, Unterscharführer Brutscher, moved the gun into position on the road, the ammunition flew out of the carrier and soon the order rang out, "Enemy tanks directly ahead, range twenty two hundred, impact fuse, fire!" The command had scarcely been given when the first round roared out of the barrel. The impact appeared in the midst of the mass of tanks and vehicles; a vehicle was left halted. Those of the crew who could, ran for their lives. Round after round, either impact fuse or armor piercing, struck the enemy column, which was forcing its way with great difficulty through the rising terrain. Then the motorcycles and Spähwagen moved out to finish off the confused enemy forces. "Peter"'s gun crew were unable to directly ascertain the results of their fire but that did not detract from their contribution to the success; a total of 48 tanks and 100 other combat vehicles were later counted on the battlefield. The danger to the Division's left flank had been removed, and the advance towards Tarnopol could resume.

The following is an excerpt from a report by the chief of 2./SS-Pz.Jäger-Abteilung, SS-Hauptsturmführer Böhmer, on a fight near Mszaniec-Ditkowce on 3. 7. 1941: "2./SS-Pz.Jäger-Abteilung was attached to the SS-Regiment - NORDLAND marching as the vanguard of the Division on the Zloczov—Tarnopol road. At approximately 10.00 hours, when about 2 km. west of Zborov, the Regiment was diverted to the north to advance through Zalosce to Noviki and link up with the spearhead of 9. Pz.Div. which was engaged in combat there. The Regiment was formed into three Kampfgruppen, the company advancing with Kampfgruppe Polewacz, and the medium platoon, of which I was a member, providing the advance guard.

While passing through Olejow, the advance guard came under light gunfire, which did not stop the advance. During a halt prior to entering Olejow a change of orders was received. Kampfgruppe Polewacz was given the assignment of securing Zalosce to the north and east. For this purpose the medium gun was detached to 1./SS-NORDLAND. The company which had given up its gun to 1./NORDLAND followed with Kampfgruppe Fortenbacher which had received orders to push through Brovika to Noviki. As it passed through Maniuki, Standartenführer von Scholz' company was moved to the front. On reaching the north end of Mszaniec the following picture presented itself: 1 gun of 8./SS- A.R. 5

and 1 platoon 4./SS-*NORDLAND* were already in position and firing on the enemy, which, consisting mainly of tanks and artillery, was defending on Hill 428 (about 3 km. southeast of Mszaniec). At the request of the commander of III./A.R. 5, I moved the platoon on the north edge of Mszaniec to the left in order to provide cover for the artillery setting up position in the town. I moved the other two platoons through Mszaniec in order to reach the most favorable position from which to fire on the enemy. An Untersturmführer of 15./SS- *NORDLAND* reported that a small hill about 400 meters northwest of Ditkowce was already in our hands. I then decided to place the second platoon in position on this hill and intended to stagger the medium platoon forward along the main road to provide flanking fire. This intention was, however, not carried out, as during the time I was briefing the 2nd platoon, the medium platoon moved over, setting up position about 1600—1800 meters south of Mszaniec, where they were already very close to the enemy. The planned action took place to be sure, but the medium platoon was in position too close to the enemy and in grave danger; but as it turned out, that was all the better. From a range of 500—800 metres we opened fire on the enemy. We discovered that the hill on which 2. Platoon had taken position was in the midst of a cornfield which was still full of Russians, who now opened fire on the guns and several men from 7./SS- *NORDLAND* who had taken up positions there. The chief of 7./SS-*NORDLAND* was killed and at the Scheidt gun the gun commander and two men were wounded. SS trooper Dlugosch was also killed there. Gunners Schütze and Zeile were killed when a shot from a Russian tank struck the upper shield and ammunition boxes of Steinfeld's gun; Steinfeld himself jumped to the gun and continued firing alone. SS-Rottenführer Lorenz showed particular guts; after his number 1 and 2 gunners fell out, he continued firing alone, though he was already wounded. He declined first aid, saying that there was time for that later. He had the medic pass him ammunition and continued firing until he collapsed. The town of Ditkowce, which was full of Russians and from which the Company was taking heavy fire, was fired on using H.E. and set ablaze. In addition, 5 enemy tanks and various artillery tractors were destroyed and machine gun and rifle nests silenced with H.E. rounds. The medium platoon also shot up an enemy column of about fifty vehicles with tanks and guns. At approximately 18.00 hours, the medium platoon was moved up to Brovica as advance guard and destroyed an infantry gun with a direct hit. The crews of 3 tanks which were advancing behind the gun then climbed out of their vehicles and fled. The tanks fell undamaged into our hands. The enemy near Mszaniec had been estimated at the strength of a division. In the night we advanced farther, right up to the outskirts of Noviki. The battle ended at about 18.30 hours. In this action the company had fought almost exclusively without infantry support."[1]

As well as achieving their first success as soldiers, the Division's young volunteers were introduced to the horror of war at the outset of the Eastern Campaign; a horror to which even the experienced frontline soldiers reacted with shock and revulsion. The Division's motorcycle patrols scouting ahead of the advance through Lemberg, reported from Leichenbergen thousands of murdered civilians in the courtyard, halls and cellars of the GPU prison: innocent Ukrainian victims of the retreating Soviets.[2]   The men of the *WESTLAND* Regiment also received an example of the bitterness that the fighting would entail; the Regiment's commander, SS-Standartenführer Wäckerle, and part of his staff, were shot from behind by Russians at dawn on 2. July as they drove off to provide cover to the north of the advance route. They were buried by their comrades the same day in the presence of the Division commander, who acknowledged Wäckerle's heroic death in a special order.[3] SS- Standartenführer Diebitsch was named as temporary commander of the *WESTLAND* Regiment.

On 4. July, the Division staff was located in Tarnopol. The Corps Headquarters of XIV. Panzerkorps had likewise taken quarters there. In the morning, the Division commander was ordered before the commanding general. General von Wietersheim gave him an oral briefing on the complete situation and explained the goal of Army Group South; to attack the retreating enemy with Panzergruppe 1 from the north and throw him back across the Stalin Line, encircling him west of the Dnjepr. In addition, XIV. Panzerkorps, after pushing back the enemy forces opposite it, would wheel north in order to complete the envelopment on the northern wing of the army group.

In connection with the situation, General von Wietersheim made General der Waffen-SS Steiner aware of the contents of an OKW order issued to corps commanders, concerning the "qualification of war jurisdiction in the area of Barbarossa". It stated that punishable acts committed by members of the Wehrmacht against the civil population would not result in prosecution. The commanding general certainly did not expect the answer which Steiner then gave him,"No rational unit leader could comply with such an order. Under those circumstances even the best units would run wild and morale would suffer. Discipline would decline and with it the moral worth and combat value of the unit would disappear. On these grounds I feel justified in referring any offence against the inhabitants to the military courts for prosecution."[4] The generals were also in agreement concerning the second OKW order which stated that all captured Soviet commissars were to be shot by their captors on the spot; they wished the war to be conducted fairly, "as it has always been the practice of our army to do." The subordinate commanders never learned of the orders issued by the Wehrmacht High Command.

Tarnopol—Satanov—Husyatin—Proskurov

It poured rain. Usable roads quickly became morasses of mud. So XIV. Panzerkorps decided to deploy on a wide front across the Slutsch and open this sector for the following 17. Armee. As the Corp's southern group, the *WIKING* Division was to advance to the Slutsch with two assault groups, a main column to Satanov and a secondary column to Husyatin. It was important to force a crossing over the Slutsch and push on in the same direction to Proskurov.

However, reconaissance at dawn on 5. July reported to the Division large enemy forces on the move. Aerial reconaissance reported: long enemy columns on the Kopyczynce—Husyatin road, on the rail line numerous freight cars.[1] The advancing Division ran into the enemy forces and became embroiled in heavy fighting. After II./*WESTLAND* broke into Touste, Oberführer Phleps, the new Regimental Commander who had just arrived, took command of the *WESTLAND* Regiment. At midnight, the experienced staff officer sent the Kampfgruppe, with the reinforced I./*WESTLAND* as the new vanguard, into Husyatin with the object of winning a crossing over the Slutsch there. In fact, von Hadeln's battalion took the crossing near Hsuyatin by surprise attack and stormed through the town to the outskirts. III./*WESTLAND* followed while the last battalion, II./*WESTLAND*, which had turned to secure the southern flank, became involved in heavy fighting in which SS- Hauptsturmführer Miklos, chief of 5./*WESTLAND*, was killed.

But the enemy did not give up. Newly arrived Soviet units went to the attack southeast of Husyatin but were repulsed by II./*WESTLAND*. The situation became ever more critical. The enemy, now concentrated in the south, attempted to take possession of the bridge over the Slutsch but was repulsed by 9./*WESTLAND*. All of 7. July the battle swayed back and forth. Then an advance guard of 1. Gebirgsdivision arrived, relieving the situation.[2] Now II./*WESTLAND* could be relieved and the Battalion freed to join the resumption of the advance southeast towards Olkovice, which was to begin at 20.45 hours. On the following day, the enemy was shaken off and after being relieved by 5. Gebirgsdivision the Kampfgruppe prepared for the advance on Proskurov after the enemy opposite I./*WESTLAND* had also been driven back to the northeast. The way east was now open. At 19:30 hours, the vanguard of the Kampfgruppe met the Division's main column, which was advancing by way of Kusmin, at Rosiosna and took the town the same evening.

The fighting on the Slutsch near Satanov was equally bitter. On 5. July, as the Division's main column marched east, the advance guard, the reinforced II./*GERMANIA* under the command of SS-Hauptsturmführer Kreuzer, was encircled by retreating Russian columns after it had stumbled onto them in the early morning fog. Fortunately, III./*GERMANIA*, held up by a combat of its own, was in the right place to launch a timely attack and free its encircled comrades.

The advance on the Slutsch now continued as an undertaking by the reinforced II./*GERMANIA*. As a precaution, a reconaissance troop of Pioniere and artillery and a platoon from Bridging Column Pi 5 were added. The enemy had apparently reached the safety of the east bank with strong forces. The bridge itself appeared to be intact. Advancing members of the lead company tried to take the bridge by surprise attack, but at the last minute it was blown up. Speed was now essential if the Soviets were to be prevented from digging in. The commander of the advance guard, SS-Sturmbannführer Jörchel, recognized the opportunity and threw the Pionier platoon of his leading company across the river on inflatable rafts. The covering artillery of I./A.R. 5 had moved quickly into position and was firing on the opposite shore before the Russians recognized the danger. The remainder of the battalion quickly followed, climbed the east bank and attacking with assault parties drove the Soviets from the nearest houses. From there they attacked as planned in an attempt to reach the eastern edge of the town. This attempt succeeded but the Soviets were not shaken off. They dug themselves in several hundred meters east of Satanov and with reinforcements rushed from the east began to lay a ring around the weak bridgehead. II./*GERMANIA* went over to the defensive and dug in. During the night of 5./6. July, work went ahead on the construction of a temporary bridge and further reinforcements from the *GERMANIA* Regiment were moved across the river. The reinforced Gefechtsgruppe von Scholz was likewise moved into this sector so that following the completion of the bridge, it could follow Gefechtsgruppe *Germania* across. For the time being it deployed in the woods and hollows on the west side of the river and later reconnoitered both flanks and its rear.

Meanwhile, during the night the Russians launched repeated attacks against II./*GERMANIA* on the east bank. Reserves had to be sent in. In the morning, as anticipated, the enemy began air reconnaissance over Satanov. Shortly thereafter the first enemy warplanes appeared and attacked the defenders on the eastern side of Satanow and the bridge with bombs, without, however, hindering the crossing by *GERMANIA*. By midafternoon on 6. July, strong elements of the Regiment were already across the river. A battalion of artillery was on the east side of the river and set up in firing positions in the bridgehead, while the other two battalions were firing on enemy movements in the rear from their positions on the west bank.

On the morning of 7. July, following a short bombardment by A.R. 5, the planned attack from the bridgehead by Gefechtsgruppe von Oberkamp against the enemy positions was launched, driving the enemy back several kilometers. The attack was supported by Luftwaffe warplanes. By the evening, the - *GERMANIA* Regiment, after bitter fighting, had pushed the enemy back so far that a motorized follow-up appeared possible. Therefore, the regimental commander sent a fast battalion consisting of two Kradschützen companies, 2./Panzerjäger-Abt. 5, an infantry gun platoon and a Flak platoon from 1./Flakabteilung 5 under the command of Hstuf. Kreuzer, to immediately pursue a path cross country to Kuzmin. But it was too soon. In the evening dusk the battalion ran into the withdrawing Russians, were attacked by them and forced to go over to the defensive. During the fighting, Ostuf. Kesper, the chief of 15.(Kradschützen) Company and an outstanding officer, was killed. There, near the old Russian border, he was buried in a soldier's grave. The battalion withdrew under cover of darkness to a line of hills to the west and set up defensive positions. In the morning, reconnaissance revealed that the enemy had withdrawn. Aufklärungsabteilung 5, reinforced with heavy weapons, in particular 1. Battery Flakabteilung 5., a light battery and Panzerjäger, set out in pursuit of the enemy under the command of SS-Stubaf. Freiherr von Reitzenstein, followed closely by the again advancing Gefechtsgruppe von Scholz, into which had been incorporated the majority of the artillery. The advance on Proskurov got under way and encountered the first determined resistance near Kuzmin. The regimental vanguard attacked immediately and by 16:00 hours the town was in its hands. An assault party from 6./*WESTLAND* and 1. Platoon 3./Pz.Jäger-Abteilung 5 succeeded in breaking through near Proskurov where they linked up with the Division's main column. Shortly thereafter, the new vanguard, *GERMANIA*, also reached the objective where in the heat of battle it briefly exchanged fire with its own units. At 21:00 hours, the regimental adjutant of Gefechtsgruppe Stolz arrived at the divisional headquarters to report that the regiment near Rosintna was at the Division's disposal.

Severe thunderstorms and rain on the night of 8./9. July rendered the roads impassable. The advance was to continue at 06:00 hours but the hand of nature had made this impossible. The war of pursuit in the battle of the frontiers seemed in any case to have ended, but new battles for the Stalin Line loomed in the days ahead. The Division commander thanked all the units in a Tagesbefehl (Order of the Day).[3]

The NORDLAND Regiment Stops a Soviet Army Corps

Overall the situation at this point in time looked as follows: XIV.Panzerkorps and the other two Panzerkorps of Panzergruppe 1. had simultaneously engaged the enemy to the north near Polonje at Novograd-Wolinski and broken through the fortifications there. On 7. July, XXXXVIII. Panzerkorps took Berdichev while III. Panzerkorps, operating on the northern flank, took Shitomir on the 9th, creating a springboard for a thrust to the east and southeast. According to the plan, XIV. Panzerkorps was to be inserted between these two Corps. To this end, it was first to drive through Shitomir behind III. Panzerkorps and then veer off through Skwira to Biala-Zerkov. Undoubtedly the rapid breakthrough on the Kiev highway had also come as a surprise to the enemy. This development represented a serious threat, as III. Panzerkorp's 13. Division pursued the retreating Russians through Shitomir in the direction of Kiev along the vital north road. For the enemy it became a question of self-preservation to stop Panzergruppe I's advance through energetic counterattacks. These were launched with unexpected consistency and tenacity. At the front near Berdichev, the new 26th Soviet Army was thrown against the advancing German armoured forces. The Soviet forces which counterattacked southward were unable to halt XXXXVIII. Panzerkorps or to hinder its march into the rear of their main force west of Uman. But they did compel III.Panzerkorps' 13. Panzerdivision to withdraw to the west and go over to the defensive near Fastov where it was pinned down by furious assaults the whole day. The situation was all the more critical as 6. Armee was held up near Novo-Wolynsk and to the east by the the attacking 5th Soviet Army. The unprotected northern flank now gave the enemy the opportunity to outflank III. Panzerkorps; an opportunity which he recognized and pursued singlemindedly. In this highly dangerous situation the spearhead of XIV. Panzerkorps arrived at Shitomir. General von Wietersheim now faced a difficult decision; proceed as ordered with the decisive operation in the enemy's rear following XXXXVIII. Panzerkorps through Skwira—Biala Zerkieff, or hurry to the assistance of the hard pressed III. Panzerkorps. He decided on the move to the southeast but detached Gefechtsgruppe von Scholz (reinforced Rgt. *NORDLAND*) which was approaching in a forced march, to III. Panzerkorps. General von Mackensen immediately diverted the Gefechtsgruppe northwards to deploy along the Kiev road between Sdwish and the Terterov river in order to protect his threatened northern flank.

Standartenführer von Scholz acted quickly. First he threw an advance Battalion consisting of 15. Kradschützen Kp. with an antitank platoon and light infantry guns (1.I.G.) northwards to Orasdorin. Their orders were to reconnoitre the northern flank and to provide a forward defence for the rest of the Regiment, which was moving up through Shitomir, while it deployed.

"Situation unclear. Unidentified light signals ahead of us and to the side". So reported 2. Panzerjäger-Abteilung 5's war diary on 13. July 1941. In addition, there is a description of the events by the Commander of the advance battalion, SS- Ostuf. Klapdor:

"The *NORDLAND* Regiment, using the good Shitomir—Kiev paved road—a boon for both vehicles and men—reached the Korostychev area. On 16. July, the Regiment took up defensive positions between Sdwish and III. Panzerkorps' open northern flank. Here we saw burned-out German tanks, but continued on to reconnoitre the Shitomir-Radomysl road as ordered. The highly valued VW-Kübelwagen and *NORDLAND*'s Kradschützen Company, reinforced with a Pak Platoon and infantry guns, moved north in the oft practiced march formation. Twenty five km. north of our own positions we ran into a Panzerspähtrupp from 13. Panzerdivision. Far ahead of its own lines in the free area on the wings of a great operation, the motorized reconnaissance unit is in its element. Familiar with maps and compass, relying on the observation tactics of the Kradschützen and the courage of the drivers, we forged ahead seeking to make visual contact with the suspected enemy. But the farther north we drove, the less it appeared that we would find him there, so we turned eastward toward Radomysl which lay on our east flank. Near Glukov we reached terrain which rose to the east toward a ridge crossed by a ditch fronted by bushes and then fell away flat to the Tschepowitschki —Radomysl road. From the ditch we had a wide view of the terrain to the east. Taking position, we were spellbound by the picture which lay before us: scarcely 1,000 meters from us were Russians. In wide open peacetime formations and without any security, endless columns marched southwards. Then another column with a combat strength of a battalion appeared. I made my decision quickly; we would prepare an ambush with all available weapons. The northern and southern flanks of our positions were secured by strong patrols. At 15.50 hours, the column had passed so far as to show us their broad flank. Then disaster struck the careless Russians. Simultaneously all light and heavy machine guns, infantry guns and antitank guns opened fire. The confusion was indescribable. Shells struck amid the thick crowds and the machine guns exhausted belt after belt of ammunition. After about a quarter of an hour they formed their first organized resistance and a further twenty minutes later the first Soviet riflemen deployed to attack. Now it was time for us to disappear! The terrain which fell away to our rear facilitated our withdrawal. The first enemy riflemen didn't come until the rearguard had vacated the heights and by then all they could see of us was a cloud of dust.

A new decision had to be made when the report was delivered to the Gefechtsgruppe. The Russians' target had to be Radomysl. After consideration we decided to move up to Radomysl and regain contact with the enemy. That had to be our goal. In the late afternoon, Radomysl came in sight. The main part of the city lay on the north side of the Terterov at a large bend in the river. We were able to enter the south part of the city fairly easily using the cover of gardens and houses. The houses were deserted which was suspicious. Dismounted, we took positions at the south bank. A strong patrol under Ustuf. Pauli was to check the situation in the northern part of the city. Pauli, accompanied only by his messenger, was to cross the damaged wooden bridge first before waving forward the rest of the patrol. I decided to see for myself what was going on.

Scarcely had we started across the planks when all hell broke loose. Radomysl was in enemy hands. The only way back was under the bridge hand over hand from one beam to another. Crawling on the ground under the covering fire of our MG's we reached our bullet spattered positions, exhausted. Now it was time to get out. In groups we made a fighting withdrawal to the south away from the enemy, losing one man. But the Gefechtsgruppe now knew what it would have to deal with in the next days and could make all the necessary defensive preparations to adequately meet the forthcoming attack."

And that is how it happened. The fighting by Gefechtsgruppe von Scholz on the northern flank of III. Panzerkorps was tough but successful. The enemy attacked with great determination but made no headway. With our numerically weak forces this was an amazing result, which is not easily explained. Fortunately, in addition, there is at hand the statement by no less than the General commanding the attacking XXVIIth Soviet Army Corps, Majorgeneral Pawel Artemeko. Artemenko, born in Ssumy, Ukraine in 1896 and a soldier since 1917, was later captured by the Germans.

"The XXVIIth Army Corps stood opposite the SS-Division *WIKING* between Terterow and Sdwish. The *WIKING*'s fighting power was characterized as fabulous. One battalion of these SS would easily smash the Army's best regiments. They breathed easily again when the SS was relieved..."[1] If this general had known that he was opposed by only a weak third of the *WIKING* Division, perhaps he would have been even more amazed. In any case, the reinforced *NORDLAND* Regiment had at least held up the Soviet XXVIIth Army Corps long enough and hit it so hard that the danger to the northern flank of III. Panzerkorps was averted. The Regiment was relieved at Irpsen by a division from the German 6. Armee which had finally disengaged.

Meanwhile, General von Wietersheim's XIV. Panzerkorps had started off to the southeast as planned, without concerning itself over events on the northern flank of III. Panzerkorps. It was to take part in a strategically decisive battle.

GERMANIA Regiment's Defensive Success

After the reinforced *NORDLAND* Regiment had marched off from Shitomir to the north, the bulk of the Division reached Shitomir on 14. July and left on a night march for Skwira. As related by Panzerjäger-Abt. 5's war diary, the fine summer weather of the past days had changed to a "terrible heat" 9. Panzerdivision marched ahead. On 16. July, the advance units of the Division passed Skwira.

Events now took a dramatic turn. The march went on to Biala-Zerkieff. Heavy air attacks followed in the course of which an enemy bomber was shot down by MG fire. On 17. July, the Division took possession of Olschanka making it the base for continuation of the march to the southeast. Gefechtsgruppe von Oberkamp formed the advance guard. However, on the same morning 9. Panzerdivision's Kradschützen Battalion ran into the enemy 10 km. northwest of Biala-Zerkieff and reported the town occupied by enemy forces. 9. Panzerdivision then attacked, taking the town on the 17th and halting there. Now the *WIKING* Division had to carry the attack forward to the east while 9. Panzerdivision assembled around Biala-Zerkieff for the move southeastwards to Thalnoje (east of Uman).

On 18. July, the advance guard of the leading Gefechtsgruppe *GERMANIA* moved up along the advance route to Taraschtscha. At first it met only weak resistance and took the spread out village. Soon however, it encountered superior enemy forces and was forced on the defensive. The following elements of Gefechts-gruppe *GERMANIA* took strong flanking fire from the north. Turning in that direction, I./*GERMANIA*, commanded by Stubaf. Dieckmann, succeeded in throwing the enemy back behind the Ross sector and taking possession of the heights southwest of Ssinjawa. But the Kampfgruppen had reached their attack objectives only after great effort and were forced to dig in there. The enemy was receiving a steady flow of reinforcements and attacked in great numbers along the entire front between Kargalyk and Biala-Zerkieff. The Division was compelled to commit all of its forces.

To make matters worse, a downpour transformed the trenches and unpaved roads into deep muddy paths. All of the wheeled vehicles sank to their axles in the morass. The only vehicles able to work their way forward through the mud were the tracked vehicles of the artillery, the Panzerjäger and Aufklärungsabteilung 5's Panzerspähwagen and Schwimmwagen. So on the eve of the forthcoming attack on the night of 18/19. 7. 1941, the burden fell on the overextended *GERMANIA* Regiment, which could yet be reinforced by Stubaf. von Reitzenstein's A.A. 5, and on the artillery which was moved into position and quickly made ready to fire.

The eve of the 19th was one of great concern. Would *GERMANIA* hold and *WESTLAND* arrive on the 19th? And where was von Scholz? Surely he was in radio contact with the division. He had been relieved in his sector between Sdwish and Terterov by a division from 6. Armee and needed two or three days to link up with the Division.

19. July brought the greatest pressure on the troops and the command. The enemy stormed the Division along the entire front without pause. The main effort was directed against Ssinjawa where two Russian Infantry Divisions attacked throughout the day. But I./*GERMANIA* under Stubaf. Dieckmann held. The Russians had run into a crack unit of veteran troops. These men had fought in Poland and the west and had learned their jobs in long years of peacetime training. III.Battalion *WESTLAND* Regiment to the north was also a steady unit. Its commander, SS- Hstuf. Steinert, was an iron hard man, but caring and warm hearted and loved by his Dutch troops.

The enemy continued his assaults throughout the day on 20. 7. 1941. - *WESTLAND* finally arrived, enabling the Division to extend its eastern front and making possible the creation of a reserve, which up until now had not been available. The enemy's losses on the previous two days had been so great that he began to show signs of exhaustion. He had also apparently shifted his main effort more to the east. The Division now found the opportunity to combine the many individual orders issued into a divisional order.[2] The exact positions of the Division's units during the defensive fighting on 20./21. July were determined from that order.

Combat in the Battle for Uman

On 21. July ,the enemy resumed his attack from the direction of Kirdany on Taraschtscha. A message dropped from a Luftwaffe aircraft reported 30 tanks massed there. A Stuka attack on the tanks was requested on behalf of the Division. The attack took place during the evening hours and achieved good results.

On the 22nd, the day also began with heavy artillery fire on the Division's defensive front near Taraschtscha followed by furious attacks on I./*GERMANIA*'s front and on the neighbouring sectors. The last reserves had to be mobilized to plug the gaps in the thinly manned front. In the early morning the Stukas appeared, supporting the Division's hard-pressed infantry with attacks on Kirdany and Rokitno as well as on the wooded areas north and northwest of the town which were full of Russians. But this was the last act in the hard struggle on the flank of Panzergruppe 1. The spearhead of III. Panzerkorps, committed north of the Ross, was approaching the battlefield threatening the Soviet corps' western flank and rear. From midday of the 22nd on, the artillery fire on the Division's northern front decreased. The infantry attacks ceased. The *WIKING* Division could now hope finally to shake off the enemy and the Corps Headquarters of XIV. Panzerkorps dared commit the rest of 9. Panzerdivision's reserve units, held southeast of Biala- Zerkieff, to the decisive battle to the southeast at Uman. During the previous night, *WIKING* had moved its command post to Potoki. From there it would direct the attack by Gefechtsgruppe Stolz against the enemy's southwestern wing which had been ordered for the morning of 22. July. Panzerregiment 33 was ordered to attack from Jushkorog to Beresjanka, destroy the enemy cavalry in front of Gefechtsgruppe Stolz and then clear the heights between Beresjanka and Koshewatoje of enemy troops. It was then to occupy Luka and later march from there to Swenigorodka and join the main battle. In the morning light, the long columns of XIV. Panzerkorps could be seen from the Division's command post as they moved through Ostramobilia. At the same time in the wooded area 2 km. west of Potoki, Panzerregiment 33 was beginning to prepare for its attack. 15./*WESTLAND* had some light patrol skirmishes as it secured Angrifsgruppe Stolz' wing and flank. The attack by the Gefechtsgruppen was laid down in the "Order for 22. July 1941".[1]

Felix Steiner

Herbert O. Gille

Johannes Mühlenkamp

Karl Ullrich

Swearing-in ceremony for recruits of SS-Art.Rgt. 5

Just returned, a reconnaissance patrol reports to the Division Commander
— Summer 1941 —

On the advance
1941

Regimental shoot.
SS-Artl.Rgt. 5
at Heuberg 1941.
Staf. Gille
in conversation
with Staf. Wäckerle.

WESTLAND's
first combat
on 1. 7. 1941
east of Lemberg.
From left to right:
Staf. Wäckerle,
Hstuf. Paetsch (Ic),
Hstuf. Schalburg (O1)
(partially concealed),
Brigf. Steiner,
Hstuf. Ziemssen
(Adj. WESTLAND)

The commander of the NORDLAND
Rgt. von Scholz as (later) Obergruppenführer
and General der Waffen-SS

The commander of the WESTLAND
Rgt Artur Phleps a.k.a. Stolz as (later)
Obergruppenführer and General der Waffen-S

An unidentified group of infantrymen. Without such men the success of the WIKING
Division would not have been possible.

August 1941: The battle for Dnepropetrovsk

First aid for the wounded.
The tireless efforts of the medical services saved the lives of many men.

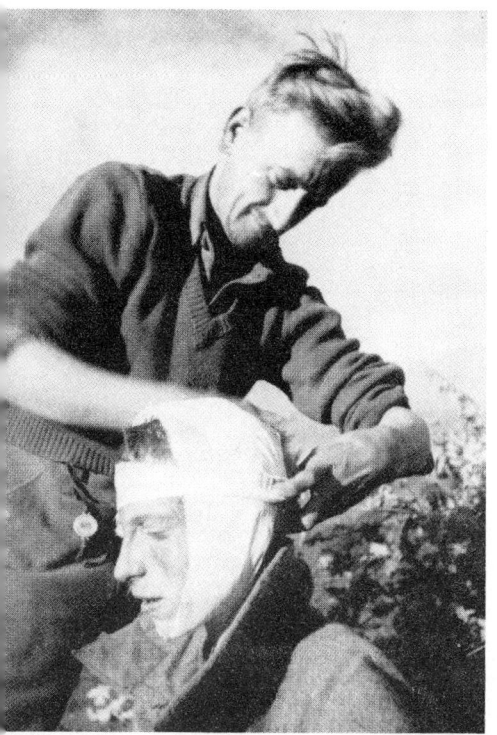

August 1941: Footbridge over the Dnepr.

August 1941: Foot and vehicle bridge over the Dnepr.

A rare photograph: A mortar position in the Dnepropetrovsk bridgehead
on 8. September 1941.

August 1941:
Ration carriers move up to the "red houses" in the Dnepropetrovsk bridgehead.

The beginning of the attack was delayed by the requirement for two Stuka bombing runs. From 10.00 to 11.00 hours, the enemy in front of the attack forces was exposed once again to Stuka attack. Results were not long in coming. The Panzerregiment moved to the attack supported by the Gefechtsgruppe's artillery. It quickly won territory to the east, reached Beresjanka and pushed forward to Lukianowka. The enemy fled in panic to the northwest. Cavalry units trying to reach safety in flight rushed together from all directions. Horse drawn batteries were shot up as they attempted to withdraw. On the way from Lukianowka to Luka stood abandoned antitank guns and overturned vehicles, while dead horses were strewn about. By approximately 15.00 hours, the attack forces' flank had been cleared of Russians. Part of Panzerregiment 33 now supported the attack force while the rest had already marched off to the south to Swenigorodka. The attack by Gruppe Stolz, launched around midday, at first met only light resistance; however this stiffened at the Lukjanowka—Taraschtscha road. In heavy fighting, III./GERMANIA took Lukjanowka and cleared it of the enemy. II./WESTLAND, which had formed up to the west, crossed the Lukjanowka—Taraschtscha road and infiltrated the forest to the east. There it succeeded in taking an enemy battery by storm. The gun positions were overrun in a daring attack by SS-Oscha. Peters and his company from 8./WESTLAND. As dusk fell, the company reformed in the complicated wooded terrain before Kirdany; the area was still thick with enemy stragglers. I./WESTLAND, which was moving toward Taraschtscha behind II. Battalion, took part in some brisk firefights in the forests. It was in one of these that the Chief of 4./WESTLAND, SS- Hauptsturmführer Adams, was killed in action. The night reconnaissance, as carried out successfully so often by SS-Oscha. Misling of II./WESTLAND, reported stronger enemy cavalry units in the northern part of the woods and infantry withdrawing to the north. For the next day the Gefechtsgruppe had ordered the continuation of the attack on the Kotluga sector. On 23. 7. 1941, the attacking forces came upon numerous pieces of abandoned equipment and large groups of saddled horses whose riders had fled, and by late morning had reached the south bank of the Kotluga. The north bank was occupied and defended by strong enemy forces. Powerful enemy forces were also dug-in in Bolkun and Kirdany. The commander of the reinforced WESTLAND Regiment was very concerned over the possibility of an enemy breakthrough, as no reserves were available. At noon on 24. July, however, it became apparent that the enemy opposite II./WESTLAND was pulling back. "Papa" Phleps ordered immediate attacks to the north along the entire front. "It worked!"; so noted the commander in his war diary. "At about 20.45 hours I reached the Kotluga depression in the Ross sector". At the same time the spearhead of Gefechtsgruppe von Scholz had left its previous operational area on the Sdwish near Taraschtscha and was moving through Luka towards Boguslav to take possession of the Ross river crossings there. With a Panzer Company which was left behind near Luka now under its command, the Kampfgruppe launched a thrust to the northeast. Although the advance guard succeeded in capturing the eastern end of Boguslav, it found the western part of the town occupied by the enemy. Meanwhile, III. Panzerkorps, which was advancing eastwards north of the Ross, began to make its presence felt. The enemy in front of the Division was forced to retire along the entire front.

Eight days of hard fighting were behind the WIKING Division. In nonstop fighting it had repulsed continuous attacks by powerful enemy forces (approx. 5 divisions), taken around 2,000 prisoners (of these about 1,000 by Gruppe Stolz)

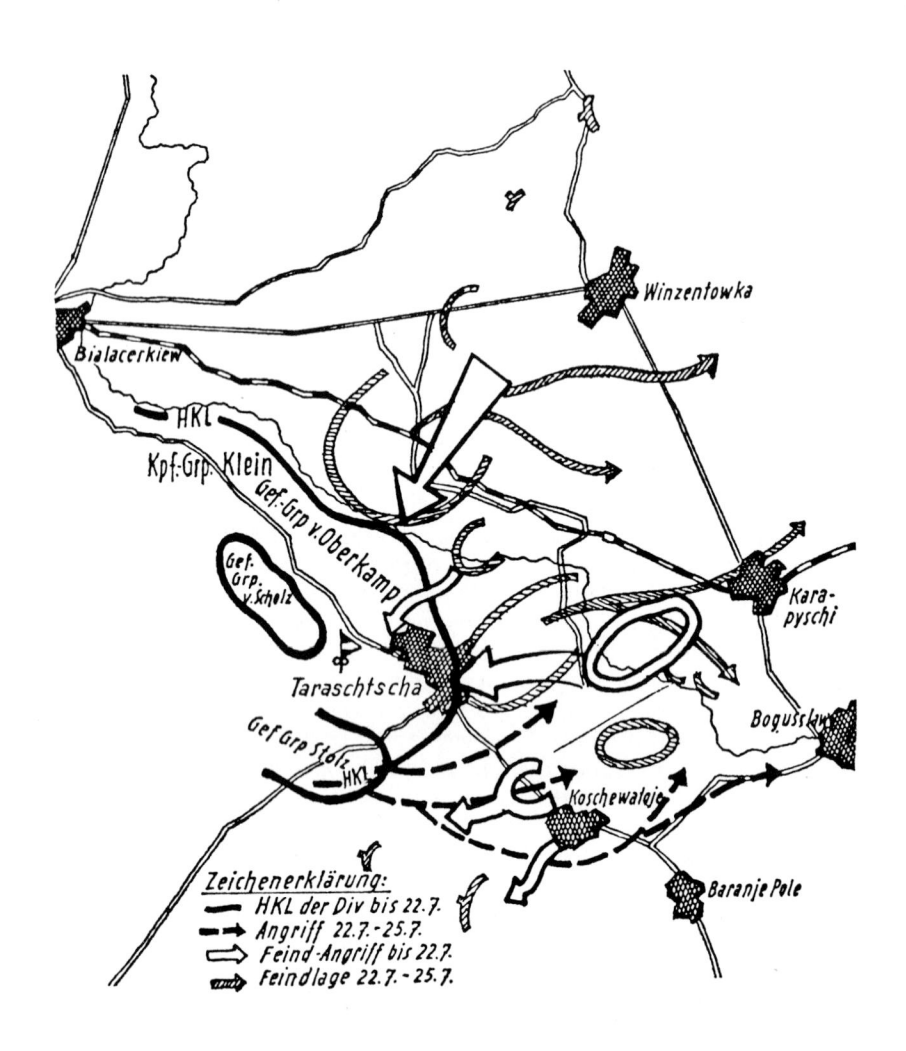

Defensive battles near Taraschtschta 22.-25. July 1941.

and captured a great deal of enemy war material. At the same time it had successfully secured the northern flank of the envelopment operation carried out by Panzergruppe 1. The Division's important part in the Battle for Uman had reached its conclusion.[2]

The Division's losses were considerable. The commanders of the WESTLAND Regiment recorded the following losses: 10 officers, 12 NCOs, 70 men killed and 8 officers, 52 NCOs and 300 men wounded. The dead, Dutch, Finnish, German and Flemish, found their final resting place together as they had fought together, along the Biala—Zerkieff road.

III. Through Smela—Korsun to the Dnepr

The following report is contained in the war diary of Panzerjäger-Abteilung 5 for 29. 7. 1941:
"Weather good. The Division has left XIV. A.K. and has been placed under the command of III. A.K.. This order has hit the men hard since they played an important role in the fighting near Taraschtscha which created the Uman Pocket. Everyone felt that the Division had been deprived of the fruits of its labour."

What had happened? The relieving offensive by the 5th and 26th Soviet Armies to avert the threatened encirclement near Uman had been fought off by III. Panzerkorps and the WIKING Division. Meanwhile, the ring around the Soviet forces west of Uman was being drawn tighter and tighter. The encircling forces were still not without gaps and required reinforcement by the now disengaged XIV. Panzerkorps and 6. Armee's southern group. But the expectation that the WIKING Division would follow south to take part in the decisive battle was not fulfilled. The enemy forces in Heeresgruppe Süd's northern flank were still too strong and posed too great a threat to the operation. Only the reinforced - WESTLAND Regiment followed 9. Panzerdivision south in the direction of Talnoje as the reserve for Gruppe Kleist. The remaining two thirds of the Division was attached to III. Panzerkorps which was attacking eastwards north of the Ross in the direction of Korsun. Its spearhead had reached the Karapyschi area northwest of Boguslav on the 26th. Through its advance to the Dnepr, the Panzerkorps was to protect the northern flank and later the rear of Panzergruppe 1, which, fighting on the reversed front, was interdicting between Novo- Archangelsk and Talnoje. Further, the Panzerkorps was to prevent the retreating Russians from crossing the river.

On 29. July, the Staff and I./WESTLAND with II./A.R. 5 moved south through Beresjanka to Talnoje. II. and III./WESTLAND followed on the 30th while the WIKING Division marched out of its assembly area with the Division Staff and Gefechtsgruppe von Oberkamp (reinforced GERMANIA Rgt. with Pi. 5 and the bulk of the artillery) on the 29th through Biala-Zerkieff to join up with III. Panzerkorps, making contact the same night near Usin. Gefechtsgruppe von Scholz with the attached A.A. 5 and III./A.R. 5 received orders to follow using the same route.

The Battle near Smela

So the Division marched southeastward behind 13. Panzerdivision and 60. Inf.Div. (mot.) in a hundred kilometre long column toward Krementschuk and Dnepropetrovsk in an effort to cut off the enemy forces falling back from Uman to the Dnepr. On 1. August, the advance halted in the hot summer weather. 13. Panzerdivision had stopped to erect bridges near Korsun. Throughout the entire day, enemy aircraft attacked 13. Pz.Div.'s columns, which were halted along the road, without inflicting serious damage. It was not until the 3rd that the first - WIKING Gefechtsgruppe was able to follow 60. Inf.Div. toward Korsun. Heavy rains had again softened the roads hindering movement. By evening the roads had dried out sufficiently to allow the march to continue. The reinforced Gefechtsgruppe von Scholz crossed the Corps military bridge near Korsun that evening. After establishing a secure position and sending patrols to the east, the Gruppe

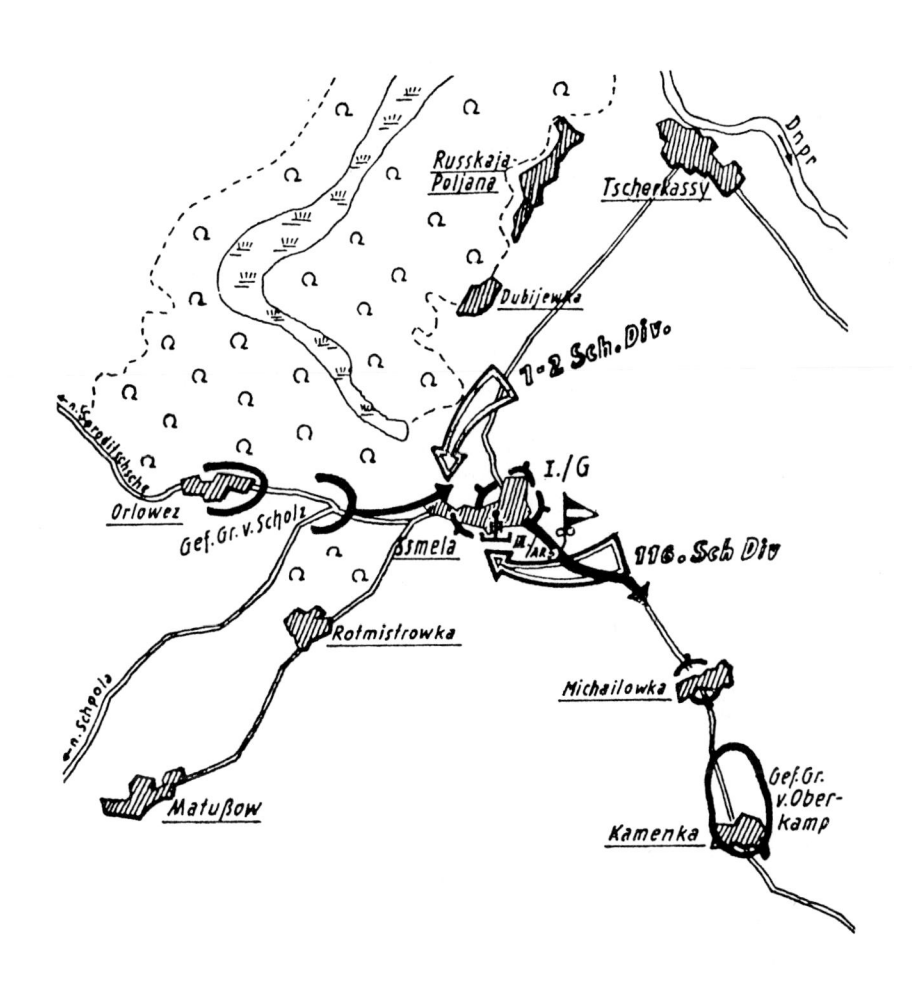

Smela Kamenka July 1941

rested for the night south of the Ross. Gefechtsgruppe *GERMANIA* with A.A. 5, Pi. 5, A.R. 5 (less 2 battalions) and the Division Staff with the Signals Battalion reached Goroditsche on the evening of 4. 8. 1941. On the previous day, III. Panzerkorps with 13. Pz.Div. and 60. Inf.Div. was diverted from Goroditsche southeastward in the direction of Telepino. The *WIKING* Division, as flanking column to the east, was sent through Smela—Kanev towards Tschigirin to advance from there southward along the Dnepr.

At 04.30 hours on 4. August, the Division Staff followed by the Ia-Staffel and the Funkstaffel with the commander of Signals Battalion 5 drove off from Smela in the direction of Kamenka. Gefechtsgruppe Gille, which was to follow, prepared to move out. On leaving the town the Division commander noticed movement on the hilltops 400 metres east of the road. Moments later masses of Russians stormed onto the road. Alertly the driver of the lead vehicle swerved into a left turn. "Everyone turn around!" yelled the commander. Only the Ia with the command section continued to roar down the road with the Kradschützengruppe in the lead. Meanwhile, both 3.7 cm. Flak opened fire independently with H.E. shells, inflicting considerable losses on the enemy infantry. The Division commander was impressed by the performance of the gun crews, who were mostly European volunteers, as well as by the guns' firepower and effectiveness. While the Kradschützengruppe was actually able to reach the woods, the Ia's vehicle took a direct hit. Quick as lightning the crew jumped out and attempted to work their way back to Smela through a cornfield. All succeeded except the Division's First General Staff Officer, SS-Stubaf. Günther Ecke. Perhaps wounded, he lost contact with the others in the thick cornfield and was killed by the pursuing Red Army soldiers.[1] The incident cost the lives of two other officers and and three men. The gun crews of 4. Platoon 1. Battery Flak-Abt. 5 were awarded the Iron Cross.

On the evening of 5. August, the advance guard drove through the town of Smela and reached Kamenka in a night march. That evening, Gefechtsgruppe Gille arrived at Smela with a battalion from *GERMANIA*, the Staff and two Battalions of A.R. 5, the Division Staff and the Signals Battalion as well as the Staff and 1 Battery of Flak 5 and went to rest positions. While Gefechtsgruppe von Oberkamp had received orders by radio to set out at 06.00 on the morning of 6. Aug. for Tschigirin via Staraja-Osata, the Division Staff intended to arrive in Kamenka an hour later to join up with the Gefechtsgruppe. But at approximately 21.00 hours on the evening of the 5th, Smela came under large-calibre artillery fire from the direction of Cherkassy, forcing the Division Staff to withdraw out of range. At 22.00 hours, SS-Standartenführer von Scholz arrived at the Division Headquarters, apprised himself of the situation and returned to his Gefechtsgruppe without having observed anything suspicious in Smela. However, before dawn on the following day, a liason vehicle from the Ib Staffel in Smela arrived, reporting that it had taken infantry fire from the area of Butki, 1.5 km. west of Smela. The Division O 3, SS-Ostuf. Wolf, his accompanying Finnish liason officer Pikkala, the interpreter and two military police had been killed by machine gun fire.

The battle near Smela had begun. Several light antiaircraft guns on the southern edge of Smela hammered away at the masses of attacking Russians. Meanwhile, A.R. 5's batteries had also moved into position and were pouring direct fire on the enemy assault columns. A Russian major, the commander of a regiment, deserted, bringing with him a map showing the Russian plan to encircle Smela. There was no more doubt, the place was surrounded on all sides by the

Soviet 116th Rifle Div. and the 672nd Infantry Rgt. While contact between Smela and Goroditsche had been broken, Kampfgruppe Dieckmann, which had been committed immediately, succeeded in reopening the road to Kamenka. The panic stricken Russians gave ground. Stukas were called in and attacked the onrushing Soviet forces north of Smela with bombs, forcing them to take cover. The - NORDLAND Regiment advanced, throwing the enemy back in the direction of Cherkassy. Smela was once again firmly in German hands.

At roughly 14.00 hours, the situation had settled down enough for the Division Staff to follow III./GERMANIA toward Kamenka. Gefechtsgruppe GERMANIA had been ordered by radio to halt there so that it could be recalled to the fighting at Smela if need be. This now proved unnecessary. General der Pz.Tr. Kempf visited WESTLAND's commander at his command post and thanked him for the Regiment's efforts. At 17.00 hours, III./GERMANIA with the Division Staff and the command agencies reached Kamenka unmolested. In the Division's rear, however, all hell had broken loose. Strong enemy forces had broken into Korsun with tanks and overrun the Supply Battalion. Cooks and butchers fought desperately for their lives. A unit of tanks from 13. Panzerdivision was able to restore the situation. Korsun was again liberated.

In view of the powerful forces of 6. Armee now following and the elements of 17. Armee which had already disengaged, the advance could be continued. The target remained Tschirigin, which was occupied in the face of weak enemy resistance by Kampfgruppe reinf. A.A. 5 on the late afternoon of 7. 8. 1941. On 8. August, Kampfgruppe Joerchel took Nowogeorgiewsk on the Dnepr while the Division cleared the territory between Tschirigin and the Dnepr of straggling Russians taking many prisoners. Thus on this day the Dnepr was reached on a broad front.[2] While there was still fighting at Korsun deep in the Division's northwest flank and 57. Inf.Div. had become involved in new fighting in the direction of Cherkassy, a vital combat sector had been secured.

Crossing the Dnepr—Establishing the Bridgehead

The situation between Boguslav and Korsun remained critical. The enemy forces already moving southward were first intercepted by the forces hastily thrown against them by the Panzergruppe in the vicinity of Olschana, 8 km. south of Korsun and near Morenzy. Gefechtsgruppe WESTLAND also played a large role in the counterattack by Panzergruppe 1's reserve units. After its temporary detachment from the Division, WESTLAND marched south toward Talnoje (10 km. south of Swenigorodka). There it joined the other units of 16. Inf.Div. (mot.) of XXXXVIII. Panzerkorps which were inserted into the front to the west to shore up the still incomplete barricading forces in the rear of the Soviet 6th and 16th Armies. On receipt of the report that strong enemy forces had broken into the Panzergruppe's northern flank, the command reacted quickly. By the morning of the 7th, Kampfgruppe Zeller had been formed from Gefechtsgruppe Stolz and the HERMANN GÖRING Parachute Regiment. This unit, possessing the strength of a division, saw hard fighting in the following weeks at Korsun, Stebleff and Schanderowka. On 16. August, the battle to secure Panzergruppe 1's northern flank ended.

Meanwhile, the great battle near Uman involving 17. Armee and Panzergruppe 1 had ended with the destruction of the Soviet 6th, 12th and 18th Armies. On 8.

August, the Wehrmacht reports were already indicating a great success. According to the reports, 103,000 prisoners had been taken including 2 Army Commanders. 317 tanks and 850 artillery pieces had fallen into German hands as well as large amounts of war material. The Soviets had attempted to break through Panzergruppe 1's encircling ring until the end. Daily they tried to wear down the surrounding forces with mass attacks, often up to ten times a day. The fanaticism of the Soviets as experienced by the Division's Kampfgruppe von Hadeln south of Talnoje, for example, can barely be described. The Soviets stormed the German positions at Ssinjucha in dense masses and were shot down in droves but repeated the attacks over and over again. It was the same around the entire encircling front in the last days of the fighting. It is no wonder that after the fighting the encircling forces were at the end of their strength mentally and physically. In spite of their attention however, hundreds and thousands of Russians succeeded in slipping through the thinly held lines or breaking through under cover of darkness. The Panzergruppe wasted no time, therefore, in following the enemy forces withdrawing to the east. It pushed on immediately toward Saporoshje and Dnepropetrovsk. 17. Armee advanced toward the Dnepr line Kremenchug—Cherkassy while 6. *Armee* directed its attack toward Kiev.

On reaching the Dnepr, the *WIKING* Division had no time to linger at Tschirigin. After clearing the terrain near the Dnepr it reached the river itself. On 12. August, a monitor and a gunboat of the Soviet Dnepr Fleet attempted to break through to the south past the Division's sector. A 3.7 cm. Pak of 14./*GERMANIA* sank the monitor with its first shot. The other vessel was sunk by I./A.R. 5, the decisive shot being fired by 2. Battery under Hauptsturmführer Hebron.

The "Passubio" Division of the Italian Expeditionary Corps, which was to relieve the Division in its positions on the Dnepr, was slow in coming, first arriving on the morning of 17. 8. 1941. Therefore, the Division was forced to pull one Kampfgruppe after another out of the Dnepr front and commit them southward toward Werschnednjeprowsk-Kamenskoje. Enduring heavy air attacks and great clouds of dust, the Division's Kampfgruppen now engaged in one action after the other, securing the territory along the Dnepr southward toward Dneproderschinsk, while 13. Pz.Div. moved forward toward Dnepropetrovsk. 60. Inf.Div. (mot) likewise moved toward Dnepropetrovsk as III. Panzerkorps' southern column and battled with Soviet forces falling back toward the city.

On 21. August, the Division's advance guard stood before enemy occupied Dnjeprodershinsk. III./*NORDLAND*'s attack, ordered by Kampfgruppe Maack to which it was now attached, was unable to progress through Kriwoje. Still in the city was approximately one division of enemy troops which was preparing to cross the Dnepr by ferry. The attack by Gefechtsgruppe von Scholz, approaching from the rear, managed to break into the northern part of the city but was unable to reach the river crossings. The enemy was still firmly entrenched in the south end of the city and their artillery on the far side of the river was able to place flanking fire on *NORDLAND*'s attack. The attack by the *GERMANIA* Rgt. was the first to make any headway. On 23. August, the Regiment forced its way in heavy fighting from the eastern edge of the city into the southern section. The Soviets defended desperately, fighting bitterly for every street. Dense minefields had to be cleared while undermined houses were blown up. On 25. August, the city was entirely in German hands. All parts of the city and the wooded areas had been cleared of enemy rearguards. Although 2,000 prisoners were taken and 12 guns and a quantity of war material captured, the desperate enemy rear guard action had allowed the bulk of the enemy forces to escape to the other side of the river.

Gefechtsgruppe WESTLAND, meanwhile, had been diverted from its withdrawal from Korsun to the south through Kirovograd toward Dnepropetrovsk and was involved near Alexandrowka and Michailowka in the fighting with enemy forces counterattacking from Dnepropetrovsk. With 60. Inf.Div. and Gefechtsgruppe von Scholz to the north, a crisis arose with the Panzer units. But the enemy appeared to be fighting here to gain time. His strong rearguards were forced more and more to pull back beyond the Dnepr, especially since III. Panzerkorps' main column with 13. Panzerdivision in the lead threatened to cut off the Soviet forces still on the south bank of the river.

Gefechtsgruppe Stolz broke into the southern parts of Dnepropetrovsk on 26. August. At 13.00 hours on the same day, the Gruppe was reunited with the - WIKING Division. The unit had distinguished itself in the encircling action near Uman as well as in its surprise attack against the enemy's flank at Korsun. Kampfgruppen von Handeln and Steinert (I. and II. WESTLAND) had launched the decisive attack by III. Panzerkorps from the south through Michailowka, helped 60. Inf.Div. (mot) take the heights there and given the enemy rearguards no rest.

The Division had meanwhile been relieved by an infantry division from 17. Armee and from 26. 8. 1941 waited for the arrival of additional forces. This cost time. To make use of this time, Pz.Jäger-Abteilung 5 was assigned the task of establishing civil order in the city. A meeting of the residents was called for 26. August. All of those residents who were prepared to could nominate someone they trusted as interim mayor. The 200 people who came, the majority being afraid to leave their houses, elected an engineer to the post. The local commander, SS-Ostuf. Rohrer, noted in his diary that the man had made a good impression. Here, as in all the occupied towns, the pictures of Stalin disappeared, his statues in public places were smashed and the party offices were taken over by the citizens. Soon a capable city administration was in place which created an unarmed force for maintaining law and order.

The Division also followed the procedures here that it had practiced in Tschigirin. A part of the advance guard was pulled out of the line. Satisfied with a reduced security force, the Division pushed strong combat forces down the Dnepr towards Dnepropetrovsk. On 28. August, Gefechtsgruppe NORDLAND reached the town of Ssuchaschewski, 3 km. west of Dnepropetrovsk. Gefechtsgruppe von Reitzenstein arrived at the Dnjepr near Taramskoje while the reinforced - WESTLAND Regiment was assembled in the Dijewka-Krinitschki area. Meanwhile, 198. Inf.Div., which had recently been placed under the command of III. Panzerkorps, and 60. Inf.Div.(mot) were making regular nightly crossings of the Dnjepr into the narrow bridgehead, relieving 13. Panzerdivision. Gefechtsgruppe von Scholz was sent across into the bridgehead as reinforcement during the night of 30./31. August and deployed next to 198. Inf.Div. and 60. Inf.Div.(mot). The enemy, meanwhile, had once again settled in on the northeast bank of Dnepr, gathered his forces and deployed his artillery which was now trained methodically on the river crossings, the town of Dnepropetrovsk, the approach routes and road junctions. In this situation the students of the former Artillery School in Dnepropetrovsk proved their worth. The enemy had soon achieved such a superiority in firepower that no one could move about the town by day and the troops in the bridgehead were forced to dig in up to their necks. The Soviets had targeted the railway bridge so precisely that repairs by day or night were impos sible. The only traffic across the river was by ferry and motorboat. Operating at irregular intervals under cover of darkness, it was shielded by the intervening houses on the east bank. The only available crossing was the foot bridge captured by 13. Panzerdivision. With only an unsecured floating foundation and under observation by Soviet artillery, the bridge was unusable by day. The troops were forced to cross the footbridge by night and risk the threat of the frequent Soviet artillery bombardments. Running across the bridge during breaks in the shelling, the men were relieved if they reached the other side unscathed. Night after night, columns of men carried munitions, rations and other items required by the troops across the bridge. Strict control and discipline had to be maintained if the threat of panic and disaster was to be averted. In any case, the men had resigned themselves to their dangerous situation as reported by Panzerjägerabteilung 5's war diary: "This morning the Abt. Commander drove off in a B-Krad accompanied by Dr. Koschemann, the unit doctor. The driver was Kradmelder Thäle. At 16.40 hours, the Commander returned to the Abt. command post completely soaked. During the return trip across the bridge they had been caught in a barrage. The driver, apparently seriously wounded, released the steering wheel. Driverless, the Krad tipped and the Commander was thrown into the water followed by the Krad and driver. The powerful current carried Stubaf. Maack under the bridge. He was able to reach a rope thrown to him by some Pioniere and was pulled out of the water. Dr. Koschemann lay motionless in the centre of the bridge. He was carried to the nearest dressing station where he was pronounced dead. Rottenführer Thäle and the B-Krad had disappeared without a trace. He had found a cold grave in the Dnepr."

During the night of 31. Aug./1. Sept., Gefechtsgruppe von Scholz (-NORDLAND Rgt.) arrived in the bridgehead and was deployed next to 198. Inf.Division. There was little cover available in the new position. The headquarters and the supply dump were sited behind the protective cover of the walls of the few stone houses south of the sand dunes about 600 metres north of the city limits. The first aide service had set up the Unit Dressing Station in the cellars. SS-Standartenführer von Scholz was an experienced soldier. He knew that in this position his troops would have to bear the brunt of the fighting. Therefore, he had them dig in as far as was possible. Every night his Infanteriepioniere laid mines in front of the Regiment's positions and later barbed wire. Scarcely had the Regiment disappeared into the thin sandy soil when the enemy launched his attack.

One of NORDLAND's men remembered: "The first glorious page in the brief history of the NORDLAND Rgt. was now written. Every morning the Russians rushed the bridgehead and tried to crush it. A weight of artillery fire never before experienced rained down on the defenders' positions. They fought bitterly, refusing to yield a meter of ground. In these days the Germans, Danes, Norwegians and Finns grew together into an exemplary European combat team. Morning after morning, they fought off with great bravery repeated Russian assaults. They were recognized by their Wehrmacht comrades as the bridgehead's strong supporting pillar in the uneven battle. While the unmolested Russian artillery commanded the battlefield from the eastern heights and supported every attack with heavy fire, the German artillery, due to the restricted supply of ammunition in the bridgehead, was of limited use. Night after night the men of the NORDLAND Rgt. patched up their battered positions and by morning the defenders were ready again."[2] A great deal of the credit for NORDLAND's performance must be given to its commander. Night after night and morning after morning, Staf. von Scholz walked or crawled through his positions, fighting beside his men and serving as an example to them during this time. From then on he was known to his men only as "Old Fritz", a name he would carry until his hero's death at Narwa. On 7. September, the entire Division crossed to the east side of the Dnepr in preparation for the attack intended to enlarge the bridgehead. In two dark nights the Division had crossed the river on rafts and ferries and moved into position on the night of 7./8. September. After numerous briefings and detailed assignments by the artillery commander, General von Roman, the divisional orders were issued for the attack on Kamenka on 8. September 1941.[3]

The Capture of Kamenka and Enlarging the Bridgehead

At 06.00 in the morning, the assault units stood ready, but still dug in in their assembly areas behind the regimental positions of 60. Inf.Div.(mot). They were prepared, as ordered, to begin the attack at 07.00 hours. At the Division command post which offered a better view of the attack sectors, the Commanding General of III. Panzerkorps, Gen.d.Kav. von Mackensen, and his staff had arrived to observe the course of the attack. As planned, Generalmajor von Roman began the attack with destructive fire on the enemy positions and artillery batteries. A half hour later, the enemy replied in such strength and with such intensity that the commanders hesitated to launch the attack at 07.00 as planned. The artillery duel continued unabated into the late morning. A number of new batteries had been discovered and these had first to be put out of action. At 11.20 hours, Staf. von Oberkamp reported in by radio pressing for the attack order to be given. The Division commander declined as the artillery battle had not yet been decided. Gruppe Stolz also felt that the decision to wait was correct. In the Division command post the Commanding General and his Chief of Staff deliberated the situation. At roughly 13.00 hours he left the command post with the words: "I realize that the attack will be very difficult. Therefore I will not demand it of you. In spite of the great difficulties which the bridgehead presents us, I would rather forego its enlargement than sacrifice a division for it." What human feelings are spoken by such words!

Half an hour later, the fire slackened. It appeared that the German artillery had gained the upper hand. Immediately the order was given for the attack by Gefechtsgruppen Stolz and von Oberkamp for 14.00 hours. Generalmajor von Roman received instructions to lay down a 10 minute long barrage with all guns on the enemy positions in Kamenka beginning at 13.45 and then to transfer his fire onto the rear of the attack sector. At 15.00 hours, Gruppe Stolz reported a rapid advance along the ridge northeast of Kamenka while von Oberkamp advised that his Kampfgruppe had broken into the town and was advancing quickly toward the town's centre. Arko.3 instructed the Corps Artillery Rgt. of the Italian Expeditionary Corps to neutralize the southern edge of Kamenka and Ssuskowskaja. At 17.00 hours, *GERMANIA* reported large numbers of prisoners and weak resistance. Parts of Gefechtsgruppe Stolz had pressed on into the northern part of Kamenka. An hour later both Gefechtsgruppen had reached the northern and northwestern edges of Kamenka. Advance elements of Gruppe Stolz had dug in firmly on the ridge. They had pushed the northern front of the bridgehead so far north of Kamenka that the Soviets were unable to affect the area deep in the bridgehead or even observe the Dnepr valley. In the evening hours, the Dnepr shore near Ssuskowskaja was cleared of the enemy by the *GERMANIA* Regiment.

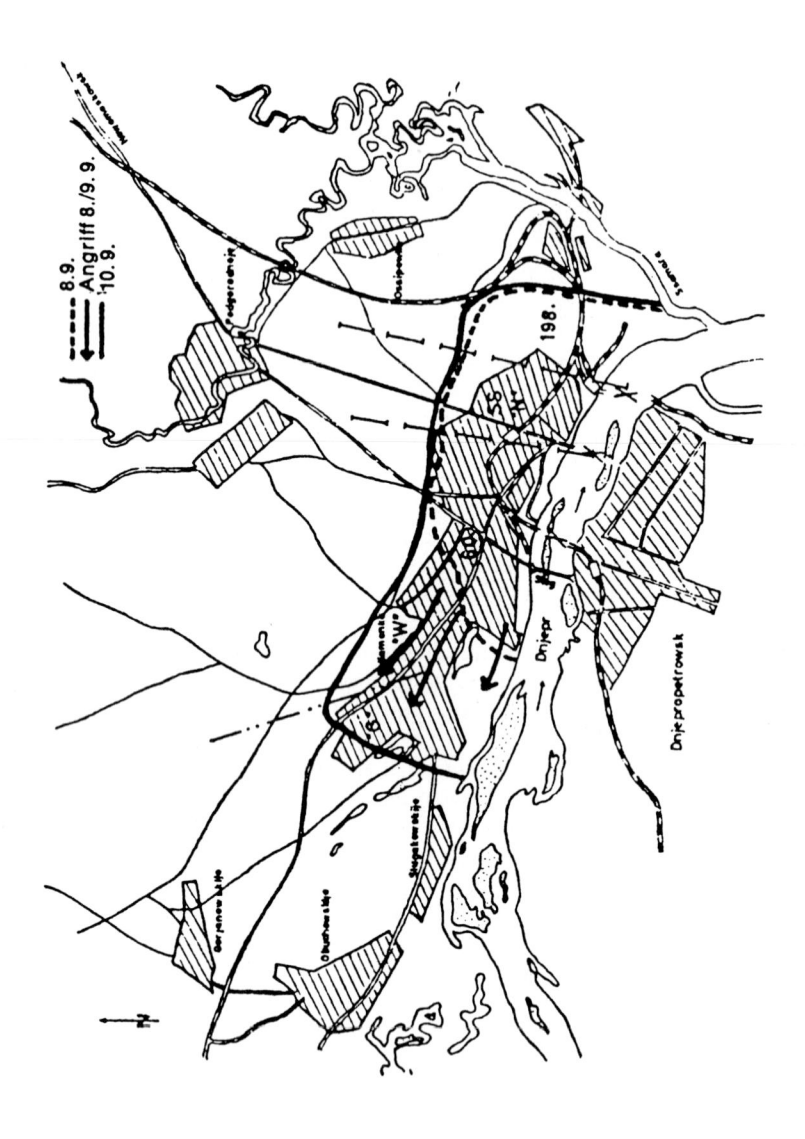

The Kamenka bridgehead

5,000 prisoners and a large quantity of war material, including several tanks, had fallen into German hands. The best news was not the success that had been won, but above all that it had been achieved with only minor losses. Following this, the fighting in the bridgehead became bearable. The Artillery Rgt. was able to push a second Battalion across to Kamenka, so that now I. and III. Battalions were located in the bridgehead.

Naturally, the Soviets did not abandon their attacks against Kamenka. Again and again they attacked in Battalion and even in Regiment strength. But the fierceness of a short while ago, when they attacked the bridgehead at any cost, had dissapated. 60. Inf.Div. could now be pulled out and marched off to be employed elsewhere; two divisions were sufficient to hold the bridgehead. By stretching its front the WIKING Division in the position to release Gefechtsgruppe Stolz as a mobile reserve for use elsewhere. When the regrouping had been completed, the Division was able to thank its soldiers for the renewed proof of their prowess in defence and offence in the following Divisional Order:

"SS Division Commander   WIKING   Div.Command Post,15.9.1941

Men of the WIKING Division!

Days of difficult fighting lay behind you. In heavy fighting the Division has repulsed daily enemy attacks, taken Kamenka, captured almost 5,000 prisoners and since then has stood in the bridgehead as the unshakeable cornerpost of this important position. Over eight enemy divisions have been smashed before the bridgehead and strong forces tied down. So by your resolute defence you have prepared the way for our comrades to push east from the Dnjepr. Your presence here will soon assist their advance. As always the Division has fought magnificently. Your accomplishments and spirit are recognized throughout the army. The enemy has felt your blows to such a degree that his propaganda has already reported you destroyed on three occasions. On the contrary, we stand with our old fighting will, ready for further action. Because of the strong bonds between all of the volunteers in our ranks, the Division has become a symbol. Whether of German, Dutch, Norwegian or Finnish origin, the WIKING Division is a symbol for all of us of our unity and common destiny. The actions by the proud Regiments GERMANIA, WESTLAND and NORDLAND, the success of Artillery Regiment 5, the reconnaissance units, the Panzerjäger, Sturmpioniere, the Flak artillery, our faithful communications men and the medical services are proof of their soldierly prowess. These units are worthy to take their place in the history of German soldiery. They have filled me with pride as have the tireless efforts of the supply and service units, who are deserving of our mutual gratitude. I know that the Division will hit the enemy hard in the coming days and add to its glory. Heil to you, Kamaraden!
signed Steiner"[1]

Kremenchug—Opening the Dnjepropetrowsk Bridgehead

On 12. September 1941, the Commander in Chief of Panzergruppe 1 issued an order of the day which indicated that events had already gone beyond the Dnjepr bridgehead.[1] On this day, after the opening of the bridgehead from

Kremenchug, the Panzergruppe, with the other two Panzerkorps (XIV. and XXXXVIII.), moved up through 17. Armee north toward Kiev. It joined up with Panzergruppe 2 advancing north to south along the east bank of the Dnepr and by 24. September had already destroyed powerful enemy forces, capturing large numbers of prisoners and masses of enemy war material. While 17. Armee advanced to the east, the Panzergruppe now wheeled and thrust toward the south with XIV. Panzerkorps. Its aim was to roll up the enemy defending between Kremenchug and Dnepropetrovsk on the Dnepr river and open the Dnepropetrovsk bridgehead and the crossings at Saporoshje. In the course of this operation, 13. Panzerdivision advanced along the ridge from Kobeljaki toward Podgorodnoje. The *WIKING* Division had released Gefechtsgruppe Stolz (A.A. 5, III./*WESTLAND*, I./*NORDLAND*, Pi. 5, Pz.Jg. 5, Flak, II./A.R. 5) from the Dnepropetrovsk bridgehead as of 23. September. This unit now moved through Kremenchug to Kobeljaki with the four Kampfgruppen of XIV. Panzerkorps and was placed under the command of 13. Panzerdivision.[2]

The Soviets did not remain unaware of this weakening of the bridgehead. By means of increased activity and attacks on narrow fronts in battalion and regiment strength they tried in vain to hinder the withdrawal of forces from the bridgehead. On 25. September, XIV. Panzerkorps began the attack on the rear of the enemy divisions in position on the Dnepr to the south and had reached Tschaplino on the 27th. At the same time as 13. Panzerdivision's advance toward Podgorodnoje—Novo-Moskowsk, III. Panzerkorps with 198. Inf.Div. and the *WIKING* SS-Division moved out of the Dnepropetrovsk bridgehead, attacking toward the east. The Italian mot. Division "TORINO", recently moved into the bridgehead, undertook a drive with limited objectives up the Dnepr.

The attack began with a short artillery bombardment on 28. 9. 1941 and quickly gained ground. A number of Russian prisoners were taken.[3] Meanwhile, Gefechtsgruppe Stolz had reached Podgorodnoje at approximately 16.00 hours and was once more under the command of the *WIKING* Division which was now a part of XIV. Panzerkorps. The Corps' commander, Gen.d.Inf. von Wietersheim, warmly greeted his old combat partners from the Battle of Uman.

If the breakout battle from the bridgehead had gone smoothly for the Division, east of the Dnjepr, Gefechtsgruppe Stolz had to endure several hot days. In order to soften up the Soviets still holding out there, it had pushed its light forces, two reinforced Kradschützen companies and Kampfgruppe von Reitzenstein (A.A. 5), forward from the ridge near Kobeljaki west to the Dnepr. Far inferior to the enemy in firepower, the light units had fallen into a difficult situation. In this phase of the operation 15./*WESTLAND* Regiment succeeded in deceiving the enemy retreating from the Dnepr into believing that a full scale Panzer assault was underway. Aided in their deception by the evening twilight, the roaring motors of the Schwimmwagen and other vehicles as well as machine gun fire from all guns sent the Russians into headlong flight.

Far more dangerous was the experience of the Company Chief of another Kradschützen company. This is his report:

"The combat duties in the Dnepropetrovsk bridgehead by my company, 15./ *NORDLAND*, ended when we were placed under the command of A.A. 5 which was located northwest of the city. So we crossed the Dnepr near Kremenchug and drove through Kobeljaki to the southeast with orders to cut off those enemy units still on the Dnepr and open the Dnepropetrovsk bridgehead from the rear. Rolling over the same crossing with us at Kremenchug were vehicles of Panzergruppe

Guderian which had taken part in the great encircling battle at Kiev. They were marked by a large letter "G" while our vehicles carried a letter "K" for Panzergruppe Kleist.

About evening we reached a hill in the area west of Podgorodnoje. The Company was halted for the night and dug in at once. Our neighbors were 15./GERMANIA to the right and 2./A.A. 5 to our left. In the Company's sector the deployment was from right to left: the Second Platoon, the First and the Third. The heavy machine gun platoon dug in behind the two platoons deployed on the right, through whose sector passed a dirt road. We knew little of the enemy. There was still supposed to be a Brigade Staff located northwest of Petrikowka, but nothing was to be seen. At roughly 22.00 hours, I once again left the position and was leaning against the side of my dugout. It was a new moon and the night was dark and still. Suddenly the bursting of a handgrenade ripped the stillness of the night. Submachine guns rattled and shouts of *"Urra"* grew louder.

We had been taken completely by surprise. Contact was lost with the Second Platoon. We could see nothing. Then 15 minutes later there was the sound of combat behind us. Vehicles burned, accompanied by explosions. Then it became quiet again; the Russians had stopped moving. The silence was sinister. Would they repeat their attacks on another position? Had the Russian unit lost forward contact? Have our units in the rear been wiped out? Does the enemy believe us to be destroyed? What has become of my Second Platoon?

I decided to first clarify the situation in our rear and attempt to make contact with Battalion; however the messenger returned without success. Then I set out myself with Uscha. Kahler in the direction of our still smouldering supply vehicles. Kahler was one of those patrol leaders whose personal courage and luck were well known. We reached the old site of the Battalion command post unmolested. But it appeared to have been transferred to the rear. The men from the supply train knew nothing about it, so we made our way back along the dirt road. Careful to avoid making any noise, bent low, we had covered almost half the way back when suddenly we heard shouts in Russian, *"Stoi—rucki werch!"* As if struck by lightning we lay pressed against the earth as a burst from a submachine gun whipped by overhead. We stayed put for a moment and then crawled sideways to the rear. There was no more doubt; the Russians located on the road had lost forward contact. They now wanted to wait there until dawn and had posted sentries. As I had previously heard no combat noise from the sector to my left, that of 2./A.A. 5, I decided to search out the company and at the same time determine how far to the side the Russians had gone. Luckily we found the company's command post with Hauptsturmführern Recke and Schnettler, but they were unable to help us as the situation in their sector did not appear to be too clear. Also they were counting on similar attempts to break through there. Disappointed, I set off with Kahler to find my own men again. It was 01.00 hours when we arrived back at my command post, an earth dugout. Nothing had changed. One could only assume that the Russians viewed the breakout as a success and assuming that no Germans were behind them they were waiting for dawn. For us everything depended on not revealing our position. The Company succeeded in regrouping into a hedgehog position without making a sound. The possibility of surprise in the grey of morning had to be used to our advantage. The first shot, fired from my dugout, was to be the opening shot of a surprise fire from all available barrels. Until then no man was to let himself be seen or heard.

During these preparations I received a report that the leader of the heavy machine gun platoon at the top of our dugout had been wounded and had collapsed near the Russians' position. We had to bring him back immediately as capture by the Russians meant certain death.

Quickly we fetched a tent square and Kahler, the messenger and I crawled in the likely direction. We found the platoon leader straight away and dragged him wounded, but without making a sound, on the tent square back the way we had come.

Back in our dugout we waited for the glow on the horizon which would announce the dawn. Every one of us realized the seriousness of the situation. Then suddenly we heard the name of our company ring through the night. "15. Company *NORDLAND!*", roared someone in a tenor voice. I shook with excitement. Should I give an answer? No, no one moves. Thank God. For the moment we must simply leave the Battalion, which is apparently searching for us, in the dark....

A short time later, we were again in danger of being discovered when from the company's left wing my name was screamed through the night. It sounded like a cry for help. Quickly I ran toward the sound and came across a completely panicked Unterscharführer, who I dragged back into the dugout. He had lost his nerve and was seeing attacking Russians before him everywhere. A few calming words worked wonders.

Finally dawn broke. On the road to our right we could see the outline of a long column. Clearer now we could see horse drawn vehicles, tractors and between them men. The closely-spaced column began far to our rear and its end was not yet visible. Finally the first burst of MG fire, the appointed signal, ripped the morning stillness. A hail of bullets showered the surprised Russians. They were completely confused and sought cover beneath their vehicles. While the first ran to the rear they returned our fire. They were answered by accurate fire from our mortars. There was a hellish racket.

Suddenly the Russians began to flee at random. Terrified screams rang out, "*Tanki, Tanki!*" Then above on the heights we saw the first Panzerspähwagen from A.A. 5 which attacked, turning the odds in our favour. But the Soviets' resistance was obstinate and lasted until late morning. In the course of the afternoon the terrain was cleared. Waving white flags, the rest, numbering in the hundreds, surrendered. The enemy's losses had been high. On both sides of the road in our sector alone we counted 163 dead. We ourselves were lucky to escape with a few wounded. Without strict discipline the number would have been far higher."

Every frontline soldier knows from his own experience now and then just how dangerous these seemingly harmless situations can be. Many such bitter combats were fought by stragglers from both sides in the rear of the large formations in these last days of September. These actions on the wings of the large operations cost the lives of many men. A dramatic example is provided by the fate of the section chief of 2./SS-Pz.Jg.Abt. 5, Uscha. Mette and his men. During the advance by Gefechtsgruppe Stolz southward from Kobeljaki, they fell out due to engine trouble along the way and had been placed under the command of a rear security unit. After repairs to his gun, Mette volunteered for a reconnaissance mission. He and his entire crew failed to return from this operation. Their fate is revealed in the following original letters:

"Dienststelle der
Fp.Nr. 20 471
E.O. 25.November 1941

Gentlemen
Hauptmann Böhmer
Fp.Nr. 43 578

In regard to your inquiry of 18. 10. 1941, which I received yesterday, I wish to inform you that there is much concerning the case in question which is unexplicable. We may be able to discover all the facts if the severely wounded SS-Man from your unit, Erich Kluss, survives. Of the incident I can tell you that on 1. Oct., my Company had to watch about 5,000 prisoners in Tschaplinka. At roughly 20.00 hours ,I received a report that a strong Russian force with 2 guns was 8-10 km. north of Tschaplinka. They had halted in a depression and planned to launch a surprise attack and burn Tschaplinka during the night. Thereupon I brought the following units in Tschaplinka to alert and then ordered the town secured:
    RAD 1/20 with 2 MG
    SS-WIKING 1/7 with 1 MG and 1 antitank gun
    own unit 2/18 with 2 MG

At about 05.00 the security forces were brought in as nothing special had occured. At 06.00, SS-Uscha. Mette and three men volunteered to undertake a motorized reconnaissance of the area in question 8-10 km. north of Tschaplinka. Ltn. Caselmann, Uffz. Fütterer and Gefr. Sönder from my unit likewise volunteered. I ordered Lt. Caselmann to be back by 08.00 as the Company had been ordered to transport the prisoners to Dnepropetrovsk on 2. October. In Tschaplinka there still remained 40 men from my unit and 100 wounded Russians. I myself had left with the remainder of my Company and the prisoners for Dnepropetrovsk at 07.00. On the 3rd, after Ltn. Caselmann had not reported back, I set out once again for Tschaplinka. While enroute I received the report from an Unteroffizier of my unit that Ltn. Caselmann with 7 SS-Men and 2 other members of my unit had been found dead on the east road leading out of Magdalinowka. It is still not clear what had induced the recon party to enter Magdalinowka contrary to my orders. I can only assume that nothing turned up in the assigned area and that they discovered the march route from civilians or were led there by the 4 straggling SS-men. The SS-men must have been picked up later as SS-Uscha. Mette left Tschaplinka with only 3 SS-men. I received further information concerning the events on 5. 10. 1941 through Ltn. Schmitz-Ost's report, a copy of which is enclosed.

                                          signed Reutter
                              Hauptmann and Company Chief

Schmitz-Ost E.O. 4.10.1941
Ltn., Leader of the Antitank Platoon
(Feldpost Nr. 23 442)

Report
On the day of the transfer of the Command Staff from Kobeljaki to Nowomoskowsk, I reached the west entrance to Magdalinowka with two guns at 12.15 hours. There I was stopped by military police and given the following report: since the morning hours vehicles were being shot at on Panzer Route K, a PKW had been captured by the Russians and at around 11.30 hours heavy firing could be heard from a range of 2-3 km. in a westerly direction. Through observation from a roof we discovered Russian soldiers with horse drawn guns. 15 minutes before my arrival, a Slovakian Major with two platoons of Slovakian troops reinforced by several members of a German Werkstatt Company had set out in the direction of the enemy. I decided to make contact with the Slovakian Major and drove after him with my guns. At the edge of a wood I met Heereshauptwerkmeister Freudenberg (L.AR.16, Feldpost Nr.23 161) who had gone through the wood capturing prisoners as well as an MG and guns. The two Slovakian platoons had advanced to their right and as I drove up to them I observed a horse drawn 7.5 cm. gun which the Russians had abandoned as they tried to withdraw. When we had taken prisoners and arrived at their position, the following picture presented itself: a gun stood, still unlimbered, aimed at Magdalinowka. The position before us had already been shelled. 100 meters to the left was a perfectly camouflaged German 3.7 cm. Pak, also unlimbered directly behind its tractor which was also camouflaged with straw. This gun had fired several rounds at the Russian position but then must have been captured. As for the vehicle, it was from the SS-*WIKING* No. 109 368. The interior of the tractor had been torn out and searched. Behind the Russian gun we found the first German dead and after further searching we found 11 German soldiers. Only SS-Man Erich Kluss (Feldpost Nr. 43 578), with knife stab wounds in the back, showed any signs of life. He was immediately taken to the Field Hospital in Kobeljaki. The dead had been killed from close range by rifle and pistol fire and some had been stabbed as well. According to the doctor they had all been killed 1 1/2-2 hours before we found them. Major Domes (1b of the fast Slovak. Division) interrogated the prisoners who were led by a Jewish commissar.

The members of the SS-*WIKING* antitank gun crew were SS-Uscha. Werner Mette, SS-Gefr. Josef Flegel, SS-Men Adalbert Leitgeb, Karl Emig, Alois Fonfara, Erich Kluss and two men whose names could not be determined. (Identity disk Nrs. 2/SS Pz.Jg.Abt. 5 Nr.312 and 2.Pz.Jg.E Abt. 5 956) The other three dead, Leutnant H.Caselmann, Gefreiter A. Sönder and Emil Fütterer were probably the crew of the PKW captured by the Russians on Panzer road K.

signature

A Destructive Battle of Encirclement

The new operation launched from the Saporoschje—Dnepropetrovsk area had two objectives. It was to collapse the enemy's entire Dnepr front as far as the Sea of Azov and attack the Soviet forces opposite 11. Armee west of Melitopol (the 9th and 16th Armies with a total of 12 fresh divisions) in their northern flank and rear and destroy them. The assignment led the Panzergruppe southward. This move was important as 11. Armee's Nordgruppe was being hard pressed by the Soviets and the 3rd Rumanian Army fighting there had already had to be reinforced by XXXXIX. Gebirgskorps, originally intended for the Crimea. The enemy was still so firmly entrenched on 11. Armee's northern front between the bend in the Dnepr and Melitopol that the arrival of Panzergruppe 1. was decisive in determining the outcome.

On 1. October, the advance guard of XIV. A.K. crossed the bridge over the Samara near Novo Moskowsk. 13. Panzerdivision was diverted southward through Rasdory while the WIKING Division had previously taken Pawlograd by surprise attack. However, the attack launched by the reinforced NORDLAND Regiment against the hill positions near Pawlograd was broken off on 4. October. After WIKING had been relieved by elements of 198. Inf.Div. on the night of 3./4. October, it followed 13. Pz.Div. which was already pressing forward to the south. Meanwhile, III. Pz.Korps which was driving near Saporoschje was deployed to smash the northern flank of the enemy forces opposite 11. Armee in the direction of Orechow. Advancing past enemy forces retreating toward the east, XIV. Pz.Korps reached Guljaj-Pole on 6. October and turned southwest through Pologi into the enemy's rear. At about the same time, III. Panzerkorps was advancing from the direction of Orechow toward Totmak and Tschernigowka while 11. Armee's two other Inf.Korps, XXXXIX. Geb.A.K. and XXX. A.K., moved to the attack, driving the enemy before them.

The WIKING Division had reached Konskije-Rasdony on 9. October and the reinforced NORDLAND Regiment had advanced farther south as far as Stara-Konstantinowka.[1] The ring began to close around the enemy; he had waited too long to withdraw. Certainly there was a wild night combat in the vicinity of Konskije-Rasdony between the reinforced WESTLAND Regiment and strong enemy columns with tanks which were trying to break out to the east, but this battle could not change the final outcome.

The blockading forces of the WIKING Division on both sides of the Melitopol-Stalino road east of Tschernigowka were witnesses to the destruction. Masses of men ran desperately here and there, leaderless and unable to organize their still considerable forces for an attempt to break out to the east. By 10.10 hours, it was over for these miserably led troops who had suffered heavy losses in men and material. 65,000 prisoners, 125 tanks and 500 guns fell into German hands. Von Rundstedt, Commander in Chief of Heeresgruppe Süd, thanked 11. Armee, 1. Panzerarmee and Luftflotte 4 for their efforts in an order of the day. Also receiving mention were, "the units of our Italian, Rumanian and Slovakian allies". At the same time the order also gave a new target, to "wipe out in tireless pursuit" the rest of the enemy army.[2]

IV. The Winter Battle of Rostov

On 10. October, the *WIKING* Division was withdrawn from the units of III. Panzerkorps[1] and was once again placed under the command of XIV. Armeekorps. It advanced along the Melitopol—Stalino highway toward Wolnowacha where it caught up with the enemy and was able to bring him to battle. Then the God of Winter intervened in the fighting. A long continuous rain came to the enemy's assistance. It transformed the narrow dirt roads into bogs and the bordering fields into swamps. The pursuing motorized units of Panzergruppe 1 found themselves in a difficult battle with the elements which again and again gave the enemy the opportunity to escape. Nevertheless, the *WIKING* Division crossed the Kalmius against light opposition and advance units reached Ignatijewka. The Division was now stretched out over 100 km. of road. Everywhere along the long road, single vehicles and small units were bogged down in the mud. Everyone was happy to reach the next village in this sparsely settled country and to be able to get some shelter and protection from the weather. The supply problems grew. Soon there were shortages of fuel and vital supplies. There was no bread and little to drink. The water was bad and sometimes even contaminated. The morale of the troops and command had sunk to zero. It could be counted on that the enemy would exploit this paralysis to overcome his present weakness. Gathering behind the next river, reinforced and resupplied he would form a new line of resistance.

In these miserable days the vast desolate countryside of the southern Ukraine between the Dnepr and the Donez revealed the full malice of its black earth. Every movement by wheeled or tracked vehicles became a laborious exercise in the muddy lanes, vehicles were ruined and fuel consumption skyrocketed. Any tank or gun that deviated from the muddy roads or tried to move into position off the road sank into the soft earth up to the axles. Vehicles which did so could often only be pulled out after strenuous efforts. The only possible means of advancing was to use the tough little steppe horses. The Russians hitched them to small carts and were able to slowly negotiate the black earth tracks of the Ukraine. Next to these, the best case was a barefoot man or one wearing light footwear.

The Division O 3, SS-Sturmbannführer and Danish volunteer Paul Engelhardt-Ranzow, made daily entries in his diary. These entries give a living picture of the daily situation:

13. October Evening: storm, rain and snow. The roads bottomless. The Russian officers and commissars have fled or been shot by their men. The soldiers give themselves up by companies. We don't have enough men to watch them or interrogate them so we tell them to simply keep heading west. Somewhere they will be rounded up. Apparently most of them disappear again. Paetsch (1c Div. der Verf.) and I carry out interrogations the entire night.

14. October Apolstolskoje, frost in the evenings.

15. October Evening Ignatijewka, only A.A. 5 forward. Div.Staff also there. Advance forward only 15 km. Div.Commander nervous and irritable. Enemy disintegrating and in retreat but we are unable to pursue. Our Division needs 136 cubic metres of fuel operating serviceable vehicles on passable roads. Today in the mud 350 cubic metres. But

we already need 700 cubic metres just to bring fuel from Dnepropetrovsk since the trains still can't come any further. So we just sit here without fuel—motorized units, tanks, aircraft. The water is very bad. I put a glass of boiled water down in the evening and the next morning the bottom of the glass was covered with a 1 cm. thick layer of oil.

16. October Still Ignatijewka

17. October Again a few kilometres to the east as far as Mokri- Jelantschik.

18. October Still no fuel. Today the 1b radioed from Guljaj- Pole that he had hauled 110 cubic metres that far. But from there to us is 200 km. When he arrived there were just 85 litres left. German readers tell a story where Russian Komsomol members apprehend a German saboteur in the Russian school we find an artillery training manual.

19. October We are still stuck fast. Division has decided to issue some of the desperately sought after fuel to a Gefechtsgruppe and a few Pioniere so that they can advance eastward toward the Krynka. The Operations Staff and Gefechtsgruppe von Scholz reach Mokri Jelantschik. The Division now covers 125 km. of road space. Fog, rain, mud!

22. October Rain the entire day. WIKING has Schachty north of Novo-Tscherkask as its target. Roads unusable. Kradmelder now come on *Panje* wagons. "Motorized" Spähtrupp A.A. 5 is sent off by horse. We get almost no bread and live exclusively on fat meat. Laboriously the Division moves east hitched to oxen!

23. October The Division has assembled enough fuel for the operation toward the Krynka. The majority still immobile. Morale lousy.

A Daredevil Dane

In these days an event occured which was not easily forgotten. At that time the 1c was facing several problems. The NORDLAND Regiment was to attack the Ukrainian city of Amrosiewka the next day without detailed information on the enemy's strength or deployment. Ranzow complained to the O 1 about the sparse reports which he had given SS-Staf. Fritz von Scholz. "Leave it to us, we'll take care of it." was the answer. In fact the Ic received a report the following morning that Amrosiewka was defended by two Russian battalions and an artillery battery. The disposition and composition of the Russian forces was given down to the last detail. There was great speculation by Ranzow. When the O 1 gave him no information he pressed his driver on the subject. He told him that on the previous evening, clothed in thick furs and accompanied by two military police, they had taken a Russian artillery tractor and stalked forward to the Soviet positions. When a sentry challenged them, the O 1 cursed the *Muschik* terribly, asking why he had called to them so late and immediately began interrogating him. Intimidated, the sentry named the password and allowed the strangers to proceed. He pulled off the same maneuvre with several officers and NCO's in the town before making off again. On 24. October, Kampfgruppe von Scholz took the town with minimal losses. The detailed briefing given by the Division Ic had substantially eased their task. When Count Ranzow interrogated prisoners on 1. November, several declared that the Commander in Chief of the Southern Front, Marshall Voroshilov, had personally inspected the city's defences a few days before. Asked by the Battalion Ia if this could be true, he replied that it was rubbish. The O 1 had passed himself off as Voroshilov during his nighttime sortie.

Naturally, this 1. Ordinance Officer is well remembered by all of the "Wikingern". He was the former Kapitänleutnant and now SS-Hstuf. Frederik-Christian von Schalburg, the spokesman for all of the Division's volunteers and their representative to the Division Commander. The volunteer mentality was familiar to him from the Soviet Winter War against Finnland where he had seen war service with the Danish Auxiliary Corps. He was born in Smiernogorsk, Siberia on 15. 4. 1906, the son of a Danish landlord and a Russian mother from Imperial nobility. He spoke fluent Russian and understood exactly the Russian mind. During the Russian Revolution he emigrated with his parents to Denmark where he entered the Royal Danish Guard as a young man. This service introduced him into high Danish circles. He became a captain and stood in high Danish service as the King's adjutant. This service made him the most qualified to represent his Danish comrades in the Division. He is credited with many daring operations such as the one at Amrosiewka.

Advance Against Stiffening Opposition

On 23. October, the weather improved. Gefechtsgruppe von Scholz could finally advance again. I./*NORDLAND* reached the road from Uspenskaja to Amrosiewka and led by its commander, SS-Stubaf. Polewacz, took the town. SS-Standartenführer von Scholz, with II./SS-*NORDLAND* under the command of SS- Stubaf. Stoffers as the new advance guard, pushed east through the woods southeast of Amrosiewka. In a rapid advance it took the heights on the west bank of the Krynka. From there the wide panorama of the hilly landscape, cut through by the Krynka and Mius rivers, spread out before the attackers' eyes. The forward reconnaissance ran into the enemy near Belajarowka. They were defending the town and were able to knock out a heavy armoured scout car belonging to the Aufklärungsabteilung. Meanwhile, the advancing A.R. 5 had gone into position with two battalions and opened fire on Kolpakowka where the enemy had retreated behind the Krynka. Immediately, II./*NORDLAND* attacked and quickly pressed into the town, which had been hurriedly evacuated by the enemy. This consisted of an enemy cavalry division which galloped off trying to reach the protection of the *Balkas* east of the Krynka. The German artillery pursued the enemy column of riders which, routed, disappeared into the river's side valleys. On the same day, Gefechtsgruppe von Scholz reached the area south of Dimitrijewka while the leading elements of the following Gefechtsgruppe Stolz got as far as Uspenskaja. 16. Panzerdivision had succeeded in occupying the town of Golodajewka on the Mius against negligible opposition. The enemy had therefore not been able to use the time he had gained while the German attackers battled the weather to organize an effective defence on the Mius river sector. In any case, he had deployed so much infantry on the heights east of the Mius that a rapid pursuit was now no longer possible.

On 29. October, the linkup between XXXXIX. Geb.Korps and 1. Gebirgsdivision on the northern flank of XIV. Panzerkorps was achieved. The enemy was now active in the air. On 30. October, the Division was attacked three times from the air and again during the night. A day later Luftwaffe aircraft appeared in the sky. Over Gefechtsgruppe reinf. *NORDLAND* Rgt.'s sector alone, German fighters shot down 5 Russian aircraft and cleared the sky of the Soviet Airforce.

"Enemy resistance stiffening before 1. Geb.Div.", reported Oberst Hans Steets, 1. Geb.Division's 1a. "The enemy holds the territory two kilometres north and northeast of the small Dimitriewka bridgehead. He is thus in possession of the commanding high ground on both sides of the Owrag river, which empties into the Mius near Dimitriewka. 1. Geb.Div. intends to throw out the enemy by attacking with two Jäer Battalions. The SS-Division *WIKING* will provide artillery support. It has sent a forward artillery spotter to Dimitriewka. The Gebirgsjäger are grateful for this comradely assistance."[1] Now the appearance of the dry late autumn weather appeared to permit further movement to the east, especially since the Division had gathered sufficient fuel. Therefore, XIV. Pz.Korps at first opened on the Mius sector. 16. Panzerdivision had created a small bridgehead near Golodajewka from which the attack could be continued eastward in the direction of Schachty. The *WIKING* Division had moved Gefechtsgruppe *GERMANIA* into the Gustavfeld—Marienheim area to provide security for the Golodajewka bridgehead. Advance elements of the *WESTLAND* Regiment had assembled near Bischlerowka and *NORDLAND* was ready in the area northwest of Golodajewka. The Division Staff, which had halted in Gustavfeld, was subjected to several attacks by enemy bombers.

Now the last preparations for the resumption of Panzergruppe 1's offensive toward Rostov-Schachty were finally complete. The renewed attack by XIV. Panzerkorps was scheduled for the morning of 5. November. From the Golodajewka bridgehead, 16. Panzerdivision was to advance east toward Agrafenowka while 14. Panzerdivision was to attack through Kirssanowka—Bolsche- Krepinskaja. Behind 16. Panzerdivision, the *WIKING* Division was to cross the Mius near Golodajewka, veer northward and guard XIV. Pz.Korps' northern flank south of Diakowo along the Zinnejanko—Novo-Alexandrowka—Astachowo road against the hill country to the north near Rowenki. In support of Panzergruppe 1's advance, 1. Geb.Div. was to launch a limited attack through Diakowo toward Darjewka tying down the enemy forces there. In his memoirs, the Division's Commander judged the situation sceptically: "A bold plan, perhaps too bold with the weak forces that Panzergruppe 1 had at its disposal. It lacked depth. As far as the Dnepr the whole area is empty. The supplying of two armies depended on a single railway line. In addition, there was the changeability of the weather. We were still in November. We had experienced enough in recent days to know what rain, snow and mud meant. As long as the enemy is still distant, such anxieties are not necessary. But what if he brings up reserves? We all had misgivings. The front line soldier knows exactly when he can risk something and when he can't"

It began on 5. 11. 1941. In two Kampfgruppen, 16. Panzerdivision made rapid progress under the covering fire of the Division's artillery. In the presence of the Panzers, the Russians kept their heads down but put up renewed resistance when the Grenadiere attempted to clear them out and open the way for their advance to the east. I./SS-*GERMANIA* tried to roll up the Russian front from Golodajewka to the south but became embroiled in tiresome fighting at every enemy strongpoint. It was here that the leader of 2./*GERMANIA*, Ostuf. Frhr. von Oeynhausen, was killed in action. The attack by the Panzers of 14. Pz.Div. turning north from Kirsanowka put an end to the nightmare. By the evening of 5. November, Kampfgruppen Dieckmann and Joerchel stood on the eastern Mius heights and had fought open the way east for the Division. Thus on the morning of 6. November, Gefechtsgruppe Stolz was able to cross the Mius heights and turn northeast toward Perwomaisk/Oktjabrisk in order to take possession of the road to Astachowo. Once again pouring rain and wet roads hindered the advance. The rills had swollen to brooks and vehicles at times had to be pushed up slippery grades until level ground was reached again.

Ghostlike Soviet Cavalry

At this point, an unusual event occured which seemed astonishingly out of place considering the mechanized nature of the battles of the Second World War: troops of attacking Russian cavalry! The war diary of Pz.Jg.Abt. 5 reported 6. 11. 1941:". . . Shortly thereafter, the lead elements of the Kampfgruppe came under attack by Russian cavalry. A short time later they had been shot down to the last man by the Gebirgsjägern . . ." An eyewitness to another attack by Cossacks on the same day was the Chief of 7. Battery A.R. 5, Ostuf. Bernau. This is his description of the attack: ". . . It was in the course of the advance toward Schachtinsk. 7. Battery had gone into position at right angles to the advance route on the eastern edge of Nowo-Krasnowka, a village of 10-12 houses. There was no firm contact with the enemy. They were trying to avoid the Division which was marching eastward in three spearheads. Together with the *NORDLAND* Regiment we were the left, northern wedge. North of us there were no more friendly troops for 40 km.. The observation post was manned by the Observation Officer, the Forward Artillery Spotter was with the infantry. I had just come from up front to see that all was well in the firing position and also to take the opportunity to visit the field kitchen for something to eat. While I was standing at the field kitchen with the Battery Officer, Ustuf. Lindner, I happened quite by chance to look toward the range of hills 2-3 kilometres north of our position. At first I couldn't believe my eyes. In the name of heaven, what is that? A closed front of horsemen burst forth from the hills and stormed toward us. I nudged Lindner who yelled: "Alarm-Cossacks!" For a few seconds everyone was paralysed. Seconds seemed like an eternity. But then the spell was broken. Ustuf. Lindner and I each ran to a gun and finally the first shots roared out in a direct fire. Meanwhile, both of the antiaircraft vehicles' (Trulu) MG's begin to hammer. The range decreases—700—600—500 metres. Now all guns are firing. A terrible sight. Horses and riders plunge to the ground, yet the cavalcade continues to storm seemingly irresistably toward us. By the time they are 100 metres away, the attack has been so decimated that it no longer poses a serious danger. Still, 70-80 Cossacks reach our fire position swinging their *Saschka* (Cossack sabres) above their heads. The majority break through and disappear beyond the next hill; the rest have fallen in battle.

We are all still quite numbed when the apparition has passed. Of the approximately 600 Cossacks, more than 300 lay dead on the battlefield. Interrogation of the survivors revealed that the Russian commander thought that the troops in front of him were his own. By the time that he recognized them as Germans it was too late to turn around, so he decided to try and ride over us. The destruction of this cavalry regiment belonging to Marshall Budjenny's army was entirely due to the devastating effect of our shells. A half year later in the Caucasus the Division would run into the Cossacks again."

6. 11. 1941 brought heavy rain and certainly marked the turning point in the Division's fortunes. On this day, which saw the first setback for the *WIKING* Division in the march to the east, there appeared another surprise. A Panzerjäger described the events in III./*NORDLAND*'s sector: "The infantrymen who had been visible on the hill moments before suddenly disappeared into their protective dugouts. Soon afterward, there appeared three then four Russian tanks on the hill at the HKL. They then drove slowly through our main line of resistance, firing their cannons at our village. My four guns opened fire simultaneously and I could clearly see that the 3.7 cm. tracing rounds were on target. I was startled to see the tanks continue on and once again circle round the infantry's dugouts. Round after round was fired by our guns with no discernable effect. The rounds simply bounced off the tanks and only a hit in the suspension or tracks achieved any results. In short, we had the first T-34's in front of us. . .''

In Combat With Superior Enemy Forces

In this phase of the fighting on 7. November, enemy bombers reappeared and attacked the march columns. Countermeasures were about zero. *WESTLAND*'s advance guard under the command of Battalion Commander Dr.Frhr. von Hadeln had reached Oktjabrisk. One kilometre to the northwest, the march column of 1. G.D. (Inf.Rgt. *Großdeutschland*) was assembling. It developed into an indescribable mix up. Gefechtsgruppe Stolz, less I./*WESTLAND*, had to be diverted south as the rapidly advancing 16. Panzerdivision was engaged in heavy fighting and needed reinforcement. Gruppe von Scholz (*NORDLAND* Rgt.) was therefore called in from the middle of the advance and Gruppe von Oberkamp (*GERMANIA* Rgt.) pushed forward as the Division's southernmost column toward Agrafenowka. Moving south of I./*WESTLAND*, it fought its way through enemy advance guards toward the east. Northwest of Oktjabrisk, 1. G.D. gradually moved forward. It also encountered a wild attack by Soviet cavalry, which was shot to pieces by a hastily assembled defence front. Enemy air attacks caused severe losses in its rear. Without a doubt the Soviets were fighting here to gain time. Their resistance became harder and ever harder. They introduced new weapons as well, including the previously unknown "Stalin Organ". They inflicted serious but not fatal losses on I./*WESTLAND*. I./*SS-NORDLAND* meanwhile, had finally won freedom of movement and was able to roll east along the wide ridges toward Ostakowo meeting little resistance. To the south, however, Russian units everywhere were fleeing into the countryside attempting to escape to the north. The Division's widely separated forces had to watch out from all sides. When they set up their strongpoints for the night they always had to take up hedgehog positions. There they lay like lost islands surrounded by ebbing breakers.

As related by Steets[1], 8. November brought recognition for 1. Geb.Div.'s unheard of efforts and accomplishments. The enemy no longer offered any organized resistance. At 15.00 hours, the interim report by Generalmajor Lanz arrived at the Geb.Korps:

"Gefechtsgruppen Kress and Picker have worn down the enemy in tireless attacks by day and night despite difficult local weather conditions and, with the direct comradely support of SS-Division *WIKING*, have driven the fiercely resisting enemy from his positions...

Shortly thereafter, the long-contested village of Djakowo was in the hands

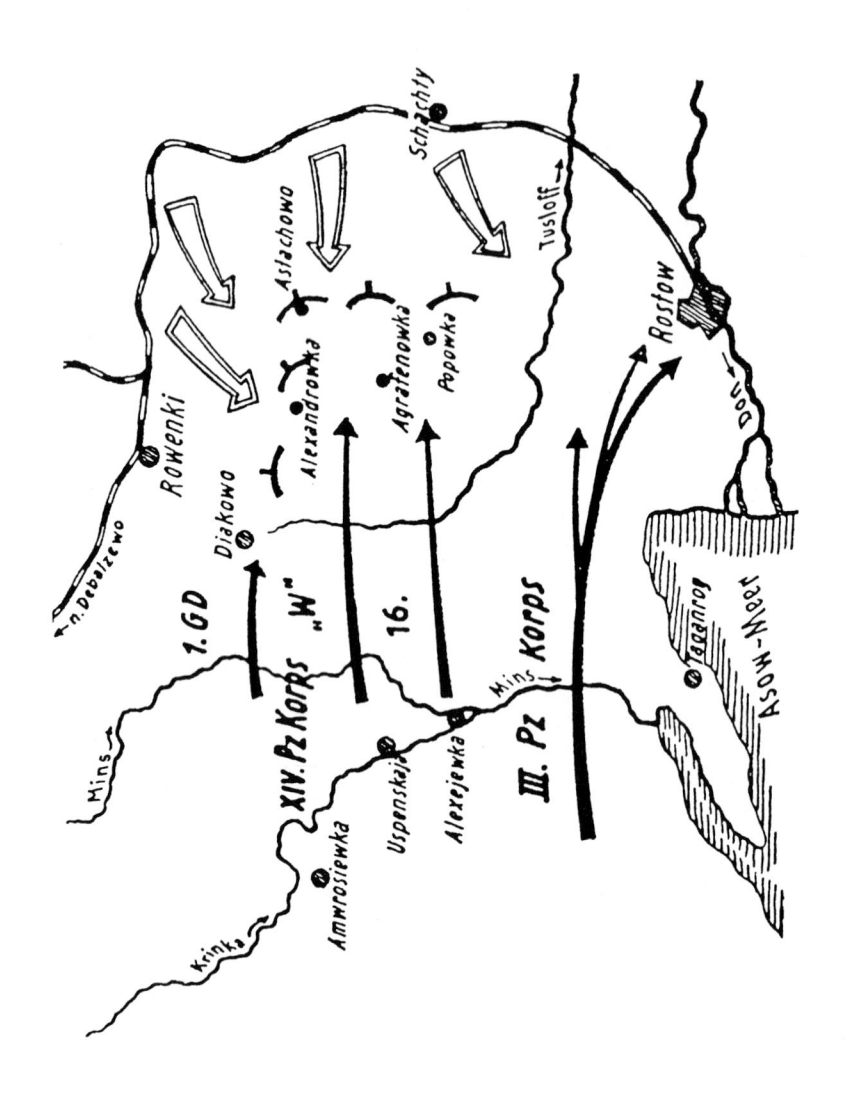

The situation November 1941

of 1. Geb.Division. Geb.Jäg.Rgt. 99 cleared the east end south of the Nagoljnaja. Geb.Jäg.Rgt. 98 took the north end of the sprawling village and stood on the north bank of the Nagoljnaja. The Lang advance battalion covered the Division's flank. Covering parties from SS-Division *WIKING* stood 8 kilometres south of Bobrikowo. In a teletype message the commanding general thanked the SS-Division *WIKING* for its comradely support in the fighting for Djakowo. The Commander in Chief, Generaloberst von Kleist, expressed his gratitude to 1. Geb.Div. in the order of the day for 9. November:
"On bottomless roads and muddy terrain, through the most strenuous efforts 1. Geb.Div. has carried out the attack against Djakowo with tireless energy. In bitter fighting, together with their comrades, the close support pilots of V. Fliegerkorps, elements of the SS-Division *WIKING* and the advance Battalion of 4. Geb.Div., they destroyed the enemy and took Djakowo. I wish to express here my special appreciation and thanks to 1. Geb.Division. The Gebirgskorps can be proud of this latest success."

16.Panzerdivision meanwhile, had run into strong enemy forces between Darjewka and Astachowo. Gefechtsgruppe Stolz had closed the gap between XIV. Pz.Korps' northern group, 14. Panzer Div., and the southern group, 16. Panzer Div., and gone over to the defensive near Popowka and Darjewka. Gefechtsgruppe von Scholz with the seconded Kampfgruppe Frhr. von Hadeln had stretched its defensive flank to Astachowo and linked-up there with the northern wing of 16. Panzerdivision on 11. November.

On 12. November, German reconnaissance pilots reported heavy movement on the railroads near Schachty and Rowenki. They had counted over 800 rail cars at one station alone. Was the transport in or out? Since 13. November, increased numbers of cavalry patrols had appeared on the Pz.Korps' flanks. New forces were being transported in! It could have no other meaning. In the next few days things were going to heat up. That meant preparation. Since the enemy now had the necessary operational reserves at his disposal, a counterblow was expected. Already on the 14th, single tanks showed themselves on the Division's flanking front. A determined Soviet attack closed the Division's march route behind Kampfgruppe von Hadeln. A counterattack threw the Soviets back toward the north. Reinforcements for von Hadeln arrived in the form of Kampfgruppe Maack which consisted of 1. Kradschützen-Kp., 15./*GERMANIA*, 1./Pz.Jäger-Abt. 5 and 3.Batt./SS Flak 5. Moreover, a cold wave had set in with average temperatures of minus 17-18 degrees. The vehicles froze up. Everywhere drivers squatted around fires attempting to thaw out the radiators. Antifreeze was nonexistant. The cold, however, gave the enemy great mobility.

On 17. November, heavy fighting broke out all along XIV. Pz. Korps' eastern front. There was a lot of action between Popowka-Darjewka and near Astachowo. According to reports, III. Pz.Korps with LAH (*SS-Leibstandarte Adolph Hitler*) , 13. Pz. Div. and 14. Pz.Div. had set out on the attack on Rostov. 60. Inf.Div.(mot) was to cover the flank at and east of the Tusloff. The battle increased in violence. On the night of 18./19. November, increasingly heavy artillery and tank fire fell on the positions of Gefechtsgruppe Stolz between Popowka-Nowo Aksai and Darjewka. On the morning of the 19th, enemy tank forces attempted to outflank the Gefechtsgruppe north of Darjewka and break through to Agrafenowka. III./SS *GERMANIA* parried this dangerous thrust. But the Gefechtsgruppe felt it necessary to create a secondary line of defence from hastily assembled staff and supply unit personnel. 2./Panzerjäger Abt. 5 helped to deepen the defence zone. On 19. November, an attack by enemy mechanized cavalry units led by tanks was broken up by concentrated artillery fire north of Darjewka. On the following day, the Soviets resumed the attack but once again suffered heavy losses from the defensive fire of II./*WESTLAND* and III./*GERMANIA*. Heavy fire from enemy tanks and a long bombardment of Darjewka indicated that the enemy was about to attack with new forces.

On 20. November, the *"Leibstandarte"* took Rostov and advanced to the large Don bridges. 13. Panzerdivision also entered Rostov but the situation there remained critical. The flanking units north of Rostov and at the Tusloff were under constant pressure from Russian infantry. Already 13. Panzerdivision was forced to detach forces from the attack force and send them to counter these assaults and protect the northern flank. The situation became ever more difficult.

Meanwhile, on the Panzergruppe's northern wing a serious crisis had developed near Astachowo. At dawn on the 18th, strong Soviet infantry forces had attacked II./*SS-NORDLAND*'s positions there. To the west, enemy tank forces attacked the positions of III./*SS-NORDLAND* on the eastern edge of Novo-Alexandrowka. The attacks were beaten off. In I./*NORDLAND*'s sector to the west the Soviets launched a determined attack against Alexandrowka with 30 tanks. Despite the antitank strongpoints there the Russians drove around Alexandrowka as they liked, overrunning several MG units. They gave up their attempt to tear open the front when three of their tanks were set ablaze. SS-Standartenführer von Scholz, with his command post in Alexandrowka, was the soul of the defence. Certainly the 19th had been a day of heavy fighting but it had seen the Soviets take a bloody beating. The fighting had also shown conclusively that the German antitank guns had little effect on the new Soviet tanks. The only possibility for success for the 3.7 cm. Pak was to hit the tracks from point blank range and render the tank immobile. It was also difficult for the medium 5 cm. guns. In order to have a chance at success they needed to be in a favorable flanking position. The new Soviet T-34 was too heavily armoured.

On the night of the 19th, II./SS-Rgt.*GERMANIA* was detached to Gefechtsgruppe von Scholz for action on the defensive front west of Alexandrowka. The remaining antitank weapons available to Panzerjäger-Abt. 5 were also thrown in and were deployed near Lilienthal west of Alexandrowka. As expected, the Soviets launched an attack there at dawn. They broke through with superior forces but were intercepted in the rear by II./*GERMANIA* commanded by SS-Stubaf. Joerchel.[1] To support the thinly manned front, XIV. Pz.Korps made available 16. Pz.Division's Panzerregiment under Oberstleutnant Sieckenius. It was employed in a counterattack on Lilienthal and the heights to the north. Although the counterattack forced the intruding enemy infantry to retreat, it was unable to force back the enemy tanks. Aware of their superiority, the Soviet tanks accepted combat and prevented a complete success. The tank duel showed clearly, however, that only the 7.5 cm. gun of the German Panzer IV could achieve results against the new Soviet tanks.

First Retreat

In Zimljanka powerful Soviet attacks shattered against the deep flank of the Panzergruppe. But in the face of the precarious situation on the army's northern flank, Panzergruppe 1 decided to break off from the enemy and conduct a fighting withdrawal toward the Tusloff sector. During the night of 21./22. November, the units of XIV. Pz.Korps disengaged themselves from the enemy. During the course of the day, all non-essential vehicles had been pulled back into the Tusloff sector. At 22.00 hours, the infantry units covered by rearguards pulled back toward the west. In fact, the Soviets had allowed themselves to be deceived. Powerful rearguards, namely III./*NORDLAND*, Pi. 5 and the Korps Antitank Battalion Rohweder, equipped with Czech tanks armed with 5 cm. cannon, remained on the Balabanoff heights under the command of SS-Stubaf. Plöw. They were to enable the mass of XIV. Pz.Korps to withdraw behind the Tusloff and occupy the far bank as planned. Oberstleutnant Sieckenius was still in readiness east of the Tusloff while the artillery had moved into position west of the river at dawn and was ready to fire. Kampfgruppe von Reitzenstein secured the Corps' northern flank north of Balabanoff and established a loose contact with Kampfgruppe von Hadeln in Zimljanka on the Panzerkorps' northern wing.

South of the Division, 16. Pz.Div., led by its energetic commander Gen.Ltn. Hube, withdrew behind the central Tusloff. Gefechtsgruppe Stolz (*WESTLAND* Rgt.) remained on the east bank on the eastern edge of Bolsche-Krepinskaja as the rearguard. The cold weather had made movement easier while the dark nights facilitated disengagement from the enemy. 2./Pz.Jäger-Abt. 5, seconded to 16 .Pz.Div., with the *WESTLAND* Rgt., had been able to leave its positions on the Popov—Darjewka—Novo Aksai line on the night of 20./21. November and withdraw unnoticed by the enemy to a defensive position on the Tusloff west of Bolsche-Krepinskaja. However, they vacated the new positions at midnight on the 22nd and at roughly 07.00 on the 23rd set out to occupy and consolidate the positions on the Tusloff. 2. Pz.Jäger Company, now attached to III./*WESTLAND*, occupied positions in that Battalion's sector.

At dawn on 23. November, the enemy found the Corps' old positions empty. Before he could decide on a follow up move, Stukas dived on the unprepared pursuit columns finding worthwhile targets along the entire front. In particular, they attacked a Soviet motorized/mechanized Corps advancing near Balabanoff and scattered it. By midday, however, the enemy had reorganized himself and as planned gone over to the attack with large tank forces against Balabanoff. The Division's artillery, with forward observers in Balabanoff, fired hell for leather. In the afternoon, a strong tank section broke into the town. Heavy fighting broke out. Every house in the long village was fought over. Rohweder's Panzerjäger lay in wait behind walls and courtyards for the Soviet tanks and destroyed them from close range. The Pioniere of Pi.Btl. 5 went up to the tanks with concentrated charges and attacked them resolutely in close combat. The Grenadiere of Kampfgruppe Plöw held the east end of the town against the masses of Russian infantry attacking in battalion and regiment strength and fought them to a standstill. The light antitank guns provided welcome support with H.E. shells. The new commander of Pi.Btl. 5, SS-Hstuf. Albert, was killed in the fighting. His place was taken by the chief of 2. Company, SS- Hstuf. Schäfer.

Now everything was on the razor's edge! At Pz.Rgt. Sickenius' command post, the Commanding General, Gen.d.Inf. von Wietersheim, was already considering the engagement, but again refrained from ordering the counterattack in the west against the Balabanoff heights which would have led to heavy losses. If Plöw could hold, the enemy would find a dug in, defensively ready Panzerkorps facing him from behind the Tusloff sector and the attempted envelopment of Panzergruppe 1 would fail. If he could not, Balabanoff would fall. Then the Tusloff sector would probably be torn off its hinges the following morning and the forces of II. Pz.Korps, still in a fighting withdrawal near Rostov, would face the possibility of destruction. But Plöw held. Balabanoff remained in German hands.

Things were easier for the Aufklärungs Abtlg. north of Balabanoff. They were able to withdraw under little pressure from the enemy and without fighting any delaying actions. Near Zimljana it remained quiet. The enemy was screening his enveloping movements against the northern wing of Panzergruppe 1 from 1. Geb.Div. standing opposite him near Diakowo.

Of the three Red Armies recently moved in from the Caucausus and East Siberia, two were employed by the enemy command in the attack against XIV. Panzerkorps' front. From these armies, two Corps with the 51st, 295th, 96th and 253rd Rifle Divisions, the 56th Cavalry Division and the 2nd Tank Brigade, were deployed on both sides of Nowo-Alexandrowska against the SS-Rgt. - NORDLAND. But the enemy had lost the battle near Balabanoff. Now he could not count on outflanking Pz.Gruppe 1 or forcing it to retreat, but rather had to launch a frontal assault against the Panzerarmee, which was deployed on the heights on the west bank of the Tusloff. The fighting near Balabanoff cost the WIKING Division a high sacrifice in blood, nearly decimated Kampfgruppe Plöw and reduced Pi.Btl. 5's strength by 1/3, including losses of 35 NCO's and men from 2./Pi.5 which was involved in the heaviest fighting. Losses were heavy but the enemy was held off. The artillery and rocket launchers roared and the Russians fled from the front lines as reported by Pz.Jäger-Abt. 5's war diary. Sharp attacks by Stukas also added to the enemy's heavy losses.

The Commander in Chief expressed his thanks to the WIKING Division, which had held out against the enemy's main effort on the northern wing, in an Order of the Day from 26. November 1941.[1]

The Panzerarmee Oberkommando 1 addressed the following message to the WIKING Division and all units:

"Soldiers of the Panzerarmee! In the winter battle of Rostow you have performed tremendously. In the icy cold, fighting day and night, you have fought off the heaviest enemy attacks and carried out smoothly the withdrawals I have ordered. This ranks with the Pz.Armee's earlier feats. Now we are going over to the defensive in a new position and we will hold it. New enemy divisions are hurrying their way here now in a forced march and will attack. I know that my brave, fast divisions will hold the position.—

Heil to the Führer!
signed, von Kleist."[2]

In the Winter Position on the Mius

The west bank of the Tusloff, due to the river's course, was not suitable for an effective defence. The river provided little hindrance to an attacker on the northern wing, particularly on 1. Geb.Div.'s front. In any case, its winding course required too many defenders. Panzergruppe 1, therefore, decided to withdraw into the Mius sector which lay to the rear. Running roughly north-south from the Don basin to the Sea of Azov, this river with its high west bank offered better possibilities for a defensive position. The Russian winter had now fully set in. The ground was frozen hard and the river was iced over. Following the tough fighting of November, the troops were completely exhausted and their weapons and vehicles were worn out. A diary entry by the Commander of the WESTLAND

Regiment gives the unit's losses from 1. July to 30. Nov. 1941: 29 officers, 65 NCO's, 347 men killed, 21 officers, 138 NCO's and 920 men wounded. Taking into consideration 29 missing, the total equals exactly 50% of original strength!
So the retreat into the Mius sector, ordered by the Panzergruppe on 1. December, was an unavoidable necessity. Panzerarmeebefehl Nr.41:
"On the night of 1./2. December the Panzerarmee will withdraw XIV. Panzerkorps and the right wing of XXXXIX. (Geb) A.K. into the Mius position. There it will establish an effective defence and hold the position at all costs. Rearguards are to be left behind to remain in contact with the enemy. Pursuing enemy forces will be allowed to walk into a prepared field of fire."[1]
We now know that 1. Panzerarmee, as it was now called, had decided to withdraw at its own risk in the face of the threat of destruction by the enemy's threefold superiority. It is also known that the Army High Command, especially Hitler, had been opposed to the idea. The conflict reached such proportions that the highly respected, operationally superior and sensible Feldmarschall von Rundstedt had angrily resigned his position. In General Steiner's opinion the example of 1. Panzerarmee demonstrated for the first time here in the south the total misjudgement of the enemy's situation and strength. In the future this would lead to the continuous underestimation of the enemy's forces and the overestimation of the German. The complete neglect of preparations during the summer for a winter war could not now be made good in a few weeks. In consequence, the nearly burned-out troops were advised to help themselves. They did so by taking advantage of their limited opportunities and calling on all their improvisational skills as well as their will to survive.
At first it was a matter of setting up the defensive front behind the Mius as ordered by 1. Panzerarmee. This was laid down by the Panzerarmee in time with the help of men from the labour service who were readily available. The improvised positions had been hastily prepared by blasting them out of the frozen earth. To the north, the recently arrived Slovakian Fast Division had already occupied the Mius sector north of Golodajewka and linked up with 1. Geb. Div. which was withdrawing toward Dimitrijewka. It was the sole unit on this sector of the front which according to Generaloberst von Kleist's statement,"had rushed here and could intervene in events". The Slovakian Fast Division was a new unit inexperienced in combat and thus required firm support. Its commanders were former Imperial Austrian Army officers and troop leaders, its soldiers well trained, frugal and well-disciplined. Now and then they lacked the necessary hardness, but at this moment they were a welcome and necessary reinforcement for the Armee's front which was already stretched far enough.
The withdrawal from the Tusloff position was unhindered by the enemy, who was exhausted after his bloody assaults of the previous days. As per the orders of 1. 12. 1941[2], the Division moved back by Kampfgruppen into the Mius positions. There they were directed by parties of guides so that no lengthy orders from the unit commanders were required. The necessary corrections were dealt with by the troops themselves.
There was no doubt that the new positions on the west bank of the Mius were favourable. They looked down along long sections of the HKL on the enemy, who in the northern sector of the position either had to remain on the eastern heights 600 metres away or climb down into the Mius valley. WESTLAND Regiment's positions in the south of the Division's sector lay on level ground. Located on the edge of the long village of Alexandrowka- Alexejewka, the positions were espe-

cially rugged and because of the numerous *kate*, were very comfortable for the defenders. Moreover, they could receive flanking support from the artillery of 16. Pz.Division. The only weak position was that of the *GERMANIA* Regiment near Russkoje. There the Mius flowed deeply notched between high banks, offering the Soviets the possibility of approaching the Mius valley unseen along a forward road. For the defence, a sharp bend in the Mius created a dead area which made a full view of the valley impossible. It was also impossible to effectively defend this area from a forward position. It would have been too isolated and would have lacked artillery support.

The Russians quickly recognized this position's weakness. They had not pursued from the Tusloff to the Mius as energetically as they had before at the Tusloff, where they had hoped to catch the German defences behind the river. Now they took their time and felt their way carefully along the Mius especially since the German positions remained hidden from their aerial reconnaissance. They also came only in small groups, so as to offer no worthwhile target to the German artillery. The mass of their forces still lay in the rear. But the Russians had not given up. The defenders of Russkoje, reinforced I./*GERMANIA* under its circumspect commander Stubaf. Dieckmann, sensed this. At its side was III.Abtlg. SS-A.R. 5 commanded by Stubaf. Schlamelcher, which had fought side by side with its comrades from the infantry in earlier battles. As well, II./*GERMANIA* to the north near Berestowo, which lay in the path of a Russian assault from the Rotowka area, would be Slovakian unit, defending west of Golodajewka near Bischlerowka, would also be affected by any Russian attack on the Russkoje position.

Meanwhile, the Grenadiere had their hands full setting up bunkers and strong points in their new positions as the ground was frozen hard. In these days the thermometer showed 20 degrees of frost and an icy wind blew from the east. Explosives and digging tools were scarce. Nevertheless the Grenadiere toiled and sweated in the cold. They dragged building materials from kilometres away by night to build their dugouts. The artillery had it easier. They were in covered fire positions, could stay undercover during the day and even warm themselves over carefully screened fires when the visibility was poor.

The supply services were busy day and night. When they were not employed in bringing up munitions and equipment, they were busy working on cook stoves which they fashioned from gasoline cans. Russian gasmasks were converted into warmers for the sentries, while charcoal was fashioned in the villages in the rear to provide the heat. Fortunately, the Division General Command had already sent a party to the Reich in the autumn to bring back winter supplies. It had taken great pains with its assignment and had been successful to a certain degree. Day after day the Pioniere of SS-Pi.Btl. 5 went out with the Infantry Pioniere to lay mines along the front and create obstacles in front of the threatened positions.

However, the "Wikinger" first had to beat off another massive Russian attack between Russkoje and Berestowo. From 5. to 11. December, the enemy launched attack after attack including night assaults with fresh troops. Numerous crises arose during these attacks when the Soviets climbed the steep western slope near Russkoje. They dug in strong MG positions on the bank and with numerous mortar positions on the river bed had created the basis for a storm assault on Russkoje. Soon the enemy also had tanks which had crossed the frozen Mius by night. They broke into the flat sloping positions in the western half of Russkoje from the rear and found cover there in the barns and farmhouses.

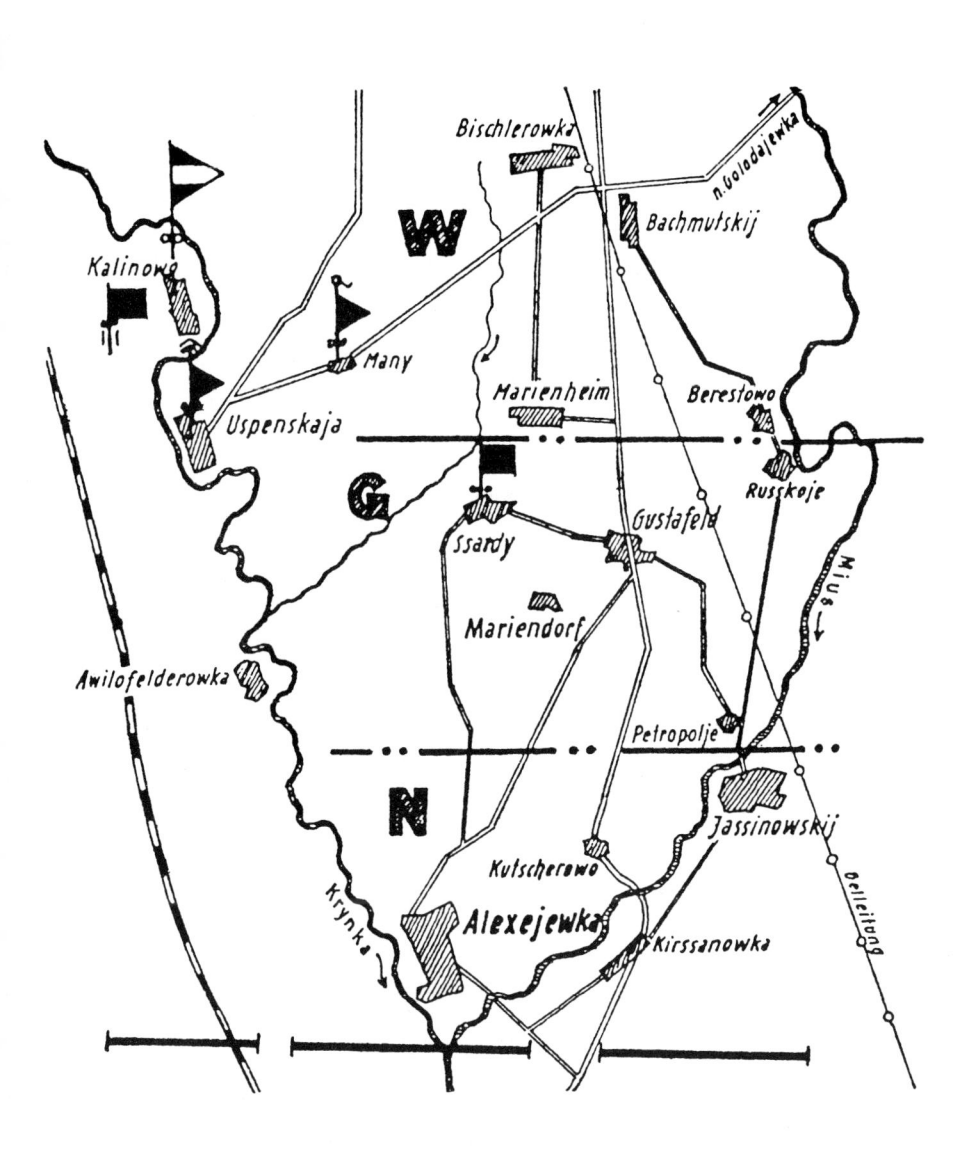

The Mius position 1941/42

But the Russians had chosen a tough opponent. The *GERMANIA* Regiment was still a master of the close combat tactics it had learned in peacetime. Every man in this unit was an experienced shock and assault trooper who had learned and mastered his handwork in three campaigns. The Russians made little impression on this unit's tight defensive positions. Providing support was the artillery of III./A.R. 5, which had learned to support motorized units with rapid fire and understood how to subdue the enemy using mobile fire tactics. In the hands of proven, decisive officers, these troops could be expected to overcome the most difficult situations. Where the enemy actually succeeded in breaking into their lines, he was immediately thrown back by aggressive counterattacks employing all available means. As a result, these battles cost the Russians heavy losses while I./ *GERMANIA*'s casualties were kept to a minimum. The enemy soon realized that he would not achieve any success here. His readiness to fight waned and transformed this dangerous and at first hotly contested sector into a fairly quiet front.

Instead, the Russians appeared to smell a chance of success against the Slovakians to the north of *WIKING*. A week later they attacked from Golodajewka toward Bischlerowa, winning the heights on the west bank of the Mius. Immediate action was necessary before the Russians could follow up with fresh troops. The *WIKING* Division gathered up the limited forces still available, a few Pioniere together with several Kradschützen, and threw them against the Soviets. The Commanding General of XIV. Panzerkorps, Gen.d.Inf. von Wietersheim, personally brought up a Panzer Company from 16. Pz.Div. and a light Zwillingsflak detachment. At dusk he sent his troops to the counterattack over the bright snow-covered landscape. With all guns blazing followed by the infantry, they roared straight toward the enemy, who had not yet been able set up a defence, and chased him back into the Mius valley.

But the front continued to remain turbulent. On the night of 26./27. December, the enemy once again tried his luck near Berestowo in II./*GERMANIA*'s sector. SS-Ostuf. Juchem lead an immediate counterattack which drove the Russians back across the Mius. And it was the Heavy Battalion of SS-A.R. 5, supported by III. Battalion from the direction of Gustavfeld, which caught the enemy in the open and caused him heavy losses. As previously arranged, both battalions concentrated their fire near Berestowo spoiling the enemy's withdrawal. One month later the Soviets attempted the same maneuvre after II./*GERMANIA* had been relieved by I./*WESTLAND*. The results were the same. Subsequently this sector too became quiet.

During the Russian night attack on Berestowo on 26. 12. 1941, the Division had a rare guest. Reichsführer-SS Heinrich Himmler had come to 1. Panzerarmee on Hitler's orders to visit the troops and convey his greetings. The visit did not run according to program. Himmler had wanted to arrive at the Division on the morning of 26. December but had underestimated the length of the trip under the prevailing weather conditions. Fetched by *WIKING* Division's 1. General Staff Officer in a cross country capable vehicle, the Reichsführer was forced to get out several times and help push their way out of mud holes. He arrived angry and tired at the command post in Kalinovo. Himmler requested that the Division commander see to it that there be proper roads behind the front. Himmler had discovered at first hand the great supply and transport difficulties that the Division had to contend with. He also learned for the first time that for weeks the troops had been forced to live on nothing but millet gruel and sticky potatoes as well as bread made from a corn mixture. The entire capacity of the single rail line which brought supplies to 1. Pz.Armee and 17. Armee was almost completely reserved for men and fuel. This was especially so since the continuous changes in weather between thaw and -30 degrees presented tremendous difficulties for the operation of the locomotives. Himmler, therefore, ordered the construction of a road which was completed in 1943.

Then came the Russian attack on Berestowo. The Division's guest witnessed the fighting and saw firsthand the actions and responsibilities of the participants. After the counterattack launched at 05.00 hours had succeeded and the enemy had been thrown back, peace returned to the command post. At approximately 10.00 hours, Himmler and the Div. Adjutant drove to Stalino airport where his Condor aircraft was waiting. The troops themselves had not caught sight of the Reichsführer-SS. The Division Commander conveyed his greetings in a Divisional Order of the Day.[3]

An High Ranking Visitor from Finnland

In January 1942, Gen. Lt. Oequist, the Finnish liason officer in the Führer's headquarters, paid the WIKING Division a visit. A short time before all the Finns were withdrawn from the Division, the guest let it be known that a self-contained Finnish battalion was being raised. All of the Finnish officers, NCO's and men presently integrated in WIKING were required to form the core of the new battalion. During the whole time of their membership in the WIKING Division, the Finns had occupied a special position. They were Finnish nationalists and sworn enemies of the Russian in his latest manifestation as the bolshevik. They faced no inner conflicts when they donned German uniforms and joined the Germans in the field against the Soviets. The Finnish government had officialy approved their decision and several weeks before the outbreak of the Soviet-German war approximately 400 volunteers had joined the WIKING Division. With a further 800 volunteers, they later formed the excellently trained and well equipped motorized battalion which rejoined the Division from Gross-Born in January 1942. In the autumn of that year the battalion was strengthened by the arrival of an additional 200 men. The battalion, consisting of four companies, was commanded by SS-Sturmbannführer Collani who proudly presented this self-contained Finnish unit to the Division's commander in Ambrosiewka.[1]

In February 1942, the Norwegian force of about 100 men was also withdrawn to its homeland, having seen a year's service. Originally 340 men strong, they had seen the war at its hardest and had distinguished themselves in the face of the enemy. The Division's gratitude went with them to their homeland.[2]

The withdrawal of these forces represented a serious loss in fighting strength which weighed all the heavier when the Division's ranks were further depleted in the heavy fighting for Rostow. Entire battalions had to be disbanded in order to keep the others combat capable. III./NORDLAND, which had fought so magnificently at Balabanoff, had to be divided between the Regiment's other battalions. In May 1942, II./WESTLAND went the same way, its units being sent to I. and III./WESTLAND. The Regiment's Kradschützen companies, all of which had lost their company chiefs, had to be disbanded. Only a motorcycle messenger platoon remained with the regimental headquarters. The Infanterie Pionier companies were also affected by these measures. They were disbanded in order to replenish the weakened combat units. Leaving the comradeship which had been forged in the previous months of combat was bitter for many, although the regiments tried to leave the smaller units together. But the needs of the Division once again forced disruptive measures.

Change of Command

The Division's personnel also received new faces. In the summer, the Division's 2. Gen. Staff Officer, SS-Hstuf. Erwin Reichel, had replaced the fallen 1. Gen. Staff Officer Ecke. He would be killed in action in 1943 on the Donez. The former Regimental Adjutant of the NORDLAND Regiment, SS-Hstuf. Kille, who would soon command the Kriegsakademie and was later killed in action, became 2. Gen. Staff Officer. The Division's 1. Ordnance Officer, SS-Hstuf. Frederik-Christian von Schalburg, was named commander of the DANMARK Free Corps. His successor as O 1 was SS-Stubaf. Wörner. The 3. Gen. Staff Officer, SS- Stubaf. Paetsch, was transferred to A.A. 5 as commander. He was later killed in action in Pomerania. His successor was the Regimental Adjutant of the GERMANIA Regiment. SS-Stubaf. Peter Kausch, commander of I./SS-A.R. 5, was named as Division Adjutant. After serving in this post for a time he returned to his previous service position.

There were also many changes among battalion and regimental commanders. The commander of the WESTLAND Regiment, actually the commander of a detached Gefechtsgruppe, Phleps a.k.a. Stolz, became the C.O. of 7. SS-Geb.Div. PRINZ EUGEN and was tasked with its initial organization. He was killed in action as commanding general in Siebenbürgen. SS- Staf. Reichsritter von Oberkamp, commander of the GERMANIA Regiment, was named as Inspector of Infantry in the SS-Headquarters. SS-Stubaf. von Reitzenstein took command of a Panzer battalion which he had set up in Germany. He was killed in action in 1944. SS-Stubaf. Plöw left for the homeland for training as a Flak commander. The commander of the disbanded II./WESTLAND, SS-Stubaf. Köller, went to the Panzertruppenschule for tank training. He was later killed as commander of a Panzerregiment. SS-Stubaf. Schönfelder was ordered to the Kriegsakademie. His successor as commander of III./GERMANIA was SS-Hstuf. Franz Hack. New regimental commanders were transferred to the Division. SS-Staf. Jürgen Wagner later took command of the GERMANIA Regiment. He had proved himself as a battalion commander in the Western Campaign and later became commander of the NEDERLAND Division, an SS-Gruppenführer and Generalleutnant of the Waffen-SS. After successfully breaking out of the Frankfurt/Oder pocket in 1945, he was captured by the English and handed over to the Yugoslavians who unjustly executed him. Command of the WESTLAND Regiment was assumed by the former Ia of the TOTENKOPF Division, SS-Ostubaf. Geisler. He led the Regiment until autumn of 1942 when he was replaced by the commander of I./NORDLAND, SS-Stubaf. Polewacz. Polewacz, a capable young commander, was killed on the Kalmück steppe in 1943. There were also many painful but necessary changes among the Company chiefs. SS-Hstuf. von Lettow-Vorbeck left the Division to take command of the FLANDERN Legion. There he was soon to be killed in action. He was replaced by SS-Ostuf. Juchem, who became Battalion Commander of II./GERMANIA in 1943 and died a hero's death near Klenowoje west of Kharkov. There were also several changes in the artillery. SS-Hstuf. Bünning became commander of I. Abteilung. SS-Hstuf. Bühler succeeded the severely wounded SS-Stubaf. Schlamelcher, who later became commander of SS-Artl. School II and died of his wounds following the war. In the Signals Battalion, SS-Stubaf. Kemper left the Division to assume command of a signals school. His successor was SS-Hstuf. Elmenreich. This summary does not claim to be comprehensive. It is merely intended to give the reader a view of the conditions within the Division's leadership.

Turn of the Year 1941/42

Christmas 1941 passed relatively quietly and with a paucity of material comforts. There were none of the special provisions with which the units of the Waffen-SS were allegedly regularly supplied. Thanks to provisions made by the Division Admin. Officer, the rations in these days, as always received from the Wehrmacht, were less monotonous than usual. He had also seen to it that a few Christmas trees were provided for some of the shelters. A little alchohol was given out which was a good thing since the thermometer had fallen to -45 degrees Celsius at Uspenskaja. But the concern which existed all along the widespread front could not be ignored. The German front still found itself in a dangerously weak condition and the enemy's combat strength was growing day by day.

In spite of the retreat, the "Wikinger"'s spirit was unbroken. The Panzerjäger Abt. even expressed a New Year's wish "to receive new antitank weapons".[1] They soon got over their disappointment. If the previous year had shown the German forces to be superior to the Russian in spirit, training and not least in weaponry, it could not be overlooked that the Soviet command was taking every measure in an attempt to reach parity. Their new tank, the T-34, was being deployed at the front en masse, their artillery shot well, and the new "Stalin Organ" was a shock weapon of great effect. The enemy infantry had been issued large numbers of submachine guns and his self confidence was improving, even if the costly mass attack tactics remained unchanged. The Soviet high command had undoubtedly learned much. In their attacks for example, they always found the correct operational positions. In contrast, the lower levels of command remained as rigid as before. Overall it could be stated that the Red Army had increased its combat skills. The Red Army soldiers had lost none of their pure soldierly qualities. It was more important now than before for the Division to emphasize the training and education of its own troops. The principles used, which are surely still valid today, were gathered from a Divisional Order.[2]

Several weeks before the arrival of the Finnish volunteer battalion, another welcome reinforcement reached the Division. At the beginning of January 1942, a brand new Sturmgeschütz Battery arrived from Germany. It had been organized by the well-proven former Battery Officer of 11. A.R. 5, SS-Ostuf. Hermann Lange, and sent to the Division.[3] But the Division could not celebrate its arrival for long. In April, all of its personnel and equipment was transferred to the *LAH* which at that time was located in the Taganrog area. A serious crisis had arisen for 17. Armee but also for 1. Panzerarmee on the Mius. 1. Panzerarmee was forced to engage in the battle with forces from its northern wing in order to assist 17. Armee.

On 18. January, the Soviets attacked 6. Armee west of Kharkov with far superior forces. They hoped to employ a pincer attack with a northern spearhead north of Belgorod and a massive thrust near Isjum in the south to break through, surround and destroy the German Corps. While a breakthrough in the north was prevented, the attack to the south was successful. The Soviets were able to break through the German positions on an 80 km. front on both sides of Isjum. Their spearheads drove about 100 km. deep into the German rear and were almost to the Dnjepr before they were finally intercepted. The entire Panzerarmee on the Mius faced the threat of being enveloped by enemy forces and thrown back against the Black Sea. Therefore, it was imperative that all of the Panzerarmee's available forces prevent the Russians from turning south from the breakthrough area and also stabilize the Armee's northern flank. The Panzerarmee stretched its long front to the limit and shifted III. Panzerkorps with seven divisions from the Armee's southern wing to the area around and west of Stolnow. But the Russians were stronger and their numbers grew from week to week. III. Panzerkorps alone was not sufficient to defeat the threat. As a result the Panzerarmee had to scrape together what additional forces were available and rush them to assist III. Panzerkorps. The *WIKING* Division also sent another Kampfgruppe to III. Panzerkorps. Under the command of SS-Stubaf. Dieckmann, the Kampfgruppe consisted of I./*GERMANIA*, 1. Battery of A.R. 5 under SS-Hstuf. Fischer and Ostuf. Lange's Sturmgeschütz Battery. The Division command believed that it had created the best mix of forces for I./*GERMANIA* to be equal to the task demanded by the serious combat situation. But events were to prove different. Immediately on their arrival, the units were thrown piecemeal into the blazing front. And it blazed in so many locations along the thinly held front! The Fischer Batterie went to XI. A.K. at Sosowijn where it proved an outstanding success but suffered heavy losses. The inexperienced Sturmgeschütz Battery was immediately sent into action alone to repel a dangerous Soviet tank assault without the infantry support of I./*GERMANIA*'s Grenadiere. In bitter fighting with far superior enemy tank forces the battery fell victim to the crushing weight of numbers. Böhmer was killed in the fighting and posthumously promoted to SS-Obersturmführer. Later, his long time Abteilungs Commander appropriately lauded this splendid officer's personality and achievements in an obituary.[4]

Kampfgruppe Dieckmann (I./*GERMANIA* with Sturmgeschütze Batterie 5) stood alone in the heart of the battle. It was decimated but through its steadfastness contributed to holding the line in this decisive sector. A Gefreiter of the Wallonian Legion who witnessed SS troops in action there for the first time gave a dramatic description of the events:[5] "From 25. February on, the Russian tanks would appear as darkness fell. They approached to within several hundred metres, fired a few shots and disappeared into the darkness.
Our patrols had a bloody fight with the Russian outposts concealed in haystacks.
The Russians carried out an unusually simple plan. They blew up our obstacles one by one. Using all their forces, they first attacked the village three kilometres to the southeast of our position which was occupied by the SS. If this position had been taken, we would have been left alone to defend the slope to the Samara which the Soviets wished to reach at all costs.

The SS force consisted of about two hundred men. They were proper daredevils. Our messenger, who maintained contact with their command post, could not get over their coolness. The Russians were thirty metres in front of them and firing from every corner. In one day the Germans had to fight off ten Russian attacks against a superiority of twenty to one. Unperturbed, they put up their defence and played cards during every free minute.

But after a week they had only an approximately hundred metre-wide exit to the west. Three quarters of these brave soldiers had been killed.

On the morning of 28. February 1942 at 05.00 hours, several thousand Russian troops fell on the fifty survivors. The carnage lasted for an hour. Only a few Germans escaped. We saw them running in our direction through the snow with the Russians close behind. They came in order to go through our own disaster..."

With I./*WESTLAND* in the "Felsennest"

I Battalion of the SS-Rgt. *WESTLAND*, especially 2. Company, also achieved great success on 27. 1. 1942 in the fighting for Berestowo. Its accomplishments were mentioned in an army report.[1] Max Stöckle, a member of the company, provided the following description of those days based on his diary entries:

"The first three weeks of the new year were spent enthusiastically preparing our front revue for the troops which was to be presented to the whole Division. The Division commander himself gave us the honour and was enthusiastic over the Russian brass band and singers, the pantomime dances, parodies and the sketch "Die Nina Neumann". A great success! However, when 3. Company and the *WESTLAND* Battalion went back to their positions, the members in the revue did not want to stay behind. On 23. January, we moved back into the positions between Berestowo and Badmutzki. The Finnish Battalion were our neighbors to the right. How many remember the *"Felsennest"*, as we then named this position? It was relieved in rotations of a week. In this hole one couldn't undress so we cowered "fully robed". The table was 30 cm. high. Our rations were similarly limited; a spoonful of jam, a small piece of bread, a mess tin lid of warm food. The mice literally ate the bread right out of our pockets and ran quite unconcerned across our coat collars. The lice were unspeakable. In a homemade mill (wood in a tin can with holes) we ground corn by hand and boiled it in snow water. All of this was done under a smokey lamp which made everyone's eyes water. It was a real feat: a fish can with a cleaning rag wick, filled with kerosene. Where did we get kerosene? We tapped it from an unpressurized oil pipeline laid west of Berestowo. In the "Felsennest" it was usually freezing cold. Although we had a metal stove there was no fuel. For days on end we couldn't leave the hole as the Russians fired directly from Berestowo on the entrance. At night the position above us was also occupied. It had to remain empty during the day as it was in full view of the enemy who literally fired at every man.

On 27. 1. 1942, we were relieved from the "Felsennest" for a few days. For "relaxation" as it was called. But strong enemy fire on Berestowo boded no good. Everything was immediately made combat ready. Then the Russians attacked in battalion strength. A partial break-in was cleared by a counterattack. This cost us many dead.[2] On 29. January, we moved back into the "Felsennest". On the 30th we took fire from a "Stalin Organ". The Russians attacked. The attack was repulsed. Our artillery played a major role. Half of the Russians remained on the battlefield. On 9. February, we had been in the "Felsennest" for 16 days. From then on plenty of "Eastern Front grumbling". On the 10th it began to thaw. Then light rain even began to fall. Water stood in the "Felsennest". The word went round that we would be staying here another three weeks. The night of 5./6. March was one of the worst. A terrible snowstorm raged. One couldn't raise his head above the parapets. Weapons and equipment as well as the bunker entrance were snowed in.

On 10. March I entered: from 9. to 10. March 1942 we are to be relieved. But nothing happens. The Russians call across to us with loudspeakers: "We wish the *WIKING* Division a happy return home and all the best. Your relief will not see home again. Tell them at home of the beautiful Soviet paradise." They can't deceive everyone into believing that they are that nervous "over there". Perhaps they were eager to see the WIKING Division depart. Flares rose constantly into the night. A prisoner revealed that a German attack was expected. Russian flyers dropped leaflets: "The WIKING Division will be relieved on 21. March. A happy return home." Until that time no more attacks took place."

"On 15. 3. 1942, I. Battalion was relieved. Battered and tired we moved back on foot toward Ambrosiewka. Weapon cleaning, fresh water, peace! We have genuinely earned it.

Naturally nothing comes of the prophesied relief. Now we squat in the Badmutzki sector. On 12. May, the Gruppe Uscha. Donderer is posted to 5. Company's Pioniere Platoon. The conversion of the WESTLAND Regiment into a so-called light regiment with two battalions of five companies begins. 5. Company becomes the heavy company with a Pioniere platoon, an infantry gun platoon and an antitank platoon. A two week Pionier training course is taken with the Pionier battalion at Uspenskaja. Then it's back to Badmutzki where on 2. July the last attempted Russian breakthrough takes place. An enemy Artillery Regiment fires on our positions like madmen. "Stalin Organs" join in. Uncountable enemy aircraft are above us. The Russians storm determinedly toward us. Two thirds of them are wiped out. All hell has broken loose. Later the "coal shovels" circle overhead and drop their loads. However, on 1. 8. 1942, the advance begins again."

The fighting west of Stalino dragged on through the whole following month until the detached units, or rather what was left of them, were able to rejoin the Division.

Bringing Men and Material up to Strength

During these actions the uneasy eyes of the commander of 1. Pz.Armee, which remained on the Mius, were directed to the north. The troops themselves were not uneasy since they knew nothing of the dangerous situation. The Commanding General of XIV. Pz.Korps, Gen.d.Inf. von Wietersheim, came on three consecutive days for discussions. The subject was the precautionary measures which would have to be taken in the event that the northern flank had to be extended west to prevent a threatened encirclement. At this time XIV. Pz.Korps was largely immobile with unserviceable motor vehicles and three quarters of the guns were without tractors.

Walter Kopp, a Hauptmann in General Staff training who had been ordered to XIV. Panzerkorps to take the place of the Ic who was home on sick leave, remembers: "From the middle of March, the WIKING Division had taken over the entire sector on the Mius. On the west terrace of the Mius valley they had dug in individual strongpoints in the clay and held. They didn't defend themselves from a permanent position but lived at first with the residents of the HKL until they were billeted out.

For XIV. Pz.Korps, the WIKING regularly provided good results from short and long range reconnaissance. Particularly impressive was a sortie to count traffic on the major rail line between Millerowo and Rostov in the area north of Schachty about 150 km. east of the front lines. This reconnaissance group was not an isolated operation. The WIKING Division was also regularly active in short range reconnaissance. Prisoners were usually brought back from these operations."[1]

As the new year announced itself, awakening nature presented new dangers. The frozen river broke up and the waters climbed. Ice floes were driven by the

After a hard battle—Comrades of the Army and *Waffen-SS* share a break in the fighting.

Irrepressible infantrymen.

Soldiers are always hungry.

Watch on the Dnepr 1941.

Gunners

Advance road in the Ukraine.

Light field howitzer in a firing position.

Comrades of the ammunition section of 7./Art.Rgt. 5.

In the Mius position winter 1941/42

The "Alkazar" of Berestowo

The motorcycle messenger section of II./NORDLAND's bunker.

The "Felsennest"

Jürgen Wagner,
commander of the *GERMANIA* Regiment

Johannes Mühlenkamp,
commander of the *WIKING*'s Panzers.

SS-Aufklärungsabteilung 5 on the attack 1942.

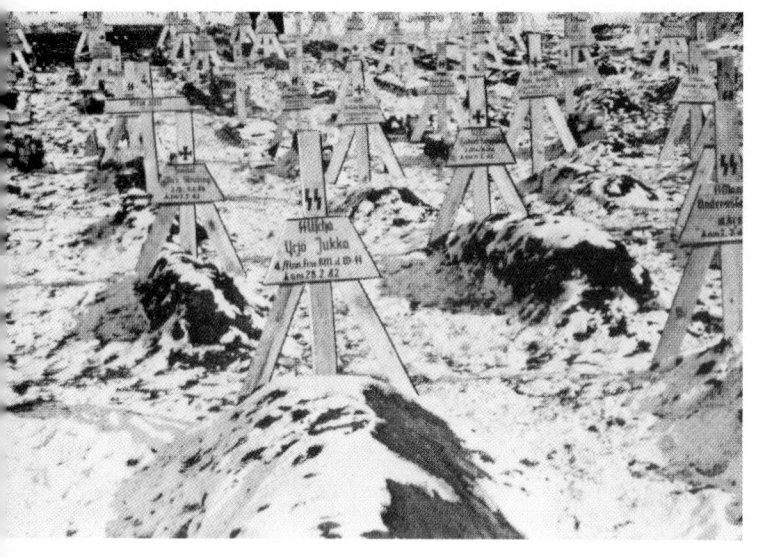

The cemetery at Ambrosiewka. In the foreground the grave of a Finnish volunteer.

"String pullers" transferring a line.

Pioniere constructing a bridge.

"*SS-Division WIKING*". Painting by E. Thöny, Munich.
(Division commander Steiner gives orders for the next action.)

Landscape near Neftjanaja in the Maikop oil region in August 1942.
Painting by former Division member Jörg Willand.

At the Don bridge
near Rostov
in July 1942.

26. July 1942:
Advance through Bataisk
(Rostov) to the south.
Red Army prisoners
stream to the rear.

Observation
in a sunflower field
near Maikop.

river against the bridge supports which began to burst. If the few bridges did not hold, the entire supply situation would be in question. The Pioniere kept watch night and day to blast apart the piled-up ice and keep the water from jumping the river's banks. After several difficult days the danger was past.

Now it appeared that the winter's concerns would be lifted. The technical chief and the unit's weapons official drove to Krakau and Berlin. They took with them a list of vehicles and weapons which were urgently required if the Division was to become a serviceable and operational unit again. It was known that in such cases the personal efforts of energetic personalities served to facilitate processing by the supply bases at home and smooth the quick transport by rail to the front.

Immediately after the cold had passed and the roads gradually began to dry, there set in a busy period of organization and consolidation throughout the whole Division. New infantry weapons came comparatively quickly to the front in order to carry out the reorganization of the Grenadier Regiments (mot) as ordered by the Army High Command. The MG company was again dispersed among the rifle companies, each of which subsequently received a heavy platoon to which a light mortar platoon was added. Instead of the MG company, each battalion received a heavy company through the disbanding of regimental units. These consisted of an 8 cm. mortar platoon, a 5 cm. antitank platoon and a Pioniere platoon. The Regiment's infantry gun companies received a platoon of heavy infantry guns. These were excellent weapons which proved very popular with the infantry and quickly earned the respect of the Russians. Then the Division set up its own assault troop training based on the lessons learned in the past year's hard fighting. Its combat techniques and weapons were far superior to the Russians'. Its main weapon was the light machine gun, around which were grouped the submachine guns, snipers, mortars and the hand grenades for close combat. Soldiers with submachine guns and hand grenades formed the assault troop while the remainder were the covering troop. This organization and equipment was made the basis for all combat school training. The regiments were all allotted time for training in small units in the numerous *Balkas* behind the front. To prevent weakening of the defensive front, the gaps left by the departure of these units were filled by supply service personnel. The commander of the supply services himself went into the trenches to gather experience on the spot and learn first hand the needs of the troops.

The depleted I./SS-*GERMANIA* had meanwhile returned and was rebuilt and reequipped as one of the Division's assault battalions. The appropriate training was immediately started and when completed was as good as any in peacetime. The officer corps under the extremely capable and creative SS-Stubaf. Dieckmann was ideally suited for such a task.

Finally the long-awaited Panzerabteilung 5 commanded by SS- Sturmbannführer Mühlenkamp arrived at the front. It consisted of about 60 medium and heavy tanks with the necessary infantry and supply services. The unit had been well prepared for its future duties by its commander. SS-Stubaf. Mühlenkamp would prove to be an able and daring Panzer commander. He possessed marked battle instincts which always led him to find the enemy's weak spots and used his experience and circumspection to lead his Panzers through every combat situation. Mühlenkamp understood the techniques of holding the high ground and used his head and heart to lead his troops in a superior fashion. He became commander of Pz.Rgt. 5 when *WIKING* became a Panzerdivision in 1944 and later Division Commander. His final position' was as the Waffen-SS Inspector of Panzertruppen. His Panzer battalion decisively strengthened the Division's combat power and provided the penetration and firepower which had been missing in the previous months, costing heavy losses. The Russian campaign had demonstrated that motorized units without tanks were always inferior to the stronger enemy units. Experience had shown that even with great bravery and steadfastness this technical disadvantage always cost a high sacrifice in blood. The commander of Gefechtsgruppe Stolz before Rostov, had already implored the Div. Commander, "Send Panzers, Herr General,[2] otherwise this wonderful outfit will go to the dogs!" Now they were there and the whole Division was filled with pride and confidence.

Attack on Rostov

As the corn began to ripen and the fields changed to yellow, the Division was preparing for the start of the offensive on the southern wing of the southern front which was to follow that which had already begun on the northern wing. 1. Panzerarmee had passed command of the Mius front to 17. Armee's Armeegruppe Ruoff and had moved north with its operations staff. In the former corps area, LVII. Panzerkorps had taken over from XIV. Panzerkorps. 13. Pz.Div., 5 SS-Div. (mot) WIKING and 298. I.D., which was known to the Division from the fighting at Dnepropetrovsk, stood under the command of General d. Pz. Truppen Kirchner. Under Kirchner and his Chief of the General Staff, Oberst i. G. Joachim Ziegler, the WIKING Division would soon get into its stride.[1]

On 16. July 1942, the Division was relieved on both sides of Golodajewka by the Slovakians and Gebirgsjägern of XXXXIX. Gebirgskorps. On 18. July, it began to shift to the south into the area northwest of Taganrog. Here, LVII. Panzerkorps was to open the Ssambek bridgehead and drive toward Rostov with its fast troops, the WIKING Division and 13. Panzerdivision. It hoped to take the city in a rapid envelopment and break open the door to the West Caucausus for Armeegruppe Ruoff.

For this assignment the Division had once again been divided into Kampfgruppen. But it could not yet employ all of its units in the upcoming battle. The WESTLAND Regiment, III./NORDLAND, and the Finnish Battalion had to give up their vehicles to the other units in order to make them fully mobile. They were to remain in the old combat zone until they were outfitted with new vehicles. After training in the Mokryj- Jelantschik area they were to catch up to the Division in a forced march. For the first phase of the summer campaign the Division was once again formed into three Gefechtsgruppen roughly of brigade strength, as they would be called today. This battle configuration had proven itself in the summer of 1941. Then, however, the Division had to fight within a Panzerkorps mainly with its infantry and artillery. Armoured units only came to its aid in the most serious situations. Now the Division had its own Panzer battalion at its disposal, albeit with a limited number of tanks. The tanks were the steel point and the core of Panzerkampfgruppe Gille, which was to open the way to the Caucausus for the Division. This configuration was later changed when the completely different foothills country of the East Caucasus demanded new combat tactics. The structure of the Division's Gefechtsgruppe was optimised for attack in open country. This made it possible for the Division to smash the enemy on the spot with a powerful blow, fight deep in the enemy's rear and as the situation developed, change the point of main effort if an opportunity presented itself. This configuration was ideal for pursuit but would have to be changed in the case of defence. The leaders of the Gefechtsgruppen were again the proven regimental commanders von Scholz and Wagner. The Panzerkampfgruppe was led by Gille, the commander of Artl. Rgt. 5. At the Division command post was located the Luftwaffe liason unit, which directed the operations of a Gruppe of VIII. Fliegerkorps which would be supporting the Division.

When 198. Inf.Div., under the command of Pz.Korps Kirchner, left the Ssambek bridgehead on 21. July 1942 to attack enemy positions, it met only weak rearguards. The enemy had withdrawn his other forces into the Tschaltyr sector near Rostow. The Gebirgskorps which had been deployed through Golodajewka southeastward toward Rostov also met only weak resistance. Here too, the enemy had withdrawn to the southeast.

On the evening of 21. July, the WIKING Division moved up behind the onrushing 13. Pz.Div. under Generalmajor Herr and advanced in a northeasterly direction north of the Ssambek—Sinjawka—Tschaltyr road. The Division marched the whole night. Forward reconnaissance found the Tschaltyr sector in the area of Krym so strongly occupied that a frontal assault appeared to offer no hope of success. According to the organizational order of 21. 7. 1942, "Gefechtsgruppe Steiner" was composed of Kampfgruppen Dieckmann, Stoffers and Weitzdörfer. Kampfgruppe Stoffers actually consisted of I./NORDLAND while Kampfgruppe Weitzdörfer was II./NORDLAND. Kampfgruppe Dieckmann's composition was as follows: Pz.Abt. 5, Command Staff KGr. Dieckmann, I./GERMANIA, 2./Pi. 5, 1 Battery III./A.R. 5, Div. Command Staff, Command Staff A.R. 5 as well as an 8.8 cm. battery from Flak-Abt. 241. Together with the remaining Wehrmacht units, they were assigned the attack on and capture of Rostov. After the artillery had moved into position it was ready to fire and at 05.00 hours on the morning of 22. July, began firing for effect. Opening fire from partial cover, Panzerabteilung Mühlenkamp laid down a barrage which the assault battalions used to conquer the first line of antitank ditches and trenches between Krym and Ssultan-Ssaly. After capturing this bridgehead, the attack deep into these positions could be planned. Under covering fire from the artillery the Pioniere had soon bridged the wide antitank ditches. Attacks by close support aircraft and Stukas were arranged with the air liason officer so that the attack on Leniawan could begin.

The taking of the antitank ditches, which the WIKING Division crossed between Ssultan-Saly and Krim, is certainly well remembered by many Kameraden. The action is described in the following combat report:

"The leading elements of the Pz.Abt. had reached the antitank ditches. Deploying in full breadth along the ditches they fired with cannon and machine guns on every position they could spot on the opposite side. As usual, we Pioniere held the required distance and waited in our Volkswagen behind the adjutant's tank. From it we received the order to immediately drive forward as far as the lead tank, taking demolition charges with us, and to cross the antitank ditches. Slalom style we drove forward, working our way up behind cover and stopping behind one of the first tanks. Oscha. Holzinger's fast group soon had the necessary material ready and then came the delicate jump through the minefield. We hadn't known that there was a minefield until we were in the middle of it! Then came the move into the rear. The front meanwhile was almost quiet and the gunners peering through their sights gave us covering fire.

In order to complete our task of making a crossing for the Panzers, we had to blast the walls of the antitank ditches. The first charges were laid in their holes and covered over. Then we took cover. A suitable detonation tore the walls of the

The attack on Rostov July 1942

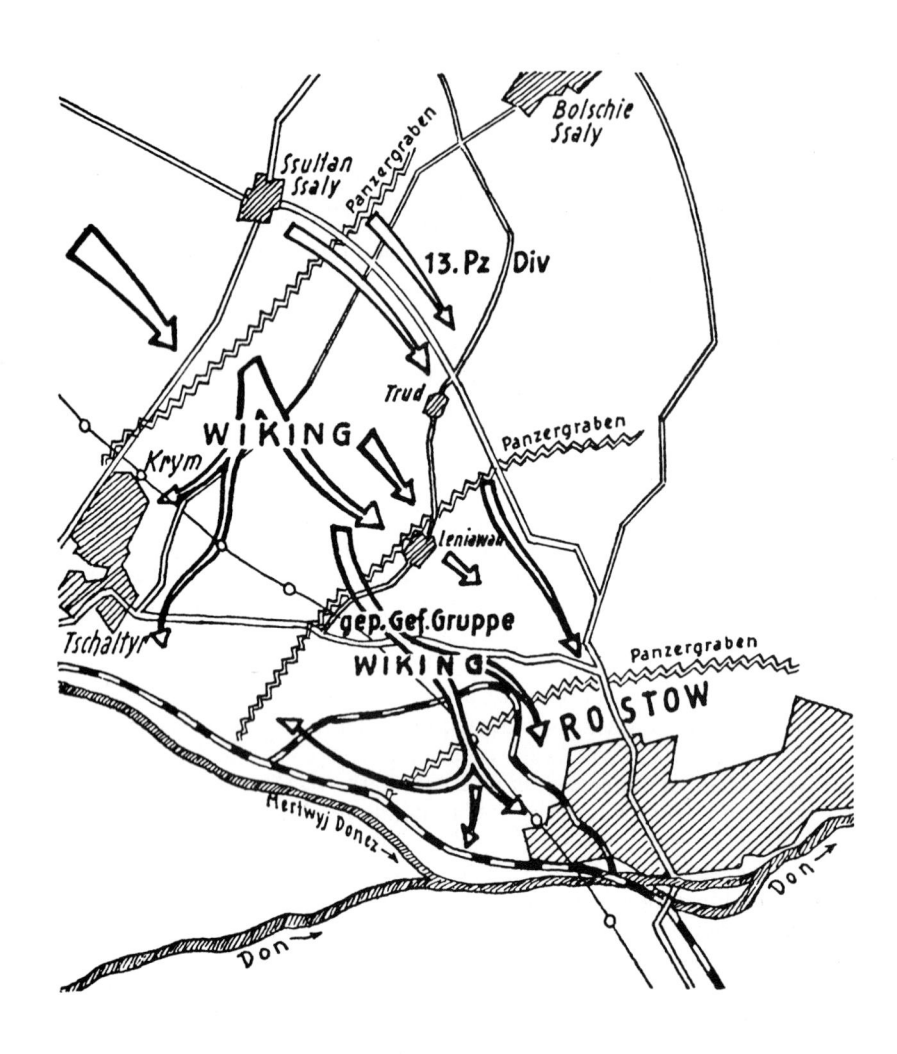

ditch, collapsing the earth back in. This was carried out at several levels on both sides.

A Grenadiere company now came forward, advanced through our holes and secured the far side. Gradually other units moved forward and sat as spectators.

The collapsed earth did not reach far enough for a crossing so a Luftwaffe unit was tasked to bring up tree trunks, beams etc.. Soon the required material was at hand. A layer of beams, a layer of earth and over that more of the same. Using this trick the bottom of the ditch was raised. A Panzer dared make the first attempt. While we nervously watched every move it tipped forward and rolled over our planked bridge which became noticeably lower. Then it climbed the other side at breakneck speed. It was dog's work leveling out the approach because it was very hot, but we had finally done it.

Now the terrain behind the ditch was searched for mines and a passage marked out. Several mines were removed. The Pz.Abt. set itself in motion. Clouds of dust rose over the land and mixed with our sweat.

A second line of antitank ditches followed the first. We rushed feverishly toward the city. Of course we didn't have to think much about battle order. We drove spread out far and wide across the Ukrainian plains with each vehicle practically with a whole football field for itself. Moving in this fashion the enemy artillery could scarcely do us any harm.

After the second came the third tank trap and in many places there had even been four trenches."

At approximately 13.00 hours, following the taking of the first antitank ditches, Pz.Abt. 5 was able to take advantage of heavy Luftwaffe air attacks on Leniawan to launch its attack on the second enemy position. Immediately after the Luftwaffe aircraft had flown off, under a barrage by the entire artillery force the Panzers were able to break into the enemy positions. In the meantime, KGr. Stoffers (I./NORDLAND) had taken Ssultan-Saly without a fight. It was to remain there with KGr. Weitzdörfer until the 23rd when it was to follow KGr. Dieckmann. On the evening of 22. July 1942, Leniawan fell and the third enemy trench position near Sapadnyj was reached. This was also protected by a wide antitank ditch. During the night the Division commander briefed his officers in a sand hut on the rail line near Sapadnyj for the attack on the third enemy position planned for the 23rd. The reconnaissance of the defence position conducted during the night by KGr. Dieckmann revealed it to be thick with Russians. Apparently they were soldiers fleeing the area before Leniawan who were seeking cover from air attack. Dieckmann and Mühlenkamp quickly agreed on the battle plan for the following day. Under the cover of the western flank, the Panzerabteilung with two mounted assault companies was to thrust at first light to the antitank ditches and provide cover for the infantry's attack. Then the Panzers would roll up the ditches from west to east and with a further Panzerkampfgruppe cross the cleared area of the ditches and push on with mounted infantry to the western edge of Rostov.

The surprise assault went as planned. The Russians sitting in the trenches in the third position were taken completely by surprise and surrendered en masse. SS-Stubaf. Mühlenkamp was able to push into Rostov in the late morning. Gefechtsgruppe Wagner followed and took over security in the city, whose entrances had been blocked-up. As the city streets had also been blocked, the Panzers decided to turn around and leave again. While they searched for a route around the city to reach the Don, a pilot dropped a report, the contents of which were confirmed by radio. The report stated that the enemy columns, which were approaching from the west through Tschaltyr, had hoped to reach the west sector of Rostov but had been thwarted.

The enemy now prepared to ford the Don about 15 km west of Rostov. The Panzerabteilung did not wait for further orders from Division. Instead it radioed to Division that western Rostov was not passable for combat vehicles and that they would fight their way along the Don with the intention of reaching the ford reported by the pilot. The Kampfgruppe's commander Hans Dorr, who had reached Rostov at 16.00 hours on the 23rd, had discovered to his dismay that the Soviets had destroyed all the Don bridges several days before. The city was now in flames.

With Mühlenkamp's taking of Kalinin, the Tschaltyr position was now finally opened from the rear. Attacking there, the infantry of 298. Inf.Div. had been decisively relieved. They and the *WIKING* Division had captured numerous prisoners and a large number of antiaircraft guns which had already been smashed in the enemy positions by Stukas. The spoils were great. On 24. July, the OKW could report, "As announced by a special bulletin, units of the Army, the Waffen-SS and Slovakian troops, supported by the Luftwaffe, have broken through Rostov's strongly defended, deeply emplaced defence positions along the whole front and after hard fighting have taken the important transport and port city."[2]

V. FORWARD TO THE CAUCASUS!

The cornerpost of the Soviet retreat across the Don to the south had collapsed. Now it was important to overtake the retreating enemy and bar him from withdrawing to the safety of the Kuban and the forests of the Caucasus. The "big picture" looked as follows:[1]
"Feldmarschall List (Army Group A) had come up with a suitable plan using the forces available and in accordance with his orders contained in Order Nr. 45. Armeegruppe Ruoff, the reinforced 17. Armee, would launch a frontal attack southward from the area of Rostov toward Krasnodar. To the east, the fast units of von Kleist's 1. Panzerarmee, followed on the left wing by Hoth's 4. Panzerarmee, were assigned the task of breaking out of the Don bridgeheads and driving toward Maikop as the other spearhead. In this fashion, cooperation between Ruoff's slowly advancing Infantry Divisions and Kleist's fast units would result in the encirclement and destruction of the enemy forces believed to be south of Rostov. The task of securing the flank for this operation fell to Generaloberst Hoth's 4. Panzerarmee on the left wing. Its first target was Woroschilowsk. Following this plan the attack toward the south was launched. It began an extremely dramatic operation which was of decisive importance for the course of the entire Eastern Campaign.

While Armeegruppe Ruoff was still struggling for Rostov, elements of 1. and 4. Panzerarmee had advanced up to the Don. Already on 23. July, 23. Panzer Div.'s Kradschützen Battalion had succeeded in crossing the river near Nikolajewskaja and setting up a bridgehead on the south bank of the Don. Only three days later, a Kampfgruppe from 23. Panzerdivision pushed southward and crossed the Sal near Orlowka. From there, XXXX. Panzerkorps with 3. and 23. Panzerdivisions advanced on the Manytsch sector. The Russian command demonstrated that it was determined not to allow its units to be encircled again. The Soviet General Staff and the troop commanders held firm to the new, but fundamentally old, strategy which had defeated Napoleon: to lure the enemy deep into the vast Russian land and split his forces before falling on him on a wide front at the moment when he was overextended.

For the German forces the country south of the Don presented entirely new combat conditions. 500 kilometres of steppe had to be crossed before facing one of the world's mightiest mountain chains which stretched between the Black and Caspian Seas before the advancing German troops.

The steppe country north of the Caucasus offered the Soviets excellent opportunities for defence. The countless large and small rivers which flow from the Caucasus watershed into both the Black and Caspian Seas were obstacles which the enemy could hold with comparatively weak forces.

As in the desert, here in the steppe the march route followed a path between souces of water. The war was being fought in an alien world. Anyone who crossed the 700 km. long Manytsch, left Europe and entered Asia. The river is the border between two different parts of the world."

In the coming months, the *WIKING* Division was also to move into this country which was so completely new to the European volunteers. It had been a daring but successful operation which had brought about the fall of Rostov. The Russians had expected an attack but not in this manner. The German assault had taken them completely by surprise and forced them to prematurely evacuate their pivotal point on the Don. Now the infantry of XXXXIX. Gebirgskorps, following in a forced march, had to open the way over the Don and take Bataisk on the south bank to provide freedom of movement to the south for the Panzerkorps. Already on 25. July, the Commanding General of XXXXIX. Gebirgskorps, General d. Geb.Tr. Konrad, was with the Division on the north bank of the Don to assess the situation, examine attack options and prepare the assault.

In Giant Steps across the Steppe

On the morning of 25. July 1942, following a heavy bombardment by about 40 batteries on the positions on the south bank of the Don, the attack against Bataisk was launched. Stuka attacks followed. Under cover of this curtain of fire, XXXXIX. Gebirgskorps succeeded in crossing the river with three divisions and entering Bataisk. This success was due not least to the "Brandenburgern", who, led by Oblt. Grabert, stormed the long slope to Bataisk, establishing a bridgehead. They risked their lives to hold there for twenty four hours until LVII. Corps crossed the pontoon bridge with 13 Panzers on the evening of the 27th. WIKING followed across at 0400 hours on the morning of the 28th. As ordered, the Division turned north of Bataisk to the north toward Olginskaja. With the Panzergruppe it marched forward toward Kagalnizkaja where they overtook the enemy and brought him to battle. Here there developed a fierce fight with enemy rearguards in the evening which was decided by 21.00 hours. As the enemy was obviously fighting to win time, spoiling attacks were expected during the night. The pursuit continued on the morning of 29. July. 13. Panzerdivision was no longer on the left as it had veered east in order to open the way to the south for 1. Pz.Armee across the Manytsch and Sal rivers. As 13. Panzerdivision was now part of 1. Pz.Armee, the WIKING Division was alone following the retreating enemy toward the Kuban.

The further south the troops advanced, the more the country changed. The villages were prettier than in the Ukraine, the roads better and the countryside was covered with golden corn and red tomato fields. In the village gardens the trees were heavy with ripening fruit. Everything the heart desired was there: melons of a size never seen before, apples, pears and other delicious fruit which made the hungry soldiers' mouths water. Every pause was used to gorge on the fruit and quench their thirst. It was very hot and dusty; so dusty that the only features recognizable through the thick layer of dust on the faces of the young European volunteers were their eyes. Everyone felt that this Panzer war was the best way to fight. Speed was the answer. Short but fierce combats with quick decisive blows by heavy artillery and Panzers crushed all enemy resistance. Enveloping movements, outmaneuvering the enemy; that is how the days passed.

Soon it had become customary for the Luftwaffe commander from Zerstörergeschwader 500, Major Diering, to land at dawn at the command post by "Storch". He would take part in the briefing and issue orders to his liason officer accordingly. As the Panzerkampfgruppe deployed, it would be accompanied by an air patrol of two ground support aircraft. These would call up the remainder of the unit's aircraft, which were on alert at Rostov, when heavier air support became necessary. In a short time this close coordination between air and fast ground forces had proven to be an ideal method. This combat tactic of combining fast ground forces and escorting air forces may have been in the mind of the Oberbefehlshaber der Luftflotte 4, Generaloberst von Richthofen, when he had the OKL set up this "Close Support Fliegerkorps." Unfortunately, due to future developments in the course of the war, the conditions which favored this type of

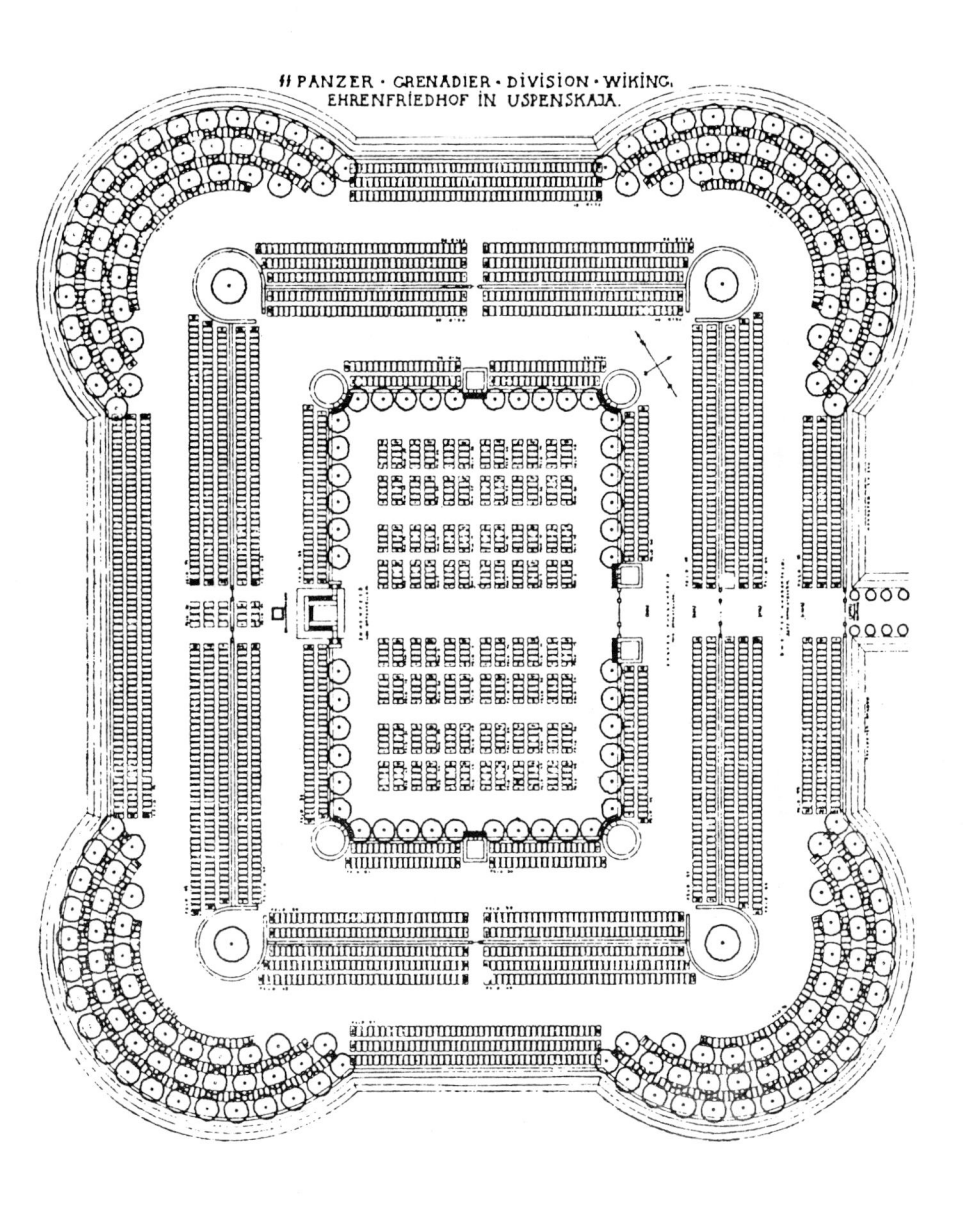

A diagram of the Pz.Gren.-Division *WIKING*'s
soldier's cemetery in Uspenskaja.

air-ground cooperation never again prevailed.

At that time in the Caucasus, however, these tactics proved a brilliant success. The Soviet rearguards were unable to occupy one position for long or mount any effective resistance. They were bombed out, shelled by Panzers and pursued by the fast infantry which forced them to be constantly on the retreat. If the Division had not taken breathers during the night they would have been far ahead and isolated in the Kuban. During the pursuit the Luftwaffe commander continually reported that the Division was moving in a flood of Russians which was rolling toward the south. His expression was one of concern that all might not be going well. But it was obvious that stiffer resistance could be expected in the Kuban. The Russians were retreating there in order to regroup. This they did with great discipline, marching day and night. But they reached the Kuban too late.

At roughly 18.00 hours on 28. July, Kampfgruppe Dorr crossed the Don. After a long night drive the Battalion and the Corps Staff followed *NORDLAND* in order to take Metschetinskaja by the evening of the 29th.

On the evening of 29. July, the Panzerkampfgruppe stood before Jegorlynskaja. Here the rapid pursuit came to a halt for the first time. On the Division's eastern flank Zelina also proved to be occupied by the enemy. Lead elements of 13. Pz.Div. approached the strongly occupied town of Ssalsk. Gefechtsgruppe von Scholz (*NORDLAND*) was moved forward and deployed to cover the eastern flank toward Zelina.

On 30. July, the Panzergruppe, followed by Gefechtsgruppe *GERMANIA*, advanced toward Ssred. Jegorlyk. Here they encountered a new enemy in the form of a fresh Soviet motorized brigade. This was a powerful force and during the night of 1. August it attacked with the strength of at least three battalions. However, it suffered a bloody rebuff at the hands of the infantry and during the night broke off toward the southwest. The way to Bjelaja-Glina, a small city and one of the important road and rail junctions north of the Kuban, was open. The Panzerkampfgruppe's guns reached the city, whose name means "white clay", at midday. The Panzers now recognized the possibility of an envelopment from the west. They joined up with the Dieckmann Battalion along the complex terrain to the southwest while Gefechtsgruppe Wagner occupied the enemy force of about two Russian motorized infantry battalions with a frontal attack. During this attack, SS-Stubaf. Schlamelcher, commander of III./A.R. 5 and a holder of the Knight's Cross, was severely wounded. By approximately 15.00 hours resistance was broken. Those who could not flee were taken prisoner. Among the captured equipment were about a dozen brand-new American trucks, which were most welcome. Statements by prisoners indicated the presence of a Russian General Command which had been ordered to Bjelaja- Glina. In fact, the hasty departure toward the south of a Russian headquarters had been observed but it had been too late to catch up with it. The German forces were welcomed to the small city by two elderly Cossacks in Czarist uniforms complete with decorations. Following the Russian custom they were given bread and salt.

Crossing the Kuban

For some time traffic to the northern rear units and to the covering forces on the flanks had been possible only in powerfully armed convoys. Night after night the units had to create hedgehog positions for all-round security. Armed groups of Russian stragglers hid in the cornfields, firing on anyone who stumbled into their positions.

The Division's next target was the Kuban. The Commanding General believed it was already in their hands. The Corps Order instructed the Division to take Krapotkin and cross the Kuban there. But events would not move that fast. Effective from 21. July, the Division was placed under the command of LVII. Pz.Corps. The Corps Artillery Officer, Oberst Rossmann, had brought along welcome artillery reinforcement, especially a battalion each of 10 cm. cannon and 21 cm. mortars. In addition there was a rocket launcher battalion with two 15 cm. batteries and a 28 cm. battery.

Amazed, the soldiers now passed through a completely foreign countryside. Flocks of birds of prey were common and here and there wolves crossed the path of the advancing forces. The lead elements encountered a caravan of nomads on camels who were travelling in search of new pasturelands. After passing through Ilinskaja, Dmitrijewskaja and Grigoripolitskaja the German forces reached the Kuban. After the long march across the steppe, the terrain here was completely different. The river's northern and eastern banks were up to 80 metres high and covered with oak forests. The southern bank in contrast was signifigantly lower, rising only 10 to 20 metres above the river.

Although the Wehrmacht bulletin of 4. August reported that fast units of the Army and Waffen-SS had reached the Kuban river on a broad front, the Division at first halted a measured distance from the river. Reconnoitering parties were sent forward. The decision was made quickly: the Division would not cross at Krapotkin or to the east but south of the river's large bend near Grigoripolitskaja. A Gefechtsgruppe was diverted to Krapotkin with orders to take the city and the river crossings there provided they were intact. With 2 heavy batteries, 2 light artillery battalions, A.A. 5 and one Panzer Company, SS- Standartenführer von Scholz had a considerable force under his command. The operation was a success but the bridges had been blown. The Gefechtsgruppe secured positions near Krapotkin and was relieved by the advance battalion of 101. Jg.Div. on 5. August. With the bridges blown, Krapotkin had become unimportant to the Soviets as well.

On the previous day the Division had marched off to the east. At the bend in the Kuban north of the Temisbbekskaja—Nowoaleksandrowskaja road the Division came upon a carefully constructed, strongly held enemy defence position. Reoccupied by an intact brigade, it demanded a carefully planned attack. But Mühlenkamp knew that everything depended on gaining time. He therefore bypassed the enemy position and reached the assigned target of Grigoripolitskaja on the evening of 4. August. He was followed by I./*GERMANIA* which had left the clearing of the enemy position to following units. The Russians still fought determinedly. Recognizing the favourable situation, SS-Stubaf. Dieckmann improvised. On the night of 5. August, using the cover of the wooded areas, he crossed the Kuban by way of a narrow island and on the 6th was on the river's west bank. The Panzers guarded the crossing until the infantry of Gefechtsgruppe Wagner arrived with the first batteries to reinforce the bridgehead.

Still on the evening of 5. August, 2./Pi.Btl. 5 had advanced to Grigoripolitskaja and the Corps Pionier Battalion had arrived. Both worked feverishly to throw a temporary bridge across the river. Despite many complications the events of this day had offered the High Command a great opportunity. Far behind the *WIKING* Div. followed a Slovakian fast division which had yet to appear. III. Panzerkorps went on ahead toward Armawir where 13. Pz.Div. had established a bridgehead on 3. August. As before, the goal remained Maikop, whose oil seemed to draw the

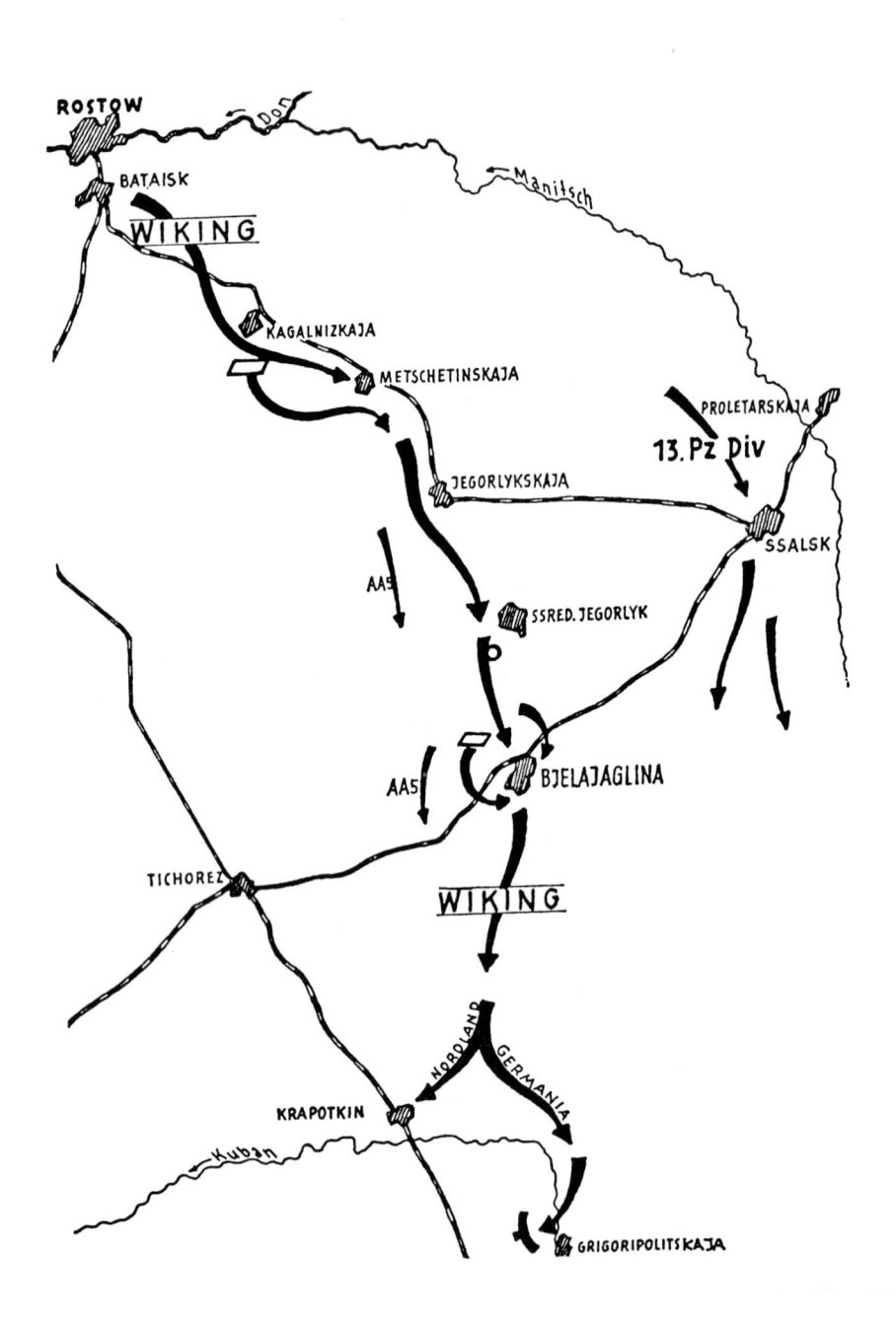

The advance to the Kuban

units like a magnet although as an operational target it was unimportant. Gen.Major Herr's 13. Pz.Div. was to storm Maikop on 9. August.

The Battle for Krapotkin

The *NORDLAND* Rgt.'s battle for Krapotkin was a notable achievement. On 5. August, a report from the Führer's headquarters declared:
" After heavy fighting the important railway junction at Krapotkin on the Kuban was taken by storm by a unit of the Waffen-SS."[1]
Stubaf. Engelhardt-Ranzow on the staff of SS-Staf. von Scholz described the fighting in detail:
"On 4. August, Gefechtsgruppe von Scholz marched west along the Temisbbek-skaja—Krapotkin rail line and at 10.00 hours passed Kawkasskaja where the men gorged themselves on apricots. West of the city the Gefechtsgruppe was engaged by Soviet scouting forces. From the high bank of the Kuban we saw Russian trains steaming off toward the south from Krapotkin one behind the other. 7 Battery of III./A.R. 5 was able to engage in target practice on them in the truest sense of the word. A munitions train caught fire and exploded, its signal flares rising high into the air. II./*NORDLAND* was halted on the western edge of Krapotkin and had to fight hard there. I. Battalion under Stubaf. Polewacz attempted to enter the city from the north but became involved in fighting with a long Russian column of about 4,000 men which was approaching from the north. With help from A.A. 5 which attacked from the western flank, the enemy was finally routed. However, I./*NORDLAND*'s attack from the north was unable to help II./*NORDLAND* to move forward. Then von Scholz himself took the initiative. He mounted a company of II./*NORDLAND* on the tanks of the seconded Panzer Company and drove at the head of this battle group through Russian-occupied Krapotkin to take the rail and road bridges by surprise attack. As the lead Panzer drove onto the approach to the bridges, they were blown up. We saw two gigantic explosions and two oil and gasoline storage tanks blazed. At 10.00 hours on 6. August, Krapotkin was firmly in our possession. The Russians did not try at all to recapture the city, since with the destruction of the bridges it was now useless to them as well. On the evening of the 5th, our Gefechtsgruppe was relieved by the advance guard of an Infantry Division and on the 6th, the Division was pulled out to Grigoripolitskaja.[2]

In Grigoripolitskaja meanwhile, things had become very lively. 6. August had begun with a heavy barrage by numerous Russian batteries on the Division's units northeast and northwest of the city which were preparing to cross the river. The Russians had also moved forward heavy motorized artillery although this still lacked infantry support. It was possible to extend the bridgehead in a semicircle from 500 to 1,000 metres as far as the edge of the thickly-wooded bank. Although the Soviets were not in the picture regarding the bridgehead, their artillery fire struck the German batteries on the eastern bank of the Kuban with astonishing precision. When these moved positions, shielded from the Russians' view by the thick forests along the Kuban, the enemy artillery fire followed them with great precision. This was more than suspicious. There was no doubt that the fire was being directed from Grigoripolitskaja. At noon, two Russian artillery observers were discovered in the church tower in the German occupied city. A patrol called on the Russians to surrender but they answered with pistol shots. So the pair were overcome in close combat.

By 7. August, the pontoon bridge built by the Pioniere was ready and could bear Panzers and heavy artillery. At 05.00 hours, Panzerabteilung 5 was the first across the bridge. Following a Stuka attack on the enemy batteries, the Panzers moved out of the bridgehead against the enemy gun positions. The Russians fled in terror and clouds of dust marked their flight. Several batteries fell intact into German hands.

The forward edge of the bridgehead now lay so far forward that the Division could form its Gefechtsgruppen unmolested and move off toward the southwest as ordered. Wild confusion reigned over the enemy. With Gefechtsgruppe - NORDLAND in the lead, followed by Gefechtsgruppe Wagner and Staf. Gille with his Gefechtsgruppe bringing up the rear, the Division's advance continued; at first to the north toward St. Otrada then along the Armavir—Krapotkin—Gulkewitschi railroad. Here the Division formed up into two Gefechtsgruppen in order to cross the Laba sector near Temirgojewskaja and Pertoparjovskaja on a broad front. The nearly 30 km. long section of track along the Division's advance route was dotted with smashed and burning freight cars which were loaded with valuable arms and equipment. The Luftwaffe had wrought this carnage. A report dropped from a Luftwaffe aircraft indicated that the crossings in the Laba sector were still intact. In response, Gruppe von Scholz was diverted toward Temirgojewskaja and Gruppe Wagner toward Petropawlovskaja with orders to seize the bridges there during the night and to establish bridgeheads on the far side of the river. The first Gruppe, which included the Division Ia-Staffel, was delayed. The Russians had hastily thrown up a defence position from Kasanskaja to Tifliskaja as far as Laba. It was manned by units they had snatched up including Marines from the Black Sea forces which were intended as reinforcements for the Kuban. But Standartenführer von Scholz quickly recognized the improvised nature of the Soviet defences as his scout parties had reported heavy movement in the enemy positions. He decided on a breakthrough at night toward Temirgojewskaja. The Panzerabteilung was made ready and after a short briefing by von Scholz and despite the dark night it smashed through the thin enemy lines on a narrow front. NORDLAND followed, assault parties enlarged the gaps to the north and south and during the night I./NORDLAND took Temirgojewskaja, which was still thick with Russians. Assault parties pressed toward the bridges in an attempt to capture them.

A report by W. Tieke, one of the Panzergrenadiere of 3. Company I./NORDLAND, provides a picture of the events on that dramatic night:

"At about midnight, I./NORDLAND stood before Temirgojewskaja. In all probability there were still powerful enemy units there. Quietly the men of I. Battalion armed themselves for the night attack on the Laba bridges. In the lead was 3. Company led by Hstuf. Bluhm, followed by the heavy company's Pionier platoon. Like ghosts the men of the "Third" raced through the town. Then an MG burst out. Russians and Germans race toward the bridge. Behind the Soviets, seven men of 3. Company run across the bridge toward the other side. Then the bridge is blown up. Seeing that they are cut off, the seven go into hiding. Russian MG's hammer away to their left and right forcing the "Third" to take cover in the sand dunes on the north bank. Things appear desperate in Temirgojewskaja until 3. Company finally masters the situation. Two Danish volunteers, Carsten Rassmussen and H. J. Petersen, were killed. Gradually our heavy MG's and the mortar section succeed in silencing the enemy MG's. Behind us I. Btl. clears the town in close in fighting. The Pioniere's first attempt to throw a foot bridge across the river fails. Again 3. Company opens fire with all weapons. The second attempt succeeds. Singly our Grenadiere run across the narrow planks of the bridge which crosses the 30 metre wide river. By daybreak the entire Third is across and has rescued the seven men from their dangerous situation." But the bridgehead was not to be held.

The Russians also resisted near Petropawlovskaja and blew the bridges in advance. Further reconnoitering of the Laba river downstream by a scout party reported favourable crossing opportunities 10 km. west of Temirgojewskaja. After an obstinately defended line near Mogila had been broken there was no opposition. Near Tenginskaja a ford was found and also uncounted vehicles belonging to the Latvian residents of the *kolkhozes* who had been forcibly evacuated there. The Division seized the opportunity and sent Panzer Abt. 5, which had taken Tenginskaja at roughly 11.00 on 8. August, into this sector where Pioniere had been able to repair the lightly damaged bridge. On the 9th, Kampfgruppe Polewacz (reinforced *GERMANIA* Rgt.) and later *NORDLAND* crossed the Laba there. The Wehrmacht bulletin on this day stated:

"Fast units of the Army and Waffen-SS crossed the Laba river and are now on the attack toward the west in the direction of Maikop."[3]

The following excerpts illustrate what was involved in the Kuban crossing. The Chief of 1. Company *GERMANIA*, SS- Hstuf. Hans Dorr, who was to die as a holder of the Swords in April 1945 after being wounded for the sixteenth time, kept a detailed diary. His entries are so precise that their worth is indisputable. In those days he made the following entries:

3. August "Dmitrijewskaja—Grigoripolinskaja

Never before has a German soldier been here between the Caspian Sea and the Black Sea. Desolate steppe, only partly, then good country.

Heavy rainshowers, good following the heat and dust. The advance to the Kuban is in its final hours. Speculation at the Div. Com. Post. Finally a decision: Advance on G., where no bridge available. Russians on the retreat. We are in pursuit. Over the Kuban by inflatable boat, coup de main style. A wonderful success for our battalion. . .

4. August Grigoripolinskaja

During the night, the enemy attempts to throw us back toward the other bank. Combat with knives, bitter hand to hand fighting. But we hold. I take over command in the bridgehead. Build a large bridgehead from the small. We can't do it with the Btl. alone. Attack by *NORDLAND* on Krapotkin fails. 13 Pz. likewise. Hold the bridgehead at all costs. Establish the small B.H. again, 7. Company comes as reserve. Hard night.

5. August Grigoripolinskaja

Enemy attacks beaten off at 02.00-02.50- 04.00 and 05.00 hours. 1. Company holds fabulously. The men, Malenki for example, are great. Crossing point under fire. At 08.15, 3. Company goes to the attack. Has success. The Russians pull back a bit. Obstinate enemy. Fanatics from Baku. At 12.00, 5. Company and I./A.R. 5 finally arrive and go to the attack. Bridgehead is enlarged. We have the good observation position in the church once more in our hands. . ."

7. August, Dorr reported the Russians' withdrawal by night and his departure with the Panzers at 05.00 along the rail line in the direction of Krapotkin.

The Laba Sector and Belaja

Carell continues the narrative[1]:
"At the head of LVII. Panzerkorps the WIKING Division sheered off to the southwest in the direction of Tuapse. Under the command of General der Waffen-SS Felix Steiner, the Baltic, Scandinavian and German volunteers gathered in the Division penetrated to the northwest and southwest parts of the Maikop oil region."

Krasnodar and Maikop fell on 8. August, the latter to 13. Pz.Div. under General Herr. Parts of WIKING, including I./GERMANIA, reached Maikop on 10. August.

After crossing the Laba sector on the 9th, SS- Standartenführer Gille once again took command of the Panzerkampfgruppe. Instead of Kampfgruppe Dieckmann, I./NORDLAND was integrated into the Pz.Kampfgruppe. Following in the advance were Gefechtsgruppe GERMANIA, called in from Petropawlovskaja, and Oberst Rossmann's heavy artillery and rocket launcher battalion. Von Scholz's forces would follow once again as a Gefechtsgruppe. He and his men had accomplished much.

In these days the Panzerkampfgruppe drove through the masses of still retreating Russians who scattered before the Panzers and disappeared in the fields of sunflowers. Guns and vehicles were abandoned where they stood. The Division had no time to recover them. It had to continue without delay and after a short rest reached the Belaja river on the morning of 10. August. Although there were no bridges in this sector, the night reconnaissance had reported the area unoccupied and residents stated that the river would be fordable there. For this operation the Grenadiere of I./NORDLAND were mounted on the Panzers. Following the Kampfgruppe was a company of the famous BRANDENBURG Regiment. This company, the 7th, was a special unit outfitted with captured Russian vehicles. Its soldiers wore Russian coats and helmets bearing the emblems of the Soviet Army. The Panzerkampfgruppe's assignment was to advance southward along the Belaja between the forest's edge and the river, take the village of Pschechskaja and capture the Belaja bridge near Beloretschinskaja before it could be destroyed by the Russians. This bridge and the Armavir—Tuapse line railroad bridge were of decisive importance for supplying the Caucasus. Welikoje, to the north of the crossing scouted by the Division, as well as Beloretschinskaja were occupied by the enemy, who had established bridgeheads there. This operation, to penetrate between two bridgeheads behind the enemy front and to roll them up, was daring and very risky. The Division had intercepted a radio message from the enemy 7th Guards Cavalry Brigade, whose duty station was located in Twerskaja. The message relayed orders to attached units to hold themselves ready at the edge of the forest east of Pschych for an immediate counterattack against the advancing German Panzer column southwest of Welikoje. Patrols were to be sent as far forward as the mouth of the Belaja.

The "Brandenburger"s Coup de Main

Now it was important to act quickly. If the Division delayed, the enemy could swing out to the attack at any time. At dawn, A.A. 5 was committed toward

Welikoje with orders to take possession of the crossing there. The Panzerkampfgruppe was to ford the river south of Welikoje while the *BRANDENBURG* Company was to move up to Pschechskaja. Masquerading as a retreating Russian column, it was to pass through Pschechskaja and take possession of the rail bridge without delay. The Panzergruppe would then follow, take the town and relieve the "Brandenburgern". To reinforce the Kampfgruppe, the Division had a 28 cm. rocket battery follow so as to have from the first moments the most powerful artillery support possible available at Pschechskaja.

Early on the morning of 10. August, the Grenadiere forded the Belaja under the cover of fire from the watching Panzerabteilung 5. In many places the water was shallow, permitting vehicles to cross. In other places it was up to the hips of the Grenadiere. The water, was ice cold and quickly woke up the tired soldiers. The heat, sometimes 40 degrees in the shade, soon dried them out again.

Then *BRANDENBURG*'s 7.Company set off. Exhibiting all the signs of terror and disintegration they drove past several Russian artillery positions at a hellish pace. Their cries of *"Tanki, Tanki"*, their terrified faces and frantic gestures to the rear produced real panic in the loitering Soviets. Now they began to run. The horse-drawn guns made off at a gallop. The heavy motorized artillery drove off at full speed. Officers and commissars who tried to rally the "Brandenburgern" who were fleeing in panic toward Pschechskaja with threats and exhortations were themselves induced to panic: "Save yourselves if you can!".

In Psecheckskaja the company overtook a Soviet heavy motorized artillery battalion which was leisurely moving into position behind the Belaja. They were surprised by the "Brandenburgern" who fired on them with their vehicle mounted machine guns, scattering them. The guns were left abandoned. A pair of sentries on the rail bridge were speechless when a Russian rifle company jumped from their vehicles, rushed across the bridge and took up positions on both sides. The sentries were thrown to the ground and disarmed. Meanwhile, the "Brandenburgern" had removed their Russian coats and now fought in Wehrmacht feldgrau uniforms. Before the enemy could grasp the situation, the Panzers rushed into Pschechskaja. They roared between the cavalry units already at the edge of the forest northwest of Beloretschinskaja and the outposts dug in on the bank of the Belaja. The Division Commander following behind the Panzerkampfgruppe saw men rushing about at the edge of the wood 500 metres away. At the same time he came under mortar fire. Rounds landed ahead and behind his truck which was moving at high speed. The tipped-down windscreen was shattered and the Division Commander slightly wounded. Close behind followed the commander of the heavy rocket battalion. Directions and a short briefing on the Russian concentrations took only a matter of minutes. The 28 cm. battery soon cleared the forest's edge.

Conquest of the Maikop Oil Region

The situation in Psechechskaja was already cleared up. Gille had the town firmly in hand. Prisoners came in from all sides, but the Division had to continue on. Unhindered by the enemy, the advance guard of Gefechtsgruppe Wagner arrived in Psechechskaja which was a beehive of activity as the tank commanders saw to their vehicles, had them refuelled and took a bit of a breather. At midday they went on. Gille was once again in the lead, this time with Mühlenkamp, Dieckmann and I./A.R. 5. They moved down a forest road along the Pschych toward

Advance into the Maikop oil region

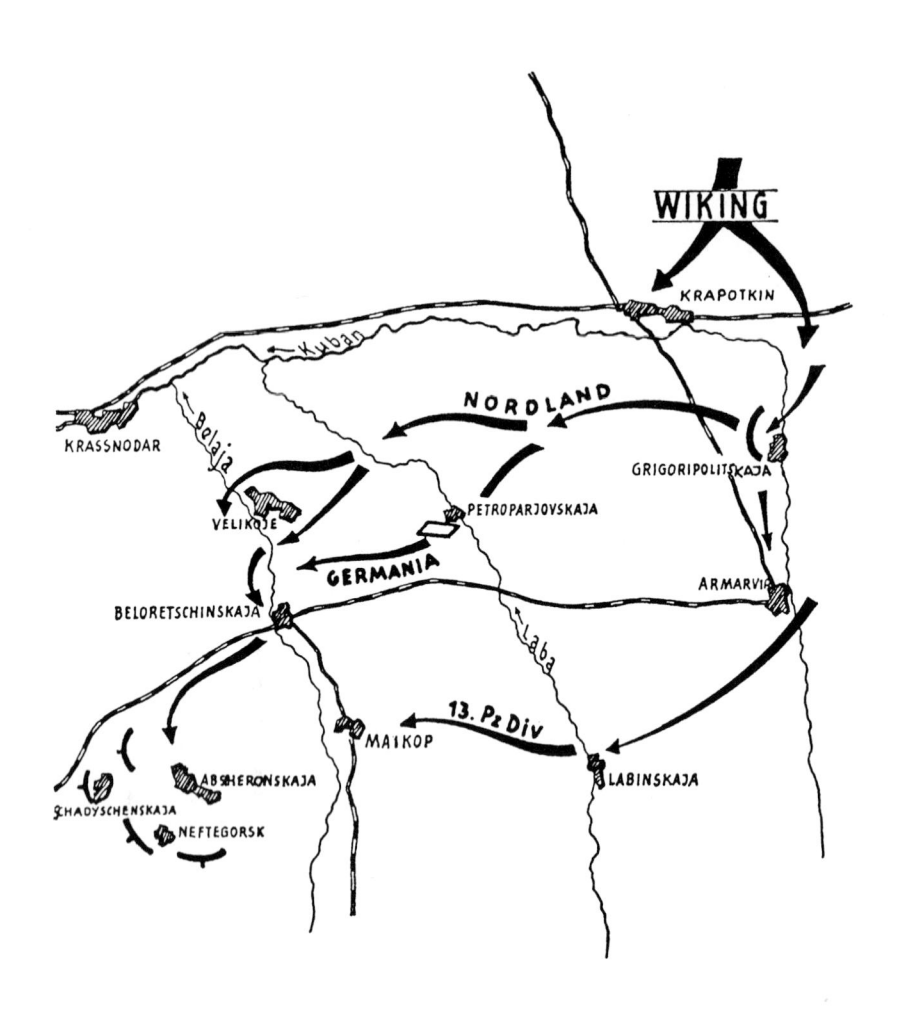

Kabardinskaja with Chadyshenskaja on the Maikop—Tuapse road as their target. With the Division in Chadyshenskaja, it would stand in the centre of the Maikop oil region. The oil wells were not in Maikop but on the ridge of hills northwest of Chadyshenskaja near Absheronskaja and further to the east.

Worth mentioning is the order which came directly from OKH and which had been passed on to the Heeresgruppe with great urgency. The Division was to send a battalion to Maikop, the exact composition of which was specified, although 13. Pz.Div. already stood just outside Maikop. The order had obviously long since been overtaken by events. In this context the special "oil salvage company" must be mentioned. Comprised of highly valuable oil specialists and technicians, its orders were to follow the army into Maikop and get production going as soon as possible. What a strange front line unit! The company, without any experience of combat, promptly ran into a Russian ambush in the Giaginskaja area and were shot up. In any case, there was no oil produced during the Division's stay in this area.

On 14. August, I./*GERMANIA* took the Muk refinery where it set up defensive positions for the night and sent reconnaissance patrols out to scout all sides. Close behind followed the bulk of the reinforced *GERMANIA* Rgt. under the command of Stubaf. Joerchel and behind it the Division Ia Staffel and Oberst Rossmann with the Mörser Battalion. A few kilometres east of Twerskaja there was an unexpected halt. The noise of heavy fighting could be heard ahead. Joerchel was detached and diverted to the northwest. His leading troops had gone over to the defensive in the face of large enemy forces. Gefechtsgruppe Commander Jürgen Wagner sent up his nearest battalion and had it advance through Kubanskaja toward Twerskaja where it reached the Pschych finding only weak resistance. It was halted there as the situation grew more serious by the hour. Mortars fired wildly and masses of Russians attacked fanatically. The situation was clear: The enemy Cavalry Corps wanted to push through Kubanskaja in a concentrated attack and win the major road between Maikop and Tuapse. To do so it first had to overcome Joerchel's II./*GERMANIA*. This he was unable to do. Rossmann's 21 cm. Mörsers began to fire shell after shell from close range, which exploded in the treetops of the forests north of Komsomolzkaja. Then the rocket launchers joined in, providing support for the infantry and any hope of success for the Russians was finished. Attacks near Twerskaja were also repulsed. The rest of the 116th Cavalry Division turned aside through Linejuaja. Just as the fighting here abated somewhat, the completely reequipped Finnish Battalion reached the Division at Kubanskaja. A brief order and the Finns drove to Linejuaja. They were placed under the command of the Mühlenkamp Panzerabteilung which had remained near Twerskaja. Mounted on the Panzers, the Finns raced off toward Linejuaja with unbelieveable elan, scattering the Russians. The 7th Soviet Guards Cavalry Korps was smashed. Hundreds of stragglers and surely several squadrons in the rear slipped away in the darkness to the safety of the forests after the conclusion of the fighting. Artillery Regiment 5 had every reason to be pleased with itself and its success.[1]

VI. BATTLE IN THE CAUCASUS

With the fighting at Linejuaja, the Division's battle for the Maikop oil region had ended. It had been dramatic enough and a tense time for the troops and command alike. Now it was important to take possession of the oil district and organize the Division for the defence of this large area. The continuation of the attack toward Tuapse as demanded by the command was unthinkable considering the state of things. Even in peacetime, a march by a heavily motorized Division with its approximately 2,000 heavy vehicles and numerous other trucks and motorcycles on narrow winding roads through the forested mountains of the West Caucasus would have been a tiresome effort with many difficulties in the style of Hannibal's march across the Alps. It would only be possible to reach Tuapse if the Division were conveyed to Chadyshenskaja by train, unmolested by the enemy. The enemy, however, surely had no idea of providing such cooperation. He offered resistance wherever he could. This showed itself in the next days.

Transition to Defence

Graf Engelhardt-Ranzow, transferred to von Scholz's staff on 21. August, noted in his diary that the Division Commander had ordered a conference with all of his officers. The meeting was called to explain to them the necessity of going over to the defensive.

The conference took place on 23. August 1942. He mentioned moreover, that "an old Cossack officer had to instruct our soldiers in patrol duty. The western European soldiers marched through the forest like a herd of elephants. He showed us how to walk carefully forward 10-15 steps without disturbing a branch or making a sound. Then we were to stand still and observe, particularly in the treetops, where Russian snipers often sat."

In fact, with limited forces the enemy had been able to block the single road to the Black Sea. From the hills on both sides of the march route and from the air, he was able to inflict considerable casualties on the Division. In consideration of this situation, the Division Commander was not overly adventurous. He halted the Division's forward unit, I./SS- *GERMANIA*, near Chadyshenskaja. Feeling their way along the advance road to Tuapse, the Battalion's men discovered, as expected, barricades and demolished bridges ahead of their vanguard. The area was occupied by fresh, combat-ready forces which had dug in in forest positions. The commander decided on his own authority to go over to the defensive. The operation toward Tuapse had now become a matter for the Gebirgstruppen who were following the fast units. Included in this force was 101. Jägerdivision under Generalmajor Dietzel and his Ia Major Ludendorff.

In any case, the arrival of the Gebirgstruppen was not imminent. On the other hand the new motorized *WESTLAND* Regiment arrived in the Division's area of operations just in time to help secure its vast sector. *WIKING* was far ahead of the other fast units which had remained behind the Belaja in the southern Maikop and which were ready for the march into the East Caucasus. The Division stood alone in the Caucasian forests and had to secure the Maikop oil wells within a radius of almost 130 km. until the expected arrival of the Gebirgstruppen. Naturally, only strongpoints could be held. Each mountain village became a small fortress which was secured toward the enemy and to the sides. Contact between the garrisons was possible only with strong convoys. The whole area teemed with Russian units of varying strengths which at first were scattered with no central command but which still posed a serious danger to the weak German battalions. There were almost daily skirmishes which cost unnecessary casualties. Particularly hard hit were the supply services which had to bring rations, equipment and fuel into the strongpoints. Eventually they had to be provided with strong escorts. The NORDLAND Regiment secured the former advance road with Kampfgruppe II./ NORDLAND under Stubaf. Stoffers on the bare hilltops west of Kabardinskaja. Further north on a similar high point was Stubaf. Polewacz with I./NORDLAND. The Finns (III./NORDLAND) covered the northern flank near Linejuaja and Twerskaja. Everywhere oil drilling installions were being dismantled as planned and in places some were still ablaze. 800 metres to the west of Gefechtsgruppe Scholz, the Soviets had dug in. This combat zone was covered with thick forests whose narrow paths could usually be crossed only by panje horses. The terrain was thus eminently suitable for guerrilla warfare, offering ample opportunities to those familiar with the area and demanding a high sacrifice from strangers. Moreover, the West Caucasian residents here were in no way peaceable. The majority were "red" oil workers from various parts of the U.S.S.R. who had joined or were forced to join the Soviet forces. Some served as leaders in these units.

Kampfgruppe Dieckmann had it better in its positions near Muk on the road from Chadyshenskaja to Tuapse. Although the Soviets were active nearby, there was a secure line of communication to the rear and it had heavy weapons available for defence should the enemy attack. To the south, Kampfgruppe Schäfer (Pi. 5) and Patloch of A.A. 5 occupied the Neftjanaja district. This was a typical Soviet industrial city with numerous oil installations, government buildings, refineries etc., as was usual here. Everything was astonishingly primitive but obviously functional.

To the east, the GERMANIA Rgt. and the Headquarters Staff occupied Schirwanskaja. It was a typical Caucasian village, whose residents seemed untouched by Soviet collectivization and lived their lives on secluded forest farms. They belonged to the Kabardiner people who had lived here in freedom for centuries. This area was joined with the Black Sea coast by a road through the Poshet valley and a mule track through the village of Tuby. Here the enemy showed himself to be particularly aggressive. Moreover, he had been receiving new arrivals of men again for the past several weeks. Ambushes and attacks by independent units, particularly near Samurskaja, were the order of the day. The Pioniere had it no better. The Battalion Staff was in "quarters" on Caucasian farms where the inhabitants sympathised with the Germans and treated them as guests, but a completely new style of fighting had begun for the companies. The smallest units were responsible for maintaining a watch over this vast area. On 22. August, 3. Company, reinforced by a light Flak platoon from Flak Abt. 5, relieved the Aufklärungsabteilung of 97. Jäg.Div. in the middle of the virgin forest. Its mission was to seal off the inhospitable valley to the south. The action consisted of armed reconnaissance, securing of supply and defending against the enemy attacks which, usually launched at night, had cost the lives of many Pioniere.

On 23. August 1942, the first members of XXXXIV. Jägerkorps under General de Angelis arrived from Absheronskaja. The Jäger had a long march behind them but were unprepared for a mountain war, as it had been planned to employ the Division in the foothills. Now it had to wait eight days for its mountain equipment to be transported forward. The 97. Light Division was known to the WIKING Division from 1941. Its Jäger were mostly Bavarians from the Isar-Inn valley whose homes were in Lenggries, Bad Tölz, and Tegernsee. At that time it had belonged to 17. Armee and was one of the units involved in the Uman battle. It was valued as a proven, trustworthy Division. 101. Jägerdivision on the other hand, was new to the Division. In the following days it relieved I./*GERMANIA* near Muk on the Tuapse road with Jägerrgt. 229. On the 28th, following a powerful artillery barrage, it attacked along the road toward Tuapse with both Regiments 228 and 229. The enemy defended tenaciously. The Jäger's attack broke down.

On 26. 8. 1942, 3./*WESTLAND* was on guard duty in Dadrowskaja in the midst of the mountains. One of the unit's men wrote enthusiastically in his diary of the magnificent country.[1] But he also reported on the increasing partisan activity in the area. Munitions and supplies could be brought in only by oxcart with a strong escort. Nevertheless, they were continually ambushed. Of course it was difficult to discriminate between partisans and regulars belonging to straggling Soviet units.

At this phase of the campaign the *WALLONIEN* Legion, at this time still a part of the army, was attached to the Division. This volunteer battalion was located in Rashublenny where it once more distinguished itself.

The High Command now had to revise its opinion that the attack on Tuapse would be a cakewalk. The weak frontal strength of the Jäger and their heavy losses were a clear message. But they had not given up the hope that with fast units they could regain the type of free wheeling operation that had been so successful on the Kuban steppe. Therefore, 17. Armee held onto the *WIKING* Division even though it was operationally idle. In any case, it served the purpose of securing the mountain operation's deep flank.

The attack through the rugged forests and mountains of the forests of the Caucasus bogged down under growing losses, and the onset of bad weather had reduced hopes for an early success. In these circumstances the High Command became more convinced that it could do without the Division in the West Caucasus. It was needed badly in the East Caucasus where 1. Pz.Armee's offensive toward the Grossny oil region was also bogged down.

From the Caucasian Forests to the East Caucasus

The transfer began on 16. September. The Division was relieved by units of 17. Armee with the exception of the GERMANIA Rgt. which could not yet be released rom its position near Samurskaja. The Division Ia, Reichel, personally bid - GERMANIA farewell. On the 17th, the Division marched in Gefechtsgruppen through Maikop—Labinskaja along the Armawir—Newinnomysskaja—Mineralnyje-Wody railway into the area northwest of Prochladnaja in the East Caucasus. On 19. September, it left the command area of LVII. Pz. Korps:

"SS-Division Wiking   Div. Comm. Post, 23. 9. 1942
— Ia —
In the following the Corps Order of the Day of the Commanding General of LVII. Panzerkorps, General der Panzertruppe Kirchner, is sent for presentation to the troops

For the Division Command
The First General Staff Officer
signed Reichel

Copy

The Commanding General   K.G.St., 19. September 1942
of LVII. Panzer-Korps
Corps Order of the Day
    Effective from 19. 9. 1942, the SS-Division WIKING leaves my area of command. I would like at this time to express to them my thanks and recognition for their first-rate accomplishments and brave actions during the march to Rostow and the Caucasus. My best wishes go with the Division for the future.

Sieg Heil to the Führer
signed Kirchner"

It required four days for the Division to reach the new land on the border between Europe and Asia, a hot untamed frontier. It had once been occupied by the freedom-loving Caucasian races who had passionately defended their homeland against foreign conquerors. The Karatschaj-Tschetschenen and Tscherkessen had been rebellious people settled by the Czar of the Terek Cossacks. But following the Second World War they were persecuted and moved out by the Soviets. Moved from a land where it was always spring. The abundance of tropical flowers and the lush fields still lay on the far side of the high mountain massif, 1,200 km. long and 130 km. wide, which separated them from the area of operations. Unlike the Alps, this mountain chain had no basin or mountain lakes. Instead it was wild and rugged with deep gorges from which rose a dense network of rivers flowing to the north. In particular the Terek and its many tributaries divide the foothills of the Caucasus into several sections and define the landscape. The entire Caucasian massif was circled by a railway which began in Baku, pushed north along the Caspian Sea toward Machatsch-Kala and then northwest through the Grossny oil region via Mineralnyje-Wody to Armawir and Rostow. It served to transport oil and had one switch line to Maikop near Armawir and a second to Twerskaja—Tuapse which led through Kutaissi and Tiflis along the Black Sea coast and rejoined the main line near Baku. Too few lines ran from the East Caucasus to Ordshonikidse, Alagir, Naltschik, Pjatigorsk and Kisslowodsk. It was to this area that the Division was transferred in order to reinforce 1. Panzerarmee which was fighting there. After the Division's commanders, who had flown ahead, arrived at 1. Pz.Armee headquarters in Pjatigorsk, they had an informative meeting with the Armee's Chief of Staff, Generalmajor Faeckenstedt. As to the question of which operational goals the Armee would have, Faeckenstedt stated that he believed it would first move on Grossny and then probably the Transcaucasus. Steiner, who we have to thank for this narrative, thereupon answered that such an operation was akin to crossing the northern Alps from Switzerland to Semmering without nearly so good a network of roads, passes and railroads at their disposal. Thereupon, his partner in the discussion was said to have replied that they, meaning the army "at the top", had already been told this. Faeckenstedt referred at the same time to the topographical model of the Caucasus and pointed to the Ossetische and Grusinische highways. These march routes actually led through the mountains to the Transcaucasus. The Ossetische highway, which ran from Akbasch past Alagir upward to the 2,800 metre high Mamisonskij Pass, was 185 km. long and passable only by light vehicles and mountain troops. The only road through the pass suitable for motor vehicles was the Grusinische highway which led over heights of 2,400 metres, was 217 km. long and ended at Tiflis. The omnibus which travelled the highway in peacetime required 10 hours to travel the route. The road also contained dangerous narrow passes. South of Lars at a dizzying height there was a 2 km.-long tunnel blasted through the rock. In the valley of the Arani river the road ran along a 460 metre high precipice. Everywhere the road was vulnerable to even minor demolitions. In the face of these facts, according to his account, Steiner stuck to his guns in his conversation with the Chief of the General Staff. In reply to his objections that such a plan was pure illusion and that the advancing season already made its realization doubtful, he received the answer: "We reported all that long ago and expressed serious doubts. They simply took no notice." According to Steiner's notes he then said, "I already know what you are going to say next. You are going to ask why Kleist doesn't simply pose the vital question. The Generaloberst has considered this several times. But should he abandon the Panzerarmee in this situation? Don't you think that there are plenty of generals who would relieve him immediately and would meekly do whatever was demanded of them?" So this discussion ended exactly as those before. Basically they were in agreement. Every critical officer knew that lately there was a vast gulf between the command objectives of the General Staff and harsh reality. Here one could raise his voice only cautiously. One could resign, but had to realize that the hundreds of thousands who manned the far-flung outposts could not get away. So the Generaloberst was right not to abandon the army. He would stay and use all of his cleverness and military experience to preserve the lives of his men. And that was already difficult enough.

In his notes Steiner related further his subsequent meeting with the Generaloberst. He had been warm and accomodating as always. "His joy at meeting old comrades from the days of the battles of Uman and Rostov was genuine. Moreover he was happy over every man he received as reinforcement here in this isolated post."

The Division had been placed under the Corps Headquarters of LII. A.K. in Gnadenburg. The Division's 1. General Staff Officer had been sent ahead there. He reported back to the Division Commander in Appalanskaja and reported on the situation and his impressions: 1. Panzerarmee had not only assigned XXXX. Pz.Korps, the only forces available, to protect the eastern flank and the forces still located in the West Caucasus, but had also sent it to the attack to the southeast where it had succeeded in taking the triangle of cities Pjatigorsk—Georgijewsk—Kisslowodsk. Already on 9. August, 3. Pz.Div. had entered Pjatigorsk which had been fiercely defended by cadets from a Red Army Officer School, NKVD troops and a female battalion. The strongest resistance was met by the Corps at Baksan in the Terek sector. It possessed insufficient forces to advance as far as the Terek. For weeks the Corps had strived to cross the Terek from Prochladnaja. However the river was as stoutly defended as the city of Mosdok further to the east. The Russians had had sufficient time to carefully fortify the south bank of the Terek. Therefore, the Armee had diverted LVII. Pz.Korps, which was still operating on the Kalmuck Steppe, with two inf. divisions for the attack on Mosdok. After preparations the attack was launched on 2. September, winning a crossing and establishing a 5 km. deep bridgehead to the south. 13. Pz.Div., which had been moved up from Maikop, broke out of the bridgehead and was able to gain and hold ground near the Elchotowo heights 17 km. to the south. LII. A.K. had likewise moved out of the bridgehead with the inf.div. in an attempt to win territory to the east in the general directionof Grossny. This attack was completely halted at the edge of the high country near Mosdok and brought to a standstill. Both divisions had suffered heavy casualties. 111. I.D., which had been forced to go to ground at Mosdok, had been reduced to the approximate strength of a regiment.

A Difficult Operation

This was the situation when the *WIKING* Division arrived in the area of Apollonskaja and to the east on 20. September. 1942. On 23. September, 1. Pz.Armee had reached a new decision. The plan called for the attack on Grossny to be renewed. III. Pz.Korps which had also arrived with two Panzerdivisions and the 3. Rumanian Geb.Div. would advance along the foot of the mountains toward Ordshonikidse through Naltschik and Alagir. As the northern spearhead the *WIKING* Division was to attack from the Mosdok bridgehead and seize the Grusinische highway south of Malgobek. Continuation of the attack toward Grossny would be determined by the situation at that time.

The following is an excerpt from the Soviet history of the war concerning the battle for the Caucasus:

"Despite their losses of the past three weeks, the Fascists had achieved no decisive success and saw themselves forced to pull one of their best divisions, the motorized SS-Division *WIKING*, out of the Tuapse sector and direct it to the Mosdok area. Following this reinforcement, 1. Panzerarmee renewed its offensive..."

The terrain over which the Division would attack, and on which the infantry of LII. A.K. had shed so much blood, was unbelievably difficult. It consisted of a several kilometre wide ridge which extended from Nishny-Kurp, the southernmost village in the bridgehead, eastward in the direction of Grossny. The ridge was completely bare and climbed terrace style in high steps from 500 to 720 metres. It was crowned by the mountain village of Malgobek. An oil centre on the Grusinischen highway, it was like a white fortress which commanded the entire Terek valley and the area north of the ridge.

This bastion could not be taken from the north. Therefore, the Division was now to attack from the west and work its way up to the mountain fortress. This was especially difficult as this face was cut in a north-south direction by numerous gorges, called *Balkas*. All of this formed a natural defence position which the Soviets had skillfully used to their advantage, and which now bristled with new trench positions.

The attack, despite thorough preparations, would in all probability result in heavy losses. These could only be kept within normal limits if heavy Stuka support was available as had been the case during the attack on Rostov. The firepower of a Panzer unit could not be brought to bear here.

There was of course another possibility for success. The ridge position would have to be raised from its hinges by a quick attack in the Kurp valley. South of the Malgobeker heights the Kurp valley extended to the east in a width of 6 km.. In the west opposite Nishny-Kurp it was barricaded by a strong defensive position protected by antitank ditches. On the Grusinischen highway it was barred by the town of Ssagopschin which was located on a hill and by an antitank barrier lying behind it. An enemy brigade was dug in in Ssagopschin. In the Malgobek range of hills was a Soviet rifle division. To the south, this terrain was bordered by a ridge. It was thickly-wooded and had hills from 800-900 metres in height. This formed the southern barrier of the actual Terek and Ardon valleys on the edge of the West Caucasus, through which III. Pz.Korps was to attack from Naltschik.

The Division faced a bitter decision. How should the attack be carried out? This depended on the support of VIII. Fliegerkorps. Its commander, Generaloberst von Richthofen, suddenly appeared in the Division's attack sector with his chief of staff, Oberst i. G. Herhudt von Rhoden. However, as he explained, VIII. Fliegerkorps was needed so badly at Tuapse and Stalingrad that it could provide only limited support for 1. Pz. Armee. This would be in the form of obsolescent Heinkel types which carried only a few bombs and therefore could give only sporadic help.

In the face of these facts the Division Commander decided to carry out the attack through the Kurp valley and cover the high Malgobeker flank through containing attacks. It was, in the face of the terrain's structure, an extremely difficult decision, which would be equally difficult to carry out.

The Division's plan of attack envisioned that the *NORDLAND* Rgt. would launch holding attacks from the heights east of Nishny-Kurp along the southern slope of the Malgobek ridge. This would secure the northern wing of *WESTLAND*'s attack group. In Werchne-Kurp, Kampfgruppe Stoffers was to advance eastward along the wooded hills of the Samankul mountain range, support the attack group in its southern flank, and provide covering fire from flanking positions for *NORDLAND*'s attack as far as the top of the antitank positions east of Nishny-Kurp. The *NORDLAND* Rgt. together with a Sturmgeschützabteilung would support the main attack.

After both of *NORDLAND*'s covering positions were established north and south of the Kurp valley at approximately the same elevation as the antitank ditches, Pz.Abt. 5, under cover of artillery fire, was to establish a bridgehead across the antitank ditches. Then, with I./SS *WESTLAND* under SS- Stubaf. Frhr. von Hadeln, it would advance along the ridge from Malgobek toward Ssagopschin. There it would envelop the town from the north and bring it down from the north and east. The WESTLAND Regiment would follow the Panzergruppe across the narrow rise in the valley, advance directly toward Ssagopschin and attack, pinning down the enemy there. The southern flank of WESTLAND's attack would be covered by Kampfgruppe Schäfer along the banks of the Kurp toward Keskem and Pssedach.

On Sunday, the 27th of September, the NORDLAND Rgt. opened the attack by moving against the heights of the Malgobeker ridge. It made only slow progress. The opposing Soviet assault brigade resisted fanatically. Its soldiers had dug in up to their noses and fought desperately. I./NORDLAND sustained severe losses. The Chief of 3. Company, SS-Hstuf. Bluhm, was killed followed by the Chief of 2. Company. Losses in officers multiplied. Adjutants and ordinance officers jumped into the breach. The Sturmgeschütz Abteilung could only provide limited support since its firing position lay on the high ridge and the Sturmgeschütze could not reach the forward edge of the slopes. By 15.00 hours the battalion was bogged down. The Battalion Adjutant, SS-Ostuf. Thöny, attempted to move the troops forward.

Things went better for II. Battalion south of the valley. It was able to gain territory to the east and bring its infantry to bear quite well. Everyone dug in. If the WIKING Division was not to suffer the fate of 111. Inf.Div., everything would have to be staked on the attack planned for the next day through the valley between the two attack support positions. SS- Standartenführer von Scholz appeared to have doubts. He thought the Armee's demands pure madness and considered the idea of accompanying his soldiers and dying in battle with them. But he did not close his mind to the exhortations of his Division Commander.

On 28. September, Gefechtsgruppe WESTLAND was to set out to break through the Kurp valley toward Ssagopschin. 1. Panzerarmee's 1. General Staff Officer arrived at the Division's command post during the night in order to be able to report to the Armee on the attack's progress. On the same night, Generaloberst von Kleist sent a teletype message to the Division:

"To the Commander WIKING Div.

The entire Army looks to your Division. You have the task of paving the way for the Army toward Grossny. I expect your armoured spearhead to be at Ssagopschin this evening at 18.00 hours.

signed von Kleist[1]

Oppressive silence reigned in the Ia Staffel as the Division's General Staff Officer read the teletype. But what could be done?

At dawn the Pz.Abteilung moved to the attack on the antitank ditches. Holding the enemy infantry down with cannon fire, it crossed the antitank ditches and established a bridgehead. I./WESTLAND followed: "The first tank trap was taken at the first go with heavy losses. Russian tanks ahead and the enemy fires with Stalin Organs like mad. The WESTLAND Regiment has heavy casualties, especially II. Battalion, whose commander Steinert is severely wounded. The majority of the officers are wounded or dead. 5. Company is decimated. Hauptsturmführer Bäurle, Chief of 1./WESTLAND, takes command of II. Battalion and leads the men, who had

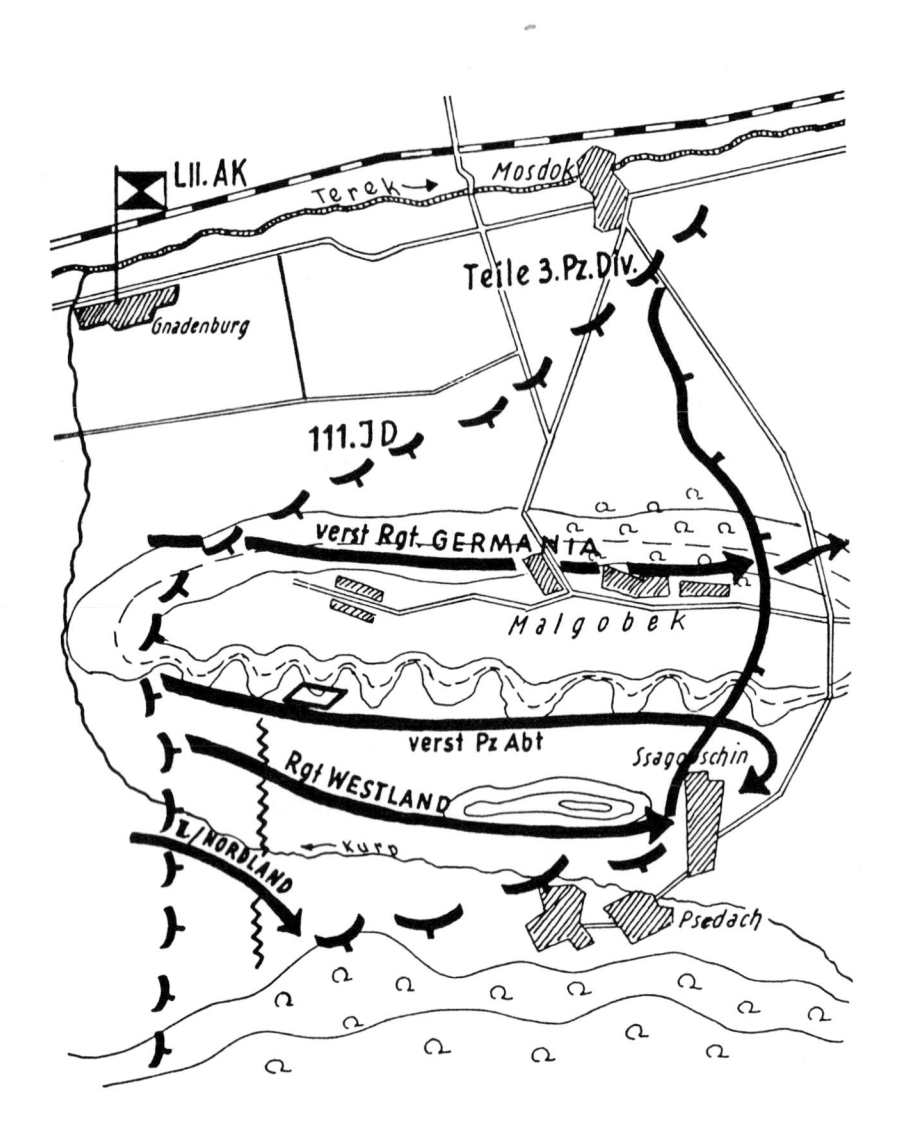

The attack on Ssagopschin and the Malgobek heights

arrived helpless and exhausted at I. Battalion's command post, forward in his own way. The dead and wounded were brought back. An advance here is impossible especially since the air is teeming with enemy American-built bombers and fighters." An eye witness report.[2] The Division Commander, nevertheless, held the view that the Regiment had not exploited the favorable situation.—

Mühlenkamp and von Hadeln now decided to advance as quickly as possible in the blind area to the right of the ridge and take Ssagopschin to the south. The speed of their advance surprised the Russians deep in the mountain position. Mühlenkamp and von Hadeln penetrated about as far as Malgobek and cleared the wide antitank ditch east of Ssagopschin from which they had taken heavy fire. WESTLAND, meanwhile, advanced frontally against Ssagopschin. The attack on the climbing terraced village came to a standstill in the face of the defending Soviet forces in approximately brigade strength. At midday the Soviets began to attack WESTLAND's southern flank from Keskem and Pssedach. Kampfgruppe Schäfer dug in on the south bank of the Kurp, covered the flank and repulsed the attack by infantry in approximately battalion strength. When dusk fell, a decision had to be made. The Division Commander, who was with WESTLAND, was called by radio. SS-Ustuf. Flügel, a company commander in the Panzerabteilung, reported. He spoke through a throat microphone: "Send a battalion of infantry, Herr General! We can make it and clear Ssagopschin this evening from the rear." However his optimism was not shared. The Battalion Commanders of II. and III./WESTLAND had hastily organized their defences. No acute danger existed there. It looked more serious around NORDLAND. It still lay before the heart of the ridge and was able to advance only slowly. The Division, therefore, had to decide what would happen with the Mühlenkamp-von Hadeln Gruppe. Under the cover of darkness, it pulled them back from their exposed position east of Ssagopschin to a defensive position between WESTLAND and NORDLAND, creating a unified arc-shaped front. Pz.Abt. 5 was to assemble in a *balka* behind the NORDLAND Rgt. as the attack reserve. The Division wanted to align itself for defence between Keskem and the ridge south of Malgobek.

These moves were carried out at dawn as planned, but with difficulty. An enemy tank force of brigade strength was approaching. It had assembled east of Ssagopschin, intending to move north of the village and fall on WESTLAND's northern flank. Still in the morning mists, the two groups crashed into each other; the Panzerabteilung which was withdrawing with WESTLAND and the Soviet tanks which were still without infantry protection. The result was tank versus tank fighting at close range. The Germans smashed through the astonished Russians. They had arrived at exactly the right time to frustrate the Russian tank breakthrough to the west. For their part, the Soviets now preferred to remain in cover east of Ssagopschin. The morning tank versus tank duel had hit them hard. Now the situation began to stabilize. The advance by NORDLAND in the valley also progressed favourably. On 2. October, II./NORDLAND linked up with I./WESTLAND on the southern slope of the Malgobeker mountain range northwest of Ssagopschin. By 09.30 hours, batteries of the Soviet 57th Assault Brigade had been destroyed and 150 prisoners taken. The enemy forces on the - NORDLAND Regiment's flank had been smashed.

The Capture of Malgobek

Although the daring operation had not led to the breakthrough toward Grossny, it had led to the capture of a vital Soviet bastion which would be indispensable as a jumping-off position for later operations. The forward headquarters also had reason to be pleased with the capture of the town of Ssagopschin. However this was not the case. In particular, the Division Commander was flooded by reproaches from the General Command of LII. A.K. because he had pulled the Mühlenkamp attack group back from its exposed position. Harsh words were exchanged and Steiner's reply was quite outspoken. The Commanding General then demanded suggestions from Steiner by 3. October for the resumption of the attack. During this conversation Steiner referred to the mountain city of Malgobek. He explained that without its capture, the Division's present forward-echeloned position would be problematical in the long run. The answer was laconic: "It will be taken by newly arriving forces." To the question, which new forces they were likely to be, the reply was as cool as it was brief: "Your Regiment *GERMANIA*, which will arrive here tomorrow."

That was the situation on 5. October 1942. Oberstleutnant Alberto Marini describes the preparations which followed:[1]

"On 3. October, the *GERMANIA* Regiment arrived. It had been reinforced by the last battalion of A.R. 5 but was without its own III. Battalion. During the night of 3./4. October, the Regiment was led into its assembly areas. It had time enough to familiarize itself with the terrain before the start of the attack on 5. October. The Aufklärungsabteilung, which had also arrived from the West Caucasus, relieved II./*NORDLAND* on the 4th in order to take over security in the south against the Mussakaj heights. II./*NORDLAND*, one of the most successful battalions, was to follow *GERMANIA*'s attack on the south slope of the Malgobek ridge. That is to say that it was proposed to carry out the main thrust of the attack with two fresh battalions, which had to take the crest of the ridge supported by two Panzer companies for every three platoons, and to echelon a relatively fresh battalion to the south.

With the exception of II. Battalion, the *WESTLAND* Regiment was ordered to remain in its positions in the hills, serving as the reserve for *GERMANIA*. The *NORDLAND* Regiment with its three battered battalions and the Aufklärungsabteilung were to remain in the valley west of Ssagopschin to screen to the south."

SS-Standartenführer Jürgen Wagner had arranged a meeting for an exchange of ideas among the leaders involved in the attack. At noon on 4. October, all of the unit leaders of the Panzerabteilung down to the level of platoon leader were gathered in the Regimental command post. There they jointly observed their attack sectors, trying to pick out enemy positions. During the night of 4./5. October, the units moved into the assembly area. According to the diary of SS-Hauptsturmführer Dorr, who had received the Knights Cross a few days before, the attack on Malgobek began at 04.30. The chiefs of the rifle companies had climbed on the platoon leaders' Panzers and the battalion commander on that of the Panzerabteilung chief. Stukas helped the attack move forward. Also taking part in the assault were the remaining forces of 111. Inf.Div. (70. Inf.Rgt.), which were involved on the northern arc. By 11.00, the *GERMANIA* Rgt. had got to within approximately 500 metres of West Malgobek. At roughly 11.30 hours, 20 Stukas appeared in the sky to the west and bombed the town, softening up the defences as requested by the Regiment's commander. By approximately 14.00, West Malgobek was free of the enemy. GERMANIA Regiment's I. and II. Battalions had taken the hard-fought-for mountain fortress. Deserving of special mention were the courageous efforts of the men of 70. Inf.Rgt. under its commander, Oberst Tronnier. According to Dorr, the GERMANIA Regiment's losses on the first day were 33 dead and nearly 200 wounded.

Following the loss of the town, the Russians immediately counterattacked with tanks along the Grusinischen highway. Moving against Gefechtsgruppe GERMANIA's southern flank, they ran into flanking fire from II./NORDLAND. The enemy attack was beaten back. On 6. October, the attack was resumed. Thick fog reduced visibility. Nevertheless, on this day the attackers were successful in capturing all of the town of East Malgobek and an area 1 km. to the east. At approximately 15.00 hours the high oil storage tank fell into the Division's hands.

Let us once again review the previous fourteen days through the diary of a "simple man"[2], who experienced the battle as a messenger:

27. 9. 42 Assembly area before Ssagopschin. Evening, we are attacked by Russian aircraft. Artillery straddles us. A confused mix-up in the corn fields. 5.Company has 1 dead—21 wounded. I. Battalion ca. 150 casualties—in one hour.

28. 9. 42 We go to the attack, 06.30 (3. Company in reserve). S is strongly fortified—tanks in front—Russian aircraft over us, like flies. They drop bombs from very low altitude and strafe. Drop phosphorous. 12.00, we are at the edge of the village. A tough fight. Finally we saw two German fighters.

29. 9. 42. We have not yet entered the village. We are to mount another attack this afternoon. American type fighters and bombers come incessantly. A damned shitty mess in these days. We lack heavy artillery and above all air support. The right flank is open, it is reported—according to statements by a deserter there is only an enemy security force there.—We are terribly filthy. The little coffee is scarcely worth drinking.

30. 9. 42 I am a messenger at the Btl. command post. 05.00 message to Company (5.)—Pioniere get ready—track noises from a gathering of tanks behind the Malgobek hills. New attack on S. The village's first line of trenches taken with heavy losses. Enemy tanks ahead of us. Stalin Organs fire.

1. 10. 42 Heavy artillery fire. Our messenger company is forbidden to use the motorcycle—every dust cloud brings down Russian artillery fire. We don't always obey—have plenty of tired bones. 5. Company's command post is on a hill to the right. With a flying start out of the cornfield up the rise—followed by Russian fire. We don't always make it to the top. One simply lets the machine fall away to the side—and into the nearest hole. Once I dropped it harshly on my chief's legs. The Russian artillery has spared me a wound. In any case I must leave the motorcycle above and return to the Btl. command post on foot.

2. 10. 42 We pull back 4 km..

3. 10. 42 We dig in again.

4. 10. 42 The usual artillery fire. GERMANIA is to arrive tomorrow and attack Malgobek.

5. 10. 42 G. attacks. Stukas come into action. After three days fighting Malgobek falls. A relief for our left flank.

10. 10. 42 I am wounded!"

The Division had now created a closed front between Keskem and Malgobek. For a while it was quiet. However, the Soviets had brought up a new Division, which was deployed east of Malgobek. It took up defensive positions and attempted to improve its unfavourable position through local attacks. In addition, the enemy had moved in several new batteries and above all "Stalin Organs". Continuing with the attack under these conditions would have been senseless, since the initiative appeared to have passed to the Soviets. In any case, there were insufficient German forces to carry out a large scale operation against distant Grossny. This had also become clear to the Armee. In any case, it seemed satisfied with the results. But the Commanding General wanted more. He demanded that WIKING take Hill 701, which lay before the Division's front. In the opinion of the commander, the hill was "without meaning" to the Division. This was because the Division could observe the Grusinische highway, which ran along its front, just as well from its present positions as it could from Hill 701. In response to the message that the Division had no more forces for the proposed attack, came the reply: "You still have a combat-ready battalion, the Finnish Battalion!" The question "What for?", was answered with the words, "For the continuation of the operation toward Grossny!" It made no difference, both the Armee and the Corps Headquarters demanded the new attack.

The Finns Take Hill 701

The Finns attacked on 16. 10. 1942 and took Hill 701. It was a heroic fight. One could not describe it better than the Finnish Obersturmführer, Tauno Pohjanletho from Sunila, Finland, already has:

Since 9. October 1942, we were supposed to attack and take Hill 701 behind Malgobek. Large and small units had attacked with partial success, but were unable to reach the crest of the hill. So on 16. October, we attacked the hill for the last time. Our Companies had been seriously reduced in the hard fighting at Terek and in the foothills of the Caucasus. Our 9th had the strength of 10. and 11. Companies together. They were merged and had a total strength of 40 men.

On 15. October, we sat at the base of Hill 701, just below the Russian positions. We had found an empty Russian bunker and crawled into it. We were hungry and things looked black. Our Battalion Commander, Stubaf. Collani, came over to us. We lit a candle. We had received no food. Instead there were a few gulps of red wine, which eased our thirst. Collani had forced himself into the bunker with difficulty. Somewhat helplessly he asked, "How's it going?" One of us murmured bitterly, "We're attacking in the morning." The mood changed. We laughed and remarked how good it was that two companies could sit in one bunker. Then we heard what the commander had ordered for the next day. An assault troop under my command was to be formed from both companies. Mühlinghaus from 12. Company would give us support with mortars and heavy weapons and a Panzer Company was to help us up the hill.

We were to launch a surprise attack without a preparatory artillery barrage. Everything was agreed. If the operation misfired, it would likely be our last attack. We knew that. There was nothing more to lose. If it succeeded, then many of us would probably be allowed to live. Our mood was determined, as it is in those situations when there is no turning back. Someone hummed the "Teufelslied". We bellowed the "Ha, ha, haah" so loudly that the Russians must have had heard. That inspired Mühlinghaus who then gave a rendition of the "Trumpet of Vionville" in French. Then we went to sleep.

In the morning there was thick fog. We waited for the time to attack. As we moved out, we were at the Russian positions in no time.
The Russians were completely surprised. We took the first trenches quickly. The higher up the slope we climbed, the harder the enemy resisted. Our shells burst on the crest of the hill, behind us lay the enemy barrage fire like a thick wall, and between them roared the firing of our tanks. Enemy machine guns and submachine guns rattled everywhere.
We were right in the midst of the enemy positions. It seemed impossible that we would go any further. Several of our Panzers tried to help us but received such heavy antitank fire from the crest that they had to withdraw to cover. The Pyyhtiäs squad received a direct hit. Gefreiter Kesti was blown into the air. To my left, Unteroffizier Metz attempted to catch a Russian hand grenade which had been thrown at us in order to throw it back. He was shot in the arm. The grenade rolled down his back and exploded between his legs. He was gone.
Unteroffizier Miettinen tried to jump forward but was shot in the stomach from point blank range. As he fell, he fired an entire magazine from his submachine gun into a Russian rifle pit. My brain was afire. I could see the fiasco and thought of the consequences. My messenger Sakari Miettinen and I jumped into a Russian hole. There was not enough room, so we lay pressed to the earth in the open without cover. Half a metre above us the machine gun fire whipped through the air. Ahead of us lay a Russian under cover in a foxhole, his submachine gun lay on the its edge. I waited until he moved a little, saw a cap, a Mongol skull and emptied my magazine. Then I crawled toward him. He would move no more. In wild bounds, we rushed to the crest of the hill. On the run, we put three antitank guns out of commission with hand grenades. Now our tanks could move ahead. Mühlinghaus came with them. They threw full magazines for our SMG's and hand grenades to us. We captured a whole company of Russians who were completely shaken. Then we cleared the crest of enemy troops. We captured a number of antitank rifles, two heavy infantry guns, numerous heavy machine guns and other infantry weapons. We had finally taken Hill 701, on whose slopes so many of our comrades would forever sleep. With six men we sat on the hill and removed the steel helmets from our sweating heads. In our dirty shaking hands we were holding our first cigarettes when it started up again. The Russian artillery flashed on the ridge. In a victorious mood we paid little attention to it. Then our valiant company headquarters section leader, Unteroffizier Sahlmann, collapsed. His last words were, "Look here, this is how German youth dies."
The next morning the Russians attacked again and again. They were beaten back. Three T-34's were hit and set afire by our Panzers. Our artillery assisted. I now commanded 10. and 11. Companies which together had a strength of 12 men. Oberleutnant Pallesche of 9. Company and our Oberleutnant Mühlinghaus of 12. Company had caught it. They joined the dead Finns.
But Hill 701 remained in our hands."
The Finns got no rest. Together with Panzerabtlg. 5, which counterattacked again and again, they fought off the Russian attacks. Here the Russians attacked with T-34 tanks. Three to four times a day they raced over the deeply dug in Finns and battled on the slopes with the German Panzers. The result was bitter tank versus tank fighting at close range. Soon the south slope of the Malgobeker ridge had become a field of tank wreckage. In the north the Division was flanked by Flak guns. From the rear fired the Finnish Pak, fighting individual duels with the onrushing Russian armour. But the Soviets got no further and every attack suffe-

red new losses. A brutal will must have driven them forward since for them every attack was a wild ride to certain death. The Division too had suffered heavy losses in the murderous fighting, particularly the NORDLAND Regiment which defended Malgobek's southernmost slope. But gradually these attacks died away as the Russians could deploy no more tanks here. As a result of the attacks by III. Pz.Korps toward Alagir-Ardon, the Soviets had been forced to transfer their main effort to the south.

Defence between Fiagdon and Alagir

The waves created by the differences with the Corps Headquarters had reached as far as the Pz. A.O.K. 1 and the Chief of the General Staff. Soon after the conclusion of the successful battle near Malgobek, the Chief of the General Staff, General der Inf. Zeitzler, arrived at the Pz. A.O.K. 1. He requested a meeting with the Division Commander of SS-Division WIKING on 20. October at Armee Headquarters in Pjatigorsk. He apparently had the impression, that a serious conflict existed between A.O.K. and the Division, and was surprised to discover that this was not the case. In any case, there had been differences of opinion between the Corps Headquarters and Division concerning the necessity of the last costly battle. The Division Commander could not be convinced that the pursuit of an offensive in the direction of Grossny was still possible or even necessary when it would demand such a high sacrifice, the wearing down of an entire division. In particular, the commander of the WIKING Division felt responsible, not only to the Army but to the Finnish government and people, for the preservation of the Finnish Battalion. This view found the complete understanding of the Chief of the General Staff and led to a frank discussion between General Steiner and the Army Commander in Chief in the presence of General Zeitzler which smoothed the waves. On this evening General Zeitzler expressed a confident opinion on the situation on the whole Eastern Front and also optimistically assessed the situation at Stalingrad . Four weeks later, however, he had to correct his view.[1] During these days a crisis had just arisen with III. Pz.Korps on the Terek front. Its three divisions had advanced across the Ossetische highway toward the Fiagdon in the direction of Ordshonikidse. While 23. Pz.Div. had been unable to overcome the Russian resistance north of Fiagdon, 13. Pz.Div., the WIKING Division's old battle comrades, had succeeded in entering Gisel and pushing advance elements to the limits of Ordshonikidse. There they ran into a counterattack by superior Soviet forces. The division was encircled between Ordshonikidse and Gisel. At that time, 23. Pz.Div. was so tied up that it could not release any forces to free the encircled division, while the Rumanian 2. Gebirgsdivision did not have the combat forces required for such a difficult task. The WIKING Division would have to provide the help. III. Panzerkorps' situation was critical enough. Troops from its supply units had just been able to establish a thin defensive front in the Basorkina and Fiagdon hills in order to prevent the Soviet forces from marching unhindered to the Ossetischen highway. The entire Terek front hung by a thread. Elements of 50. Inf.Div. were hurriedly flown in from the Crimea and relieved WIKING in its positions near Ssagopschin. As the Division's Kampfgruppen were relieved, they set off on a forced march southward toward Alagir. But all of this had cost time, too much time...

Meanwhile, the first of the Division's self-contained Kampfgruppen had been relieved. On 16. November, Stubaf. Stoffers with his well tested II./NORDLAND,

Stubaf. Mühlenkamp with the reinforced Pz.Abt. 5, and III./A.R. 5 arrived in Alagir after a strenous march via Prochladnaja. They immediately went to the attack against the western side of the Soviet encircling ring north of Gisel.

The attack by the Stoffers Gruppe took the Soviets by surprise and was successful, especially since 13. Pz.Div. attacked simultaneously at Gisel and was able to press the Soviet forces hard. While 13. Pz.Div.'s rearguards still held temporarily near Dsuarikau, and the bulk of its forces were still gathered west of the Ossetischen highway, a new front was formed between Hochgebirge and Samankul through Fiagdon and Ardon. This front was held at first by three German divisions; WIKING in the south, 23. Pz.Div. in the centre and 13. Pz.Div. on the northern wing. Two new Gebirgsdivisionen secured the deep flank to the Caucasus mountains. After the encirclement of Stalingrad, 23. Pz.Div. was transferred to 4. Panzerarmee. WIKING and 13. Pz.Div. stretched their sectors and held shoulder to shoulder in heavy fighting against furious attacks by Soviet forces supported by tanks. The Soviets, recognizing the hopelessness of the present situation, changed their plan of attack. With great difficulty and under extreme hardship, the Soviets began to move their attack forces through the valleys of the Caucasus mountain ranges. Their aim was to drive up to the deep southern flank of 1. Panzerarmee, and then from the north, that is north of the Terek in the southern Caucasus, to create a pocket around 1. Panzerarmee.

In those days, the SS-Div. WIKING (mot) was renamed. As of 9. 11. 1942, on orders from the Führer and Supreme Commander, it carried the unit designation, "5 SS- Pz.Grenadier-Division WIKING". No longer were the men in the infantry regiments designated as "SS-Schützen" as before, but "SS-Panzergrenadiere".

On the northern Alagir front the enemy had shifted his point of main effort to the Ardon. Not a day passed in November 1942, when the enemy did not attack with superior forces the elements of 13. Pz. Div. there. And there was no evening, when the Germans' sole reserve, Hauptmann von Gaza's Pz.Grenadier Battalion, did not counterattack to throw the enemy back from his newly-won positions.

Things were quiet before the Division's front, however the situation on its flanks was becoming more dangerous. At first, the Soviets attempted to smash the front's southernmost corner pillar near Dsuarikau. But here he ran into a steel-hard opponent. The Division's well-proven battalion, I./GERMANIA under its commander SS-Stubaf. Dieckmann, as well as II. Battalion, were masters of the situation. Unfortunately, the recently added Rumanian companies often fled in the face of the attacking enemy. Reunited with GERMANIA, they felt secure with their German brothers in arms and performed their duties bravely. Nothing much happened on the Ossetischen highway either. There, I. Battalion of Gebirgsjäer Rgt. 99, well-trusted by WIKING's commander and attached to the Division since 4. December, interdicted south of Alagir. Steiner had no cause to be disappointed. Again and again the Jäger held out against attacks by far superior Soviet forces. The enemy troops were part of the Soviet 351st Rifle Division, almost exclusively from a young age group who had previously been members of the Soviet "Ossoviachim" youth group. "A counterattack on 8. Dec. succeeded according to plan with the support of an attached platoon of SS-Pionier Battalion 5", whose fighting spirit was favourably mentioned. Here too, the Rumanians, who had been deployed on the Battalion's flank, were an unsteadying factor.

More and more, the enemy threat to the mountain front's flank showed itself further to the west between Ardon and Uruch. At the beginning of December the enemy was active south of Karman—Dsindshikau. Also appearing there were

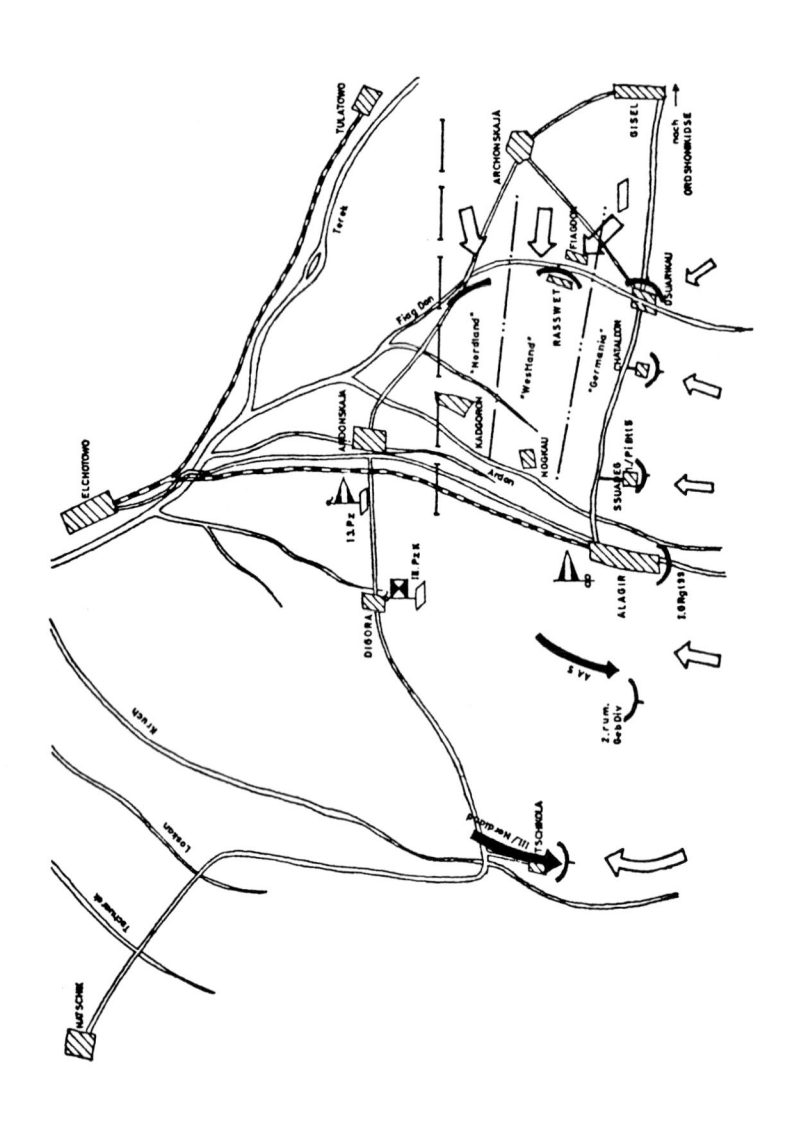

The situation near Alagir November 1942

NKVD units, which attacked to the north with great bravado. But the Soviets had been unable to bring any artillery and only a few tanks with them through the trackless forests and over the mountains. The Panzergrenadiere of the WIKING Division had long since lost their fear of attacks by infantry alone. SS-Stubaf. Paetsch, the commander of the sector near Karman—Dsindshikau, and his veteran SS- Aufklärungsabteilung 5 had the situation well in hand and held the attacking Soviets in check. The manner in which Soviet military historians present the changeable fighting in the period between 19. Nov. and 23. Dec. 1942 will surely interest the reader. The complete reproduction of a lengthy extract from the chapter titled, "The Counterattacks by the Northern Group of the Transcaucasian Front in the Direction of Alagir—Naltschik", may be justified because its contribution, whose objectivity and self-criticism is impressive, allows the accomplishments of the WIKING Division to be seen in the correct light.[3]

"On the Fascist side of the Alagir front stood the 13. Div., the 23. Div., and the 2. Rumanian Mountain Division. The enemy regrouped and reequipped the battered elements of the 13. Div. and the 23. Tank Div. Utilizing the favourable terrain, the combat engineers built a strong, well-prepared defensive position in the sector 15 to 18 km. east of Alagir. Because he feared Soviet attacks there, the enemy hurriedly transferred the motorized SS-Division WIKING from Malgobek to the Alagir front.

Because of the weakness of the reconnaissance, these measures were not discovered in time. This worked to the disadvantage of the Soviet counterattacks.

On 19. November, the Soviet units went over to the offensive toward Alagir. They overcame the enemy's bitter resistance and moved slowly forward. The Fascists possessed a marked superiority in tanks and undertook frequent counterattacks.

The Soviet tank forces deployed in this sector were unable to make any significant contribution to the progress of the counterattack as a result of the difficult terrain conditions in this area and the poorly organized coordination between them and the artillery, infantry and air forces. Nevertheless, the soldiers of the 5th Guards Tank Brigade were able to break the enemy resistance in one sector, destroy 15 tanks and 4 batteries of artillery and mortars in heavy fighting, advance 4—5 km. and take an important hill. The bitter fighting on the Alagir front lasted until 23. November. The territorial gains of the Soviet troops, however, were insignificant, and the offensive was not expanded.

The commander of the Northern Group decided, therefore, to temporarily suspend the attack in this direction and to strike another blow. In response to this decision, the units on the Alagir front ceased offensive operations on 23. November and began preparing for the new operation. But this time the Soviet forces needed only three days time and renewed the attack on 27. November.

This overly hasty changeover succeeded, because the enemy had begun to pull back his forces to a new defence sector. In doing so, the Fascist German command shortened the defensive front, releasing 23. Panzerdivision. It was transferred to General Manstein's group, which together with the Tormosiner group, was preparing at this time to go to the aid of their units surrounded at Stalingrad. To create this group, the enemy command had pulled together tank and motorized units from various sectors of the front. While 23. Panzerdivision was transferred to the Stalingrad front, the WIKING Division was relieved in the Malgobek area by 50. Infantry Division. It had previously been in the Crimea but was now inserted into 1. Panzerarmee.

The Northern Group's units identified the beginning of the enemy's withdrawal and on 27. November went over to the attack. The Group smashed the enemy's screening forces and began to successfully move forward in the direction of Alagir.

But the enemy, who had pulled his units back into the Ardon sector and thrown the SS-Division *WIKING* into the front lines of the defence, halted the Soviet units in this sector.

On 30. November, on orders from the high command, the Northern Group's units broke off their attack and temporarily went over to the defensive in order to prepare for a new attack against the units of the German *III. Panzerkorps* in the direction of Alagir-Naltschik.

On orders from the Commander of the Northern Group, the attacking force for the blow toward Alagir-Naltschik consisted this time of 3 Rifle Brigades, 1 Rifle Division and 2 Tank Brigades. The offensive was to consist of two thrusts. One would be carried out from the area west of Archonskaja toward Tschikola with elements proceeding toward Alagir. The second would be launched from the area northwest of Sadon and likewise move toward Tschikola. The forces carrying out the attack from the Archonskaja area would go over to the offensive first, followed one day later by the forces attacking from the Sadon area.

The operation began on 4. December following brief preparations and continued until 9. December. The attack was unsuccessful as there had been insufficient preparation and the forces involved were too weak. On 9. December, the Soviet forces broke off their attack in the direction of Alagir-Naltschik and went over to the defensive. They prepared for a further attack which began at the end of December.

In order to shorten the front and release the *WIKING* Division, the enemy pulled his forces out of the Ardon—Alagir—Digora area on 23. December and back into prepared defensive positions in the Elchotowo—Tschikola sector. The *WIKING* Division was quickly transferred to General Manstein's group.

When the units of the Northern Group noticed the enemy's withdrawal, they went over to the pursuit but were unable to get far as they ran into stubborn resistance from the new, prepared defensive positions in the Elchotowo sector.

With this ended the counterattacks by units of the Northern Group in the direction of Alagir-Naltschik..."

Battles in the Tschikola Valley

On 14. December 1942, General d.Kav. von Mackensen, the former Commanding General of III. Pz.Korps, was recalled from this position to take command of 1. Pz.Armee. He replaced the Armee's long time Commander in Chief, Generaloberst von Kleist. Von Kleist became Commander in Chief of the German forces operating in the Caucasus.

In the course of these personnel changes the former commander of the *WIKING* Division, Felix Steiner, was appointed to command III. Pz.Korps. SS-Brigadeführer and Generalmajor der Waffen-SS Herbert Gille, who had been commander of the *WIKING*'s artillery regiment during two long years of war, took over the command of the Division.

In these days the defensive battles of 2. Rumanian Gebirgsdivision under its able commander, Generalleutnant Dumitrache, were in the focus. They succeeded despite difficulty and hardship in preventing enemy breakthroughs near Durdur. Then the enemy attacked further west from the narrow Tschikola and

August 1942:
On the road in the
forests of the Caucasus.

July 1942:
I./SS-Pz.Rgt. 5 in the
area of Belaja Glina.

July 1942:
I./SS-Pz.Rgt. 5 on the
attack south of Jegorlyk.

The Finnish motorcycle
messenger Pekka Kurvine
on the Ossetische road
in the East Caucasus 194

Men of
III./*GERMANIA*
advance toward Mosdock
under the protection
of their own tanks.

On guard
in the Caucasus.

December 1942:
One of the high peaks
of the Caucasus
seen through a battery
commander's telescope.

Flak firing position
in the Caucasus
October 1942

Winter 1942:
Action in the
East Caucasus

SS-Sturmbannführer Christian Frederik Schalburg, Division O 1 and later commander of the *Danmark* Corps.

On the advance to the West Caucasus, August 1942. Oberführer Gille issues new orders.

Aerial photograph of the *WIKING* Division's military cemetery at the rail station in Uspenskaja/Ukraine.

Hand-over of Finnish volunteers by Felix Steiner to the Commander in Chief of the Finnish Army, General Malmberg, on 11. 6. 1943 in Hanko/Finland.

The WIKING Division cemetery in Uspenskaja/Ukraine.

Gun crew near Pjatigorsk January 1943

Radio operators in action in the Malgobek area.

On the heights
at Terek
before the Caucasus
in Autumn 1942.

The mud
wins again.

In the Caucasus
November 1942.
Becoming acquainted w
the camel as a pack anir

A seventeen year-old volunteer of the WIKING Division.

Europe in action on the 3.7 cm Flak: from left to right: comrades from Finland, Sweden, Norway and Volksdeutsche.

cm. Flak on the rail transport from the Caucasus to the Kalmuck steppe.

Knight's Cross holders from the *WESTLAND* Regiment: from left:
SS-Hstuf. Walter Schmidt (Oak Leaves), Commander of III. Battalion;
SS-Ostubaf. (later) August Dieckmann (Swords), Commander *WESTLAND* Regiment;
SS-Hscha. Albert Müller, Platoon Leader 4./*WESTLAND*

SS-Hscha. Willi Esslinger, Pz.Jg.Abt. 5, reviews the companies
with the Abteilung commander after receiving the Knight's Cross.

Uruh valleys with a fresh Guards Rifle Division. They faced only weak security forces from the military police south of Tschikola and a Georgian auxiliary unit near Chasnidon.

The Chief of the General Staff of III. Pz.Korps, Oberst von Dawans, gathered together all the available forces, a Sturmgeschütz battery which was at hand and the last company of military police, and immediately sent them to counterattack in the Tsckikola valley where the Russians had broken through the Rumanian positions. They succeeded in freeing their surrounded comrades but were too weak to stop the superior forces of the attacking Russians. They retreated to the town of Tschikola which lay close to III. Pz.Korps' only road in the Alagir—Zraudon valley. So the *WIKING* Division had to go their aid. However, only one battalion could be released; III./*NORDLAND*, the proven Finnish battalion. The reinforced Kampfgruppe Collani, consisting of 1. Pz.Gren.Btl., 1/3 of the *NORDLAND* Rgt.'s Infantry Gun Company, two Panzerspähwagen, two Flak guns and a battery of light howitzers of A.R. 5, reached a point not far from Tschikola and immediately went to the attack. Assault parties pushed into the village and cleared it of the enemy in hard fighting. They then deployed in defensive positions on the heights south of Tschikola. A Finnish company went to the aid of the Georgians near Chasnidon. The company attacked the eastern flank of the Soviet Guards Regiment in the Uruh valley causing it to withdraw. The situation there was also restored but in the long run had become untenable.

VII. RETURN TO THE DONEZ

On 22. December, the Corps' front was shortened, the Ossetische highway given up and all units of III. Pz.Korps pulled back into a new position between Durdur and Elchotowo. Several days later the Corps had to release 5. SS-Pz.Grenadier Division WIKING. During the Christmas period the Division was relieved from its positions for the march to Prochladnaja. From there it was transported to 4. Pz.Armee in the direction of Stalingrad.[1]

Departure from the Caucasus

"In the GERMANIA Regiment's command post", wrote Pi.Company leader Günther Wanhöfer in his book "Pioniere nach vorn![2] ", "were gathered all of the unit commanders and commanders of strongpoints belonging to this sector. After brief greetings the grim-faced Regiment Commander opened the briefing. He began with an overview of the situation on the entire southern front, referring particularly to the extremely dangerous situation at Stalingrad. After reviewing the local situation, he revealed the High Command's intention to immediately withdraw the units which were deepest in the Caucasus area. After a three day retiring movement, in which the attached Pionier companies would form the rearguard, the Division would be moved out and deployed in another position. There were no doubts that the most difficult days of this campaign could well lay ahead. Due to the developments at Stalingrad, the Army of the Caucasus was likewise in danger of being cut off. In addition, the imminent arrival of winter had to be reckoned with. Large scale motorized movements were expected. "We begin the withdrawal movements today at 18.00 hours." These words from the Commander struck the officers present like an electrical charge. In a few hours the troops must be ready to march, followed by disengagement from the enemy. After the company commanders returned to their strongpoints, preparations for the withdrawal began immediately... Not until the last infantry units have pulled back past the highway can the Pioniere leave their positions and break contact with the enemy. On the road they form, as the last German unit, the rearguard. Now they stand at the fork in the road waiting for the platoon which has been placing obstacles on the road. A clear star-filled sky arches magnificently above them. Again and again they look up. They also look to the houses they have abandoned. However they are swallowed in the night as are the mountains with their shining fields of snow and ice. Tomorrow is Christmas eve. They would have happily stayed in their accomodations in the village. There at least they could have spent a few hours inside at Christmas..."

During the summer and hard fighting in the autumn, the Division had suffered heavy losses. The Panzergrenadiere in particular had been hard hit. The number of Panzers available had also shrunk to just a few. A considerable number were in the repair shops. Many had been written off as total losses.

As for the men of the Division, they were as imperturbable as ever. Their fighting spirit remained unbroken. In all situations, in defence, counterattack, on flat or mountainous terrain, they understood how to find their way and had become a high quality unit. Within the Division's units, comradeship had grown during the last bloody battles at Malgobek and Fiagdon. There was now scarcely any difference between the foreign and German volunteers.

COPY
English radio broadcast—Night of 13.-14. 2. 1943
If the German army is successful in carrying out an orderly withdrawal from the Caucasus, it is entirely due to the efforts of the SS-Division WIKING. But this division too will be destroyed.

III./SS Artillery Regiment   5 Abt. Comm. Post 22.2.1943
to
7., 8., 9 and HQ Batteries
Copy sent for your information.
                     a.B. signed

The concern of the Finns had naturally increased as the situation on the Eastern Front deteriorated and the likelyhood of victory by the German-Finnish allies was placed in doubt. The Finns were worried that they would never see their land of a thousand lakes again. This question was also raised by General Tavela, a Finnish liason officer with the OKH. He had visited his fellow countrymen just after the heavy fighting near Malgobek and had personally witnessed their ordeal at Hill 701. He was also depressed by the high casualties which this excellent battalion had suffered there. The decision to order the Finnish contingent back into the fold of the Finnish army may well have been made at that time. Shortly after Talvela's departure, the Finnish Oberleutnants Ladan and Tenomoa came to the Division Commander and asked if they could be released by the Division and return to their homeland. The Commander promised them to do all that he could in order to accomodate their request.

The gaps in the Division's ranks had just about been filled by men returning from the hospitals. In the Waffen-SS military hospital in Kislowodsk the Finns had received excellent care from the Finnish nurses Liisa and Laine-Maire, since their homeland generally provided for their care. In the front lines however, it was the Baroness Ruth von Muck who tirelessly saw to the well being of the Finns in the military hospitals. She had already accompanied the volunteers of the 27th Jägerbataillon to Germany in 1915 as a nursing aide. With them and now with the Finnish volunteers of the Second World War she had won a legendary reputation. Now she followed her nation's volunteers to the Caucasus, to care for the wounded and bring them a little piece of their homeland.

Change of the Year 1942/43—The Race to Rostov

The operations on the south of the Eastern Front had taken a crisis-filled turn at the end of 1942. Now the consequences of the failed operations in the summer of 1942 became apparent. In the Caucasus, 17. Armee was at a standstill before the snow-covered mountains between Maikop and Tuapse. Continuation of the attack on the Black Sea coast was impossible due to the Armee's strength situation and the unfavourable weather. In the East Caucasus the operation against Grossny had failed. Both Armies, 17. and 1. Panzer, had been forced onto the defensive.

When the WIKING Division arrived in Simowniki in the last days of December, it saw itself already forced on the defensive. The units had to go straight from the transport trains to the counterattack against attacking Soviet forces. It had walked into the centre of a steady retreat by 4. Pz.Armee which, following a brief offensive toward Stalingrad, had itself been forced on the defensive. The most that it could

Battles on the Manytsch January 1943

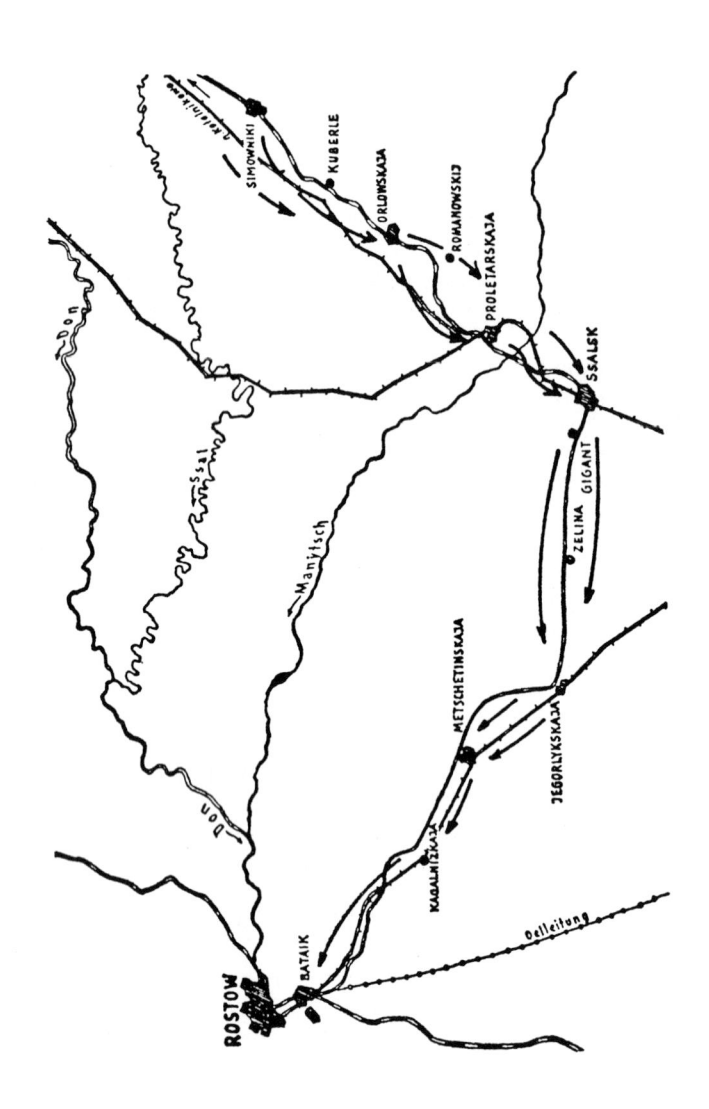

do was to support the endangered southern flank of Heeresgruppe Don against a threatened Soviet encirclement from the south. Now began a retreat from sector to sector, from Kuberle to Rostov. This led to a relentless struggle in the severe cold on the open snow-covered steppe for possession of the few villages there. During the day the German forces struggled against the superior mobile forces of the Soviets and during the night moved back to the next settlement. It was a mobile war on the steppe which forced the troops to call on all of their strength and demanded the utmost of their steadfastness and combat skills. The Division stood this test as well.

In the past months many changes had taken place within the Division. SS-Standartenführer von Scholz had been posted and on the northern sector of the front had laid the foundations for the future *NORDLAND* Division. SS-Ostubaf. Geisler, commander of the *WESTLAND* Regiment, had taken ill and was sent back to Germany. Command of the regiment was taken over by the commander of I./*NORDLAND*, Stubaf. Polewacz, a man who had distinguished himself by his tactical abilities, circumspection and energy. Command of the *NORDLAND* Rgt. was taken over by Ostubaf. Joerchel, former commander of II./*GERMANIA*.

Meanwhile, the fate of Stalingrad had been decided as the lead element of the Division, I./*NORDLAND*, arrived in Kuberle. On 28. December, with the rest of the Regiment, it was moved out to Simowniki in order to set up defensive positions there. On 31. December, the Soviets attacked. The leader of II./*WESTLAND* at that time, SS-Hstuf. Dietrich Ziemssen, reported:[1]

"On 30. 12. 1942, II./*WESTLAND* was transported to Simowniki in two trains. Rumanian troops without weapons, without officers and without order streamed toward the west; there was no front here now. The staff of Armeegruppe Hoth had left Simowniki before noon, but the Ic had remained to brief the officers of the Waffen-SS units. That meant making it clear that they could count on pursuing Russian units arriving at any time. Meanwhile, II./*WESTLAND* had used the past several days to set up undisturbed their defences in the long strung-out village. It was supported by I./A.R. 5 and a mixed Flak Abteilung from the Luftwaffe. The 8.8 cm. guns were installed in the front lines where they were welcomed by *WIKING*'s men as support against the enemy tanks.

The elaborate telecommunications net left behind by Hoth's staff later proved invaluable in the defence against the mass Russian attacks.

During the night, Russian tanks followed by infantry in trucks entered the town. As ordered, they were not molested by the gun crews in the HKL, who had made their positions as invulnerable as was technically possible.

The tanks were destroyed "by hand" by the mobile Pak of the Heavy Company, while the Soviet infantry held out in places until noon 31.12.1942. This combat in the "heart of the battlefield", was fought mainly by Company Sergeants with their supply train crews; in addition, the last of the battalion which was unloading also destroyed some of the enemy tanks...

The destroyed advance group was followed in the next days by 5 Russian divisions with their respective brigade units. These stormed Simowniki in dense waves of tanks and infantry up to 3 km. in width. Later they were joined by artillery.

The outstanding cooperation between *WESTLAND*'s Grenadiere and their versatile Heavy Company, which had been strengthened with the addition of captured weapons, the Wanhöfer Pionier Kp., I./A.R. 5 and the Flak Abteilung, ensured that the 2 to 3 assaults that the Russians mounted daily collapsed in front of the HKL.

Particularly heroic was the nightly defence against Russian assault parties by the widely separated machine gun positions.

The threat of being outflanked on both sides led the High Command to order the evacuation of Simowniki. This order was carried out with reluctance since the troops were well dug-in and were prepared mentally and physically to fight here."

On Christmas Eve the thermometer showed -30 degrees. The Panzergrenadiere had no time to celebrate. A battle along the Manytsch and a struggle near 4. Pz.Armee's deep southern flank had begun. It was the Division's responsibility to guard that flank. WIKING accomplished this by occupying strongpoints in the villages and crossroads on 4. Pz.Armee's southern flank and in doing so, parried the Soviet's flanking maneuver. There were daily crises.The Manytsch proved to be a last bastion which gave the Division a certain support and enabled it to regroup its forces.

In these days, SS-Ustuf. Lüers, who was returning from home leave, reported to the Forward Direction Centre for Personnel in Transit in Rostov. There he was ordered to the higher SS and police officers. The Division's personnel returning from leave were assembled there, about 300 men in all. The city resembled a witch's cauldron. The public houses were open and Germans, Rumanians and Italians celebrated and enjoyed themselves. The ration strength was supposed to number 140,00 men but it seemed that no one could be found who would take over the security of the city and other important points. Naturally the "Wikinger" took over the task. As the sole officer among the men on leave, Ustuf. Lüers endeavoured to bring about an early return to the Division. When the commander of transport offered a possible ride back, patrols scoured the city's theatres, public houses, movie houses and bars to notify as many of the Division's members as possible. How many "Wikinger" were at the station for departure? Wehrmacht and Luftwaffe officers who were sceptically observing the operation doubted that it would be many. At approximately 17.00 hours, 230 men had arrived at the station. A steady flow of additional soldiers arrived until by 18.30, when the train pulled away, there were 296 "Wikinger" sitting in the cold compartments—and singing! On the following day they were back with their units and the Division was approximately 300 men stronger.

On 18. January, the NORDLAND Rgt. stood in Proletarskaja with the two other Gefechtsgruppen guarding the flanks. Powerful enemy attacks were repulsed. Gigant, Zelina and Jegorlykskaja were names well-known to the Division from its offensive in the south. Now they reappeared in the WIKING Division's war diary and were the scene of bitter fighting by the Kampfgruppen during the race to Rostov. It seemed as if the fighting of the summer was mirrored in the names but with the front moving in the opposite direction. However, the Germans fought better. They did not allow themselves to be overrun so easily as the Russians had. Again and again a neighbour stood ready to parry a breakthrough or an outflanking, keeping the way through the Rostov bottleneck open for the approaching 1. Panzerarmee, whose advance elements were near Belaja-Glina.

However, the troops were hard pressed. The enemy had learned. He crossed the open steppe with small units of 30-40 troops, spaced up to 100 metres between men, "weaseling" their way between the scattered villages. Against such tactics, machine gun fire, artillery fire and bombing attacks lost some of their effectiveness.

The German slow retreat in small units was described in a report by Werner Meyer, who at the time led 1. Platoon of 1. Company of I./SS-*GERMANIA*:[2]

"After an ice-cold night drive, I./*GERMANIA* received orders in the morning to take up position on the edge of the village of Baljabanow and simultaneously hold the bank of the frozen Metschetka against the enemy's attacks. "The 1st Platoon, battle strength 1 : 1 : 9, will defend the left wing in the area of those shot up houses, establishing contact to the left with *NORDLAND*. Both Zwillingsflak must also provide them cover!" How long is this suposed to last, the Platoon Leader wants to know. "Until Sturmbannführer Dieckmann personally orders us to pull back. Vehicles remain with the Company."

The Company departs, leaving behind a small detachment of 10 men. We grab our MG's and look for suitable positions. Digging in is out of the question since the ground is frozen hard. Therefore we go into the wrecked houses. Franz Homolka, the "Reichsrottenführer", establishes contact with *NORDLAND* and even locates part of the Regiment. "Untersturmführer, they have orders to pull back under heavy enemy pressure", he reported somewhat indignantly. "So what? We remain until orders come from battalion." Hopefully they haven't forgotten us...

A little later, the dance begins. Ivan attacks past our nose against *NORDLAND* and succeeds in forcing our neighbour back. We turn a little, and now the Russians are marching along before our "front", direction Germany. We fire, but the Russians scarcely take notice of us. Then we get on their nerves and they try to set up their heavy machine guns on the opposite side of the road.

Uscha. Wolpers crawls excitedly up to the Platoon Leader: "Heavy machine gun ahead of us!" The Platoon Leader looks where Wolpers has reported: there, 20-25 metres away, the Russians are peacefully setting up their gun. "Those idiots, move the gun forward!" Carefully we stalk up to a firing position and after four or five shots the war is over for the gun crew. "Let's get out of here Wilhelm, a few more shots and they'll have spotted us." But the Russians had discovered us and Uscha. Wolpers received a grazing head wound which bled terribly. Rottf. Homolka dragged in a man with a serious bullet wound in the upper arm. "Franz, take the wounded to Company. Explain the situation to the Chief and ask whether we're permitted to pull back." Wolpers doesn't want to go with them." Then take the other one and come back quickly!" Homolka packed the wounded on a sled and weaseled off between the wrecked houses.

A Krad pulled up behind us. Oscha. Klaus Frahm from the Fourth jumped out. "I'm supposed to check on you to see if you're still allright. You must hold until 10.30 hours at all costs!" Then he roared off again.

Meanwhile, we lay well-hidden in a farmhouse, firing on the Russians who stubbornly continue to pass by us at close range.

Finally Homolka comes back. "We may pull back if we are unable to hold out any longer. Dieckmann was at the Company command post and sent me right back." "Thank God! Move back individually. Franz, we'll stay until everyone is away and take Wolpers with us."

The few men disappeared; we provided covering fire and then dragged Uscha. Wolpers with us. We brought him to the Company but he died several days later in hospital. During the Company's retreat, Franz Homolka received his sixth wound, a shot through the hand. But we brought everyone out!"

On 4. February at 15.30 hours, the Division set off from Swoy Trud in the direction of Rostow. The rearguards stood in Nowo- Bataisk. Oblt. Obermeyer's Kampfgruppe barred the way on the left flank near Olginskaja. It bravely fought off the Russian advance along the Don with its Flak units. Günter Jahnke, at that time the Adjutant of I./SS-A.R. 5, reported on his return to Rostov:

"During the night of 3./4. February, orders reached I./A.R. 5 to withdraw and cross the Don bridges near Rostov. It thus appeared that things were going well again. Everyone breathed easier and was happy that these days and nights of continuous fighting while moving in long and short leaps in the direction of Rostov were over. The grim cold and usually strong east wind made spending the night in the open or staying outside for long nearly impossible. Trying to observe to the east in one of these storms made one's eyes water. The tears were literally frozen by the cold. Both we and the Russians tried to reach a village, a *kate* or a barn by dark, where at least we could sleep without fur hats and more important, where we could find a warm place to thaw out. It happened more than once that friend and foe, heavily clothed and difficult to tell apart, moved into the same village at dusk. Then there would be a short scuffle and usually we came out on top. The Russians had to go back into the cold. We figured that the Russians were more accustomed to the inhospitable climate than we were.

The enemy attacked the weakly guarded villages fairly regularly; occasionally the gunners were able to support the Grenadiere with direct fire.

Now came the last hurdle across to the sanctuary, at least for the time being, of the Don. But we were short of fuel. The men of the refuelling Staffel, who had accomplished so much in the past weeks, had not arrived as anticipated on the previous day or during the night. They could not all have fallen out. There must, therefore, have been a great mixup on the supply roads and especially on the bridges. But where could we get fuel? Even the most well-intentioned units were unable to lend us any due to their own shortages. There was nothing else to do but "organize" and our reserves were used up.

When the fuel trucks had still not arrived on the morning of 4. February, the commander, SS-Stubaf. Bünning, gave me the order: "Drive back, look for our fuel trucks, bring them here, but in any case bring back fuel!" A not exactly pleasant, but necessary order because we had brought our trucks, tractors and guns this far and wanted under no circumstances to leave them behind now. So off I went. Near the front the roads, or better the terrain which resembled roads, were comparatively empty. But the further we drove, the more crowded they became. First the train of *WIKING* Division's vehicles, then the Wehrmacht units' and the rear services. Wherever the "road" came to a bottleneck such as a bridge, *Balka* or crossroad, things got balled up. Officers and military police attempted to restore order to the confusion and get things moving again. To avoid the congestion we drove mostly next to the "road" on hard frozen side roads or across open fields.

As we drove off, I had said that I honestly thought that we would have little hope of finding I./A.R. 5's three or four fuel trucks in this jumble. They could have broken down, been shot up, be under repair or not even be on the way. Search, search...

But as so often happens, fortune smiled on us. We caught the supply column near Bataisk. Our men had been forced to drive far to the rear, as the fuel dumps near the front were already empty, and then look for us. They are deserving once again of our thanks for their accomplishments. Exhausted, they have worked hard and cared for their comrades. It has always been a mystery to me how the supply services found us in critical situations after frequent changes of position. But they always did it.

We turn around and go back to the battalion as fast as the roads permit. We arrived at the battalion just as it was moving back. The trucks were fueled up and we were able to take everything back with us. The remainder of the trip went grimly but slowly forward, that is backward. As we stood at night once more on the dam south of Rostov, taking cover from the wind behind our truck, I looked at the time—23.00 hours, still the 4th of February. I fetched a bottle of Schnapps and said to my driver, "Come, there's still time to have a Schnapps. Today's my birthday."[3]

In the late morning on 5. February 1943, the Division reached Rostov. The Soviets had lost the race.

One day before, the Division had left the units of LVII. Panzerkorps. The Commanding General expressed his thanks in an order of the day:

"The Commanding General   K.G.St., 4. February 1943
of LVII. Armeekorps (mot)

To the SS Panzer Grenadier Division WIKING. Today the SS Pz.Gren.Div. - WIKING leaves the units of my Panzerkorps. From the first day of its attachment to the last, the Division has been admirably successful in bold attacks and determined defence in continuous, weeks-long battles under unfavourable weather conditions against an always numerically superior enemy. It has always proved to have an outstanding fighting spirit which has caused great damage to the enemy. Thanks to the Division's excellent composure, the enemy has been prevented from attaining his goal—breakthrough and envelopment. So today I watch the brave men of the SS Pz.Gren.Div. WIKING leave my forces with a heavy heart. My thanks and full recognition go equally to the officers and troops. My best wishes go with the Division on its way to new battles and successes.

Heil to the Führer!
signed Kirchner"

While the majority of 4. Panzerarmee's units had marched off to the west to form up between the Mius and the Dnjepr for a counterattack against the Soviet forces which had begun to cross the Donez near Isjum prior to an advance toward the Dnjepr, the WIKING Division marched north toward Stalino to the hard-pressed 1. Panzerarmee. Waiting for the Division near Amwrosiewka on 8. February 1943 was the Division Commander who had led III. Pz.Korps back from Terek north toward Rostov. He had meanwhile handed command of the Pz.Korps back to Gen.Lt. Breith.

In the Caucasus and the flanking battles south of the Don, the Division had lost three highly valuable commanders with promising futures who had belonged to the Division's initial group of officers. The young commander of the WESTLAND Regiment, SS-Obersturmführer Harry Polewacz, and the longtime commander of the Regiment's I. Battalion, SS-Sturmbannführer Frhr. von Hadeln, who was scheduled to train as an officer of the General Staff, were killed on the same day at the same position. Prior to this, the longtime battalion commander in the - WESTLAND Regiment, SS-Sturmbannführer Steinert, was killed in action in the Caucasus. All three had established their battalions and stamped them with their personalities. Their names will forever be associated with the history of the Division.

The Division's 1. General Staff Officer, SS- Sturmbannführer Reichel, took over command of the WESTLAND Regiment. SS-Hstuf. Walter Schmidt, proven as a Company Chief and Regimental Adjutant, took command of I./WESTLAND while SS-Hstuf. Koop did the same with III. Battalion. Taking Reichel's place as 1. General Staff Officer was SS-Stubaf. Schönfelder, the Division's 2. General Staff Officer.

Even before he was presented the Oak Leaves to the Knights Cross personally by Hitler in the "Wolfsschanze" on 5. February, the *WIKING* Division's commander, SS- Gruppenführer and Generalleutnant der Waffen-SS Felix Steiner, had learned that he was to be assigned to set up a new Panzerkorps. This assignment would only leave him a short time with his old Division. Steiner has described in detail the impressions he received in the Führer Headquarters in his book "Die Freiwilligen". (The Volunteers) [4]

In Combat with Armoured Group Popoff

On 8. February 1943, the Division passed through Amwrosiewka on the march toward Stalino, taking a well-earned rest there. The new orders read: "March toward Stalino—Konstantinowka. Further orders there from III. Pz.Korps." SS-Gruppenführer Steiner flew on ahead of the Division on 10. February and found an urgent radio message for the *WIKING* Division at 1. Pz.Armee's headquarters:
"Pz.A.O.K. to Div. WIKING
Urgent!
Powerful enemy forces, Popoff Tank Group, across the Donez near Isjum advancing southward toward Krasno—Armaiskoje. WIKING Division to immediately turn to the west. Attack toward Krasno—Armaiskoje.
Mission: Contain the Popoff Tank Group.
signed von Mackensen[1]

The situation was highly threatening, the danger had become acute. Up till now the Armee had still been able to ward off its enemy from Lissitschansk to Kramatorskaja. It did not, however, possess the strength to throw him back across the Donez. Now it had no more forces, other than the just arriving *WIKING* Division, to hinder its threatened outflanking with the obvious aim of throwing the German forces back against the Sea of Azov. The Division, whose leading elements must have just reached Stalino, was halted by radio. In Stalino the Division received the brief orders to turn toward Selidowka—Krasno-Armaiskoje. A new advance guard was formed. It was led by the *NORDLAND* Regiment's commander. The artillery was regrouped. The forward located *GERMANIA* Rgt., which now was to march at the rear, had to turn around on the road. The Division rolled toward Krasno-Armaiskoje.
A look at the "big picture" at this phase of the war:
Heeresgruppe South had some anxious hours. In the next days it had to decide whether its Eastern Front, namely 4. and 1. Panzerarmee, would be able to stand the Russian pressure and nail down Tank Group Popoff near Krasno-Armaiskoje, thus retaining for the Armeegruppe its operational freedom of movement. It had ordered 4. Pz.Armee to assemble between Saporoshje and Stalino for an attack toward the north or northeast, while the recently attached Armeeabteilung Kempf, securing its northern flank through limited attacks toward the southeast, would form the northern army in the planned pincer attack. The Armeegruppe hoped to be able to halt the enemy, who had crossed the Donez on a wide front, cut off his spearheads and smash the main body of his forces between the Donez and the Dnjepr. As the operation developed and moved northward toward the Donez, 1. Pz.Armee was to move against the first enemy battalions near Kramatorskaja and on the Kriwoj-Torez, achieve the destruction of Tank Group Popoff, advance through Slawjanka and gain the Donez near Isjum. All of these plans

were dependent on Tank Group Popoff being held near Krasno-Armaiskoje—Grischino.[2]

On 10. February 1943, the Division turned toward the west as ordered. As its advance guard rushed past the Galluzinowka highway, it passed long columns of Italians who were fleeing from Selidowka. They were obviously striving to reach the safety of the Woltschja sector and were trying to get as far to the south as possible. Selidowka appeared to be free of the enemy. The NORDLAND Regiment's reconnaissance platoon pressed forward along the road to Krasno-Armaiskoje and, unmolested by the enemy, reached the hills before Wosdweshenskij. The advance guard under SS-Ostubaf. Joerchel succeeded in taking Datschanskij. Also grabbed quickly, after a light skirmish with weak enemy forces, was Hill 180, which offered a commanding view of the surrounding terrain. From the hill the men observed a group of tanks which had driven south on the Krasno-Armaiskoje road and reached the rail stop north of Gubin. Surprise fire from the advance guard's artillery startled the Russians and forced them into cover. Joerchel immediately took advantage of this opportunity to send III./NORDLAND toward Gubin on a side road so that it could arrive before the Russians occupied the town. In doing so, he created the base for NORDLAND's other battalions to continue the advance to the north.

On the morning of 11. February, the NORDLAND Regiment dug in on the Gubin line and west of the road to Selidowka, preventing a breakout by the Soviets from Krasno-Armaiskoje to the south. During the night of 12. February, Kampfgruppe Schäfer with the rest of Pi.Btl. 4, advanced toward Swerrew barricading the field road and rail line from Krasno-Armaiskoje to the southwest. A.A. 5 moved forward through Nowo-Troizkoje toward Sergejewka in order to secure the Division's flank to the north and west. The WESTLAND Regiment was turned sharply to the north with orders to reach Lissowka Rownyj and there to barricade the road to Krasno-Armaiskoje to the north and in the direction of Konstantinowka. At dawn, the rest of Gefechtsgruppe GERMANIA left Selidowka with orders to advance through Troizkoje east of Postyschewo toward Grischino and take possession of the village. The Division's artillery, with the attached Flakabtlg. 5, received instructions to open fire at dawn from its positions on Krasno-Armaiskoje with the intention of deceiving the enemy into believing that there were much stronger artillery forces facing him than was the case. Gille attached one artillery battalion each to Gefechtsgruppen WESTLAND and GERMANIA. South of Krasno-Armaiskoje he set up artillery strong points with the heavy battalions, Flakabtlg. 5 and the rest of the light battalions. They were to carry out the bombardment on his orders which also included NORDLAND's heavy infantry guns in the firing plan. During the whole day he directed the artillery fire in such a fashion that the enemy must have automatically believed that there were several artillery regiments opposite him. It was, therefore, not at all strange that the Soviet commander reported to his Army Group by radio:

Have been attacked by 5 SS-Panzerdivisions, can hold only with difficulty. Assistance urgently required.
Long live Stalin![3]

In fact, on 14. February the Soviets near Grischino were attacked only by SS-Pz.Gren.Regiment GERMANIA, which also succeeded in entering the northern section of Grischino and taking up defensive positions there. When German artillery and an army Flakabteilung also made themselves felt from Rownyj, the

Soviets must have believed that there was a whole SS-Panzerkorps with the - *WIKING* Division at that point. The enemy no longer attempted to push with his leading forces alone from Krasno-Armaiskoje toward the south. In addition, on this day he appeared to be having supply difficulties and was waiting for deliveries of fuel. However, these had been discovered on the road to Krasno-Armaiskoje by 11. and 7. Pz.Div.'s standing patrols of scout cars and completely destroyed. For kilometres the road was littered with burning vehicles and the winter landscape was brightly lit by flames from the blazing fuel.

Meanwhile, the fighting for Gubin and the railroad junction to the north continued. Enemy tanks attempted daily to break into Gubin but were driven out again and again by the Finns, who were entrenched in the houses and fired on the tanks with infantry guns, Panzerfaüsten and Pak. The battle there was a fight for every house. Enemy forces which had gained some territory from III./*NORDLAND* were thrown back in a counterattack with submachine guns and hand grenades. The Regiment had created such a powerful antitank strongpoint that attempts by the Soviets to roll over it were unsuccessful. At midday on the 13th, the enemy attempted a wild tank charge through Rownyj toward Novo- Ekonomitscheskoje. A group of approximately 12 tanks with mounted infantry reached the centre of Rownyj. There they were destroyed one after another by 8.8 cm. Flak guns which the *WESTLAND* Regiment had carefully deployed with the Rgt.'s Panzergrenadiere at the entrance to the town and within the town itself. The survivors fled back to Krasno-Armaiskoje in panic. The prisoners taken were hand-picked soldiers, mostly former *Komsomol* members and excellently equipped. They belonged to the 9th Independent Guards Tank Brigade. The information obtained from the Russian Lieutenant P., who was captured near Ssachalin on 13. February, is contained in the *WIKING* Division Ic's interrogation report:[4]

Statements by Russian prisoners indicated that Krasno- Armaiskoje was occupied by the IV.th Guards Tank Corps of Armoured Group Popoff which had dug in approximately 120 tanks in the city's industrial section. Concentrated bombardment was making life there hell for the Russians. After Krasno-Armaiskoje was taken, over 80 damaged tanks were counted there. A later radio message by the Soviet commander to his superiors, which reported only slightly more than 50 tanks available, confirmed the prisoners' statements.

The End of Armoured Group Popoff

On 19. 2. 1943, the troops were made aware of a call by the Führer and Supreme Commander in a speech concerning " a battle of worldwide significance" requesting that the German soldiers give their last.[1] On the same day, the attack preparations by Heeresgruppe Süd had progressed so well that 4. Pz.Armee was able to go to the attack to the northeast on 20. February 1943. The time to attack Armoured Group Popoff had now also come for 1. Pz.Armee. Between the 11th and 19th of February, the Russian force had demonstrated an almost unintelligible passivity. Not only was it immobile near Krasno-Armaiskoje but also the disintegration of its other tank groups to the south was slowly taking place. In any case, the Xth Tank Corps, which was assembling near Dobrapolje north of Grischino for a further advance, was not yet available and the IIIrd Tank Corps, which had been directed from Kramatorskaja to Stepanowka, was not yet on hand when 1. Pz.Armee's XXXX. Pz.Korps smashed into these concentrations on 18. February. With 7. Pz.Div. advancing toward Dobrapolje, the *WIKING* Division attacked from the south with the *WESTLAND* Regiment in the northeast and the *NORDLAND* Regiment in the south. Supported by Pz.Abt. 5 and a Kampfgruppe from 7. Pz.Div., it concentrated on Krasno-Armaiskoje and destroyed the remaining forces of the Soviet IVth Guards Tank Corps there. Weak Soviet forces, with the Commanding General, were able to escape to the north at the last minute. Simultaneously, the *GERMANIA* Rgt. and the *NORDLAND* Rgt., which had moved quickly through Krasno-Armaiskoje, smashed the 7th Ski Brigade which was defending Grischino. Near Postyschewo and Krasno-Armaiskoje the Panzergrenadiere of the *NORDLAND* Regiment were eyewitnesses to a terrible sight. In the villages lay numerous German soldiers, Todt Organization members and Wehrmacht Women Auxiliaries who had fallen into the hands of soldiers of Armoured Group Popoff and been mutilated and sexually assaulted in a barbaric fashion.

On the evening of 19. February, Grischino was also in German hands. Here and near Krasno-Armaiskoje, the bulk of Armoured Group Popoff, in any case its tanks, had been destroyed.[2] With its destruction, the threat to the southern wing in this sector was averted.

The Division now had an open road to pursue the enemy forces retreating in the direction of Gawrilowka and northward toward Barwenkowo. Its path led across the Byk near Kriworoshie directly north toward Alexandrowka on the Samara, while the spearhead of its neighbor to the right, 7. Panzerdivision, advanced through Stepanowka. On the left wing, 11. Pz.Div. pursued the Soviet IVth Tank Corps toward Oktjaberskij in the direction of the Suchoj- Torez.

The Division Ic explained the enemy's situation as contained in part 1 of the Divisional Order of 21. 2. 1943:

"On 28. February, the enemy occupied Krassnoarmaiskoje with 5 units (9th, 12th, 14th Guards Tank Brigades, 3rd Guards Motorized Brigade and 7th Ski Brigade). Our own attack on the morning of 18. February took the enemy by surprise. Uncertain as to the strength of our attacking forces, on 19. 2. the enemy command ordered that our forces which had entered Krassnoarmaiskoje be destroyed without, however, sending the appropriate reserves to IV. Guards Tank Corps fighting there. Rather, on the 19th, Armoured Group Popoff continued assembling the Xth Tank Corps in the area of Dobropolje and at the same time ordered the withdrawal of the IIIrd Tank Corps from Kramatorskaja. Armoured Group Popoff first became aware of the loss of the towns of Krassnoarmaiskoje and Grischino on the morning of 20. February. At the same time, the IIIrd Tank Corps' assignment to march through Alexandrowka to Stepanowka had been rendered impractical by Gruppe Balck's attack. The offensive was resumed on 21. February with 7. Pz.Division attacking from the Dobropolje area to the north and northwest and 11. Pz.Division from the area west of Alexandrowka northward in the Lwlowka—Oktjabrskoje area. This forced the enemy to change his original decision to prevent any possible German withdrawal to the west through a surprise attack in the Slawjanka—Petropawlowka area. At midday, Armoured Group Popoff had ordered its units, which were now having serious fuel and supply problems, to retire into the Gniluscha area, while the remainder of the 7th Ski Brigade and 9th Guards Tank Brigade were facing destruction in the western part of Krassnoarmaiskoje."[3]

On 20. February, 4. Pz.Armee had commenced the attack on Pawlograd while the Corps' western wing, 1. Pz.Armee's XXXX. Pz.Korps, was already advancing toward the Suchoj-Torez sector on both sides of Barwenkowo. The rest of Armoured Group Popoff followed closely behind the Xth Soviet Tank Corps which was withdrawing rapidly toward Barwenko. The IVth Guards Tank Corps was finished. Its three Guards Tank Brigades, one motorized Guards Brigade and particularly the 7th Ski Brigade, which had been assembled in Krasno-Armaiskoje and Grischino for the advance to the south, had been smashed. All that was left were the small numbers of troops who had managed to escape from the pocket. The Division took hundreds of prisoners and captured numerous tanks and large quantities of material.

The battle for Grischino had been hard on both sides. The enemy's 7th Ski Brigade which was holed-up there fought stubbornly and bitterly. The remainder of the *GERMANIA* Regiment had launched a surprise attack on Grischino from the north on 14. February and after tough house to house fighting had driven the enemy toward the southern section of the town. *GERMANIA* was unable to finish off the tank-supported enemy until 19. February. Not until the attack by Gefechtsgruppe reinf. *NORDLAND*' from the southeast through Krasno- Armaiskoje toward the southern edge of Grischino could the Soviet forces be worn down and overcome. The attack cost the *NORDLAND* Regiment heavy losses.

In the Suchoj-Torez Sector

On 22. February, the Division arrived in the Byk sector via Leninski—Kriworoshie encountering no resistance. A reconnaissance in force carried out by Panzerabteilung 5 and 7. Pz.Div.'s Panzerregiment through Kriworoshie also failed to make contact with the enemy. The Soviet Xth Tank Corps, which had originally been assembled 30 km. east of Grischino for the advance toward Slawjanka, was hurriedly withdrawing to the north. In addition, no enemy forces could be found in the Ssamara sector near Alexandrowka or to the west. The Division's advance went ahead smoothly through Novo-Petrowka, across the Ssamara and into Alexandrowka. On 23. February, the reconnaissance forces first became aware of renewed Russian resistance south of Barwenkowo and on the Suchoj-Torez. The Division's western flank was becoming longer and required strengthening. The Division command was forced to assign Kampfgruppe Schäfer, reinforced with Flak 88's, to secure the sectors on the Ssamara and between the Ssamara and the Suchoj-Torez and to carry out reconnaissance to the west. On 24. February 1943, the Division's advance guard was passing through the village of Bogdanowka when it was attacked by a Soviet tank force. Caught by surprise, the *WESTLAND* Regiment nevertheless succeeded in gaining the north edge of the village and holding its ground there. The Regiment's II. Battalion, which had pushed on to the west, was overrun by enemy tanks, sustaining heavy losses. It was saved from total destruction when it managed to withdraw east into Bogdanowka. The pursuing Soviet tanks now ran headlong into fire from the 24 guns of two artillery battalions. In the face of this concentrated fire, the enemy abandoned his attempt to break into *WESTLAND*'s flank and made off to the north at high speed. The Soviets had rejoined the battle near Baranowka. The sounds of battle were also heard south of Baranowka in 7. Pz.Div.'s sector and the muzzle flashes of tank cannon were seen on the Bogdanowka—Baranowka road. 7. Pz.Div. was also engaged with Soviet forces.

After shaking off the enemy near Bogdanowka, the Division deployed once again for the advance on the Suchoj-Torez sector. The *GERMANIA* Regiment was redirected to the northeast to attack the flank of the enemy forces which were engaging 7. Pz.Division. Part of the Regiment was able to enter Bogdanowka but its main force had to pivot to the north toward Podolje—Archangelskaja from where it was taking heavy flanking fire. Initially the Regiment was stopped in front of the enemy positions in the hills. The WESTLAND Regiment, which was advancing toward Zyglerowka, was also halted before the strongly-held sector. South of Zyglerowka, setting up of the artillery positions was in full swing when the commander arrived and gave orders for the rest of the NORDLAND Rgt. to cross the river near Ssemenowka and attack the enemy positions on the north bank from the west. Pz.Abt. 5 was to smooth the way for the Regiment on the north side of the Suchoj-Torez into the enemy's western flank. The plan succeeded with minimal casualties. The commander of the WESTLAND Regiment wanted to be on the spot to direct the holding measures by his flanking battalion near Alexandrowka in support of NORDLAND's attack. While on the approach road, his vehicle was hit by an antitank round from the direction of Archangelskaja. The commander was struck in the head by shrapnel necessitating his immediate evacuation to Dnjepropetrowsk. Before leaving, this excellent officer and long-time assistant to the Division Commander insisted on reporting to Steiner. Several days later SS-Stubaf. Reichel succumbed to his severe wounds.

The attack by Gefechtsgruppe NORDLAND was amazingly successful. By evening, the Regiment was deep in the enemy's flank in the Suchoj-Torez sector. In the twilight, the enemy abandoned his positions in panic and fleeing broke up into individual groups of infantry and tanks. Without having sustained significant casualties, the Division's regiments crossed the Suchoj-Torez sector on a wide front and stayed on the retreating enemy's heels until darkness fell. On the next day they advanced toward Wjel. Kamyschewicha unhindered by the enemy and advance forces reached the southern shore of the Donez west of the bend in the river near Isjum. There the Division halted the attack and went over to the defensive. Meanwhile, further to the west 15. Inf.Div. struggled toward the Donez as 4. Pz.Armee's western flanking division.

A great operational success had been achieved. The coherence of the southern front on the Donez—Mius had been restored and the onrushing Soviet forces brought to a halt. But the Division had suffered heavy losses in officers, NCO's and men. On 4. March, the Division's commander commemorated the hero's deaths of Commanders and holders of the Knights Cross, SS-Ostubaf. Polewacz and SS-Stubaf. Reichel, Commanders and holders of the German Cross in Gold, SS-Stubaf. Frhr. von Hadeln, SS-Stubaf. Steinert and SS-Stubaf. Krocza, as well as holder of the Knights Cross, SS-Hauptsturmführer Pförtner. The Commander expressed his praise to the troops in the following Order of the Day:
"SS Panzer Grenadier Division Div.HQ, 4. March 1943
WIKING
Comrades!
After a long and difficult fighting withdrawal, which was necessary because of the serious situation on the Don front, the Division has turned in an instant and has struck decisive blows against the previously scarcely hindered enemy.

Near Krassnoarmaiskoje, the Division first halted and then as part of XXXX. Panzerkorps, side by side with its comrades of 7. and 11. Panzerdivisions, destroyed the most powerful part of the Russian operations group, the Popoff Tank Army. Today we stand once again on the Donez, the Russian Popoff Tank Army is smashed and the Russian 1st Guards Army and 6th Army are in retreat. The German soldier has triumphed once again.

Once more, the Division as always, has done its duty, fought triumphantly in a vital position and won new glory.
In these days you have truly fought for and advanced the destiny of your country. It will one day thank you. Today I want you all to be satisfied with my thanks and greatest appreciation as well as pride in your accomplishments.

signed Steiner"[1]

At the beginning of March 1943, after gaining the west bank of the Donez, the Division had gone over to the defensive on the southern and western slopes in the sector west of the bend in the Donez near Isjum and Protopopowka. In front of the Division's positions, the bank sloped to the north and east. On the enemy side, a thick forest blocked the view of the terrain. It appeared to be deserted but was occupied by attentive Russian snipers who continually kept the German side under surveillance. They served as a reminder to the Division's Grenadiere that a new enemy, one of undetermined strength, had taken over the defence of the Donez.

In those April days a period of quiet had settled over Heeresgruppe Süd's entire front. Kharkov had been retaken on 16. March. East of Kharkov the Donez had been reached on a broad front and Bjelgorod captured. The armies could certainly use the rest they had won, as indications of new operations were visible on the horizon.

Departure of the *NORDLAND* Rgt. and the Finnish Battalion

From 16. April, the Division was gradually pulled out of the front and transferred to the Losowaja—Michailowka area as a reserve force. There the Division could rest after nearly three years in action and bring its personnel and equipment up to strength. Replacement officers and NCO's arrived from the homeland. The Division was desperately short of personnel. New men were placed in responsible positions. SS-Sturmbannführer Dieckmann had taken the place of the fallen SS-Stubaf. Reichel as commander of Pz.Grenadier Rgt. *WESTLAND*. SS-Stubaf. Joerchel commanded the *NORDLAND* Regiment while SS-Staf. Jürgen Wagner once more led the *NORDLAND* Regiment. In place of SS-Stubaf. Mühlenkamp, transferred to Berlin, SS- Stubaf. Köller took over the leadership of SS-Pz.Abt. 5. The previous Pionier Commander, SS-Stubaf. Schäfer, was preparing for a new assignment. His successor was to be SS-Hstuf. Eichorn. Proven men were placed in command positions. SS-Hstuf. Dorr had taken over I./*GERMANIA*, SS-Hstuf. Juchem II./*GERMANIA*, while SS-Hstuf. Hack led III./*GERMANIA* as before. In the *WESTLAND* Regiment, SS-Hstuf. Sitter was commander of I. Battalion while SS-Hstuf. Schmidt had taken over II. Battalion. In accordance with RF-SS, RF/V/ 40 24/43, as of 18. 3. 1943, *NORDLAND* was withdrawn from the Division to form the cadre, as SS- Gren.Rgt. 2 *NORGE*, of the III. (germ) Pz. Korps. III.Battalion *NORDLAND*, the Finnish Battalion, was removed from the regimental units and transferred. "As the Battalion's two-year committment neared its end," wrote Prof. Dr. Mauno Jokipii in his essay[1], "the Germans had come early in March after the men had received leave in Finland, to discuss a continuation of the agreement. From the German standpoint the Battalion had a symbolic value which could be utilized for propaganda purposes. On the Finnish side, there was no hurry to renew. The Finnish government, however, with its then Prime Minister

Prof. Edwin Linkomies and Foreign Secretary Dr. Henrik Ramsey, sent an unofficial representative, the Rector of the University of Helsinki, Prof. Rolf Nevanlinna, to Berlin in early 1943 to ascertain the wishes of the Germans. He received the appropriate information from the Chief of the SS-Head Office, General Gottlob Berger, and conveyed it immediately back to Finland. Following the expiration of the agreement, the Finnish Battalion was released via Reval to its homeland. The Battalion was not embarked for Helsinki, where a danger was seen of air attack, but quietly sent to Hanko. A parade was held deep within the country at Tampere on 3. 6. 1943. The men received a month's leave; however, their future fate was still undecided." After prolonged negotiations between the governments, the German side waived its request, "for the Battalion, in order to spare the Finnish volunteers the moral dilemma." (Jodl) Finally, the Battalion was "disbanded with modest ceremony at Hanko on 11. 7. 1943."[2] Its members were immediately inducted into the Finnish army.[2]

The Arrival of the Estonian Battalion

Instead of the Finnish Battalion, a new battalion, the Estonian Volunteer Btl. NARWA, reached the Division. It had formerly been I. Battalion of the 1st Regiment of the Estonian Legion.[1] At its head was SS-Hauptsturmführer Georg Eberhardt. This unit's officers had enjoyed a basic military training in the Estonian army and were career officers or front line soldiers experienced in partisan warfare and of high fighting quality.

At this time, the former commander of the WIKING Division, who had led it since its establishment, handed over command to the former commander of Art.Rgt. 5, SS- Brigadeführer and Generalmajor der Waffen-SS, Herbert Gille. The departing Division Commander, Felix Steiner, was to take over III. (germ) Panzerkorps. First, however, Steiner flew to the Finnish Battalion's dismissal where he handed the battle-tested unit over to the Finnish army with words of heartfelt thanks and affirmation of their brotherhood in arms.

It was easy to see that the quiet on the Eastern Front would not last for long. In the south the party had ended in a draw. In spite of all the successes and failures, victories and defeats, at the end of this stage of the campaign the enemy occupied the same positions as in 1942 without having reached a decision. But the situation had changed fundamentally. The Soviets had made decisive gains in personnel and material while the Germans had experienced a considerable loss in strength. And time was pressing for both sides. Both of the opponents faced the problem of how they wished to conduct the war. The answer to this operational question was easy for the Soviets. Considering their potential superiority and the necessity to improve their position, they could and must remain on the offensive. In contrast the OKH faced two alternatives; attack again although the German forces could expect no further significant growth or go over to the defensive. To attack entailed significant risks. The option of defence foresaw the enemy assaulting fortified positions on this heavily defended front, that is, the beginning of a war of attrition. In view of the enemy's greater potential and the German need for economizing, this appeared to offer the German forces a better chance for success. For whatever reasons, and despite voices of warning, the OKH decided on a new offensive.

This led to the German attack at Kursk. The Panzer units of Heeresgruppe Süd as well as those of 9. Armee in the north which had just been reequipped and brought up to strength were so depleted in the first days of the assault that they never regained their former combat strength. Before the attack began on 4. July 1943—certainly too late as the Soviets had been able to make extensive preparations and call up reserves—the Division, still near Losowaja, was moved up to the Donez front. There it stood in the area northwest of Slawiansk as the Armee reserve and later together with 17. Pz.Div. under XXIV. Pz.Korps as Heeresgruppe reserve although the OKH had not released the units for general use.

Since the winter of 1941/42, the area of the Donez north of Slawiansk and near Isjum had been the Soviet's base of operations for an offensive against the German forces on the Mius. They had attacked here in the winter of 1942 in an attempt to drive Heeresgruppe Süd back against the Sea of Azov. They had also attacked in the winter of 1943. The objective of the Soviet drive toward the Dnjepr had been to lift the entire German southern flank from its hinges. As before, Slawiansk and Isjum remained sources of danger. If the Russians possessed forces for a preventive attack on the German assembly areas for the Kursk offensive, as undoubtedly they did, this would be the area where the blow would fall. Thus this area remained a source of concern for the OKH. At this time XXIV. Pz.Korps was deployed in this area and it was in the right place.

However, on 5. July 1943, the first day of the Kursk offensive, it was moved from there by Heeresgruppe and ordered north through Kharkov behind Armeeabteilung Kempf whose attack had bogged down after several days.

By 7. July, it was already obvious to this attacking Gruppe as well as to 4. Panzer Armee to the west that the attack was a failure. Certainly the troops had given their utmost and achieved significant tactical successes, but the operation as a whole was a failure. "But the decision by the Armeegruppe's High Command not to break off the attack prematurely, and perhaps just before the conclusive victory was achieved, remained firm. It still held XXIV. Panzerkorps with 17. Pz.Div. and the *WIKING* Division in reserve as its trump card. This Corps had been the subject of a fight between the Armeegruppe High Command and Hitler since the beginning of the offensive or actually since the pre-attack preparations. One must remember that we always took the point of view that we had to stake everything on the success of this operation, even at a considerable risk in the Donez area"; so wrote Feldmarschall von Manstein in his book "Verlorene Siege" ("Lost Victories").[2]

VIII. THE DEFENSIVE BATTLE FOR KHARKOV AND ISJUM

On 13. July, Manstein requested the employment of the Corps, and with it the *WIKING* Division which was assembled 50 km. west of Kharkov, in the already lost battle. However, the Corps had to be turned around on the 16th and marched southward again as quickly as possible toward Isjum. The enemy had gathered strong forces there and was threatening to go over to the offensive. The leading elements of *WIKING*, now the Corps' front column, reached Aleksejewskoje on the Bereka on 17. July. Persistent rain had transformed the roads into morasses and the units became bogged down. Precious hours were lost. On the same day, following a one and a half hour barrage, the Russians attacked across the Donez west of Isjum, driving 46. Inf.Div. from its positions. The Division's expected Kampfgruppe, Kampfgruppe Dorr with Pz.Abt. 5, reached the Wjel-Kamyschewycha area during the night of 17./18. July. With scarcely a pause, it went to the attack on the morning of the 18th, assaulting the town of Ssredkj on the west bank of the Donez which had been taken by the Russians. There was no time for a lengthy reconnoitering of the area. Kampfgruppe Dorr had to operate almost blindy, having only the reports from elements of 46. Inf.Div. to go on. It had decided to first retake Ssrednj and then veer toward the northwest in order to roll up the Russian bridgehead from the flank. The *WESTLAND* Regiment's I. Battalion was to follow toward Ssrednj. The attack was a success. Ssrednj was retaken and I. Btl./*WESTLAND* moved in to clear the town while Kampfgruppe Dorr had already turned toward the northwest. Now fully committed, the Kampfgruppe received heavy flanking fire from long range. Numerous mortar batteries rained shells of all calibres on the troops. Heavy antitank fire forced the accompanying Panzers and Sturmgeschütze to seek cover in the terrain. In addition, the deeply scored terrain hindered a quick attack. Losses mounted. The Danish Obersturmführer Korsgaard fell at the head of his company and next to him his Company Officer, SS-Ustuf. Bade. The commander of the Kampfgruppe, SS-Stubaf. Dorr, was wounded once again, his place being taken by SS-Ostuf. Iden.

The attack faltered. Attempts to get it going again were unsuccessful. The Dutch Sturmbannführer Stroink, who had been ordered to the *GERMANIA* Regiment to become familiar with the duties of battalion commander, reported:"The attacking units were at full strength. After a long period of rest the mood and morale of the troops was good. The unit was excellently trained and consisted mostly of battle-proven soldiers. SS- Sturmbannführer Dorr's leadership was clear and circumspect. All of these factors plus the anticipated support by artillery, Panzers and Stukas led to the expectation of a complete success. However, the attack failed to reach its goal. By the evening of 18. July, the originally 700 man strong unit had been reduced to 150 men." What was the reason for this bitter failure? The troops were experienced and the leadership proven. But they had been left insufficient time to carefully prepare the attack and to coordinate thoroughly the support of the heavy weapons with the movements of the Grenadiere.

A quick attack west of Isjum had certainly been necessary after the Soviets had dug in on the west bank of the Donez on 17. July. The haste which the General Command of XXXX. Pz.Korps had demanded of the approaching attack forces was understandable. The breakthrough through 46. Inf.Div.'s smashed front into the rear on the 18th had to be expected. But help was already near and a counter-attack after defeating the Russian breakthrough attempts would have been easier

Battles in the Isjum area July 1943

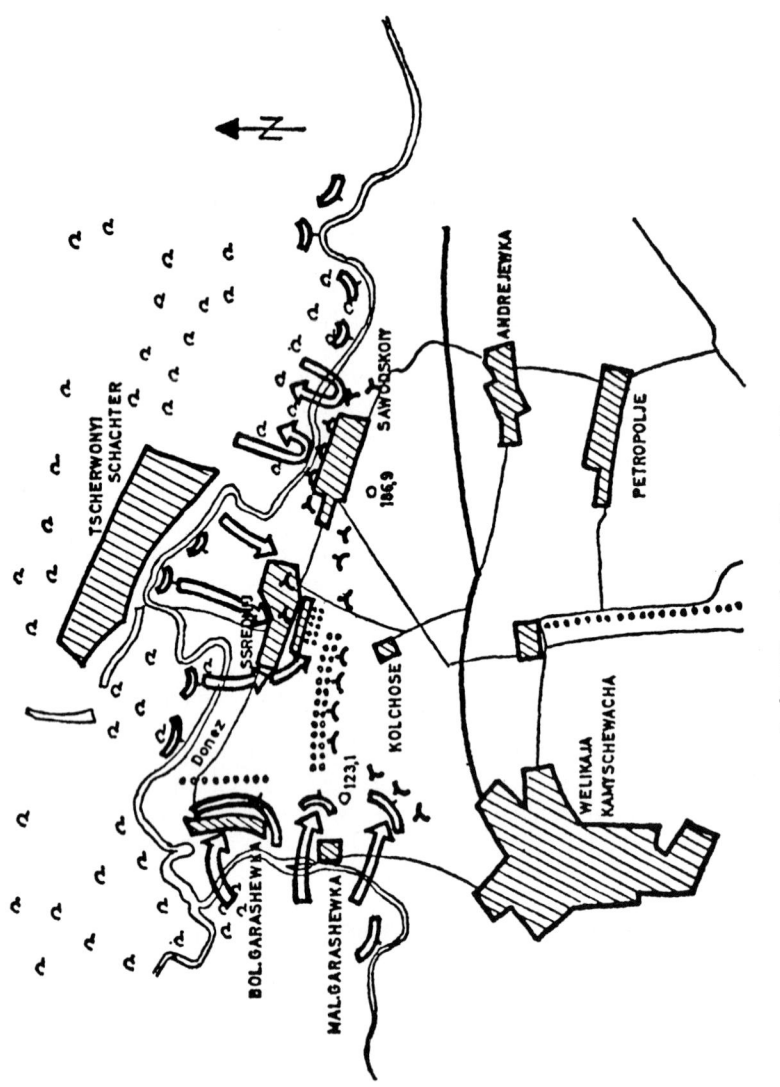

and more successful than an unprepared advance by inadequate forces into a narrow bridgehead commanded on all sides by enemy artillery. The deployment of both divisions of XXIV. Pz.Korps standing by in Kharkov was prevented, however, allowing the enemy to win further territory south of the river.

The Division, since 19. July organized for defence north and northeast of Wjel.Kamyschawycha in close proximity to the Russian bridgehead, reacted well to the situation under the leadership of Generalmajor der Waffen-SS Gille. This was demonstrated in the dramatic events during the days of fighting which followed. On the early morning of the 19th, Russian tanks felt their way forward near Ssrednj and ran into the alerted 1. Company of Panzerabteilung 5. Allowing the tanks to pass, the Company destroyed several from behind and engaged the remainder which had fled into Ssrednj in close combat in the town. By approximately midday all seven Russian tanks had been destroyed.

The Estonians' Baptism of Fire

At noon on this day, the dreaded catastophe appeared to be at hand. The Estonian Pz.Gren.Btl. NARWA, which was dug in on Hill 186.9 near Sawodskoij east of Ssrednj, was attacked and overrun by approximately 100 tanks. Despite desperate resistance by the Estonians and the destruction of numerous tanks, a weak force penetrated toward the south. There the enemy tanks were destroyed by artillery fire from close range. During these fierce individual combats between groups of Estonians against tank formations and the batteries of A.R. 5 against the enemy tanks which had broken through, the "Wikinger" proved to have the better nerves. By the evening of the 19th, the danger of a breakthrough here had been averted. But at such a sacrifice! The commander of the NARWA Battalion, SS-Hstuf. Eberhardt, had been killed in close combat. Many Estonian officers, NCO's and men died soldiers' deaths with him. This volunteer unit had passed its baptism of fire in heroic fashion before the entire Division. No Estonian had abandoned his position. Every strongpoint had been fiercely defended. The determination of the Estonians to hold the front at any cost had proved stronger than the force of almost 100 Soviet tanks.

Front line soldiers are their own strongest critics. Since it is not the object of this division history to write an heroic epic, the words of a Hauptsturmführer are presented. He described the events of the night of 19./20. July in his diary as follows:

"A relieving attack on Ssrednj is ordered for the night. I personally don't think much of the idea, since as everybody knows, a tank man is nearly blind at night. Now there is nothing to be seen through the hatches. The mess begins when the Sturmgeschütze lose their way and lead the Pioniere in the wrong direction. I must add, that the attack was carried out by two Panzer companies and a Sturmgeschütz battery. The Pionier battalion attacked as infantry. It is thus no wonder that things went wrong. The Panzers crashed around endangering their own troops and vehicles. In the end no one knew where the other was. Panzers got stuck in the ditches and bunkers in the fruit gardens. All in all it was a mess. When Dieckmann came I reported to him that everything had gone to shit. He then drove forward himself in his Volkswagen. But his appearance alone did not help.

Why had it not worked? For one thing, too many tanks were deployed for this operation. Secondly, the tank crews were unacquainted with the terrain. As mentioned above, some of the crews lost their way. Others remained stuck in the local area. Thirdly, communications were not secure. There was no contact between the Panzers and the commander of the Pionier battalion. Fourth, the planning for the mission was not clear. The Pioniere chiefs didn't know which sections of the town they were to attack. Compass bearings were not laid down. Fifth, as a result of the general confusion, eventually everyone was firing at everyone and thus the operation ended in failure..."[1]

The Battle for Golaja-Dolina

The first phase of the battle on the Donez had ended. The crisis had surely not been averted, but the Soviet breakthrough had not succeeded. On 17. July, the Russians had broken through in the Division's old territory near Golodajewka on the Mius. The breakthrough was smashed by the attacking II. SS-Pz.Korps which had hurried south from the attack area near Belgorod. Afterward the situation on the Donez between Slawjansk and the Bereka was as tense as before. New Soviet forces were reported there. They belonged to Marschall Koniev's front which had been inserted into the southern front southeast of Kharkov.

On the Donez, XIV. Pz.Korps had a chance to take a breather, regroup and hastily tend to the wounds it had received in the fighting. Fourteen days later the Soviets attacked southeast of Isjum forcing a 12 km. wide and 10 km. deep penetration on the road near Slawjansk. On 3. August, the village of Golaja-Dolina was the scene of heavy fighting. The attack forces of XIV. Pz.Korps rushed in from all sides in an attempt to restore the situation. A Kampfgruppe from 17. Division succeeded in a bold thrust toward Golaja-Dolina in destroying 23 enemy tanks and achieving a local success. The Division's reinforced Regimental Kampfgruppe *GERMANIA* with attached Panzer forces hurried from the northwest in order to attack Golaja-Dolina from that direction. By late afternoon the village was firmly in German hands. In the evening, 1 Company of Pz.Abt. 5 set out in pursuit of the fleeing Russians, dragging the neighbouring battalion of 17. Pz.Div. along and helping win back the road southeast of Golaja-Dolina.

On 4. August, the attack in the direction of the Donez through the high country south of the Donez hills was to be continued. The diary of I./SS-Pz.Abt. 5 reported:

"4. 8. 43

At dawn briefings for the continuation of the attack. Present are the unit commanders of the forces employed, the Division Commander of *WIKING* and the Commanding General of XXXX. Pz.Korps, General Heinrici. There are differences of opinion over the plan of attack. A Kampfgruppe from 17. Pz.Div. is to attack Hill 199.5 from the south. Gefechtsgruppe *GERMANIA* is to simultaneously advance from Golaja-Dolina past Hill 199.5 to the west in the direction of the Donez and throw the enemy back behind the river."

The attack went forward energetically. The range of hills northwest of Golaja-Dolina was quickly taken. As the attacking forces began to cross these they took unusually heavy artillery, antitank and tank fire. They were pinned down in the positions they had reached in the burning heat.

At 15.30 new orders by radio:

"...Pz.Abt. 5 is to attack with artillery preparation with mounted infantry of II./GERMANIA in the direction of the Donez. SS-A.A. 5 will be deployed from the north in support of the attack.—Attack begins at 16.00 hours."

Time was short. Once again preparations were hurried. The infantry rushed to the running tanks and climbed aboard. At 16.00 hours the attack rolled out.

SS-Hstuf. Wolf Schneider described his impressions thus: "At exactly 16.00 hours we drove across the hills towards the northwest. As we pressed forward there, we were subjected to fire the like of which I had seldom experienced on the Eastern Front. A virtual wall of fire rose high before me; fountains of dirt in between the flashes of exploding shells. I see 5 of our tanks ablaze. Shot up, my brain registers automatically. Then I hear over the vehicle's radio the orders to pull back to the jumping off points. I have 3 vehicles left. The Grenadiere have taken heavy casualties. Mounted on the tanks, they were unprotected from the shrapnel until they took cover on the ground.

The whole attack was simply useless. We unit commanders had feared this."

The Defensive Battle for Kharkov and the Dnepr

The *WIKING* Division was pulled out of the fighting in the night and transferred again to the north toward Bereka. There it waited ready to go for two days. The enemy had struck north of Kharkov and broken through to the southwest between Armeeabt. Kempf and 4. Pz.Armee during the night. Motorized units marched from south to north on the road to Kharkov. The Heeresgruppe sent in the available reserves. Marching from the Mius front, forces of the Divisions *TOTENKOPF* and *DAS REICH* passed the Division's operations area. Enemy aircraft were constantly in the air dropping bombs. The *WIKING* Division had to wait and let everything pass. This took several days.

On 11. August, the road was finally free for *WIKING*. Destination: the area northwest of Kharkov. The front was ablaze there! The extent of the Soviet numerical superiority showed itself for the first time. Despite their losses in men and material in the previous days of fighting in the Kursk salient they had become still stronger. They had inserted a new front, the Steppe Front under the command of Marschall Koniev, behind the Donez. This constituted a severe threat to the flank and rear of the German offensive forces north of Kharkov.

The inevitable happened. The enemy struck back near Bjelgorod and several days later renewed his offensive on the Donez. In protracted and bloody fighting, he pushed forward toward the northern wing of the Heeresgruppe and forced its southern wing to retire toward the west sooner than had been anticipated.

On 12. 8. 1943, coming from the Donez, the Division reached the area northwest of Kharkov behind the SS-Divisions *TOTENKOPF* and *DAS REICH*. Things there had meanwhile taken a serious turn, with the enemy threatening to envelop Kharkov from the north. North of the Kharkov—Ssumy rail line the Division immediately ran into a powerful enemy force attacking in the direction of Kryssino—Olschany. The result was heavy back and forth tank fighting there and northwest of Olschany which was decided in the Division's favour. Persistent counterattacks succeeded in holding the enemy in check there despite his great numerical superiority. This lasted until the situation on the flanks of 8. Armee forced the evacuation of Kharkov on 22. August. The decisive factor had been the addition of the forces of the Russian Steppe Front which joined the attack on the city from the east.

On 12. August, the *WIKING* Division's main force had reached Olschany, relieving the security forces of the SS-Pz.Div. *DAS REICH* for use elsewhere. The Division had orders to align its defences on the range of hills north of Sinkowsky as far as Hill 222.4 which was still held by a reconnaissance patrol of the *DAS REICH* Division. But the Russian advance guard also had designs on capturing the hills. On the 12th it came down to the customary footrace with the enemy for possession of the common objective. *WIKING* immediately played its strongest trump. It deployed the Panzerabteilung on a broad front, attacked toward the centre of the range of hills and, in a fast armoured charge, occupied them before the enemy arrived.

On the following day the village of Klenowoje, which still lay ahead of the front, was to be incorporated into the defence. I./Pz. 5, II./SS *GERMANIA* under SS-Hstuf. Juchem and 2./*NARWA* under Ostuf. Heder were to take the village in a swift attack before stronger Russian forces were moved in. However, it was already too late. The attack succeeded in reaching the southern edge of Klenowoje but the resistance there was so strong that a further advance without new preparations would have been senseless. At noon on the same day, the Kampfgruppe renewed the attack as ordered. Once again without success! The Kampfgruppe was able, however, to disengage from the enemy under cover of darkness and pull back to the positions on Hill 209 where it dug in during the night.

The attack had cost a high sacrifice in Panzers and Grenadiere. The commander of II./*GERMANIA*, SS-Hstuf. Juchem, was missing and the war correspondent Kurt Eggers was killed.[1] The Battalion was left with a fighting strength of barely 100 men. They held a 2.5 km. wide sector. "But", wrote a survivor, "I have not met a man who had become despondent over it."

As expected, the enemy moved out of Klenowoje on 15. August and launched a counterattack. There was great alarm along the whole front. But for the time being, the area of concern was possession of Hill 209.5 where the weakened II./*GERMANIA* had been reinforced during the night by a company from the *NARWA* Volunteer Battalion.

For the first time, the Soviets once again fielded powerful infantry forces. Again I./Pz.Abt. 5 succeeded in stealing unnoticed behind the hills and drove out of a fold in the terrain into the attacking Russians. Soon the front ahead of Hill 209.5 had been cleared of the enemy. They had either been shot down or had fled to the safety of the village of Klenowoje. But there were rumblings on the Division's western flank. There the men of 2./*NARWA* under Ostuf. Heder waited on Hill 202.4. In the evening, enemy infantry attacked in battalion strength accompanied by tanks. Once again it was the Division's tanks which had to help. At 23.00 hours, two companies went to the counterattack toward Hill 202.4 with all guns blazing. The Soviets, who had just begun to make themselves at home there, fled in panic. Here too they abandoned a quantity of weapons and material.

The following morning was quiet. The Grenadiere were dug in deep in their positions. The Kampfgruppe could be satisfied with the results of the fighting. But this had all been just the preliminary round. Here, as they always did before a large attack, the Soviets had first felt out the front with exploratory attacks by entire battalions with tank support.

On 18. August, things became bitterly serious. The barrage began at dawn. The Soviets first attacked Hills 228 and 209 on a broad front and after an hour their tanks and following infantry had pushed ahead as far as Hill 209.5. Panzerabteilung 5 launched an immediate counterattack. A *Tiger* company was rushed forward. A great tank battle developed along the entire front. The focal point of the enemy attack lay at first near Hills 228 and 209.5. Of approximately 100 enemy tanks, 84 were destroyed. The positions were held for the time being. In the evening, however, Hill 209.5 was lost, although the attacks by the tank units of two Soviet tank corps were again beaten off.

According to a report by SS-War Correspondent Dr. Richard Stürmer, Armee-Headquarters 8 sent its thanks to the WIKING Division in the following teletype message on 20. 8. 1943:

> "In the past several days the Corps has recorded two great successes: 1. The defensive victory by the SS-Pz.Gren.Div. WIKING, which after the engagement by the Tiger Abteilung resulted in the destruction of 84 enemy tanks. The daring advance across the Merla by SS-Pz.Gren.Div. TOTENKOPF. My thanks and my complete appreciation to the command and the troops.
>
> signed Woehler
> General der Infanterie
>
> I am pleased to be able to convey to the attached Divisions and Korps units the preceding letter of appreciation from the Commander in Chief of 8. Armee.
>
> signed Breith
> General der Panzertruppen and Commanding
> General of III. Pz.Korps[2]

Relative peace lasted at the front until 21. August. The hard-hit enemy had halted. But the situation for the Division's neighbour to the east, 3. Pz.Div., was highly tense. It was forced to retreat toward the southwest in the face of far superior enemy forces. II./SS-*DEUTSCHLAND* of the *DAS REICH* Division, which had hurried from 8. Armee's western flank, temporarily filled the resulting gaps. On 22. August, Kharkov was evacuated on orders from the Heeresgruppe but against the directions from the OKH. The evacuation took place literally at the last minute.

On 23. August, the Soviets attempted to break through Pz.Gren.Rgt. *WESTLAND*'s positions to the south in order to bypass Kharkov and cut it off from the north. Despite heavy mortar and artillery fire and the employment of large numbers of infantry, the enemy failed to achieve even a modest success. But the Regiment's old positions near Sinkowsky had become untenable. The Division had to pull back its eastern wing toward the edge of the woods south of Olschany. As a result of the rebuff suffered on the 23rd, the Russians did not follow up here but for the first time mounted heavy raids with night bombers on the night of 25./26. August. The enemy was fully prepared for the attack with all types of weapons, from tanks and infantry, to his air force units, being employed.

The pressure on the eastern flank became ever greater. The enemy appeared here on the 28th with tanks and received a bloody beating losing 8 T-34's. The escorting infantry in battalion strength left behind approximately 100 prisoners on the battlefield.

"Gruschki Grave!"

On 31. August 1943, the great Russian offensive against the Division's southward bending eastern wing began. The assault was aimed directly toward the Kharkov—Poltawa rail line. A tank attack by Pz.Abt. 5 restored the situation. A

Soviet battalion was destroyed in the fighting. But the enemy stuck to his guns. At the junction with 3. Pz.Div. he forced a threatening penetration which required decisive measures by the High Command. The SS-Pz.Gren.Rgt. *DER FÜHRER*, with the attached *Panther* battalion from the SS-Pz.Div. *DAS REICH*, which was hurrying forward, was to parry the Soviet thrust. On the morning of this day of heavy fighting, I./*GERMANIA* with the attached 4. Company of Pz.Rgt. 5 had received orders to fall on the northern flank of the enemy's breakthrough and halt him there. SS-Ostuf. Hein, the chief of 4./Pz. 5, reported on the operation:

"On the night of 31. Aug./1. Sept., 4./Pz. 5 was seconded to I./*GERMANIA* and was to set out immediately for the Battalion in the direction of the "Gruschki Grave". These were the orders which I received that night which simultaneously placed me in command of 4./Pz. 5, whose chief, SS-Ostuf. Jessen, had been wounded on the previous day.

4. Company was only conditionally operational and desperately needed an overhaul of its radio equipment. But we rumbled off in the night to the assigned location, reported in with the Battalion and set up a hedgehog defence with the Company before getting a bit of much needed sleep.

The morning fog had just moved off when we received the bad news of the confirmation of a Russian breakthrough at the junction with 23. Pz.Division. Immediate measures were necessary. Along the rail line to Poltawa we went into an ambush position in a section of terrain similar to ancient burial mounds which was marked on the map as "Gruschki Grave". Far and wide nothing was to be seen of our own units. The hills, which lay ghostlike before us in the morning twilight, showed us the direction from which the enemy must come.

The motors are switched off. We can hear the ringing march noises of a powerful approaching tank force. A few moments later we can see approximately 40 enemy tanks with infantry loaded like flocks of pigeons, pressing toward us over the hills. They have already deployed. "Ridge 12...range 1,000. Armour piercing—fire!" The commander and crew react quick as lightning. 4 shells, 4 hits, 4 burning enemy tanks. The Red Army men jump off in panic. All of this happens in seconds before our eyes. Time is not measureable, so tense is the situation. 11 burning T-34's and 4 immobile tanks block the Russian attack. In reverse, the enemy quickly pull back behind the hills. My men jump from the turret hatches shouting loudly from excitement over the victory. But they are already anticipating the next attack from the hollows on both sides of the hills. Quickly targets are assigned. Hand signals take the place of the unserviceable radio as the enemy's new enveloping attack begins.

It works like clockwork! As perfect as a sand table exercise. The enemy is once more beaten off. 2 T-34's are left burning, 2 stand motionless. A KV-II rolls its fifty-two tons past us at high speed. "Turn around and let's go." We are behind him ready to fire. "Range 250 metres". Fire, a hit, it bounces off! Four times this macabre spectacle is repeated. Then "Hurrah!" The Russians have bailed out and the KV-II is ours. We move forward. Then the Russians climb back in. Turret at 6 o'clock and we're ready to open fire again. The Russians turn leisurely and show us their side. A shot! He burns. But it is our last round of armour piercing...

No radio contact with the Battalion, all shells expended, meanwhile at 11.00 hours we are chased like rabbits by 20 enemy tanks. But we succeed in reaching the protection of the raised rail line where we are met by by our approaching 3. Company who take care of the enemy tanks. We report to Battalion. Quick repairs to our guns, our radios are put in service and as evening falls we roll into a new position 2 km. south of the previous battleground. Nothing happens during the night. We close up our positions. The vehicles are well-camouflaged. A night's sleep does us good. By first shooting light we recognize the enemy, who has camouflaged himself with straw and is deployed in readiness in our old position.

We call battalion, requesting reinforcements. We must get this enemy. We all want to take advantage of this opportunity. There is a sense of urgency. The wounded chief of a Sturmgeschütz battery from *DAS REICH* reports to me. We plan the attack using a sand model. With all nine gun commanders we climb the rail station tower. An artillery spotter turns up. The targets are quickly made out and assigned among seven commanders. Two remain in reserve. The artillery observer will fire a smoke screen. At 11.00 hours our vehicles roll to the attack. Under cover of the smoke screen we reach our designated firing positions, 500 metres from the enemy. "Fire!" Immediately 9 enemy tanks are burning. 4 T-34's try to escape but are destroyed from the rear. A pair of armoured scout cars try to zig-zag their way to the cover of the hills. We take target practice on them and roll up a Soviet trench where the escorting infantry have dug in. Now the way is free for the *DER FÜHRER* Regiment's planned counterattack which is laid on for the afternoon. As long as we hold "Gruschki Grave".

In Combat with Partisans and Enemy Paratroops

After the setback which he had received in and around "Gruschki Grave" on 1. and 2. September, the enemy was more cautious on the Kharkov—Poltawa rail line. Until 6. September, he cautiously followed the *WIKING* Division which was withdrawing toward Walki—Tschubowo—Poltawa. Not until the 7th did the enemy push toward the Division's new defence position near Walki. There, with strong infantry forces dug in, all heavy guns moved up, and after careful preparations, the Soviets launched their attack hoping to achieve the desired breakthrough. After heavy fighting, he had received a bloody rebuff. Protected by its mobile rearguards, *WIKING* was able to withdraw toward the west with the enemy unable to mount a new offensive. The Soviets were not ready again until 19. September. The Soviets were now concentrated and prepared for a major offensive toward the Division which was set in positions between Chorol and Subny. Once again the Soviets had the same massive array of infantry and heavy weapons but this time also tank forces and aircraft! Again the result was three days of unimaginably hard infantry and tank combat. Once again the "Wikinger" held and were able to withdraw without too much difficulty through Irklejew toward the Dnjepr. On 27. September, after six weeks of hard fighting, they crossed the Dnjepr near Cherkassy.

After vacating the area of Kharkov, 8. Armee went over to a mobile defence. As a rule, this meant fighting during the day and moving at night as the *WIKING* Division had done. Sleep was scarce and short in those three weeks in which the fighting alternated between quick counterattacks and ambushes by armoured forces against the advancing enemy and battles on a wide front from hastily reconnoitered, quickly occupied positions. 8. Armee's condition was such that the positions could usually be only thinly manned. Again and again the masses of Soviet infantry charged to the attack. Fighting them off demanded that the German forces stretch their physical and psychological strength to the limit. One crisis followed the other. But eventually the soldiers and commanders proved once again that they were superior to the Soviets tactically and in combat skills. On the battlefield they remained masters of the situation, although operationally the enemy dictated the rules of engagement. The gaps in the front, such as those in the Division's neighbouring sector, that of 4. Pz.Armee, were gradually closed in the course of the withdrawal. In these battles which sapped the troops mentally and physically, 8. Armee alone had to cover an area of 210 km. with 12 Infantry and 5 Panzer Divisions, although their actual strength was the equivalent of approximately 8 full-strength divisions. In addition, on 3. September at the suggestion of its neighbour to the right, *XI. Korps*, the Armee ordered that XI. Korps pull back its front and with it *WIKING*'s right wing. The result was an impossible front line along the HKL for the Division which appeared as a right angle exactly at the focal point of the entire front! In the weeks which followed, the enemy charged the thin lines holding these positions again and again with a sixfold superiority in men. However, the Armee preserved its integrity, inflicting heavy losses on the enemy and in doing so gaining a substantial amount of time up until 27. September 1943.

But was the enemy on the Dnjepr really so spent that his forces would be unfit for a long time for operations before this river barrier? Would the time gained be used by the Germans and stand them in such good stead that they would be able in the long run in strong positions behind the Dnepr to withstand attacks by the far superior enemy forces?

When the troops of 8. Armee, including the *WIKING* Division, reached the Dnepr, they found there neither a sufficient number of prepared crossings for a withdrawal on a broad front, nor the preparations or covering forces which would enable them to set up for defence in the new positions. Construction of new crossings was out of the question. Instead of being able to busy themselves with at least improving their positions, the troops now had to fight for them. Enemy paratroops contested their possession of the area. This action by the Soviet 1st, 3rd and 4th Guards Parachute Brigades took place on 24./25. Sept. in the area between Cherkassy and Kiev near Kanew. They made things difficult for the units of XXIV. Panzerkorps but were beaten off. Attacks against III. Pz.Korps to the south were made by weaker forces, perhaps in preparation for a large landing by the Soviet 1st, 2nd and 4th Airborne Brigades with heavy weapons and tanks in the area of Moshny. These forces were put out of action by the SS-*WIKING* Division during the course of 25. September.[1] Partisans made life difficult from the first moment. Russian combat units had already dug in in several bridgeheads on the western bank of the Dnepr and were ready for action. The way to and across the Dnepr had been even shorter for the enemy's pursuing fast battalions than for the pursued, who had lost valuable time crossing the few bridges and in marching into their new sectors. The battle on the Dnepr was nearly lost before it began, since nowhere were the Germans able to crush the enemy bridgeheads and throw the enemy battalions back across the river.

The *WIKING* Division had crossed the Dnepr on 27. September near Cherkassy and had the luck to reach its positions largely unhindered and without fighting. There it grappled for several days with enemy parachutists, who were destroyed. Several days before, the infantry divisions of 8. Armee had crossed the Dnepr near Kremenchug, Cherkassy and Kanew. Among them was the Bavarian 57. Infantry Div. which was to be the Division's northern neighbor. Therefore, it may be of interest to learn of the impressions and opinions of this unit when it arrived behind the Dnepr. The 1. Gen.Staff Officer, Oberst i.G. Hans Schmid, reported as follows:

"The crossing by 57. I.D. near Kanew was completed on the evening of 23. September. The Division's front was 20 kilometres long. The Division's fighting strength had been weakened by the months-long battle against an enemy superior in men and material. The infantry battalions are at only 20—40 percent strength. Fighting morale has sunk. Within the unit is an apathetic indifference. The troops have lived under conditions in which the most primitive essentials of life have been lacking. They had hoped to find prepared positions behind the Dnjepr where they could have a rest from fighting. But they found there neither prepared positions nor a reception party other than the Russians. The result was to dash their spirits to the ground. Harsh words of embitterment and lack of faith in the High Command were voiced by the troops." The Division's former commander, Gen.Maj. Trowitz added:

"Short of men, digging all day, a huge sector of the front to defend and no sleep at night; no man can do that."[2] With these terse words Trowitz characterized the condition of the overburdened troops and their morale. There was also the reason that the previous feeling of general superiority over the Russians no longer existed. This statement may be a blow to 57. Inf.Div. but is based on reports from numerous units and was the subject of confidential communications by the commanders.

IX. THE DEFENSIVE BATTLE ON THE DNEPR

On 1. October, even before the WIKING Division had moved into its new positions, I./SS-Pz.Gren.Rgt. GERMANIA, which had been detached to serve as Corps reserve for III. Pz.Korps, found itself once again on the attack against the enemy bridgehead across the Dnepr north of Kanew. Here the pursuing Soviets had crossed the Dnepr and occupied the hills west of the river. A counterattack by 57. Inf.Div. failed as did that of 3. Pz.Div. on 26. September. The enemy had dug in at this bend in the river near Silischtsche and so reinforced it that a new attempt to throw him back across the Dnepr only appeared possible with the deployment of strong forces. The battle here was renewed on 2. October and taking part in 3. Pz.Div.'s area was the WIKING Division's Reserve Group Dorr. The following is a short combat report by SS-Hstuf. Dorr which tersely describes the dramatic assault:

"1. October 1943
08.00 hours. Enemy attack near I./GERMANIA beaten off. At 10.00 hours another enemy attack repulsed with support from Sturmgeschütze of 3. Battery, Sturmgeschütz Battalion 261. A number of prisoners taken in the counterattack.

2. October 1943
05.15 Preparatory artillery fire begins.
06.35 Gruppe Dorr goes to the attack.
07.00 The attack makes good progress.
By 07.30 the Kampfgruppe has already taken the first objective by storm. The neighbours to the left, Kampfgruppen Brandt and Ekkert, are halted by heavy antitank fire from the flank. Of their 14 Panzers, 6 have already been knocked-out.
Gruppe Dorr holds the positions that have been overrun. Infantry of Kampfgruppe Dorr take cover in the captured trenches and successfully repulse repeated enemy counterattacks." (condensed version)[1]

Attempts by 3. Pz.Div. between 08.40 and 11.00 hours to relieve I./GERMANIA failed. Not until the evening could Kampfgruppen Brandt and Ekkert win ground to the east, after first returning to their jumping-off points. A quarter of the bridgehead was taken from the enemy. At 18.30 hours a surprise attack by an armoured Grenadier unit succeeded in making contact with the cut-off elements of I./GERMANIA. The wounded were evacuated. They stated that the enemy had attacked with far superior forces, simply overwhelming I./GERMANIA and causing heavy casualties. Many wounded were bayonetted by the Russians. During the course of the night the rest of Kampfgruppe Dorr succeeded in fighting its way out, bringing the dead with it. At 20.00 hours, I./GERMANIA was pulled back to Studinez as a reserve. Its combat strength was 11 men. The Battalion Commander's report closes with the sentence: "Particular recognition is due 3. Sturmgeschütz Btl. 261 commanded by Oberleutnant Dräger and the readiness for action of Oberwachtmeister Petrowic of the same battery." The commander of 3. Pz.Div. acknowledged the actions of I./GERMANIA under the command of Hstuf. Dorr in writing:[2]

Thus began the battle for the bridgeheads. Elsewhere, as here near Studinez, the attacks by the Germans were unsuccessful. The weeklong fighting between the Donez and Dnepr had so worn down the troops and weakened their fighting strength that they were no longer capable of greater efforts in the attack.

Within the *WIKING* Division meanwhile, further personnel changes were taking place. SS-Standartenführer Jürgen Wagner, the longtime commander of the *GERMANIA* Regiment, had left to set up the *NEDERLAND* Pz.Gren.Brigade. He was replaced by SS-Obersturmführer Fritz Ehrath, formerly of the *DEUTSCHLAND* Regiment. As before, the *WESTLAND* Regiment was led by SS-Obersturmführer Dieckmann. On 10. October, this veteran regimental commander was killed in action in the heavy bridgehead fighting on the central Dnjepr for the so called Fuchschwanz (Foxtail) Island. The award of the Oak Leaves with Swords to the Knight's Cross had not reached him at the time of his death.

At the beginning of November 1943, *WIKING* was reclassified as an SS-Panzerdivision although it was not yet reorganized as one. Essential elements were still missing which they had not yet been able to transport from the homeland. Originally the Division belonged to III. (germ.) SS-Pz.Korps as the third unit with the newly formed SS-Pz.Gren.Div. *NORDLAND* and the SS-Pz.Gren. Brigade *NEDERLAND*. III. (germ.) SS-Pz.Korps had been formed in the autumn of 1943 but was not yet ready for operations. As a result of the tense situation at the front, Heeresgruppe would not release *WIKING* which delayed its reorganization as a Panzerdivision. It was now hoped that this could be accomplished at the front. Therefore the Division was assigned an apparently quiet, though lengthy, sector on the Dnjepr, while SS- Sturmbrigade *WALLONIEN*, recently formed in Germany, was brought to Korssun. Thus, in spite of its designation as "5. SS Pz.Div. *WIKING*", the Division's makeup was still that of a Panzergrenadierdivision. With the added forces the Division could have devoted itself to its reorganization as a Panzerdivision and carried out its combat assignments as well. But things were to work out differently.

The Battles on "Foxtail Island"

At the beginning of October, the Division's sector on the Dnepr Front became active once more. In front of the mouth of the Rossawa the enemy had dug in on the large Dnepr island, the so-called "Foxtail Island", and was reinforcing his forces there. All the signs pointed toward an attempt by the enemy to cross the river and attack, especially since the Soviets had already acquired a small bridgehead on the Rossawa. In order to deprive the enemy of his base for this attack, the German High Command ordered an attack on the bridgehead and the island on the Dnjepr behind it. The attack took place on the night of 7./8. October. Taking part in the attack from the the Bavarian 57. I.D. on the Division's left was Gren.Rgt. 164. Both battalions of the *WESTLAND* Regiment, supported by several swim-capable tanks, engaged in bloody fighting on the Dnjepr island. As previously mentioned, SS-Obersturmführer Dieckmann fell on the fourth and last day of the battle which saw the enemy thrown back to the eastern bank. Not only the Division was hard hit by this painful loss. His successor was SS-Ostubaf. Marsell. Meanwhile, the operational situation on the Dnjepr stiffened day by day. On 17. October, General Koniev's 2nd Ukrainian Front thrust from the bridgehead between Kremenchug and Dnepropetrovsk toward the junction between 1. Pz.Armee and 8. Armee. Attacking with far superior forces, the Soviets forced 8. Armee to pull back its southern wing toward Kirowgrad. Heeresgruppe Süd immediately employed XXXX. Pz.Korps in a counterattack which cut off the enemy spearheads. But 8. Armee had to scrape together all available forces to protect its southern flank. On 24. November, followed a new, deeper penetration near Kremenchug. The enemy had also created a bridgehead near Cherkassy. The Heeresgruppe's central front faced a growing and ever worsening crisis, especially since the commanders of the 2nd Ukrainian Front steadily fed new forces into the breakthrough positions.

The situation on the northern wing appeared even worse. The enemy had also attacked here on 3. November near Kiev. With powerful forces the enemy had first created a bridgehead on both sides of the city then broke through the elements of 4. Pz.Armee there, throwing all of 4. Pz.Armee back toward the west and northwest. The 1st Ukrainian Army had followed energetically, reached Fastow and Shitomir, and was advancing with considerable forces toward Korosten. The entire Heeresgruppe faced the threat of being enveloped in the north of the widely stretched front and of being broken through in the centre near Kirowgrad. In this highly dangerous situation the Heeresgruppe acted swiftly. XXXXVIII. Pz.Korps, quickly thrown together south of Shitomir, succeeded through seesaw fighting in advancing northward and throwing the enemy back. At the beginning of December, Radomyschl and Shitomir were retaken. Likewise, the enemy was beaten back near Berdyczow and east of Brussilow. However, further east near Fastow and Biala-Zerkieff, he had doubled his strength. But on the whole, the acute danger of being enveloped from the north and thrown back toward the Black Sea had been averted. Aware of the enemy's capability of rapidly redeploying his battered units, the Germans had to expect renewed action in the near future on the Heeresgruppe's northwest flank. Meanwhile, on 8. Armee's northwestern wing, things had developed more quickly and even more dangerously.

Sturmbrigade *WALLONIEN* Reaches *WIKING*

The SS-Sturmbrigade *WALLONIEN* emerged from the *WALLONISCHEN LEGION*, known from the summer campaign of 1942. At the conclusion of the fighting in the West Caucasus in the winter of 1942/1943, the Legion was returned to Belgium to reform and recruit new members. Although possessing only four companies of infantry, it also had several infantry guns, Flak and antitank guns, Sturmgeschütze and Pioniere; altogether a unit which would be welcome reinforcement for the Division. Its commander, Oberstleutnant and SS-Ostubaf. Lucien Lippert, was a career officer in the Belgian Army who had graduated from the Military School in Brussels at the top of his class. At age 29 he had become the commander of this young unit which was his own creation and for which he lived and fought. An idealist of truly knightly appearance, two thirds of his 2,000 volunteers consisted of young workers and sons of artisans, but there were many members of the nobility and the Belgian middle class, sons of diplomats, officials, and industrialists including several wearers of the Jesuit Schools' Gold Medal. With these sociological ingredients, these Wallonian volunteers fit well into the *WIKING* Division. They formed a unit which was animated by the will "to gloriously represent our nation amidst the twenty peoples which have come to fight; by this means do our duty, which is to fight for Europe; to succeed in earning an honourable place for our nation in the continental community which must emerge from the war, and finally to create combat troops whose weight will guarantee social justice when we finally return to our homeland after the end of hostilities."[1] As a result of an agreement between the Wehrmacht High Command and the Army Chief of Staff on one side and the Reichsführer-SS on the other, the Wallonians were taken into the Waffen-SS effective 1. June 1943. At the beginning of November 1943, the SS-Sturmbrigade WALLONIEN began its march to the WIKING Division reaching it in Korssun. In July 1944, the unit was enlarged and reorganized as 28. SS-Freiwilligen-Panzer-Grenadier-Division WALLONIEN.[2] The Brigade was motorized and excellently equipped with over 340 vehicles of all types. It was deployed in WIKING's Dnepr front along the Olschanska, securing the Irdyn Marsh. There the Brigade had time to once again accustom itself to the still unfamiliar conditions on the Eastern Front.

Battle at the Irdyn Marsh

The remnants of the Russian parachute brigade which had landed south of the mouth of the Rossawa at the end of September and been routed by 57. Inf.Div. before it could assemble, had joined forces with the powerful partisan units of the Soviet partisan chief Bjelow. In the Irdyn marsh they were dug-in in a deep system of fortifications which would later form an essential basis for the creation of the bridgehead near Cherkassy. Scarcely had the SS-Brigade set up in its defensive positions in the Bol. Staroselje—Dnepr sector when it carried out a well-prepared reconnaissance of the area. During the course of this operation, the Brigade pressed into the wooded country near Bol. Staroselje on 22. 1. 1944 and near Baibussi on 3./4. February. It was able to destroy most of the fortifications there and fill the Soviet units in the Irdyn Marsh with respect. The members of these partisan bands were volunteers and convinced Komsomol members who represented a powerful addition for the Soviet command, particularly here in the Ukraine.[3] Armed with light machine guns, submachine guns, and automatic rifles, the partisans had available trained combat engineers and mining units and were capable of taking the place of regular Soviet infantry.

The Soviet units in the Irdyn Marsh maintained a mostly defensive posture. They launched their first attacks following orders from the Soviet Army command. On 20.11.1943, the enemy had already attacked near Cherkassy. 57. Inf.Div., which had been moved in from the Dnepr front near Kanew, was just able to hold but could not prevent the establishing of a Russian bridgehead. On 24. November, the Soviets had also gone to the attack near Kremenchug, forcing back XI. A.K. which was defending south of Smela. Following that, the situation northwest and southwest of Smela was one of frequent small clashes. But essentially the area was quiet until the Soviets launched a surprise attack from the Irdyn Marsh toward the Smela—Gorodischtsche road on 15. 1. 1944. They reached Teklino and the village of Buda Orlowezkaja. Only an immediate counterattack could save the situation. The attack toward Buda Orlowezkaja was carried out by elements of 57. Inf.Div. while Sturmbrigade WALLONIEN, supported by the Division's artillery, moved against the fortified forest area near Teklino. The attack succeeded. In four days of hard fighting the enemy was driven back into the Irdyn Marsh, his fortifications there destroyed, and the situation restored.

A great Russian offensive appeared to be imminent. And it came. However, it came not from Cherkassy, but with powerful forces from deep behind the front near Kremenchug. The attack smashed open a wide breach between Kapitanowka and Rotmistrowka on the right wing of XI. A.K. opening the way into the rear of 8. Armee's northern wing for the waiting fast units of the 5th Guards Tank Army. As the Russian infantry armies pushed back XI. A.K. and the 4th Guards

Army pivoted to the north, the enemy tank forces advanced further north via Swenigorodka in order to link up with their tank forces moving south from the area of Biala- Zerkieff. Followed by the 27th Army, their objective was to encircle the northern wing of the German 8. Armee and the eastern wing of 1. Pz.Armee.

X. THE CHERKASSY POCKET

On 27. 1. 1944 the Division, via the communications network, had already received the division report that enemy forces had occupied Schpola. A reconnaissance carried out immediately to the southwest reported enemy tanks northwest of Schpola and near Swenigorodka. Meanwhile, a new and highly alarming report arrived from Ssteblew where the Division's Replacement Training Battalion and Pionier Combat School under the command of SS-Ostuf. Heder were located. According to the report, individual enemy tanks had moved into Boguslaw. The immediate reconnaissance carried out there and to Medwin revealed enemy forces present in both localities. By the evening of 27. January, the Division had determined that two enemy tank forces were operating in its rear from a southern as well as northern direction, and were attempting to encircle the German forces standing between Smela and Kanew.

The picture became clearer for the Division on 28. 1. 1944 when during the night the alert units which the Division had formed from the supply services were attacked by enemy tanks south of Olschana. To the northwest, the Division's Replacement Training Battalion and Combat school in Streblow had already been involved in heavy fighting with the enemy tanks and had formed a hedgehog defence there. On this day, XXXXII. A.K. defending the front to the north between Kanew and Kagarlyk was attacked on a broad front and was forced to withdraw toward the Rossawa sector during the night of 30. January. The task of defending to the east between Gorodischtsche and the eastern wing of XXXXII. Korps would inevitably have fallen to 389. Inf.Div. and 5. Inf.Div. with the seconded Sturmbrigade *WALLONIEN* as well as the *WIKING* Division's SS-Pz.A.A. 5. But this would have meant giving up the remaining positions on the Dnepr which had become militarily worthless. On orders radioed from OKH the commanding generals of XXXXII. and XI. A.K. were forbidden to do this until replacement forces arrived. The High Command therefore left the Corps on its old front in the southwest and north while it frantically searched for new forces with which to create a new western front. The cornerposts of this new front were to be the villages of Ssteblew in the north and Olschana in the south which were being defended by Kampfgruppe Heder and the supply services from the *WIKING* Division. Precious time was lost which gave the enemy the opportunity to tighten the encircling ring from the west and strengthen it in depth. Moreover, his object was unmistakeable; to break down the large pocket which until now had been self-contained. The hard struggle for Olschana lasted until 5. February. The *WIKING* Division's supply services reinforced by the Estonian *NARWA* Battalion and 3. SS- Pi.Btl. 5 which was deployed in the sugar factory, held against far superior enemy forces from 28. January until 5. February and finally set up a hedgehog defence. During the night of 5./6. February, the Kampfgruppe evacuated its positions as ordered and at 02.30 hours broke through to the Division, its men returning to their units as planned. The front near Sstreblew held for days until it could be covered by XXXXII. A.K.'s HKL on 3. February. But between the two villages the enemy broke through, advanced as far as Kwitki, took Schanderowka on the 5th and from there pushed further east into the centre of the pocket without meeting significant opposition.

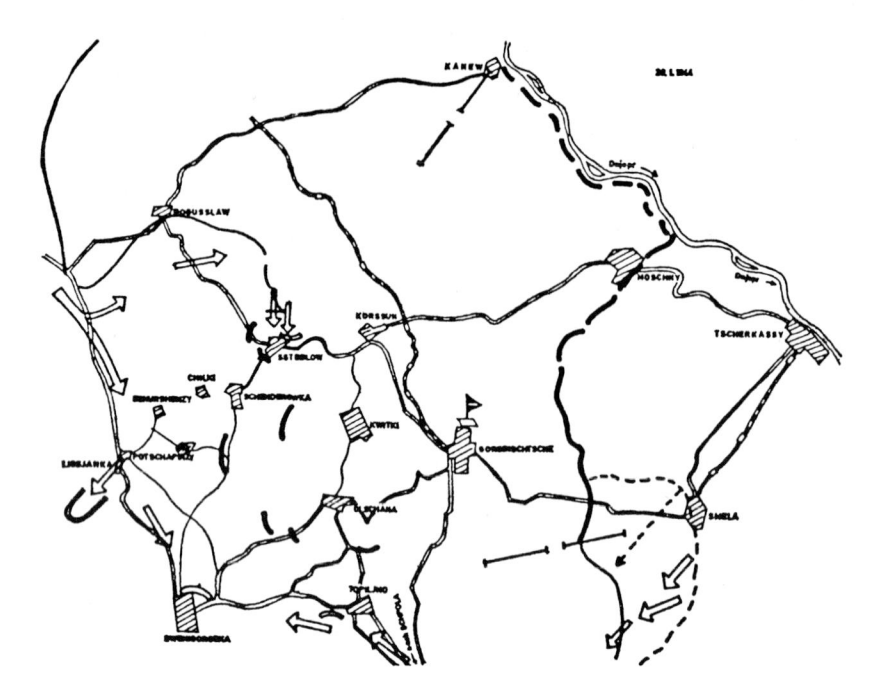

The Cherkassy pocket 28. January 1944

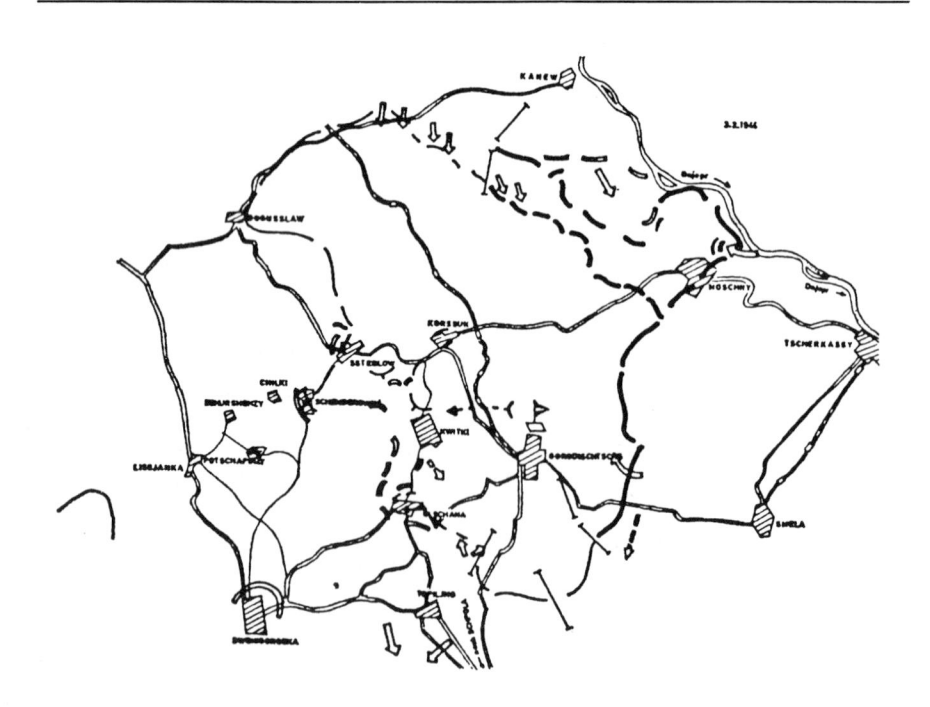

The pocket on 3. February 1944

The Pocket Wanders to the West

On 31. January, the chain of command was reorganized as the A.O.K.8 on this day had named a commander in the pocket. He was the Commanding General of XI. A.K., General Stemmermann. However, for this new task he had neither a staff nor the signals organization required to command such a widespread front. Instead he received the categorical order from the OKH to hold his old positions. A truly tragic human situation and an unsolvable military assignment!

On 7. February 1944 at 11.40 hours, the A.O.K. gave the General freedom of action in the following teletype:

"Relief advance by III. Pz.Korps toward Morenzy. Gruppe Stemmermann will shorten the front lines and move with the pocket in the direction of Schanderowka in order to be able to break out toward the relieving forces at the proper time."[1] (Further revealing radio messages compare Div. Chronicle Inf.Rgt 249/II, Pages 125-133.)

Now there was movement in the previously frozen front. The already long overdue measures were now singlemindedly and energetically carried out in order to secure the western front of the pocket. However, the confined area, the few roads and the muddy routes made the necessary regrouping immeasurably more difficult. The stand-fast order from the OKH was bearing its first bitter fruit.

The villages which had been lost in the west now had to be retaken in costly fighting: Schanderowka, Komarowka, Novo-Buda and Chishinzy. The Division took Schanderowka and Komarowka with the *GERMANIA* Regiment while 72. Inf.Div. captured Novo- Buda and Chishinzy. The fighting now went on for every foot of ground. The enemy defended stubbornly. His tank forces provided energetic support. But the Kampfgruppen of both divisions succeeded in making the impossible possible. However, their losses soon exceeded that which was bearable.

On 9. 2. 1944, the commander of the Pz.Abtlg., SS-Stubaf. Köller, assigned the chief of 1./Pz.Rgt. 5, SS-Hstuf. Wittmann, to form an infantry company from all elements of the battalion which were not in action. This company had a strength of 4 officers and 220 NCO's and men and was divided into four platoons. The armament of each platoon consisted of 3 machine guns and the rest with submachine guns, rifles, pistols and handgrenades. This rifle company had to face heavy fighting from 11. until 17. February. Initially deployed at the enemy bridgehead near Ambrusino, with the breakout from the pocket it took over a security sector on the left and right flank. After six days of fighting casualties were 2 dead, 17 wounded and 35 missing.

During the fighting for Novo-Buda, the Pz.Abtlg. was also in action. When the enemy attacked the southeastern edge of the town with 2 battalions on 13. 2. 1944, he was able to break through in several places due to the gaps in the strongpoint system built by the Germans. After SS-Stubaf. Schumacher counterattacked with 2 Panzers and had thrown the enemy from the village, the Russians renewed the attack with 15 tanks assaulting the southwest part of Novo-Buda. Thereupon, Schumacher decided to halt this tank breakthrough with his 2 Panzers and destroy the 8 T-34's which had already entered the village. After successfully carrying this out he reached the southwest exit of Novo-Buda where he was able to destroy 2 further T-34's. On the following day the Russians attacked with 11 tanks. Schumacher decided to drive into the enemy-occupied southern part of the village with 2 Panzers in order to take the enemy from the flank. Antitank fire damaged the other Panzer's cannon so that at first Schumacher's was the only one ready for action. He destroyed 7 enemy tanks and with his last three H.E. shells forced the crews of 3 attacking tanks to bale out. Meanwhile, another Panzer arrived as support enabling Schumacher to set the 3 abandoned tanks afire and to knock-out another which had attempted to move from the village and surprise him from the rear. For this feat Schumacher, promoted to SS-Obersturmführer, received the Knight's Cross.

In expectation of certain relief, the encircled troops abandoned all unnecessary vehicles so as not to reduce their mobility. The total congestion and poor condition of the roads also led Sturmbrigade WALLONIEN to get rid of any ballast from its vehicles while leaving behind any vehicles which were not fit for a 30 km. trip through the mud. Leon Degrelle reported:

"The road from Goroditsch to Korsun which was to be used for the last breakout attempt was already jammed with long columns. Thousands of trucks, one behind the other on a 20 km. stretch of road, skidded over the black holes in the road which had been transformed into a gigantic cesspool. The heaviest artillery tractors attempted laboriously to clear the road. The great accumulation of vehicles could not have offered the Soviet airforce a better target. Their aircraft buzzed over the pocket like angry wasps, diving in squadron strength every ten minutes in low-level attacks on the vehicles mired in the mud.

Trucks burned everywhere.

The thick, deep mud was ground up to such a degree that after a short time passage had become impossible.

However the attempt had to be made. The way across the open fields meant bogging down after one or two hundred metres. The road was no longer passable. At least a thousand trucks were stuck fast and had to be set afire to prevent them from falling into enemy hands... To protect this giant transport of more than ten thousand vehicles via the shaky planks of a miserable rail line, our troops had to hold fast under all circumstances for a few more days against the Soviet assault."[2]

The Wait for Relief

The pocket became ever smaller. In a few days 54,000 men had been pressed into an area 7 by 8 km. and looked in deep depression toward their last hope to the south and west. They waited for relief. It was the same as in Stalingrad.

"Stalingrad Number 2" was also the subject of leaflets dropped by the U.S. Airforce which mentioned among other units, the SS-Pz.Div. WIKING and the SS-Brigade WALLONIEN.[1] Also dropped were different types of Soviet leaflets and "passes".

The Soviet front propaganda was comparatively coarse. The methods of the so-called "National Committee for a Free Germany" were somewhat more sophisticated, although they certainly made no impression on the men of the Waffen-SS. As far as can be ascertained, the NKFD's leaflet operations began with messages addressed to the "Officers and soldiers of the 72. I.D., 57 I.D., 389. I.D.,SS-Division WIKING and attached units" from Röckl and Büchler who were leaders of the "Alliance of German Officers" which was part of the NKFD.[2] Allegedly on the personal orders of Stalin, General Seydlitz and the Army Group's Political Officer Watutin with escorting officers went to the Cherkassy pocket and on 8. 2. 1944 wrote to the commander of 112 I.D. and to Oberst Fouquet of the staff of 112 I.D.. General Korfes wrote to Gruppenführer Gille, commander of the

IN LETZTER MINUTE!

Offiziere und Soldaten im Kessel!

Ihr verbringt hier Eure letzten Tage. Die Liquidierung des Kessels durch die russischen Truppen geht ihrem Ende entgegen. *Korsun-Schewtschenkowsky*, wo sich die Hauptkraft Eures Widerstandes konzentrierte, ist in russischer Hand.

Was brachte Euch die Ablehnung der russischen Kapitulationsbedingungen?

Ein Blick auf die Karte sagt alles.

Lage am 9.2.-   Lage am 15.2.   Sowjettruppen

In den letzten Tagen ist Euer Kessel auf einen verschwindend geringen Raum zusammengeschrumpft. Euer Untergang ist nahl

Auf einen Ausbruch durch eigene Kraft hofft Euer Kommando längst nicht mehr. Es redet Euch jetzt angesichts der erfolglosen Ausbruchsversuche ein, Hilfe käme von außen.

Laßt Euch gesagt sein: *Jeder Versuch, zu Euch durchzubrechen, ist absolut erfolglos und kostet der deutschen Wehrmacht nur neue ungeheure Opfer.* Es ist nicht das erste Mal, daß Euro Kessel zum Grab wurden, sowohl für die Eingekesselten, als auch für die «Entsatztruppen». Erinnert Euch nur an Stalingrad und Kirowograd! Glaubt nicht, daß die SS-Division «Adolf Hitler» Euch retten wird. *Die Rote Armee ist stark genug, sie und Euch zu vernichten.* Von den sechs Panzerdivisionen, die anfangs noch zu Euch durchschlüpfen wollten, sind auch nur traurige Überreste übriggeblieben.

Eure Hoffnung auf Hilfe von außen ist also Selbstbetrug und bedeutet Selbstmord!

Einzig und allein die Gefangengabe kann Euch noch retten!

Alle, die sich *freiwillig* gefangengeben, erhalten laut Befehl des Oberkommandos der Roten Armee Nr. 1470 vom 12. Juli 1943 *Vergünstigungen.*

DEUTSCHER OFFIZIER! DEUTSCHER SOLDAT!
Zögere nicht länger! Noch steht Dir der rettende Weg in die Gefangenschaft offen.

Beschreitest Du diesen Weg nicht beizeiten, dann findest auch Du in diesem Hexenkessel Dein Grab!

A Soviet leaflet dropped into the Cherkassy pocket directed at the surrounded German troops. The leaflet invites the Germans to surrender stating that continued resistance is suicide.

SS-Division *WIKING*, on behalf of Seydlitz.³ Naturally no one knew at first how seriously to take these types of demands or even if they should be answered. Seydlitz even went so far as to speak to the surrounded troops with a loud hailer from the front lines. With such methods the first great attempt by the National Committee to move a German unit to capitulate had failed miserably.⁴

Everyone still hoped for relief and the command trusted in the radio message from AOK 8 which the Chief of Staff Speidel communicated to General Stemmermann among others on 13. February:

"Breith's leading elements have reached Lissjanka. Vormann advancing from Jerki bridgehead in direction of Swenigorodka. How is the situation there? All the best for a successful outcome.

Speidel⁵

The "successful outcome" in any case would not be decided quickly. All indications were that it would be seriously in doubt. Feldmarschall von Manstein certainly had the necessary men to open the pocket from without. But between it and the rapidly approaching relief forces had been deployed two Soviet Tank Armies; Koniev's 5th Guards Tank Army in the south and Watutin's 6th Tank Army in the north. These would have to be smashed in order to reach the pocket. During his return from the fruitless debates in the Führer Headquarters, when Manstein first received reports of the Soviet breakthroughs in the north and south and the union of strong tank forces near Swenigorodka, he had acted without delay. He had ordered 8. Armee to pull three Panzer divisions out of the front and assemble them in the direction of Schpola. 6. Armee was to give up the fresh and battle ready 24. Pz.Division. With these forces, Generalleutnant von Vormann and the Corps Headquarters of the XXXXVII. Pz.Korps were to carry out the attack between Schpola and Swenigorodka as soon as the forces could be assembled. At the same time he ordered III. Pz.Korps with a further four Panzerdivisions and a "heavy" Panzerregiment to attack eastward from the area of Winograd.

That was a powerful force which could probably have defeated the Soviets. In spite of the muddy roads and the comparatively long march, things at first went like clockwork. And they probably would have continued to go well had the OKH not once more, in a disastrous fashion, interferred with the units' command. On 3. February, Gen.Ltn. von Vormann's southern group with the 3., 11., 14. and 24. Panzer Divisions was assembled south of Schpola and near Jerki 9 km. south of Swenigorodka. In any case the 3., 11. and 14. Pz.Divisions had come from heavy fighting and still had elements involved in the battle to the east and were thus only partially usable. Von Vormann's group had had to attack on 26. 1. 1944 northeastward toward Kapitanowka in the direction of XI. A.K.'s broken southern wing in order to close the gaps there forced by the attacking Russians. An armoured group from 14. Pz.Div. was successful in making contact with XI. Armeekorps. The group was separated from the division and had to remain in the pocket. However, galloping past the group's firing cannon was the Vth Russian Guards Cavalry Corps with the 11th, 12th and 63rd Cavalry Divisions which pressed forward toward the west. Trailing infantry attempted to keep the gaps open and became involved in heavy local battles with the German Panzer units of XXXXVII. Pz.Korps. So for example, General Unrein's 14. Pz.Div. was still free in the break in area on 10. February. 24. Panzer Division, hurrying from 6. Armee, was unbroken and stood assembled and combat-ready on 3. February near Jerki. It had laboriously covered more than 300 km. northward over muddy roads in order to be in position in time to attack. With its firepower it would probably have been in a position to smash the Russian Tank Corps opposite near Swenigorodka and lead forward the following divisions of XXXXVII. Pz. Korps. But unexplicable orders from FHQ ordered 24. Pz.Div. back to 6. Armee. Awaited with great hopes in the pocket, XXXXVII. Pz. Korps had also lost its sole immediately available assault force and was damned to teeth-grinding inactivity. Due to the loss of time in bringing up 11. Pz.Div. to relieve 24. Pz.Div., the longed-for breakthrough toward Swenigorodka was no longer possible.

III. Pz.Korps, which was to carry out the attack from the west, was also in position in time. It had available outstanding and combat-capable units. The 16. and 17. Pz.Div., the SS-Pz.Div. *LAH* and the following 1. Pz.Div. were all combat proven operational units with years of Russian front experience. All possessed powerful Panzer units. In addition came the Bäke Heavy Panzer Regiment with 34 *Tiger* and 47 *Panther* tanks. This was a terrific combat force which could well cope with the powerful Soviet forces. However, misfortune also plagued this promising operation. The OKH had ordered the attack to be carried out at first toward the north instead of directly toward the east. Instead of opening the pocket directly from the west it wanted to envelop the enemy in the north and in his western flank; thus two operations in one: to open the pocket and at the same time carry out offensive operations.

After initial success, this operation also failed. On 15. February, 8. Armee radioed to General Stemmermann in the pocket:

"Operational capability of III. Pz. Korps reduced. Gruppe Stemmermann must break out and reach Hill 239 near Dshurshenzy with own forces. Link up there with III. Pz. Korps.

I. A. signed Speidel[6]

But still lacking was the approval of the OKH. Once again Feldmarschall von Manstein intervened at the last second and radioed to Stemmermann at 15.00 hours on 16. 2. 1944:

"Password freedom. Target Lissjanka.'"[7] In doing so the Feldmarschall took up the password given in the orders of XXXII. Armeekorps from 15. February, 20.00 hours, by the Commanding General Lieb at Schanderowka. With this brief order the fortress on the Dnepr from which Hitler had envisaged the retaking of the entire bank of the Dnepr had fallen. The last act of the Cherkassy pocket could begin.

The Last Act

On 8. February, the representative of the Soviet Supreme Commander, Marshall of the Soviet Union Zhukov, the Commander of the Troops of the First Ukrainian Front, Army General Watutin and the Commander of Troops of the Second Ukrainian Front, Army General Koniew, had prepared an ultimatum to the commanders of the 42. Armeekorps, 11. Armeekorps, the 112., 88., 72., 167., 168., 57. and 332. Infantrydivisions, the 213. Security Division, the SS-Div. *WIKING*, the *WALLONIEN* Brigade as well as "to the entire officer corps of the German forces encircled in the area of Korsun—Schewtschenkowsky."[1] On the same day it was carried over to 112. Inf. Div.'s sector of the front by an emissary. Charter members of the "Alliance of German Officers" Steidle, Büchler and Stöckle called for the acceptance of the Soviet ultimatum in air-dropped leaflets.

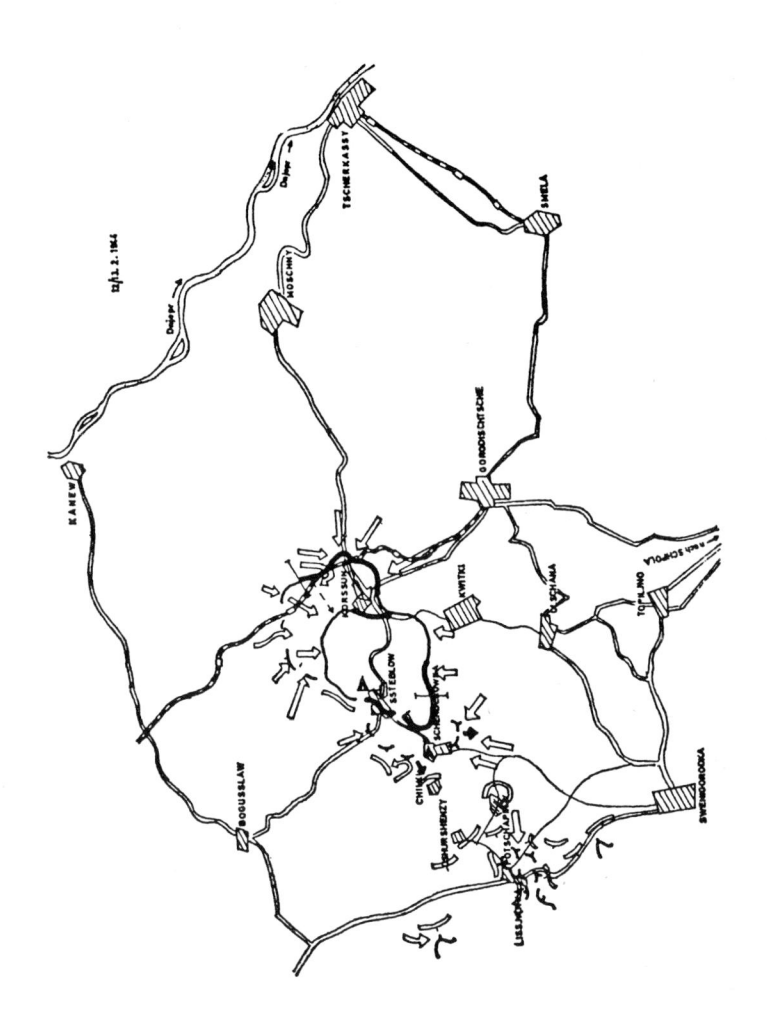

The pocket wanders toward the southwest 12./13. February 1944

The surrender of the pocket was, however, unanimously rejected.[2] We know with what relief the surrounded troops—from Grenadier to General—had received von Manstein's break out order. But we also know of the deep concern of the leading corps and Division commanders over the expected coming events.

On 15. February, the last briefing for the WIKING Division took place in Schanderowka. The commander issued brief and clear orders and made no long speeches. Léon Degrelle, later successor to SS-Ostubaf. Lippert who was killed in action during the breakout, who was present at the briefing, remembers the following words:

"Only a desperate effort can save us now. Waiting is pointless. Tomorrow morning at 05.00 the fifty thousand men of the pocket will go to the attack toward the southwest. Breakthrough or death. There is no other solution. Troop movements begin tonight at 23.00 hours."[3]

Gille, therefore, harboured no illusions. In the High Command of the 8. Armee they did not see things so clearly. Otherwise the radio message already sent by Generalmajor Speidel to General Stemmermenn on 15. February could not be explained. Undoubtedly the commander in the pocket planned correctly and in good faith that he would find III. Pz.Korps on the Dshurshenzy hills. This did not hold true. On the following day this fateful error led to catastrophe.

Manstein's laconic order to break out gave the encircled men the direction toward Lissjanka. But there were no crossings prepared there for 50,000 men. The relief forces themselves could hardly be expected to provide their own crossings. But they carried out their difficult duty and with their limited means built an emergency bridge. But the accumulated units of the encircled forces backed up before the Gniloi Tikitsch. Behind them were the Russians, on their flanks the Russian tanks, before them a raging river. Panic among the backed-up masses of men was unavoidable.

In the pocket General Stemmermann had taken all available measures before 15. 2. 1944 in order to push his units as far to the west as possible. Naturally that could take place only after an attack. The base for the planned breakout, the village of Schanderowka, had been taken by storm on 11. February by SS- Pz.Gren. Rgt. *GERMANIA*. The following report was provided by the former Company Commander of 1./*GERMANIA*, SS-Ostuf. Werner Meyer:

"Late in the morning, Sturmbannführer Dorr had called in the Company Chiefs of his I. Battalion *GERMANIA* and stood with them in the dreary winter weather behind a haystack east of the village of Schanderowka. I. Battalion had the task of taking the village. From there the breakout from the pocket was to happen. Suggestions here, suggestions there. Dorr, Klein, Sören Kam, Martin Kruse and I agreed to attack by night.

Who will take the lead? When no one appeared enthusiastic Dorr ordered: Lead First Company, I will go forward with them. Company in file. Klein follow likewise in close file, Kam in reserve. We'll break through left of the village near the large *Balka*, turn right toward the village and take it. The whole operation using surprise. In the village the First Platoon left of the road, the Second to the right.

After darkness fell, the companies prepared themselves. The missing platoon from 1. Company had meanwhile arrived. Silently the Company moves in the darkness into the large *Balka* toward the Russian positions. It snows and blows heavily.

Stubaf. Dorr and I scout ahead. We are almost at the end of the Balka deep below the road and deliberate how we should continue. Then two Russians who have apparently become curious appear on the horizon above us. We get them but not without noise so Dorr orders: Out, let's go, let's go, into the position and then on!

With a roar and wild firing we break into the position. A pair of weary sentries scarcely defend themselves. Hand grenades into the bunker and then across the road. The Second and Third can do the rest!

On the other side of the road the Company assembles briefly and immediately attacks the meanwhile-awakened village. A few metres from the village house-high flames hiss from the ground causing momentary panic. We had not seen that before. But the flamethrower went out again; it was stationary with a trip wire. It caused little damage since its firing height was set for tanks and could do us little harm on foot other than frighten us. The First reached the village. The Second has meanwhile arrived and the street fighting begins, in which both Companies are experienced. "Otto, alternate as usual, one house for you, one for me!", I yell to the Chief of the Second. "Will do!", calls back the Schleswig-Holsteiner."

On the same day, Novo-Buda, the flanking village to the south was attacked by Gren.Rgt. 105 of 72. Inf.Div. under the command of Major Köstner. The Regiment's carefully planned and energetically executed attack was successful. The WALLONIEN Sturmbrigade followed on foot, relieved the Regiment and defended the village against furious counterattacks until the breakout began. Killed in the fighting was the Belgian Brigade Commander, Lucien Lippert. His brave countrymen and fellow volunteers carried his corpse with them to safety as far as Gniloi Tikitsch to the other side of the lines.

The breakthrough divisions formed up on 16. 2. 1944. On the northern wing was Korpsabteilung B (112. I.D.) under the command of Oberst Fouquet. Assembled north of Chilki, it had taken part in the capture of Schanderowka, Chilki and Komarowka. In the centre to the south was 72. Inf.Div. and on the southern edge of the village 5. SS-Pz.Div. WIKING whose line of attack paralleled that of 72. Inf.Div. past Hill 239.0 to the south.[4]

Beside Sturmbrigade WALLONIEN in Novo-Buda there remained on the eastern front 57. Inf.Div. with its front to the southeast and east; south of it was Kampfgruppe Dorr of the WIKING Division with the remainder of 14. Pz.Div.'s Pz.Gren. Battalion which had broken through and remained in the pocket. The northern flank was held by 88. Infantry Division.

The pocket had now become so narrow that vehicles could scarcely still move and troop movements could be made only with great difficulty. On 10. February Korssun had to be evacuated. With that, supplying of the pocket by air ceased. Approximately 4,000 wounded were assembled in Schanderowka.

Shortly before the breakout, another serious crisis arose. At the junction between 57. Inf.Div. and 88. Inf.Div. Soviet tanks broke into the rearguard positions and pushed through toward the southwest. An immediate counterattack by a small Panzer group from the WIKING Division threw the enemy back and restored the situation. Léon Degrelle described the events:

"The WALLONIEN Sturmbrigade received orders to arrive by dawn at the head of the breakout force in order to take part in the ultimate attack. Salvation or destruction. Through the terrific confusion, with Soviet tanks everywhere which had been drawn to the last thousand German vehicles, we pushed on quickly to the southwest. Behind us the noise was deafening. Schanderowka had held less than an hour. The Russians had already moved past the village. Their tanks rolled toward us for the ultimate showdown. The German Panzers were sacrificed in a

desperate counterattack. They fought one against ten as Marschall Ney's troopers had done a century before east of the Beresina.
I saw them just before they threw themselves on the enemy. The young Panzer soldiers offered a splendid picture. In their short, black, silver trimmed uniform jackets they stood in the Panzer cupolas knowing that they were driving to certain death. Several proudly wore the black and silver Ritterkreuz at their throats, a shining target for the enemy.
None of these outstanding fighters appeared excited or agitated. They rolled on their tracks across the snow through the confusion of the retreating army. Not a Panzer, not a man would return. Orders were orders. The sacrifice was complete. In order to gain one hour, the hour which might enable ten thousand European and German soldiers to be saved, the German Panzer soldiers died to the last man south of Schanderowka on the morning of 17. February 1944."[5]
The report by 57. Inf. Div. was somewhat less emotional:
"Early on 16. February, the Russians pushed into the movements of 57. and 88. Inf. Divisions with tanks. The breakout was sealed off."[6]
Stoves said it bluntly: "After the last Panzers of the WIKING Division had once again cleared up the situation east of Schanderowka through a courageous counterattack, and in doing so saved 57. and 88. Inf.Div.'s which were together in bitter fighting as rearguards, the leading elements of Gruppe Stemmermann under General Lieb moved out almost noiselessly without preparatory fire at approximately 23.45 hours."

Breakout to Freedom

On the evening of 16. February, the breakout divisions stood ready to attack toward Hill 239.0 as ordered by XXXXII. A.K. in the Chilki area on the southern edge of Schanderowka. All movements were carried out as planned. The reinforced SS-Pz. Aufklärungsabteilung 5 under command of Ostuf. Heinrich Debus took over the lead of the WIKING Division. It was to advance through Chilki north of enemy-occupied Komarowka toward the attack target followed closely by a Kampfgruppe from the WESTLAND Regiment under SS-Stubaf. Walter Schmidt. To the south stood Sturmbrigade WALLONIEN commanded by SS-Hstuf. Degrelle. It had moved up from Novo-Buda at dawn in the direction of Potschapinzy to screen Kampfgruppe GERMANIA withdrawing southward from the pocket under SS-Ostubaf. Fritz Ehrath. "Using only close combat weapons, the brave Grenadiere of GERMANIA destroyed 24 Soviet tanks and in bitter close quarters fighting prevented the splitting of the pocket."[1]
At the main dressing station in Schanderowka, the chief of the First Aid Company and the WIKING's Divisional Medical Officer, Dr. Thon, had loaded the wounded. They did not wish to see them fall into enemy hands. One group of 140 men was laid in the Division's tracked vehicles and waited under command of SS-Hstuf. Dr. Isselstein. A 100 severely wounded men of the Division, in addition to 30 wounded from Korpsabteilung B, were loaded on panje wagons and followed under the command of Dr. Thon. Kampfgruppe Dorr with I./GERMANIA and attached Kampfgruppe were to cover this column.
Everything was accomplished with complete order despite the congestion, the Russian artillery fire and spoiling attacks by Russian tanks.
In a "Combat report on the Abteilung's breakout on 16. 2. 1944" to SS-Pz.Aufklärungsabteilung 5 on 7. 3. 1944, SS-Ostuf. Debus, commander of the

146

lead Gruppe, reported on the course of the fighting by his unit.[2] On that bloody morning the following units veered southeastward through snow flurries and reached the covering forest south of Potschapinzy.

The bulk of 72. Inf.Div. was likewise left standing before the Dshurshenzy—Potschapinzy road. Following behind the WIKING Division, it had become backed up there. Firm control over the units had become impossible as they bunched up. To add to their misfortune during the march, 14 T-34's appeared from a Balka and overran the column of WIKING Division wounded which was just passing. SS-Hstuf. Dr. Isselstein fell with his wounded comrades. Dr. Thon succeeded in reaching safety with a few dozen vehicles and their wounded. Later he even succeeded in crossing the river. But panic among the concentrated masses could no longer be prevented.

Stolid as a Panzer" marched "Papa" Gille and his staff with the bulk of the WIKING Division up to the Gniloi Tikitsch. With hand-held weapons the Division had thrown back the enemy infantry, beaten off attacking cavalry again and again and through the roaring tank fire had forced a way through the midst of the enemy. Already the safety of the western bank of the small river beckoned. Surely everyone could almost grasp the freedom before them. It was scarcely 150 metres! But at the river they found none of their security forces and no crossings but rather began to take flanking fire from the north and south. The first men were already diving desperately into the water. Many reached the safety of the western shore but many drowned in the flood of the swollen river.

Only two of the WIKING Division's units remained relatively unaffected by the dramatic proceedings at the crossing: 1./SS-Pz.Abt. 5 and the SS-Sturmbrigade WALLONIEN. Separated from the Division, they waited in the cover of several woods until darkness on 17. February and arrived in Lissjanka with only the weapons they could carry, but without heavy losses.

The Pz.Abteilung's war diary recorded:

"16. 2. 1944

The enemy attack toward Novo-Buda intensifies. Russians retake the southern part of the village at dawn. During the day two Panzers remain with I./SS-GERMANIA as security.

15.00 hours the ordinance officer from GERMANIA arrives at the command post and brings the orders to break out. I./SS-Pz.Rgt. 5 has to disengage at dusk at approximately 19.00 hours and move to Schanderowka. Further orders to follow from Division in Schanderowka.

Commanding officer and adjutant reach Schanderowka at approx. 17.00 hours in order to oversee preparations for the breakout by part of the Abteilung which is still in Schanderowka.

The commanding officer immediately goes to Division and on his return issues the following order:

Following the return of the Kampfgruppe from Novo-Buda the Pz.Abteilung will march immediately to the northern part of Schanderowka and stand ready there to break through.

At 19.20 hours follows the departure of all of the

Panzer forces, organized as follows:

1 command Panzer
2 Panzer IV
4 Panzer III
6 Sturmgeschütze

Immediately behind the Panzer forces follow the wheeled components.

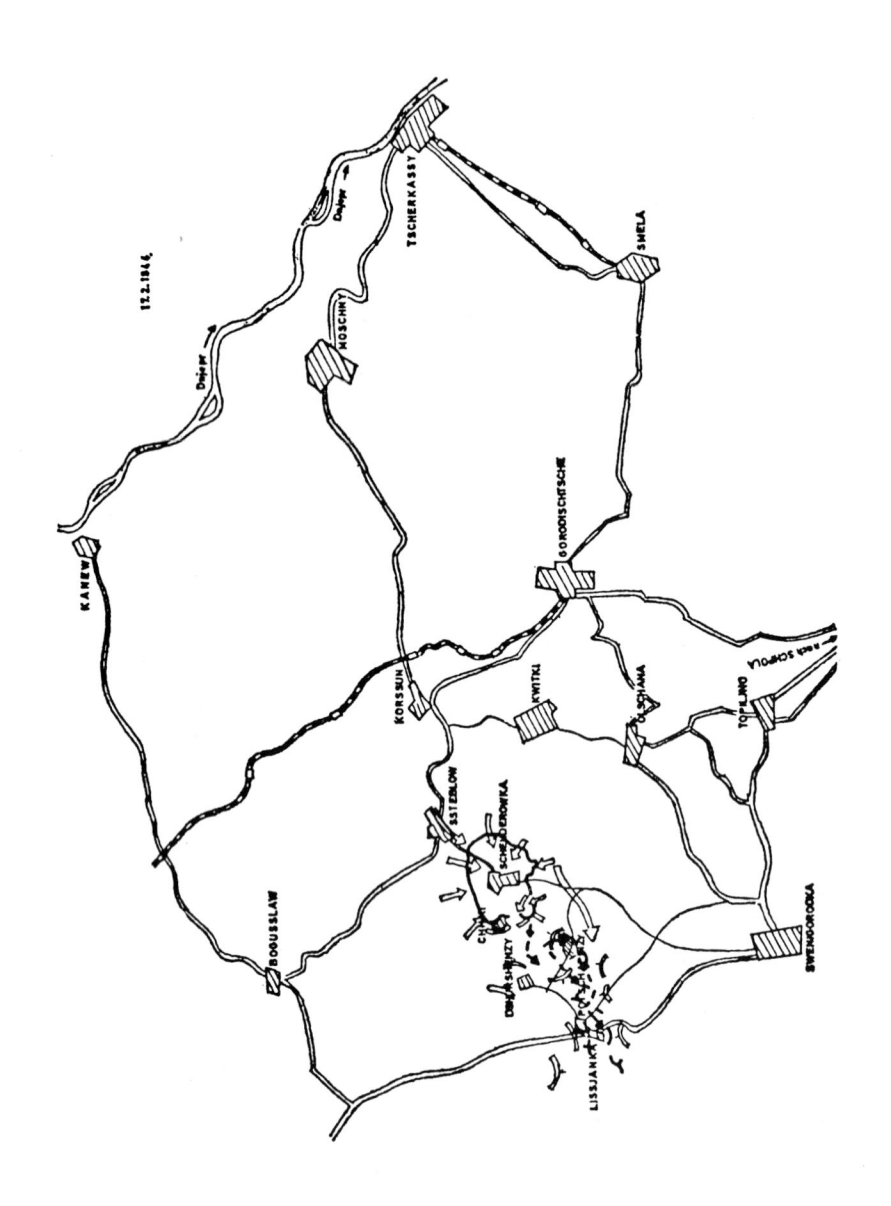

The breakout on 17. February 1944

Making headway is very difficult since the roads are completely jammed with horse drawn vehicles.

At 21.00 hours the Abteilung reaches the western edge of Schanderowka. While crossing the brook on the west end of Schanderowka, the command Panzer breaks through the bridge. Repairs to the bridge which would allow Panzers to cross take too much time.

All traffic is halted. The Panzers must be towed singly across the bridge by an 18 ton tractor. The last Panzer passes over the bridge at 01.45 hours.

17. 2. 1944.

At 02.10 hours the Abteilung set out on the ordered breakthrough. Road conditions very poor. First enemy resistance southwest of Chilki. Here the last of the Abteilung's wheeled vehicles were destroyed, since further progress was impossible due to the deep ruts and mud.

Enemy tanks moved out from Komorowka and tried to prevent the breakthrough with heavy fire. SS-Ustuf. Schumacher was committed with all of the Panzers south of Chilki in order to destroy the enemy tanks appearing from Komorowka. 2 tanks were destroyed.

The command Panzer had to be blown up due to track damage.

The commanding officer and adjutant climbed into Ustuf. Schumacher's Panzer. Schumacher then took over command of the remaining Panzers.

Commanding officer and adjutant attempted to hold the men together but due to the complex situation this was not possible.

The commanding officer climbed aboard an 18 ton tractor as this was the only vehicle which could make headway over this terrain.

Enemy tanks appeared from the north, moving southwards and fired with machine guns and cannon at the Panzers moving southwest toward Lissjanka as well as at the vehicles which had been able to fight their way this far.

Near the wooded area east of Dshurshenzy, where the tractor had to cross an open area, it was fired on by enemy tanks and received a direct hit just behind the driver's seat. The commanding officer, SS-Stubaf. Köller, was killed.

At the tip of the wood east of Dshurshenzy enemy tanks, which had come from Dshurshenzy, once again appeared. The Panzers were unable to climb the hills which rose from the tip of this wood so they were blown up.

The men of the Abteilung fought their way through individually. By the evening the majority of the Abteilung had reached Lissjanka. The adjutant had been wounded in the course of breakthrough."[3]

Sturmbrigade *WALLONIEN* was also lucky. Its commander, SS-Hstuf. Degrelle, wrote:

"While we waited for darkness (near Oktjabr), the three thousand survivors who lay strewn about our wood were divided into groups by the NCO's.

All arms of the services were represented...

Without food or drink we had survived since morning on a few handfulls of snow. But the snow had only made us more thirsty. We huddled together as closely as possible in our protective holes so that we could warm ourselves a little.

Above all we waited fearfully for the end of this terrible day. Not until the tank on the hill could no longer see our movements did we dare leave our protective positions.

At half past five we set off in close order...

Led by scouts we moved two kilometres farther along a path which led through the swamps.

Even there the mud came up to our knees.
The Russians had not noticed us.
We climbed up a snow-covered bank. On the other side a stream sparkled in the moonlight. One after the other we crossed over on a very slippery beam. Then there was wild excitement. Three shadows with steel helmets suddenly appeared before us. We fell into each other's arms, laughing, crying and jumping about after which the entire weight of our fear and all of our pain fell away.
It was the first outpost of the Germans from the south."[4]
Equally moving is the description found in the extremely colourfully written book "Verbrannte Erde" (Scorched Earth) by Paul Carell:
"And far and wide no crossing. No foot bridge.
1. Panzerdivision's bridges and an emergency footbridge built by the Jena Pioniere Btl. under the protection of the last Grenadiere of *LEIBSTANDARTE* lay two and a half kilometres further north. 2,500 metres! But no one knew this. And everyone had only one urge: get across the river, to the other side to where the Soviet tanks could not follow.
These thoughts left no place for calm consideration. The great disappointment on Hill 239 had destroyed the men's confidence. They felt abandoned and betrayed. They quarreled and cursed. They wanted just to get away, just to get out of this damned hell!
The thermometer read five degrees below zero. An ice-cold wind swept across the land. But what could be done? Four T-34's drove to within a few hundred metres of the tightly-packed mass of men and fired with H.E.. Horrible. Groups of thirty to forty men ran blindly into the icy water.
They drowned in groups. The bodies of horses floated among the ice floes. It was only thirty metres. But to cross the thirty metre-wide flood required strength and clear thinking. The damned panic!...
Where the *WIKING*'s units reached the Gniloi Tikitsch General Gille chose more rational measures. He stood on the bank in a short fur jacket with his knotty walking stick. 4,500 men, 70% of the Division, had come this way. He did not want to see them suffer heavy losses now. He had the last tractor drive into the river. It was to serve as a sort of support for an emergency bridge. But the current tore it away. *panje* wagons which were pushed into the river were likewise swept away by the gurgling water.
Then Gille singled out the non-swimmers. Chains of swimmers and non-swimmers alternately were formed. The General himself led the first chain into the water. But halfway across the river the third man let go. The living bridge broke apart. Shrill curses. Cries. The non-swimmers were carried helplessly away by the current. General Gille's Ia, Obersturmbannführer Schönfelder, admonished the men. A new attempt. But this also resulted in too many drowned.
Hauptsturmführer Dorr arrived with the rearguard. On boards and poles they dragged the last surviving wounded from the column through the snow. Dorr's Grenadiere, together with a group from 14. Panzerdivision which had broken into the pocket, had provided protection for the column of wounded. *WIKING* had suffered its highest losses of the breakout defending against the murderous tank attacks on this column.
And that group at the river? What did they intend to do? It is the Belgians of the *WALLONIEN* Brigade. They have brought the body of their fallen commander, Oberstleutnant Lippert, on a *panje* wagon with the wounded. After the column was shot up by the Soviet tanks, four men carried the dead man with them. He

would not fall into Russian hands. The four men swam across the river with the body wrapped in a tent sheet. On the other side they dragged him through the snow up the icy bank until they reached the security of III. Panzerkorps' lines.

Gille's 1st Orderly Officer, Hauptsturmführer Westphal, now tried to bring the last Panzer III across the river. But the attempt failed. Westphal had to swim the Gniloi Tikitsch too."[5]

Once again, on 16. and 17. February, III. Panzerkorps had tried to ease the situation of the men surrounded in the pocket. The Bäke Heavy Panzer Regiment was sent into action from Chishinzy toward Dshurshenzy. It made little headway but at least it tied down the enemy tanks. On the night of 16./17. February, two Pz.Gren. battalions of 1. SS-Pz.Div. *LAH* from Oktjabr assaulted the enemy blockade ring which separated the encircled from the rescuers. In vain! And too late. The battalions were halted before Hill 239 with bloody losses.

General Stemmermann, commanding the breakout forces, fell—contrary to the libellous statements made later—near Potschapinzy. He and his staff were killed by antitank fire.

Yet almost 70% of the soldiers entrusted to him were saved despite the difficult situation. More than 34,000 men reached the safety of the western bank of the Gniloi Tikitsch including the rearguard and 57. and 88. Inf.Div.'s which had found an emergency bridge near Lissjanka. However, 20,000 in one day remained on the battlefield, drowned, fallen exhausted or wounded into the hands of the Russians. Only a handfull survived Russian captivity. The enemy's promised "passes" once more proved to be shameless lies.[6]

An interesting document[7], a radio intercept by the "Deutsches Nachrichtenbüro" for the information of the Führer Headquarters on 18. 2. 1944, quotes a Soviet special bulletin of the same day. The reader, knowing the facts of the events in and around the Tscherkassy pocket, may form his own opinion as to what extent this Soviet disclosure corresponds to the truth.

Since the performance of a unit is nothing other than the sum of the performances of all of its soldiers down to the last Panzergrenadier, it seems appropriate to recall the individual accomplishments of an SS-Oberscharführer in those days. They are typical of many similar performances by the men, NCO's and officers in the Tscherkassy pocket and in addition are convincing proof of the spirit and attitudes which animated these men:

"On 13. 2. 1944, SS-Oscha. Fiebelkorn destroyed 3 T-34s during a tank battle. On the following day, powerful tank forces repeated the attacks on Novo Buda, during which the Kampfgruppe which Fiebelkorn was assigned to under the command of the then SS-Ustuf. Schumacher, destroyed a further 11 T-34's. During the course of the fighting, Panzer 112, commanded by SS- Oscha. Fiebelkorn, received a hit in the motor compartment and immediately began to burn. As they abandoned the Panzer, all of the crewmembers were wounded. Fiebelkorn, last to leave the Panzer, broke an ankle jumping from the tank. The crew forced their way through to the battalion command post and were sent that evening to the unit medical officer with the supply vehicles.

As the dressing stations could accept no more wounded, the company's wounded men stayed with the battalion. Each unit was responsible for evacuating its own wounded from the pocket. After the Panzers and infantry had set out, an 18 ton tractor with three machine gun crews drove slowly behind the combat forces as protection for the wounded. Following it were three tractors carrying the wounded and the train of other vehicles. After approximately 7 km., the tractor in which the commander and Oscha. Fiebelkorn were riding was struck by two antitank rounds forward on the right side. The commander was killed and most of the wounded received additional wounds. After the firing diminished, the wounded were loaded onto *panje* wagons and the march continued. They reached the first wooded area southeast of Dshurshenzy. As the leading Panzers reached the edge of the wood they suddenly came under flanking fire from the hill from 14 T-34's. In the course of the ensuing tank fight the enemy tanks withdrew. Fiebelkorn lay under cover in the wood. I got him a vehicle with a driver and four horses and asked Fiebelkorn to get through on his own. I said to him that we had almost reached our goal. After I had got him the team he drove on about 1 km. farther. There the driver simply left him standing and attempted to get through the heavy defensive fire alone.

Fiebelkorn called for help and was lifted from the vehicle by an unknown SS-Sturmbannführer. Just as he got down, the vehicle received a direct hit and was blown to pieces. Fiebelkorn crawled into the cover of a hole and lay there for several hours. He asked passing comrades to take him with them but none were in the position to do so. With sunrise Fiebelkorn worked his way farther forward. He encountered two more wounded soldiers who he took with him.

In the morning hours of 18. February, Fiebelkorn realized that he had gone astray and found himself in the enemy positions. Since the large snowdrifts offered the possibility of them not being seen, the men dug into the snow and again waited for darkness. When the time came and they could break out, Fiebelkorn cheered up his two comrades and they crawled farther forward. Shortly thereafter, one of the wounded men died. Moments later the other died as well. Fiebelkorn crawled on alone and summoning the last of his strength reached a German outpost position.

In addition to the injuries he had received, Fiebelkorn froze both feet, both hands and his right knee. After reaching the German lines he lost conciousness and did not regain it until he was being taken off the transport aircraft. When I visited him he said to me that only his ambition and firm will not to leave his family without support could have enabled him to bear this trial. All that he would allow his wife, who was at that time having their second child, to know of his condition was that he had escaped the pocket and his only injuries were to his right hand."[8]

After the *WIKING* Division had escaped the Cherkassy pocket, its remaining forces were assembled behind III. Pz.Korps' front west of Risino. All had barely escaped with their lives and whatever they carried with them; perhaps a haversack and at most a light weapon, rifle, submachine gun or pistol. That was all.

On 25. February began the departure by rail in the direction of Liegnitz. Scarcely had the remnants of the units settled into their makeshift accomodations when on 13. March their expectations that the majority of them would receive home leave for the first time in three years at the front, were, at least for the Germans, dashed. The entry on that date in I./SS-Pz.Rgt. 5's war diary read "Leave only for the Germanic volunteers and the wounded." Those who had already left on leave were stopped in Silesia on orders of the Führer and brought back to Lublin. Everything thus pointed toward renewed action for the depleted Division.

On 20. 2. 1944, Hitler had presented Generals Lieb and Gille and SS-Hstuf. Degrelle their decorations at the Führer Headquarters. Gille became the 47th soldier to receive the Swords and Oak Leaves to the Knight's Cross of the Iron Cross, General Lieb received the Oak Leaves and Degrelle the Knight's Cross. The latter was able to obtain 21 days home leave for the men of his Sturmbrigade.

On the morning of 2 April 1944, the *WALLONIEN* Brigade crossed the Dutch-Belgian border to present themselves to their countrymen for the first time. In the capital Brussels, a crowd of thousands gave them a joyful reception.[9]

An American leaflet which reported the end of the Cherkassy pocket referring to it as "Stalingrad number two". Among the ten German divisions which had allegedly been totally destroyed was SS-Panzer-Division *WIKING* as well as Sturmbrigade *WALLONIEN*. The caption on page 1 declares, "Ten German divisions uselessly sacrificed."

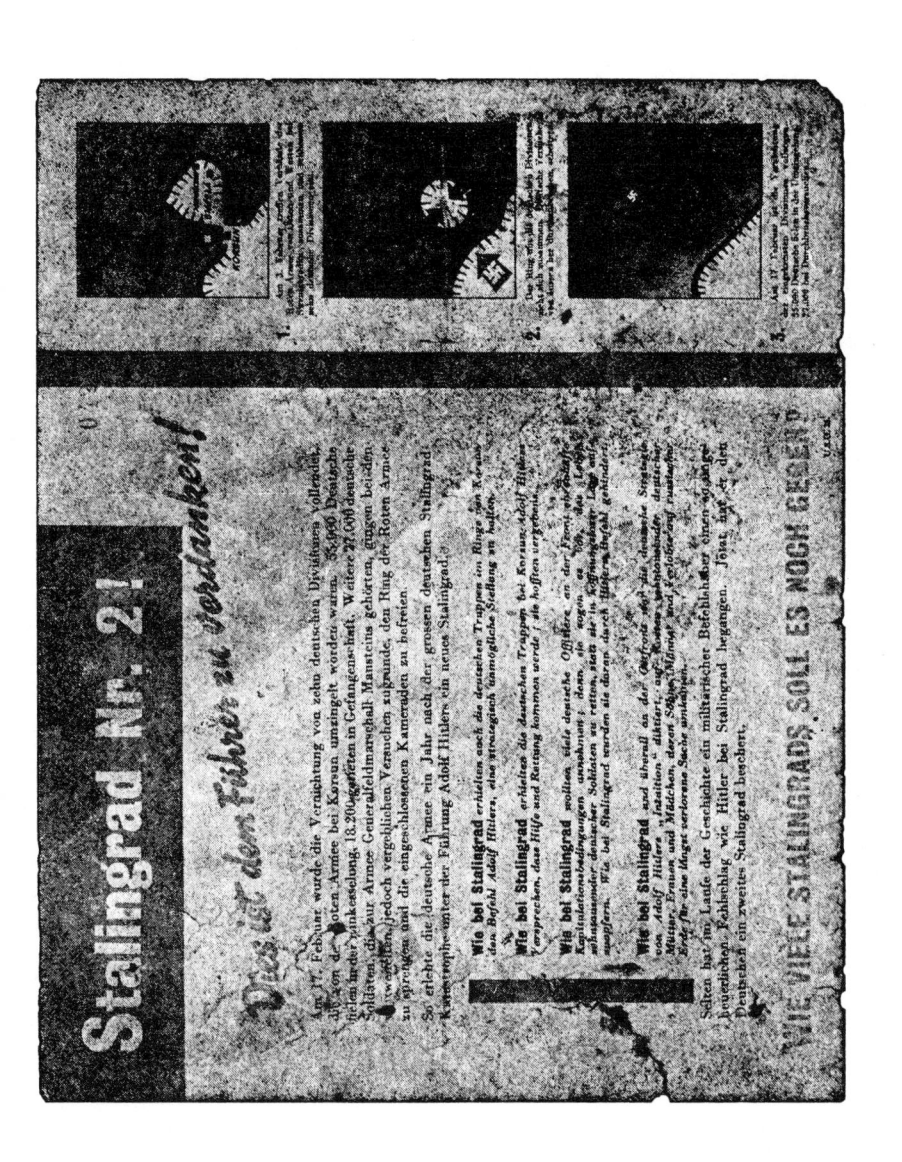

XI. "FORTRESS" KOVEL

At the end of February 1944, the WIKING Division, with the survivors who had been fortunate enough to escape the pocket, found itself in the area between Cholm and Lublin. There was to follow the rebuilding of the Division. New weapons, above all heavy weapons, vehicles and manpower replacements had not yet, arrived. Then a call from Führer Headquarters reached the Division command in Lublin on 12. March from the Waffen-SS Liason Officer, Gruppenführer Fegelein. The Division was to carry on with its rebuilding in Kovel, since it appeared advisable to place a strong garrison in this city which was located in the Pripet Marshes.

At the same time the Division Commander was ordered to proceed to Führer Headquarters to discuss the details. However, during the telephone conversation he made it quite clear that the Division still possessed no fighting capability. Other than small arms, they were lacking everything. They were also still below strength in men.

The Division O 1 was sent to Kovel to assess the accomodations possibilities there. He determined that barracks and factory buildings were suitable.

The garrison of Kovel consisted of 1 Regional Defence Rgt., SS-Kav.Rgt. 17, SS-Pol.Rgt. 17, 1 battalion of Pioniere, 1 battalion of light artillery with 6 guns, 1 light Flak detachment with 8 guns (2 cm.), 1 delousing unit, 1 care unit and 2 railway maintenance units with approximately 300 old railwaymen in blue uniforms. Total strength was between 4,000 and 4,500 men and the garrison's duties were originally seen as combatting partisans. The majority, however, were securing, against a further advance by the Soviets, a sector east of Kovel in the area of the Pripet marshes where a hole gaped in the German front. The enemy, however, did not attack this position.

Gille, who was still at FHQ, had meanwhile given instructions for preparations to begin for the transfer of the GERMANIA and WESTLAND Infantry Regiments to Kovel.

On 15. 3. 1944, Gille returned to Lublin where the first preparations were already underway. Transport had reported to the Warsaw transport commander and the necessary trains to Kovel requisitioned. During the night of 15. March, light machine guns and munitions were brought up from Warsaw.

Gille Flies to Kovel

On the morning of 16. March followed the loading of the GERMANIA and WESTLAND Regiments. Immediately afterward began their rail journey to Kovel. At midday, Gille, accompanied by his O 1, flew by Fieseler "Storch" from Lublin to Kovel.

East of Cholm Gille sighted the Division's train and circled in salute before continuing on to Kovel. They landed there as planned and set up the command post in Kovel's "square".

The continued story is taken from the personal notes of the Division's former O 1, SS-Hstuf. W. Westphal:

"At roughly midday I landed with General Gille in Kovel. We immediately went to the commander of Kovel's command post where we were received by his Ia, Oberstleutnant Reimpel, and briefed on the situation. Only three days had passed since my initial visit to the city but the situation there had changed tremendously. The securing forces to the east of Kovel had made contact with the enemy and in the face of superior forces had withdrawn slowly toward the edge of the city. They were pleased in Kovel to finally receive "reinforcement by a Panzerdivision." They did not realize that we were only several thousand inadequately armed men.

Following the briefing and after once more discussing the quarters for the individual units, I made my way to the station to receive the train which, according to the schedule, should arrive soon. But in spite of waiting no train arrived and the station manager was unable to obtain any information concerning its time of arrival.

Then finally I was called to the telephone and spoke with Dorr, the regimental commander of *GERMANIA*. Speaking by way of a railway telephone line from a train station he advised me that the transport train had been fired on by the Russians and that the train had halted. The *GERMANIA* Regiment had immediately attacked the enemy forces in order to reopen the rail line and enable the journey to continue.

For a long time this line which ran through territory occupied by the enemy was our only contact with the regiment. But it soon became apparent that armed only with rifles and machine guns it would be unable to overcome the enemy forces. Therefore the journey could not be continued. Meanwhile, *WESTLAND*'s transport train had also been beset by the enemy and the Regiment was in action. As evening fell we gradually realized that we were sitting in a city which was slowly but surely being surrounded on all sides by enemy forces. Reports from the units around Kovel also indicated that the Russians were pressing in from all sides. Four Russian rifle divisions, namely the 76th, 143rd, 184th and 320th, had been identified. On the following day, *GERMANIA* and *WESTLAND* mounted another attack and attempted once again to break through to Kovel. The Soviets surrounding the city had, however, become too strong.

In the evening came the order declaring Kovel a "fortified town" and Gille its commander."

The "fortress" was small, 2 km. long and 3 km. wide, but was protected all around by marshes through which led the few firm roads and rail lines into and through Kovel. Consequently, the city was an important road and rail junction in the Russian- Polish border area. SS-Obergruppenführer Gille requested assistance from the Luftwaffe, for without supply from the air a lengthy defence of the city would not be possible. On the following day Kampfgeschwader 55 in Demblin was given the assignment, which it carried out with great courage. Since landing in Kovel itself was impossible, supplies had to be dropped from the air. Until 7. April, Kampfgeschwader 55 dropped 270 tonnes of supplies in 255 missions despite powerful Soviet antiaircraft and fighter defences, thus carrying out the supplying of Kovel as planned. This great accomplishment was a tribute to the aircrews as soldiers and fliers.

In the "fortress" General Gille acted energetically and with circumspection in order to improve the "fortified town's" combat situation. He was assisted by his 1. General Staff Officer, Oberstleutnant i. G. Reimpel. As many men as possible were trained in combatting tanks at close range. The Pionier Battalion mined the approaches to the fortress and placed obstructions and field fortifications. The eastern edge of the city was developed into the bulwark of the defences. After several days of tireless effort the city's combat potential had been considerably increased. However, the persistant attacks on all fronts had considerably worn down the defenders. Two thousand wounded lay in the city's cellars, receiving only improvised care. To be sure, the commander radiated confidence wherever he went; however, he had doubts that the city could be held until relief arrived.

Naturally, the enemy did not remain inactive. On his part he made every effort to ensure that the "fortress" fell as quickly as possible. Powerful barricading forces to the north and west were to prevent any relief of the city. They were assisted by partisan units which were now deployed en masse, providing active support. They stopped rail traffic and blew the rail lines to Cholm and Brest-Litowsk. Bringing up the available relief forces was thus difficult and time consuming. From Cholm this was successful only under the protection of an armoured train and was slowed by the repairs needed to the blown sections of track. Immediately after crossing the bridge over the Bug at Cholm, the armoured train entered the partisan danger area. Here long sections of track had to be secured against the Pinsk marshes to the north. An Hungarian cavalry division was given the task but was insufficient and had to be reinforced by elements of the immobile Kampfgruppe Richter. Richter was commander of SS- Artl.Rgt. 5 of the *WIKING* Division.

Still the trains succeeded in reaching Luboml although rail movements were persistently harassed by attacks from low flying Soviet aircraft. On 21. March, several transports even reached as far as Maciejow where the forward elements of 131. Inf.Div. were unloaded. The new armoured III. Btl. of the SS-Pz.Gren.Rgt. *GERMANIA* which had just arrived from France and a Sturmgeschütz Battery from the following Sturmgeschützbrigade 190, were sent forward. From here on all arriving forces had to fight their way farther eastward. On 25. March, a powerful Kampfgruppe commanded by the commander of 131. Inf.Div. had assembled in Maciejow and was able to set out in the direction of Kovel. The armoured III./ *GERMANIA* drove strong enemy forces out of Tupalz. The following Kampfgruppe Naber with Gren.Rgt. 434, 131. Inf.Div. and the attached III./SS-*GERMANIA* with the Sturmgeschütz Battery set out immediately from there in the direction of Stare-Koszary and took possession of the town after heavy fighting with Soviet advance guards. The following Kampfgruppe Massell of the *WESTLAND* Regiment attacked toward the southeast with several of *WESTLAND*'s companies and SS-Flak Abt. 5 which was armed only with hand held weapons. They cleared the villages of Widuty and Milanowicze of enemy advance forces in order to take over security of Gruppe Weber's southern flank from 131. Inf.Division.

Ostuf. Nicolussi's Success

But time was pressing. Alarming reports came from Kovel. The Panzer AOK 4 therefore moved quickly and ordered an immediate attack with the forces available at the time. This began on 29. 3. 1944. The first unit to arrive in Maciejow was 8. Company of Panzerregiment 5. Its company chief was a daring officer who came from the South Tirol, SS-Ostuf. Karl Nicolussi-Leck, who had already proven himself as a Panzer leader in the Caucasus. His Panzer company was well trained and newly equipped with sixteen "*Panthers*". The company was well suited to lend support to the attack ordered against Kovel. Under the command of Oberst Naber, commander of Rgt. 434, the attack was to be carried out along the Cholm—Kovel rail line directly toward Kovel. In addition, the Nicolussi-Leck Panzer Company was to move directly toward Czerkasy, break through the antitank barrier on the hills to the west and push on as far as Czerkasy. The armoured battalion of the SS-Pz.Gren.Rgt. *GERMANIA* with 10 Sturmgeschütze under the command of SS-Stubaf. Hack was to accompany the attack while I./434 under Hauptmann Bolm with 7 Sturmgeschütze was to secure the northern flank through an attack toward the northern end of Czerkasy.

At 12.00 hours, preparations had advanced so well that deployment could begin. Oberst Naber had seconded approximately 30 volunteers from his regiment to SS-Ostuf. Nicolussi-Leck. They climbed aboard the *"Panthers"* and assumed the role of infantry support for the tanks.

At 14.30 hours, Nicolussi radioed: "Company standing on hill 600 metres west of Czerkasy. Enemy positions penetrated. Heavy snowdrifts. Will first clear the hill of the enemy and then continue the attack."

16.30 hours: "Involved in fighting for Czerkasy."

17.15 hours: "Czerkasy taken, will be cleared by infantry. 7 Pak, 4 guns, 300 prisoners. 8 tanks operational, 3 fallen out due to enemy fire, 5 stuck in the marsh."

Meanwhile, the surviving enemy infantry had evacuated Czerkasy. With approximately 1,000 men they retreated northward toward Moszczona pursued by 5 Panzers. But continuing the attack in the direction of Moszczona as ordered was unthinkable. Snowdrifts and approaching darkness as well as the orders of Oberst Naber held the Kampfgruppe in Czerkasy. After overcoming three antitank barriers and powerful infantry forces, Nicolussi- Leck did not wish to see this success slip from his hands. In an agreement with Hauptmann Bolm of I.R. 434, both officers decided to take advantage of the success and, disregarding the halt order, use the cover of the morning twilight to advance farther toward Kovel, especially since infantry reconnaissance had revealed the presence of weak enemy forces along the front. So at 04.00 hours the attack was resumed. Ostuf. Nicolussi-Leck takes up the narrative of the daring Panzer thrust toward the Kovel railway embankment, which surely must have been a coup de main unique in the history of the war:

"On 30. 3. 1944 at 03.00 hours, we had available 9 serviceable Panzers. With these I set out at 04.00 toward the embankmant deployed in the direction of the small woods right of the rail embankment behind the Panzers.

Two km. east of Czerkasy we took fire from 2 enemy tanks from the woods to the right of the embankment. After destruction of these, we lost 2 Panzers to mines during the advance to the vicinity of the Czerkasy station.

The infantry, which had remained behind during the firefight, reached the lead Panzers and set up a security screen around them which included the station area and the small wood to the east of it with the munitions dump right of the railroad. Enemy resistance was extremely weak.

At 06.00 hours the mine field was cleared by assault engineers. Hauptmann Bolm told me that he had orders to proceed no farther. I explained to him that we could halt no longer and immediately set off with mounted assault troops. I had ordered the 2 immobile Panzers under the command of SS-Oscha. Faas to proceed with repairs and at the same time to defend the Czerkasy station strongpoint and thus hold open the line for the following Panzers. In addition to this, Hauptmann Bolm placed a group of infantry at my disposal to provide close support for the Panzers.

When my armoured spearhead was within 2 km. of Kovel, I received the following radio message:

"Order from the Battalion commander, the Panzers are to halt." This message was brought to the commander of the rearmost Panzer by a messenger from Hauptmann Bolm and passed to me by radio. As my lead Panzer was already in action against enemy infantry and antitank rifle units which barred the city's northwest exit and shortly thereafter became involved in a heavy firefight with 10-12 Flak and artillery guns from the Kovel—Moszczona line, I could not possibly halt and therefore disregarded Hauptmann Bolm's message. Moreover, I was not subordinate to Bolm. Heavy snowdrifts temporarily eliminated the threat to the left flank and at the same time the barricading positions were broken through by the advanced Stecker strongpoint during which the escorting volunteer assault troops performed magnificently. We no longer had contact with Hauptmann Bolm's infantry. At approximately 07.30 we reached the railway loop and made contact with Hauptmann Stecker.

After fulfilling several requests in regard to combatting enemy forces from units defending in the northwest section of the city, I drove with 7 Panzers to Gille's command post and reported to the Gruppenführer."[1] With this daring coup de main Nicolussi-Leck had destroyed 16 antitank guns, 2-7.62 cm. Flak guns, 3 "Sherman" type tanks, approximately 30-40 antitank rifles, several mortars and light infantry weapons as well as service and supply vehicles. For this feat he received the Knight's Cross.

Quick as lightning the news of the successful breakthrough of 30. March spread through the pocket, reviving the spirits of the defenders who had become doubtful of rescue. The reinforcement by *"Panthers"* also contributed to the renewed optimism. Naturally no fundamental change in the situation was reached since the Soviets closed the ring around Kovel behind Nicolussi's Kampfgruppe and once again sealed off the city from the west.

The strongpoint which Nicolussi-Leck had left east of Czerkasy with two damaged Panzers and sixteen infantrymen of I.R.434 under the command of SS-Oscha. Faas, was now completely isolated and cut off. The armoured III./ *GERMANIA* and its Sturmgeschütze had been forced to veer off to the south as a result of heavy fire from the forest south of the Stare-Koszary—Kovel railway line. There it encountered superior enemy forces which had dug in on the northern edge of the forest zone southeast of Stare-Koszary and was only able to penetrate parts of the wood. The bulk of 131. I.D. was engaged in fighting in the southeast and northeast and the Bolm Battalion had halted in Czerkasy. Attempting to eliminate Faas' Panzers, the Russians fired with artillery, "Stalin Organs", and mortars. Russian infantry in battalion strength pressed ever closer to the defensive strongpoint which Faas had set up in the station buildings 2.5 km. southwest of Czerkasy. Fortunately, he at least had contact with 4 of the company's *"Panthers"* which were bogged down in a swamp four kilometres farther west. They had an army artillery observer with them so that Faas was able to request supporting artillery fire. But soon his situation had become so critical that the *WIKING* Division's Kampfgruppenführer, SS-Standartenführer Richter, decided to send 11. Company of SS-Pz.Gren.Rgt. *GERMANIA* under the command of SS-Hstuf. Treuker to help on the eve of 31. March. The Company successfully penetrated the enemy lines in the darkness and reached the Panzer strongpoint without signifigant losses.

But on the afternoon of 1. April, Treuker must have recognized that his Kampfgruppe was being squeezed into an ever-smaller area and could hold out only for a few more hours against the continuous attacks by several Russian battalions supported by heavy artillery fire. He received orders to break through to

SS-Panzer-Regiment 5 Kowel, den 15.4.1944
Ia / Kdr. / Eg.

Regiments - Tagesbefehl

Der Führer hat dem

SS-Obersturmführer Nicolussi-Leck,

Chef der 8. Kompanie das Ritterkreuz zum Eisernen Kreuz verliehen.
Dem SS-Obersturmführer Nicolussi-Leck ist aus eigenem Entschluss unter harten Bedingungen am 30.3.1944 der Durchbruch in die eingeschlossene Stadt Kowel gelungen.
Er hat der Besatzung die entscheidende Verstärkung gegeben. Er trägt mit seiner 8. Kompanie einen besonderen Anteil, an dem Aushalten der Besatzung.
Das Regiment ist stolz einen so verdienten, alten Angehörigen ausgezeichnet zu wissen.
Möge zu jeder Stunde dem SS-Obersturmführer Nicolussi-Leck das Soldatenglück zur Seite stehen.

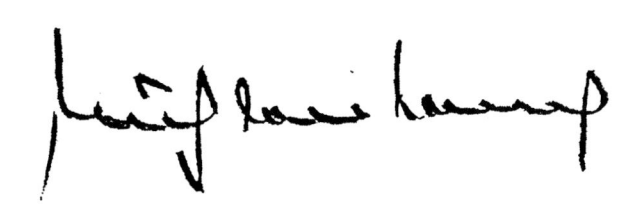

A copy of the Regimental Order of the Day commending *SS-Ostuf.* Nicolussi-Leck on the award of the Knight's Cross for his spectacular dash into Kovel.

Kovel on the following night. Treuker, however, decided to break out to the west. He was severely wounded but after blowing up the damaged Panzers brought his decimated company and Kampfgruppe Faas back to the German lines.

Things were also hot for Hauptmann Bolm in Czerkasy. The Russians also attacked here with a grim fury. Possession of the town changed hands several times until II./434, with the help of the newly arrived 7. Company of SS-Pz.Rgt. 5, retook it and decisively resolved the situation in the Germans' favour.

2. April was generally a critical day for the "relief forces". In the north and south of the narrow pipeline from Maciejow the enemy had gone over to the counterattack. In the north he stormed against Krasnoduby and in the south charged the hills southeast of Stare-Kosary, Milanowicze and Widuty in an effort to break the corridor. But he was repulsed everywhere. However, the newly arrived "Panther" company of SS-Pz.Rgt. 5 and the Sturmgeschütze of Sturmgeschützabteilung 190 had to be rushed from one hot spot to another in order to restore the situation.

It had long since become clear to the High Command that these forces would be unable to relieve Kovel. 131. I.D. was too weak and, even with the addition of Ski Battalion 2 and the Sturm-Btl. of A.O.K. 2, could not win decisively. Employment of the rest of WIKING without heavy weapons, vehicles or even field kitchens, whose artillery possessed no guns or tractors and would have had to fight on foot as would the remains of A.A. 5 and the Flakartillerie, could not be justified. Fortunately, at least the Staff of I. Battalion, the Regimental units and II. (Panther) Battalion of SS-Pz.Rgt. 5 were fully manned and equipped. Together with the armoured III./SS-GERMANIA they represented the total mobile forces of the bloodied Division. The fate of the "fortress" of Kovel would have looked bleak had not Heeresgruppe Mitte (Army Group Centre), which had been covering its deep southern flank and now had taken over responsibility for the city, taken decisive measures for its relief. In spite of concern for its own front, it deployed LVI. Pz.Korps under Generalleutnant Hossbach with 4. Pz.Div. under Generalleutnant von Saucken and 5. Pz.Div. under Generalleutnent Dekker into the area west of Kovel and gave orders that it should free the city. Until these forces could arrive, Kovel had to hold and the former "relief forces" so tie down the enemy that he could no longer continue his attack on Kovel as powerfully as before. These assignments were carried out with remarkable bravery. On 2. 4. 1944, the advance guard of 5. Pz.Div. reached the town of Smidyn (north of Milanowicze). On 3. April, the lead elements of 4. Pz.Div. arrived in Stare-Koszary. The attack was to begin on the morning of the 4th. There was already heavy fighting in Kovel.

Once again a brief description provided by the former Division O 1:

"Before us the defensive ring occupied around Kovel had been compressed more and more by the attacks of the superior enemy forces. Our command post lay so close behind the front lines that it could be reached even by enemy mortar fire.

The number of wounded was large and their accomodation posed a particular problem as most of the houses had no cellar. Providing medical care was also difficult since there were not enough doctors, bandages or medical supplies. One doctor was even flown in by supply glider.

Soon there were scarcely enough men to fill the defence ring. Companies now consisted of a few soldiers. Again and again enemy tanks succeeded in penetrating the city. The brave defenders knew that enemy infantry would follow the tanks. Several tanks stood near the command post for an hour until one was destroyed by a Panzerfaust and the other moved out of range. A third Russian tank in the city crashed from a bridge into a brook and the crew were made prisoners.

Again and again we marked on a map the position of the relief forces which were moving toward the city from the west, because we could calculate when the depleted garrison would no longer be able to hold Kovel against the continuous enemy attacks. However, no one became discouraged and everyone firmly believed that we would be relieved."

The Freeing of Kovel

At precisely 00.15 hours on 4. 4. 1944, the artillery bombardment began on the enemy positions preparatory to the large scale attack on Kovel. The attack would begin at 03.30 hours.

At that time a Kampfgruppe from 131. I.D. was to attack toward the east in order to cover the attack's flank to the south. It was to occupy the wooded area south and east of Czerkasy and reach the railroad embankment near Hp.Czerkasy.

The spearhead of the assault was 4. Panzer Division with the seconded Panzerkampfgruppe Mühlenkamp (commander of SS-Pz.Rgt. 5) which was to attack toward Moszczona and from there advance via Dubowa toward the northern edge of Kovel. Kampfgruppe Dorr with the rest of GERMANIA was to take the wood northwest of Czerkasy in the flank of 4. Pz.Div.'s attack and follow the ongoing advance. 5. Panzer Division would be employed from Smidyn against the Krühel—Szajno line in order to cover the attack from the north.

At 03.30 hours followed a heavier barrage on Nowe-Koszary by the massed artillery and an assault by Panzergrenadier Regiments 12 and 33. Koszary fell after heavy fighting. But the attack on Moszczona progressed slowly because 4. Pz.Div.'s Panzerregiment was too weak and WIKING Division's powerfully equipped II./Pz.Rgt. 5 had not yet arrived. Only after a heavy Stuka attack on the strongly-held wood south of Moszczona could the attack again move forward. At approximately 18.30 hours this town was also taken; after destroying 50 antitank guns Kampfgruppe Dorr with two Panzer companies was deployed via Nowe-Koszary toward Moszczona. With the now assembled Panzerkampfgruppe Mühlenkamp, it veered in the direction of the northwest and Kovel from where it reconnoitred to the southeast. The advance guard of 4. Pz.Div., the reinforced Pz.Gren.Rgt. 33, found itself on the Dubowa hills.

On the following day, the 5th of April, the attack was to be continued at dawn. For that purpose Generalleutnant von Saucken had ordered Panzerkampfgruppe Mühlenkamp to attack and take tha strongly-held line of hills south of Dubowa while Pz.Gren.Rgt. 33, with the help of 5. Pz.Div.'s Panzerregiment which would attack from the north, would capture the enemy-occupied town of Dubowa. With its flank and rear protected by 5. Pz. Div. it would then go to the attack on a broad front toward the northern edge of Kovel. The attack was a success and established the long strived for contact with the "fortress" of Kovel. On the eve of 5. April, a reconnaissance by Pz.Gren.Rgt. 33 had established temporary contact with the forward strongpoint of Pol.Rgt. Goltz of the fortress defences. In the course of 5. April a permanent linkup was made following 4. Pz.Div.'s attack.

At 03.15 hours the attack commenced. Two spearheads moved toward the southeast, Panzerkampfgruppe Mühlenkamp to the right with the hills 2 km. south

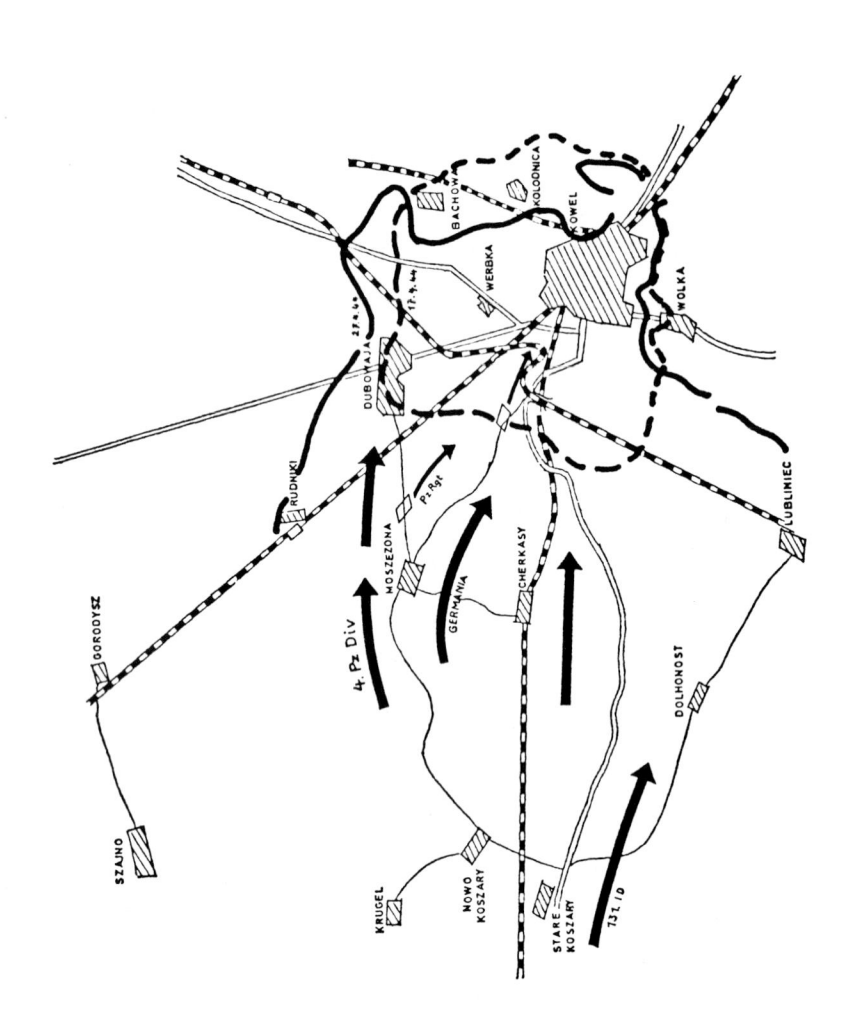

The relief attack on Kovel on 4./5. April 1944

of Dubowa as its target, and Pz.Gren.Rgt. 33 to the left toward "do Dubowej". The first goal was reached quickly after hard fighting. Now began the struggle against the enemy's outer bastion on the northern edge of Kovel which was studded with antitank guns. In a running firefight with a tank column to its right, Panzerkampfgruppe Mühlenkamp advanced toward the railroad loop northwest of the city with its left column moving along the Brest-Litowsk—Kovel rail line. In a bitter firefight, the antitank positions there were smashed while 4.Pz.Div.'s attack group penetrated from the north into the northern part of Kovel.

At 16.00 hours the breakthrough had succeeded[1] and a wide breach forced which on the following day enabled over 2,000 wounded to be evacuated to the east unmolested in the available tracked vehicles covered by 4. Pz.Division. Early in the afternoon, following the successful breakthrough, the leader of the relieving attack, Generalleutnant von Saucken, and SS- Ostubaf. Mühlenkamp arrived at Generalleutnant der Waffen-SS Gille's command post to discuss further action. Kovel was free but for the time being could only be reached from the north. So on the following day the enemy's barricade zones to the west and south were broken by individual attacks from Kovel.

On 6. 4. 1944, Kampfgruppe Dorr, which had advanced on the extreme western wing of 4. Pz.Div. and had penetrated into the northwest part of Kovel, attacked westward supported by 7. (*Panther*) Company of SS-Pz.Rgt. 5 and linked up with the leading elements of 131. Inf.Division.

On 10. April, the enemy was thrown back north of the Turja and Bachow, 6 km. northwest of Kovel, was captured. On the 12th an enemy tank attack from the east was beaten off by 4. Pz.Div. supported by a Panzerkampfgruppe from 6. Company SS-Pz.Rgt. 5. 15 enemy tanks were left on the battlefield. On 16. April, the enemy on the southwest edge of the pocket was smashed by Kampfgruppe Dorr and Pi.Btl. 50 supported by two *Panther* companies of SS-Pz.Rgt. 5. A fortified line was pushed from there to the southwestern edge of Kovel.

On 20. April, a report reached the *WIKING* Div. that its commander, SS-Gruppenführer Gille, had become the first General of the Waffen-SS to be awarded the Brillanten (Diamonds) to the Knight's Cross. After the conclusion of combat operations Gille flew to FHQ on 29. April to personally receive the decoration from Hitler.

On 24. April, the enemy south of Kovel on the hills near Lubliniec was attacked and driven back by Panzerkampfgruppe Mühlenkamp with the Regimental Staff of SS-Pz.Rgt.5, II. (*Panther*) Battalion Pz. 5, 5., 6., and 8. Companies plus the Pz.Pi.Company of Pz. 5, 2./Pz.Jäger Abtlg. 49 and II./434. In the course of the fighting, 51 antitank guns, 8 guns and 3 tanks were destroyed, the Turja reached approximately 10 km. south of Kovel and barricaded near Korodelec. Thus the defensive positions could be extended outward approximately 10 km. southeast and northwest of the city which was conclusively freed from its previously closed encirclement.

The Tank Battle of Maciejow[1]

While the *WIKING* Division was reforming and reequipping as a Panzerdivision at the Heidelager training grounds in Poland, its Panzer regiment, less I. Battalion but reinforced by III. (gep) *GERMANIA*, had been seconded to LVI. Panzerkorps. At the end of July 1944, it was standing by east of Kovel as the attack reserve and was preparing to take part in a counterattack by 4. Pz.Div., 26. I.D. and 342. I.D..

For the counterattack there were various options to be explored.
According to the situation, it had to be reckoned that in continuing their great offensive which had begun on 22. June 1944 and had been so successful against Heeresgruppe Mitte, the Soviets would launch an assault with powerful tank forces along the Kovel—Lublin rail line in order to take the Bug crossings. The assembly of forces in the forests around Kovel clearly pointed in this direction. Contrary to the popular view and the opinion of the Corps, the terrain northwest of Kovel in this season was not tank-proof. The Regiment's continuing reconnaissance revealed that the marshes were drying up more and more with the advance of summer and were becoming passable. The Commanding General, Generalleutnant Hoßbach, convinced himself personally of the accuracy of this assessment.

Therefore, the regimental commander, Obersturmbannführer Mühlenkamp, suggested that his Panzers be held under cover in the area around Maciejow so that an enemy tank attack north of the Kovel—Lublin rail line could be met and defeated.

However, before the necessary movements could be carried out, the Soviets launched a surprise attack on the afternoon of 6. July near Nove-Koszary with 17 tanks and mounted infantry. The following description of the attack was provided by the former Regimental Adjutant, Obersturmführer Lichte:

"Brilliant sunshine! We—the ordinance officer, Untersturmführer Jensen and I—had gone to pour a bucket of water over our heads to cool off. This ceremony was suddenly interrupted by an unusually heavy fighter-bomber attack. Wearing only bathing trunks we jumped into a foxhole in front of our burning command post.

In vain I cranked the field telephone we had brought with us. The lines to the companies were broken. The operations area lay under heavy artillery fire. Suddenly we heard the sound of an engine. "What idiot was driving around under this fire?" yelled Jensen. As we lifted our noses above the edge of the foxhole we saw 3 T-34's about 50 metres away. Luckily the commanders standing in the turrets were looking in the wrong direction. In a few bounds we reached our well-camouflaged Panzer which was nearby and destroyed 2 of the T-34's. The third was handled by the commander who appeared just at that moment. From this short range our shells had such an effect that all 3 tanks were blown to pieces."

In a short time this Soviet thrust, obviously an armed reconnaissance, was beaten back. The bulk of the Kampfgruppe carried out the change of positions as ordered by Corps. The regimental command post itself was transferred first to Tupaly and finally to the eastern part of Biliczy.

The enemy had surely not recognized the German tank concentrations near Maciejow when under a massive umbrella of fighter bomber attacks he launched a massive attack with several hundred tanks north of the village in an east-west direction. The Panzer crews—the commanders in their turrets, the gunners at their sights, the loaders, drivers and radio operators—could not believe their eyes when they saw the dust-shrouded steel armada drive out of the horizon like a steamroller crushing everything in its path.

The companies stood ready in their partially-covered and well-camouflaged positions so that they were able to bring concentrated fire to bear with the assurance of getting a hit. Detached from them was Obersturmführer Olin who had driven into position with several *Panthers*. This daring Finnish officer who had not returned home with his comrades of the Finnish Battalion had the assignment to

Advancing infantry
during the defensive
battles between Kharkov
and the Dnepr
on 16. August 1943.

A direct hit
by the Herzog gun
during the tank battle
near Kolchos Stalinsk
on 12. 7. 1943.

Reinforcements arrive.

Breakout from the Cherkassy pocket.

17. February 1944:
The march to freedom.

8. 2. 1944:
Goroditsche—Korsun:
vehicles which became
stuck in the mud
had to be abandoned
as the single road
in the Cherkassy pocket
had to be kept open.

16. 2. 1944:
Schanderowka.
Final preparations
for the
breakout attempt.

17. 2. 1944:
The goal is nearly reached.
Only a few were fortunate
enough to cross
the Gniloi-Tikitsch
in this manner.

Comrades of the Army and Waffen-SS

A downed German airman in the Cherkassy pocket.

Relief attack on Kovel early 1944.

Waiting for the order
"Mount up!"

Armoured
personnel carriers
of III./*GERMANIA*
on the attack
east of Warsaw.

On the attack
summer 1944.

In the trenches at Zegrce.

September 1944: Position on the Narew.

July 1944 before Warsaw: Danish volunteers prepare for a counterattack.

Machine and creature
in the mud.

Panthers
and armoured personnel
carriers advance
summer 1944.

Artillery firing position
summer 1944.

"Prepare to attack!"

July 1944: Infantry in the attack on Siedlece.

An die Führer, Unterführer und SS-Männer der SS-Pz.-Division „Wiking"

Soldaten des Todes!

Schaut Euch um! Ihr gehört zu einem Haufen, dem aus der jüngsten Vergangenheit nur die Nummer noch geblieben ist.
Ihr gehört zu einer Totendivision!
Die Zahl Eurer Toten ist um das mehrfache größer als die der Lebenden.

Euer Kampfgefährte, Euer Führer ist der Tod!

Die eigentliche Wiking-Division wurde im Februar in dem Kessel von Korsun (westlich Tscherkassy) vernichtet. Tausende Eurer jungen Kameraden fielen im sinnlosen Kampf, betrogen durch Hitlers Entsatzversprechungen, verraten von ihren Führern. Der Kommandeur der Wiking-Division, der Gruppenführer G i l l e, sein Ia Obersturmbannführer S c h ö n f e l d e r und Ic Hauptsturmführer M a i n - K u h n flohen mit einem «Fiesiler Storch» aus dem Kessel, nachdem sie ihre Soldaten verräterisch dem Untergang preisgegeben hatten.

Ihr meint, sie kamen vor das Kriegsgericht als Feiglinge und Verräter? So seht Ihr aus! Gille, der Mörder und Verräter seiner Soldaten, erhielt die Schwerter zum Eichenlaub des Ritterkreuzes. Auch die anderen Lumpen wurden ausgezeichnet.

Dafür sorgte Hitler — Hitler, der diesen verbrecherischen Krieg vom Zaun gebrochen, Hitler, der Jahr für Jahr Euch mit Siegesversprechungen und von Größenwahn überschäumenden Reden betrogen und verhetzt hat, Hitler, der Millionen deutscher Männer seinen wahnwitzigen Eroberungsplänen opferte, Hitler, der diesen nunmehr vollkommen aussichtslosen, verlorenen Krieg bewußt verlängert und Euch und Eure Heimat ins Verderben mitschleppt, nur um seine und seiner Mordgesellen Galgenfrist in die Länge zu ziehen.

Eben zu diesen Mordgesellen Hitlers, die auf Kosten Eures Blutes durch Euren sinnlosen Tod ihren eigenen unvermeidlichen Niedergang zu vertagen suchen, gehören auch Eure Kommandeure. Sie haben Tausende Eurer Kameraden im Kessel von Korsun gemein betrogen, verraten und dem Tode preisgegeben. Jetzt führen sie auch Euch in den Tod

Auch Euch betrügen sie, auch Euch werden
sie ebenso verraten, wenn es brenzlich wird!
Und darauf braucht Ihr nicht mehr lange zu warten.

Eure Tage sind gezählt!

Hier in den Wäldern und Sümpfen Wolhyniens wird Euch dasselbe schonungslose Schicksal ereilen, das Eure Kameraden am Dnjepr heimgesucht hat.

Hitler hetzt Euch in den Tod —
Eure Heimat, Eure Lieben brauchen Euer Leben!

Das haben bereits die besten, die vernünftigsten aus Eur r Mitte begriffen. So z. B. der Bataillonsführer SS-Hauptsturmführer Kurt Schröder (II./Rgt. »Germania«) rettete das Leben einigen hunderten SS-Männer, indem er rechtzeitig die Waffen strecken ließ und auf die Bedingungen einer ehrenvollen Kapitulation einging. Hunderte Verwundeter SS-Männer rettete vor dem durch Gille befohlenen Selbstmord der SS-Hauptsturmführer Dr. Walter Milsch (SS AA/5, SS PD »Wiking«) Er und seine Patienten befinden sich jetzt wohlaufgehoben in russischen Lazaretten.

Eure Kameraden in russischer Kriegsgefangenschaft rufen Euch auf, ihrem Beispiel zu folgen.

Eure toten Kameraden mahnen Euch:

Sterbet nicht für den Massenbetrüger und Mörder Hitler!

Sterbet nicht für die erlängerung seiner Galgenfrist.
Lebet für Deutschlands friedliche
Zukunft, lebet für Eure Lieben!

Darum rettet Euer Leben um jeden Preis!

Fliehet aus dem todgeweihten Hitlerheer oder gebt Euch gefangen!

Dieses Flugblatt gilt als Passierschein für deutsche Soldaten und Offiziere, die sich der Roten Armee gefangengeben.
Эта листовка служит пропуском для немецких
солдат и офицеров, сдающихся в плен Красной Армии.

A Soviet leaflet with "pass" for members of the WIKING Division which was dropped over the northwest Ukraine. The success of this action was nil since the claim made in the leaflet that Gille and his staff had fled the Cherkassy pocket by "Storch" and other claims were recognized as lies. The contents of one such Soviet "pass" are contained in Document Appendix No. 31.

open fire first and draw the enemy's attention. Cold-bloodedly Olin first allowed 10 enemy tanks to drive past and then knocked-out the first, the last, and eventually the rest. As expected, the Soviet tanks oriented themselves in the wrong direction and, strung out in a long formation, presented their full broadside to the German guns. "Open fire!" Soon after the first barrage nearly 50 Soviet tanks were destroyed. Everywhere were burning steel hulks and smouldering wreckage! One armour-piercing shell after another left the barrels of the *Panthers*'s guns. The duel lasted half an hour and ended a battle in which 103 Soviet tanks were hit and destroyed. Taking into account the damaged vehicles, the number of enemy tanks put out of action was significantly higher. Naturally some German tanks were also hit but amazingly none were total losses. Captured documents confirmed the German speculation. The goal of the Soviet tank concentration had been the rail bridge over the Bug west of Luboml, over which a bridgehead was to have been established. The decisive action by the flexibly led Panzerkampfgruppe from the *WIKING* Division had brought an important Soviet operation to ruin.

The German public learned of this exceptional defensive success in the Wehrmacht report of 11. 7. 1944:

"In the Kovel area, troops of the Army and Waffen-SS in four days of heavy defensive fighting against an assault by 10 soviet rifle divisions, 1 tank corps and 2 tank brigades have beaten off the attack and caused the enemy considerable losses in men and material. In this fighting, 295 enemy tanks were destroyed before the front and in the rear by the combined efforts of all weapons. The Rhine-Mosel 342. I.D. under the command of Generalmajor Nickel, the Rhine-Westphalian 26. I.D. under the command of Oberst Frommberger and a Kampfgruppe from 5. SS-Pz.Div. WIKING commanded by SS- Standartenführer Mühlenkamp have distinguished themselves through their exemplary steadfastness."

The commander of SS-Pz.Rgt. 5, SS-Standartenführer Mühlenkamp, was awarded the Eichenlaub (Oak Leaves) to the Knight's Cross of the Iron Cross.

Also noteworthy was the steadfastness of 5. and 6. Companies. SS-Oscha. Alfred Grossrock, platoon leader in 6. Company, and his platoon alone destroyed 26 enemy tanks. Grossrock was awarded the Knight's Cross.

After this tank battle in which the Russians had attempted to employ Guderian's tactics while Mühlenkamp had employed his Panzers as a mobile antitank front, II./SS-Pz.Rgt. 5 was pulled out of 4. Pz.Armee's front. The Battalion drove north to join its Division which was to be thrown against the enemy forces near Bialystok which had broken out of the Polish interior.

XII. FROM BIALYSTOK TO WARSAW

By 22. July, the Soviets had already reached the Bug near Cholm and established themselves on the west bank. They pressed forward quickly toward the Vistula. By the end of July, the German Heeresgruppe Mitte found itself in complete disintegration. The Armee's front was broken, its remnants streaming irresistably toward the west. Elements of 3. Panzerarmee were already in retreat through Lithuania toward the East Prussian border. 9. Armee had been smashed in the area of Bobruisk. 4. Armee's flank on the Beresina was threatened and individual Kampfgruppen were withdrawing westward. Powerful Russian units followed at their heels. Only 2. Armee on the southern wing was still combat capable and was carrying out a fighting withdrawal in the Pinsk—Slonim area. It was an unpleasant sum which Generalfeldmarschall Model, the new Commander-in-Chief, had to add up. He had just taken over command from his predecessor Feldmarschall Kleist in this desperate situation in order to unify this command with Heeresgruppe Ukraine. Of 38 divisions in the field, 28 had been smashed and the remnants of 8 divisions were in rapid retreat toward the west. 350,000 to 400,000 men wounded, killed or missing. A catastrophe on an almost unimaginable scale!

In this situation, after hastily completing its reequipping, 5. SS-Panzerdivision was rushed to Bialystok where it closed rapidly on the spearheads of the 2nd White Russian Front. Kampfgruppe Mühlenkamp with the Rgt. Staff and II. Battalion as well as the armoured Pz.Gren.Btl. III./SS-*GERMANIA* was the first unit to reach Bialystok but was immediately ordered back to Najnowka and first made contact with the enemy on 16. July near Bialowice. But the danger was greater to the rest of 9. Armee north of the Bialowice forest. The Kampfgruppe was immediately diverted there, the Division sent to Wysokie-Litewski and ordered to immediately disembark from the trains and proceed east toward Kamieniec-Litewski and establish a bridgehead across the Lesna river. Powerful Russian units were so close to the Lesna on a broad front that it was feared that this vital sector could be lost in a few hours. Once again it came down to who would be quicker.

Once again it was the Division's Panzer units which were first in contact with the enemy. I. Battalion SS-Pz.Rgt. 5 under the command of SS-Hstuf. Säumenicht was able to engage the advancing enemy forces while still south of the Lesna and thus contain them north of Widomla so that it was able to take control of the road leading from the southeast. Violent but brief tank battles developed, but the enemy was so superior in numbers that the stronger II. Battalion which had just arrived with its *Panthers* was forced to take over the sector. I. Battalion was transferred to the area east of Kamieniec-Litewski during the night in order to attack eastward with the approaching I./SS- Pz.Gren.Rgt. *GERMANIA* and take the village of Topola.

On the afternoon of 18. July, the enemy was thrown back near Topola. A Russian attack on the wood south of the village was also beaten off. The establishment of the bridgehead had succeeded at the last minute.

Now I. Battalion could once more be pulled back to Kamieniec-Litewski since the situation at the bridgehead appeared secure. However, on the morning of 19. July, it had to move further north to the Klepacze area in order to make preparations for an attack to the east. The remnants of 7. I.D. which were securing the area had run into serious trouble when the enemy crossed the Lesna near Szyszowo with powerful forces and established their own bridgehead. I./SS-Pz.Gren.Rgt. *WESTLAND* and I./SS-Pz.Rgt. 5 were given orders to throw back the enemy forces which had crossed the river and to take Szyszowo. Following hurried preparations near Hulewicze, the infantry of Kampfgruppe Sitter (I./SS-WESTLAND) attacked at 16.00 hours following a heavy bombardment. I./Pz.Rgt. 5 under the command of SS-Ostuf. Schumacher was committed via Hills 156-162 for an enveloping attack. The Sturmgeschütz Battalion commanded by SS-Ustuf. Bauer provided covering fire and pinned down the enemy. By 16.30 hours Szyszowo was firmly in German hands. The Panzers spread out to the southeast. At approximately 20.30 hours the enemy, with powerful artillery support, attempted to retake the village. An attack east of the village by an enemy combat group of approximately 1,000 men was stopped by flanking fire from the Sturmgeschütze at close range and broken up with heavy Soviet casualties.

The Division's "Toughest Assignment"

Of the Division's "toughest assignment", reported the former Division O 1, SS-Ostuf. Günter Jahnke:[1]

"On 19. July, the bulk of the Division arrived in the Bialystok area, reuniting the Division with its armoured Gruppe already fighting here. The Division operations staff rushed to make contact with the local command headquarters. Since a Divisional Command Post had not yet been set up, I escorted the Ia, SS-Ostubaf. Schönfelder, to 2. Armee's headquarters where we reported to the Chief of Staff, Generalmajor von Tresckow, for a briefing. The briefing was so unique that I remember it well, especially since several days later von Tresckow was mentioned in connection with 20. July.

The Chief of Staff, von Tresckow, gave the following situation report:

The enemy, following a bombardment lasting several hours and of an intensity not previously experienced, has launched his anticipated offensive along a broad front employing massive infantry, tank and artillery forces. Initial reports indicate that he is concentrating his heavy artillery fire on headquarters and lines of communication near the HKL. All lines of communication—wire and radio have been completely disrupted. The first reports indicate large deep and wide penetrations. The enemy appears to be marching west on a wide front. All officers are on the way in order to explore the situation. At this time the situation is unclear as never before.

Ostubaf. Schönfelder and I looked at each other. We were certainly used to some things, but such an unclear and catastrophic situation....!

SS-Pz.Div. WIKING's assignment:

Armoured group once again attached. Division to clarify situation, establish contact with our own units, determine how far west the enemy has penetrated. Attack enemy forces, disrupt enemy supply lines, cause as much alarm among the enemy as possible, conduct mobile operations in all directions in order to gain as much time as possible until our own forces can regroup and take up new positions and until relief forces have arrived. Constant contact is to be maintained with Armee for which purpose a radio section has been made available. The assignment ended with the admonition:

"Stop the enemy! There are no more forces in the west! The way to the Reich is open!"

We had already received many remarkable assignments, but this was surely one of the most difficult and uncomfortable situations and the toughest assignment which the Division had been given. But the Division fulfilled this assignment as well. For weeks we drove to the east then to the west, attacking in every direction under heaven, breaking contact with the enemy in order to fall on his rear or flank a few hours later, made "horizontschleicher" [2] (literally horizon crawls), entered villages which the Russians had just left, drove for hours without seeing a single man and in the next moment were in the "prettiest" mixup". The enemy air force made things here very uncomfortable, attacking even single vehicles.

After several days we made contact with other of our units and quite slowly built a loose front again, that is one which was stable and firmly held, which first became practical before Warsaw."

While the Sturmgeschütze had been moved forward on 20. July for use by 7. Inf.Div. in the Kamieniec Litewski bridgehead, the tactical operations staff of I./SS-Pz.Rgt. 5 was transferred to Kol. Lisowosyce. At approximately 14.00 hours, orders reached the Regiment to move immediately toward the north with the objective of intercepting the enemy who was advancing from the northeast toward the southwest threatening supply bases as well as the Czeremcha-Wysokie supply rail line. Deploying immediately, I./Pz.Rgt. 5 reached the area west of Jasieniowka. Following the return of 4. Company from the bridgehead, I. Battalion marched to Bobrowka on 21. July as ordered, making contact there with *WESTLAND*'s 5. and 7. Companies. During the course of this day and 22. July, the units fought their way further west via Zubacze to Czeremcha. Here, on 24. July, they received the order according to which the Division, "today and tomorrow is to march to the west bank of the Bug for new employment north of Brest-Litowsk."

However, Kampfgruppe *WESTLAND*, consisting of the *WESTLAND* Regiment, I./SS-Pz.Rgt. 5 and I./SS-A.R. 5, which was waiting to be relieved by other units, was still expecting heavy fighting in and around Czeremcha. In the late afternoon of 25. July, the enemy attacked with 11 tanks and approximately 200 infantrymen, pushing into the village. Concentrated fire from the Headquarters Company's Vierlingsflak succeeded in stopping the enemy's attack. I./A.R. 5 poured in direct fire. In the late morning of the following day another attack was repulsed; later that evening orders were received for all units to immediately break off and march in the direction of Tokary.

On 2. August, the Division crossed the Bug near Slezany. But they had found no ford. Ostuf. Senghas, who covered the crossing with the remaining 6 Panzer IV and 2 Sturmgeschütze, was forced to blow up the combat vehicles.

In eventful battles the Division withdrew through Sarnaki- Losice-Mordy, Sokolow, Wengrow and Greblow farther to the west.

When the Division was roughly east of Wengrow, the Russian 2nd Tank Army advanced out of the area north of Lublin toward Warsaw. At the beginning of August, three Russian tank corps had broken through farther south and their spearheads had reached the area of Okuniew—Radzymin. The Division, which meanwhile stood on both sides of Stanislawowo, received orders on 5. August to employ its armoured group in order to encircle the Russian forces. From Praga were committed 19. Pz.Div. and the Fl. Pz. Div. *HERMANN GÖRING*. In fact they succeeded in encircling and destroying the bulk of the enemy forces there.

Running into the middle of this whirlwind of Russian breakthroughs was 3. SS-Pz.Div. *TOTENKOPF*, which had been brought up to the Eastern Front from the Rumanian theatre by train. After its arrival in the Siedlce area it was immediately moved into the Stanislawowo area so that both SS-Divisions could fight side by side.

Formation of IV. SS-Panzerkorps

At the same time, the formation of the IV. SS-Panzerkorps, whose General Command had already been set up in Germany, was announced. On 8. August, Commander in Chief Model's order reached the Division which stated that the Division was to assume the role of Corps Headquarters until 10. August at 12.00 hours, since the new Corps Headquarters was not yet operationally ready. On 12. August, a special Corps order announced what had been decreed since 20. July; the former commander of the *WIKING* Division, SS-Obergruppenführer and General der Waffen-SS Gille, had been given command of IV. SS-Pz.Korps which soon would include 3. SS-Pz.Div. *TOTENKOPF*. SS-Standartenführer Mühlenkamp was given command of 5. SS-Pz.Div. *WIKING*.

The former Division Ia, Manfred Schönfelder, remembers that multi-faceted order for creation of IV. SS-Pz.Korps which caused several headaches. The order was as follows:

"The *WIKING Panzerdivision* will withdraw unobtrusively from the fighting for Brest-Litowsk, advance immediately in a westerly direction toward Warsaw, screen its southern flank against the pursuing enemy forces, link up with the *TOTENKOPF* Panzerdivision presently assembled in the Siedlce area forming IV. Pz.Korps, cut off the enemy forces which have pushed into the Modlin area, prevent the arrival of further enemy reinforcements and destroy the enemy in cooperation with our units already fighting there.

At the same time the Division Command will take over command of the newly created Panzerkorps."

Schönfelder described how difficult it was at that time simply to make contact with its new neighbour:

"Our initial worry concerned our future partner, the *TOTENKOPF* Panzerdivision, and the swift establishment of contact with it. We knew nothing of its situation, other than what was contained in our orders. It could not have been rosy, since the Russian breakthrough must have caught them in the midst of assembly or unloading. Radio communication was not available. All that remained, therefore, was to conduct an armed reconnaissance toward Siedlce.

A happy situation—or could one better call it coincidence?—had changed all of this. Namely that the enemy had not destroyed all of the permanent field communications in an east- west direction so that they could be of use to him. Perhaps they were all destroyed except that single line which the signals men now succeeded in finding against hope. In any case it was like a gift from heaven when suddenly we could hear on the other end of the line the voice of *TOTENKOPF*'s commander, Generalmajor der Waffen-SS Becker. The discussion at this vital moment enabled the first communication to be made from a distance as well as the first joint action in the sense of the order. It was the moment of birth for IV. Panzerkorps. Soon afterward the two Divisions linked up."

The thus created new unit called itself IV. SS-Panzer-Korps. At first it was a Corps in name only since the apparatus necessary for the command of a Corps did not exist. The *WIKING* divisional command had at the same time to improvise the Corps command using its own resources. During the course of the battle up to the Vistula-Narew positions, the Corps Headquarters' personnel and material was brought up piece by piece after which it was in position to take over command of the continuously growing Corps.

On 10. August 1944, the *TOTENKOPF* Division was attached, the *WIKING* Division taken over by Staf. Mühlenkamp and the command post moved to Jaktory Castle, north of Radzymin. It was of vital importance to establish a new HKL which joined the forces to the right in the Praga bridgehead (73. I.D., I. Imp. Hungarian Cav. Div., 19. Pz.Div.) and XX. A.K. to the left.

The First Defensive Battle for Warsaw

On 18. August 1944, the Russians abruptly opened fire with a heavy barrage, such as the Division had never before experienced, by mortars and artillery on the Division's entire sector. Simultaneously, Russian forces went to the attack under the protection of a smokescreen with the main effort directed toward Jadwinin and the basin terrain northwest of Cicioly—Sulejow. The Russians succeeded in breaking through the HKL. As a result they were able to push two companies into the southern edge of Tluszcz. At the Tluszcz station they set up defensive positions. Further penetrationss were achieved with tanks and mounted infantry north of Sulejow and Wolka-Sulejowska. In close combat, however, the Soviets were thrown back with bloody losses. In the course of the fighting, 17 Russian tanks were destroyed. The *GERMANIA* Regiment's 5. and 6. Companies were overrun by enemy tanks. An immediate counterattack by German Panzers brought the Soviet attack to a halt.

More dangerous were the developments on the Division's left flank. Following a several hour long barrage early on the morning of 19. 8. 1944, the Soviet 8th Army successfully attacked XX. A.K. with tank forces. The breakthrough threatened *WIKING*'s left wing with envelopment. This was pulled back with a turn to the left so that the HKL now ran from the woods north of Wolka-Kezlowska to the north through Debinki along the rail line to Zabrodze.

On the following day, 20. July, enemy fighter-bomber attacks lasting an hour prepared the way for an attack by infantry and tanks. A tank battle ensued just east of the Radzymin—Wyszkow road near Trojany. Simultaneously the German lines were successfully pulled back to the southern edge of Fabianow. In the course of the day 20 enemy tanks were destroyed, 15 by II. Battalion and 5 by I. Battalion of SS-Pz.Rgt. 5. Heavy losses to the *WESTLAND* Regiment resulted in I. and II. Battalions being pulled together in order to create a hedgehog position around Kochowo—Laskow.

At 04.00 hours the Russians attacked Laskow and *WESTLAND* carried out a fighting withdrawal toward the high terrain of Slopsc. In spite of continuous attacks by Soviet fighter-bombers and fire from all heavy weapons, the Grenadiere held. In the evening the relief of the Division from the Slopsc—Malopole sector by 1,131. Brigade under Oberst Söth began. However, the enemy renewed his attacks on Karpin and Malopole. The battle surged back and forth and on 22. August Malopole changed hands three times. After three tank battles Malopole was in German hands in the evening.

The forces of the Soviet 8th Army had the support of 100 batteries in the last days' battles; on 24. August, a Soviet concentration with approximately 150 batteries was discovered. The HKL now ran in a north-south direction from the Bug to Malopole. On the right wing was 3. SS-Pz.Div. *TOTENKOPF*.

At 03.00 hours on 25. August, a heavy barrage by guns of all calibres began abruptly on the positions of 1,131 Brigade and the Soviets succeeded in achieving several penetrations. During the entire day the counterattacking 3. Company held

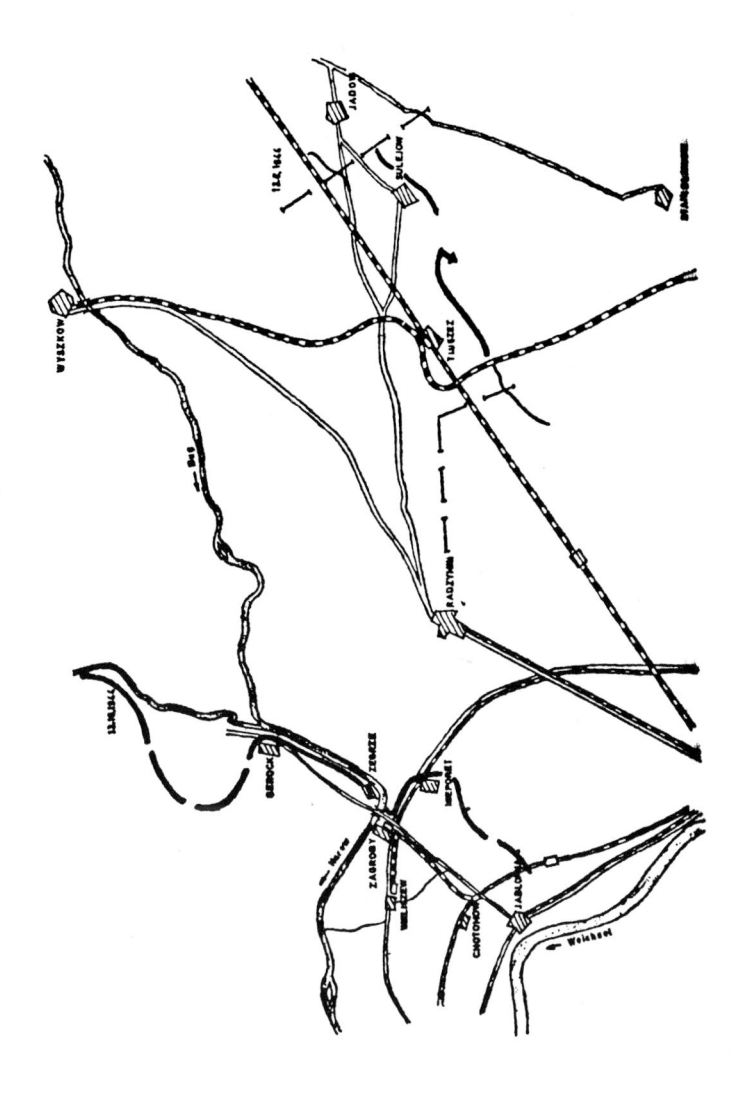

The 1st 3rd defensive battles for Warsaw Autumn Winter 1944

off enemy attacks on Hills 103 and 106 and in doing so provided support for I. Battalion 1,131 Brigade in a comradely fashion. At 19.00 hours a briefing with Oberst Söth took place during which the lines of the Slezany bridgehead were laid down as follows:

I./1,131 left shoulder following the Bug through the southern edge of the wood near Ignatow on the southern edge of Kowalicha, II. Battalion joining there through the southern edge of Ludwinow and from there back to the northeast as far as the wooded hills 1.5 km. north of Ludwinow.

After a five hour barrage, the enemy attacks on the right wing of the WIKING Division and the left wing of the TOTENKOPF Division were repulsed. Placed under the command of IV. SS-Panzerkorps were 73. Inf.Div. and the 1st Hungarian Honved Cavalry Division as well as the proven Ritter Battalion.

Therefore, on the evening of 25. August the Corps' defensive front stood from the unchanged bridgehead around Slezany to far to the northwest of Radzymin. In the south TOTENKOPF was northeast of Radzymin. In the early morning hours of 26. August, a reconnaissance patrol achieved a valuable success: it discovered that the Soviets planned to move out of Czarnow with tanks and advance toward the Bug bridge in an attempt to shake the bridgehead near Slezany. Two hours later enemy tanks advanced from Czarnow and succeeded in blowing up the bridge over the Bug when a shell scored a direct hit on a demolition charge. The premature destruction of the bridge had one other result. Since there was no ford within the bridgehead, I./SS-Pz.Rgt. 5 attacked west of Czarnow in an attempt to win a crossing over the river. However, since the terrain was "absolutely unsuitable for Panzers" the attack failed. Killed in the attack was Knight's Cross holder SS-Hstuf. Säumenicht. In spite of a defence to the last shell the bridgehead was lost. After stripping them of weapons and equipment, the men of I. Battalion blew up their 12 Panzers and Sturmgeschütze. They then left the bridgehead by scrambling across the wreckage of the 24 ton bridge. It was small consolation that the enemy had also suffered heavy casualties in the fight for the bridgehead. On 25. August, 8. Company alone succeeded in destroying 5 "Sherman" type tanks and T-34's and leaving 7 others immobile. Of these, 8 were credited to the commander, SS-Uscha. Tausend.

In the last days of August the fighting on the Corps' front died down. At the same time the first defensive battle for Warsaw ended on 30. August; two more were to come. On 27. August, the Corps was given command of 19. Panzerdivision. The Corps' sector now stretched from the Vistula near Zbytki as far north as the Bug east of Serock.

The Second Defensive Battle

The second defensive battle (31. Aug.—9, Oct 1944) began with heavy artillery and mortar fire on the sectors occupied by the GERMANIA and WESTLAND Regiments. The Soviets attempted to smash the German positions in the areas of Aleksandrow, Ciemne and south and west of Radzymin in order to force a breakthrough. They succeeded in penetrating into Cegielna. The situation in the north remained quiet. However, in the morning hours of 1. September the enemy covered WIKING's entire sector with heavy fire. Supported by fighter-bomber attacks and tanks, at approximately 10.00 hours the Soviets attacked Radzyminek and Slupno. II./WESTLAND, supported by several tanks, was able to offer little resistance to the attacking Soviets and was forced to retire to Point 104. In contrast, the Soviet attack toward Radzyminek had been repulsed after intense tank duels. At approximately 18.00 hours new fighting broke out around Wolka-Radzyminska and Slupno. Supported by 40 bombers, the enemy attempted to capture Point 104. However, every attack by the superior Soviet forces was beaten off. With heavy losses in infantry and the loss of 24 Sherman, Valentine, T-34, T-43 and KV-1 tanks, the Soviet attack was left standing before its own lines.

But the Russians stuck to their guns. After heavy preparatory fire on the entire Divisional sector lasting more than an hour, they resumed the attack at midnight on 2. 9. 1944. Near Borki the Soviets were repulsed a total of three times by the men of 73. Pz.Gren.Regiment. Not until noon on 3. September did the Soviets enter the eastern part of Borki. However, the Ritter Battalion attacked Borki at approximately 20.00 hours and threw the Soviets out. At 22.00 hours the village and positions were again in German hands.

On 3. September the Signals Battalion intercepted an interesting signal. According to the message, the Soviets intended to move via Ruda-Borki and Wolka-Radzyminska toward Nieporet. On 4. September, enemy infantry had occupied the woods north of Wolica and Wincentow as well as Dabrowa and Arciechowska-Opole. The Ritter Battalion and a company of A.A. 5 were immediately sent to the attack from the Myszniec-Wolica area in order to push the Soviets out of the woods, reach the arm of the Bug at Myszyniec-Wolica and occupy the positions there. The attack was carried out in three assault groups and made good progress. By approximately 11.00 hours, German Panzers were already northwest of Arciechow and pushing farther toward Dabrowa.

Battalion 560 under the command of Major Ritter also made good progress. By 12.00 hours Dabrowa, Radzyminska and Arciechowka were in German hands. The former HKL on the arm of the Bug was occupied by German infantry units. The attack's objectives had been reached.

But the success of 4. September was of little value. On the same day the enemy broke through near Wyskow with powerful forces and the main column marched from Wyskow in the direction of Ostenburg while secondary forces proceeded toward Serock. On orders from the Armee, the Sturmgeschütze left their duties securing the bridges near Jackowo and Popowo and set off to Wola- Mytowska. They were assigned to secure the area east of the village in the direction of Wyskow in conjunction with a Pakfront from 35. I.D. which was withdrawing toward the Wyskow—Serock road. For this reason Brigade Söth and all of the Division's security units were withdrawn from the northern bank of the Bug to prepared positions on the west bank of the Narew during the night of 4./5. September 1944. A bridgehead was established north of Serock near the 70 ton bridge.

However, the enemy had also successfully crossed the Narew approximately 11 km. north and had established his own bridgehead near Pogozelec with about 600 men. Despite strenous efforts by elements of the Division, Brigade 1,131, a battalion from Pz.Gren.Rgt. 1,007 and Pz.Gren.Rgt. 73 of 19. Pz.Div., they were unable to reduce the Soviet bridgehead. During the attack by Pz.Gren.Rgt. 73 north of Dzierzenin both battalion commanders were killed while leading their units.

The enemy's objective was to enlarge his bridgehead near Pogozelec to the north and west and above all to establish contact with his forces advancing near Serock. That meant that the *WIKING* Division's entire sector might be rolled up from north to south. On 7. September the Soviets registered a success: they successfully enlarged their bridgehead and 20 of their tanks broke through from north to south in the direction of Male. In the southern sector things were quiet at first; however, deployment of enemy artillery with approximately 180 batteries and numerous automatic weapons as well as accompanying infantry and tanks was detected opposite 73. Inf.Division. In the course of their loudspeaker propaganda, the Soviets urged the former Division Commander of 73. I.D., Generalleutnant Böhme, and his Ic to desert.

Deep Soviet penetrations in the following attacks on this sector obviously reinforced the military command's impression that this Division could no longer be looked on as reliable.

According to the war diary of SS-Pz. Rgt. 5 the German lines on 7. 9. 1944 ran as follows: "3 Pz. V from the *TOTENKOPF* SS-Pz.Rgt. secured north of Serock, north of Male 4 Pz. V and a Sturmgeschütz under the command of the Finnish SS-Ostuf. Olin, who on the previous day alone had destroyed 11 enemy tanks with his Panzer, and west of Debinki 3 Pz. V of the *TOTENKOPF* SS-Pz. Regiment. Our own security ran from Male through Budy—Ciepielinski—Piskoria to the north. The enemy position was given as: "The Division stands opposite the XX. Rifle Corps with the 55th Guards Rifle Division, the 20th Guards Rifle Division and the 7th Guards Rifle Division. The VIIth Guards Tank Corps had been badly battered in the previous month's fighting and had been pulled out at the beginning of September and transferred to the north. In its place the 28th Army was moved in from the north and deployed against IV. SS-Pz.Korps." On this day SS-Pz.Rgt. 5 issued a special order celebrating the destruction of its 500th enemy tank.[1]

In the following days the fighting swayed back and forth. 73. Inf.Div. was overrun east of Warsaw and routed. The enemy thus succeeded in achieving a larger breakthrough and penetrating to the city limits of Praga. On 14. September Praga was lost following bitter street fighting.

Through this altered situation southeast of Warsaw, on the same day at approximately 21.00 hours the HKL was taken back to the common line Serock—Zegrze—crossroad southwest of Nieporet—Aleksandrow. In this sector the *WIKING* Division lay opposite the Soviet 20th and 114th Rifle Corps with the 40th, 55th, 20th, 76th, 413th and 165th Rifle Divisions. Once again the Soviets remembered their partisan units. As revealed in intercepted Soviet communications, the bands in the forests south of Modlin were to be reinforced by parachutists and supplied with rations. In fact on 18. 9. 1944 120 Soviet bombers appeared shortly after 13.00 hours. A large portion of their supply drops missed their targets, however, falling into German hands in the Poniatow—Kaluszin—Krubin area.

Since 1. August 1944, an insurrection had raged in Warsaw under the command of Polish General Bor (Komorowski). The uprising had undoubtedly followed the hope that the Soviets, who had already advanced to the far side of the Vistula, would come to the aid of the Polish freedom fighters. Such a union would have presented a serious danger to the German front and the *WIKING* Division in particular. The Soviets had taken Praga at the beginning of September, but as everyone knows, they remained on the bank of the Vistula until the Polish uprising in Warsaw had been crushed. On 2. October, the surrounded Poles were forced to capitulate.[2] In these days and weeks it fell to the side of the western allies to support the uprising and local partisans through various operations. These consisted mostly of air drops of weapons, munitions and rations. Many of the drops went astray. From this time many of the Division's men carried American Colt sidearms.

The Third Defensive Battle.

On 9. 10. 1944, SS-Standartenführer Karl Ullrich was placed in command of the WIKING Division. The former commander of III./SS-Art. Rgt. 5, SS-Hstuf. Rudolf Pinscher, reported of this change of command:
"In October 1944, all of the Division's commanders were ordered to be at the WESTLAND Regiment's command post, which was located in Jablonna Legionovo, for 14.30 hours. I drove off at the appropriate time and with map in hand was just beginning to orientate myself in the terrain when an SPW roared past at high speed. We were just able to make out the Division pennant and several high ranking officers standing in the vehicle as it went past in a cloud of dust. This was the best possible signpost! We roared off in pursuit.

The SPW had scarcely stopped in front of WESTLAND's command post when all of the occupants jumped out and quickly disappeared into the house. I did not understand this behaviour at all but instinctively I also rushed to get into the house.

It had been the new commander, SS-Staf. Ullrich, who had roared past in such haste and to whom we were now to be presented. At the same time the situation was discussed.

The reason for his haste? While enroute the command vehicle had intercepted a radio communication, according to which, the Russians were planning a bombardment for 14.30 hours on Jablonna Legionovo, where until the previous day the Corps headquarters had been located.

The barrage began promptly. Everyone took cover and pressed tightly into the cellar of the house we waited for the firing to end. When Ivan was quiet again, the program proceded as planned. Despite his unusual entrance, Ullrich became a good, universally-popular commander."

SS-Standartenführer Ullrich was a veteran Pionier Commander and Regimental Commander with the TOTENKOPF SS- Division, where as senior officer he served for a time as assistant Division Commander. At this time the WIKING Division's new commander already wore the Knight's Cross with Oak Leaves.

Everything pointed to a new offensive by the Soviets. Field entrenching and increased patrol activity on both sides characterized the situation. Prisoners were required... Many indications led the Germans to believe that the Soviets were carrying out training in order to reinforce their units with members of the local population. On 29. September, the first enemy reconnaissance was observed, which from then on appeared daily. The nervousness increased. The sudden barrages by German and Soviet artillery became heavier. A definite focal point showed itself near III./WESTLAND. Enemy attacks were carried out in platoon strength which naturally achieved little result. The enemy was obviously feeling out the front. The battle and combat designations of the WIKING Division[2] placed the end of the second defensive battle for Warsaw (Zegrze) at 9.10.1944. On that day the Soviets screened the edge of the forest west of Pilawa with smoke. The coming day, 10.10.1944, was "Red Army Day". It was clear to the German command that this day would be a "proving day" for the enemy units. Therefore, an increased state of readiness was ordered for that day.

The WIKING Division was forced back in a desperate fighting withdrawal from the areas of Brest-Litowsk, Sokolow and Stanislawowo toward the Vistula. On 12. September, despite the fact that 19. Pz.Div. commanded by Gen.Ltn. Källner had distinguished itself in the defence of the Warsaw bridges, the Germans had been forced to give up the areas of the city of Warsaw-Praga lying east of the Vistula.

179

The IV. SS-Pz.Korps had occupied a new defensive position with its right wing on the canal north of Praga in the line Zegrze to the northern edge of Serock. Deployed from the right were 19. Pz.Div., *TOTENKOPF* SS-Pz.Division and the *WIKING* SS- Pz.Division. The Corps' neighbours were XXXXVII. Pz.Korps on the right and XX. Pz.Korps on the left. The 1st Imperial Hungarian Cavalry Division under Gen.Ltn. Ibranof, which had previously been under the Corps' command, had been pulled out for transfer to Hungary, 73. Inf.Div. had meanwhile been withdrawn for reorganization and the *HERMANN GÖRING* Parachute Division under Gen.Major Schmalz had been transferred to East Prussia in order to establish a Corps.

Even before the fighting of 25. September abated, German aerial reconnaissance revealed on the Siedlce—Kahiszyn—Novo-Minsk—Praga road surprisingly heavy motor vehicle traffic of several hundred vehicles per day which continued by night and day in the direction of Praga but whose run into the area east of Warsaw could not be clarified. The continuous flow of prisoners brought in confirmed that no weakening of the enemy infantry from withdrawal of units had resulted, since one after another the divisions of the Soviet 47th Army which had previously been in combat could be shown to have deployed in front of the right part of the Corps' front. A reconnaissance photo taken on 30. September revealed a total of approximately 165 batteries opposite the Corps' sector, the bulk of which stood opposite the right part of the sector. The arrangement of the Soviet artillery indicated a typical defensive depth of 10-12 kilometres. Particularly significant was the fact that the enemy's "Stalin Organ" rocket launchers had been placed in positions in the rear third of the enemy artillery zone. Due to range limitations their fire could reach the HKL but not into the German rear areas. From this organization it appeared that the Soviets above all wished to protect their artillery and headquarters from a surprise attack by German Panzers. German radio intelligence, which had broken new ground, particularly in the area of radio detection, and which followed the enemy from the front lines, had constructed a picture from signals traffic which also indicated a similar deployment in front of the Corps' right wing. From these peculiarities in the Soviet deployment arose the following assessment of the enemy's position at the end of September:
1. The enemy had not withdrawn any units,
2. he was bringing in a steady flow of men or material by motor transport,
3. no decisive postponement of his attack on Warsaw could be counted on for the time being,
4. the defensive organization, particularly of the artillery and army units, appeared to indicate that the expected new offensive was not imminent.

Besides, the military situation in the Warsaw uprising led the Germans to believe that the Soviets would make a renewed determined attempt to relieve the rebels after a landing operation south of the Warsaw Vistula bridges had failed to result in a decisive success.

This view of the Corps Headquarters, as the late Corps Commander, General der Waffen-SS Herbert Gille, recalled while imprisoned[4], was regularly reported to 9. Armee under its Commander in Chief General von Lüttwitz, but not shared by the A.O.K.. The Armee in contrast, thought the threat of a new attack, if at all, greater south of Warsaw and considering the weak forces there—even if behind a powerful natural barrier, much more dangerous. As a result of this contrasting assessment of the situation by the A.O.K.9 (Armee High Command - 9. Armee), 19. Pz.Div. was to be pulled out of the line and the radio intelligence platoon under the Corps' command was to be withdrawn for other duties.

Various discoveries concerning the enemy's position, among others those relating to the Soviet artillery deployment, concentration of patrol activity on the right wing and centre of the Division's sector, the arrival of two assault engineer brigades in the area of the opposing attack army and the presence of a large number of pontoons northeast of Praga, clearly indicated that a crossing of the Vistula was planned in the Division's sector. But more than anything it was the findings of an agent dropped in enemy territory at the end of September by the Ic/A.O. of A.O.K.9 in the Kahiszyn-Siedlce area which allowed the Corps Headquarters to make a new assessment of the Soviet's intentions on 6. October. The agent had discovered that the motor traffic was almost exclusively conveying artillery ammunition into the area north of Praga, while the continuous arrival of replacements was being accomplished on foot at night. The Corps' General Command's assessment was as follows:

The enemy intended to launch a new offensive in the Corps' sector. To this end he had assembled opposite its sector two to three armies with a total of 19-21 rifle divisions which had been reinforced by considerable artillery, mortar and Guards mortar units as well as by combat engineers and other army units. The grouping of the 47th Russian Army, which was preparing for the attack, with a strength of 12-14 rifle divisions and attendant units in a sector with a width of 10-12 kilometres between the canal north of Praga and the village of Aleksandrow, indicated the probable width of the attack. The enemy's preparations had reached such a stage that the Germans had to reckon that the attack could commence at any time. The attack's goal, according to the opinion of the Corps' Command, was not in the first place the reaching of the area of Nowy-Buda, but apparently the establishment of a bridgehead between Warsaw and Modlin with the object of linking up with the powerful partisan units in the forests south of Modlin, and with these enveloping Warsaw from the north and breaking through the German defensive front. The outlines of further operational objectives had not yet appeared at this point in time.

This judgement of the enemy situation—according to the records of General Gille—was reported on the evening of 6. October with the Ia-Daily Report by telephone and teletype to the A.O.K.9.. The Armee did not suscribe to the Corps' assessment, but on its part reported to Heeresgruppe that there were no indications of an imminent enemy offensive. That same night of 6./7. October 1944, it notified Heeresgruppe by teletype of its own assessment of the enemy situation, which differed from that given by the Corps Headquarters.

Considering the weakened condition of 3. SS-Pz.Div. *TOTENKOPF* and especially 5. SS-Pz.Div. *WIKING* following the just completed fighting withdrawal, the order to withdraw 19. Pz.Div., which would have necessitated covering a wider sector by both Divisions had to be challenged under all circumstances.

So in view of the anticipated enemy offensive it was suggested that:
1. 19. Pz.Div. be left in its present area of operations,
2. refrain from withdrawing the signals intelligence platoon and
3. immediately make available the ammunition necessary for the artillery defence against this attack.

Since tha A.O.K.9 did not agree with the Corps' assessment of the situation despite the detailed substantiation by telephone and teletype, the order for the withdrawal of 19. Pz.Div. was upheld and reissued. At least it ordered that the greater part of the Luftwaffe replacements, although untrained, would immediately be incorporated into the infantry divisions. The requests for deliveries of ammunition were declined. Following a discussion which took place at the Corps command post, the signals intelligence platoon was allowed to remain by the Corps Headquarters.

"For me", wrote General der Waffen-SS Gille, "the following situation resulted:
1. In my view there could be no doubt that the enemy offensive was imminent.
2. In the face of the enemy's superiority in artillery, infantry and probably tanks, any prospect of defending against the attack, if at all, would only be given if (a)there followed no weakening of our own fighting strength and (b)in the face of our own numerical inferiority, the weight of the defence could rest on the artillery, which would only have been possible with a correspondingly high allocation of ammunition,
3. As I had been unsuccessful in convincing A.O.K.9 of the correctness of my assessment, as I saw it a catastrophe in my Corps' sector would inevitably take place which would result in the loss of Warsaw, which again could not fail to have an effect on the overall situation on the Eastern Front."

In the following days and nights the enemy situation was again carefully reviewed. The clearing of minefields, the creation of new artillery positions, which had grown to approximately 230-240 batteries, as well as the decoding of a Soviet radio message gave new confirmation of the imminent attack which had to be expected for the morning of 9. October. General Gille and his Chief of Staff decided on smashing the enemy headquarters just before the attack. This could only be managed with the help of the German artillery which faced the unfavourable ratio of 42 German to 235 Soviet batteries. In three time-staggered barrages from the concentrated German artillery, enemy headquarters, artillery concentrations—in particular the automatic guns, and the infantry assembly areas were to be smashed to the extent which the ammunition situation permitted on the night before the attack commenced. The fixed fire plan had been worked out in advance by the Corps Headquarters on 8. October. On that evening, the divisions were informed of all of the details of the enemy situation and through a warning order were advised that an important artillery order was expected that night.

The three concentrated barrages apparently led to a postponement of the Soviet offensive. Statements by prisoners and especially radio intercepts appeared to confirm this. Intercepted radio communications from Soviet combat engineer units reporting their combat readiness once again allowed the new attack date of 10. October to be predetermined. Again the Corps' commanders decided to smash the Soviet attack with artillery before it began. As a result of the limited supply of artillery ammunition, however, the artillery action during the night of 9./10. October 1944 was carried out with a minimum expenditure of shells. A considerable weight of fire was directed on the infantry positions, in particular the last barrage just before the anticipated beginning of the attack. The results must again have been devastating as the Russian attack was once again postponed.

The Battles in the "Wet Triangle".

In the first and second defensive battles for Warsaw it was IV. SS-Pz.Korps with 5. SS-Pz.Div. *WIKING*, 3. SS-Pz.Div. *TOTENKOPF*, 19. Pz.Div. and other units such as the Söth Brigade and the Ritter Battalion which had prevented a Soviet breakthrough. In the period between 13. August and 9. October, the powerful Soviet assault forces were first intercepted in the area east of Radzymin and then brought to a standstill west of that city. At the conclusion of the fighting, the Division defended an HKL which ran south of Serock along the Narew, through the old Czarist fortress of Zegrze on the bend in the Narew, up to the eastern edge of Nieporet and farther in the same direction to the south.

All efforts were directed toward bringing the battered units back up to strength. In addition, the Division was sent replacements from the Luftwaffe. Many noncommissioned officers arrived this way. First, however, they had to be trained and become used to the stresses and harshness of the ground war. Unfortunately this had to take place in the front lines as individual units and elements could be relieved only for a short time for the purpose of training.

The following is a description by the former leader of Pz.Pi.Btl. 5, Hstuf. Eberhard Heder, of the fighting by the Division in the "wet triangle", in particular that of his unit in the Letniska forest:

"At the end of September 1944, the Battalion's 1. Company was employed as infantry on the Narew while the other two companies took advantage of their first opportunity to rest and refit. The armoured 3. Company had distinguished itself during the fighting for the Serock bridgehead, where it had repeatedly been employed in local counterattacks. During one such attack on 5. September, the company's brave chief, Obersturmführer Nemitz, had been killed in action.

The primary task of the Pionier battalion, with two construction battalions (including one foreign) under its command, in those days was to construct a second and third position on either side of the east-west flowing Narew.

On 30. 9. 1944, 2. Company had to be put to use as infantry and in addition was placed under the command of I./*GERMANIA* and Hstuf. Kruse in the Zegrze-Nieporet sector.

I had my hands full in order to find my way in my new assignment and to increase the Battalion's fighting strength in men and material as much as possible. But since the greater part of the Battalion was placed under other commands this did not go well.

Very soon, however, all of our plans were upset. On 10. October, a several-hour firestorm of all calibres destroyed the rustic peace in our village and announced the beginning of the third defensive battle for Warsaw. The focal point of the great offensive lay at first near our neighbouring division, 3. SS- Pz.Div. *TOTENKOPF*. Obviously the Vistula crossings and Modlin were the targets.

After the breakthrough attempt in the Legionowo area had failed, the Soviets concentrated their forces toward the northern sector of the so-called "wet triangle". The "triangle"'s base was the HKL and its sides the Vistula and the Narew/Bug which flowed by the mouth of the Bug near Nowy Dwor. On 12. October, following a mighty bombardment, the enemy succeeded in overrunning III./*WESTLAND*'s well-constructed positions which were in an arc around Nieporet and achieving a local breakthrough. This could not be straightened out as insufficient reserves were available. The enemy's superiority in men and material was too great. The order and principles of combat leadership left the Battalion nothing to do but claw in its positions and resist against the onrushing flood. Thus, under the command of SS-Stubaf. Nedderhof, the courageous battalion, just completely refitted, was smashed.

However, the sacrificial struggle by III./WESTLAND had a decisive effect on the further course of the defensive battle. It cost the Soviets so much of their strength that they were not in the position to exploit their local breakthrough and advance through Nieporet into the main defensive positions.

Still: How should the crisis be mastered? How was the new offensive expected on the following day to be met? Neither the WESTLAND Regiment commanding the sector nor the Division had reserves worth mentioning available. South of Zegrze gaped a hole in the HKL. The Regimental Commander, Sturmbannführer Hack, temporarily blocked off the area along the Zegrze-Legionowo rail line with all available units, mainly with those of the Regimental Headquarters. Amazingly he succeeded in holding his positions.

In this situation, on the evening of 12. 10. 1944, I received orders in the Division command post in the presence of the Commanding General of IV. SS-Pz.Korps, General der Waffen-SS Gille, to relieve the security forces along the mentioned rail line in the Letniska forest that same night and to defend this position. At any rate I did not have to carry this out with my own battalion but with an Alert Battalion which was being assembled at that moment from the remnants of WESTLAND's regimental units, supply service units and Flak-Abt. 5.

By about midnight three companies had been drawn up. Every one of the detailed officers and NCO's—if not every soldier, realized that a great deal was at stake and anticipating something of the threatening disaster, fought back doubt and despondency. How would this "lost crowd", who scarcely knew each other, cope with what was to come?

I set up the command post in the cellar of one of the houses of the forest settlements there, which was to be the basis of the defence. The building had previously been used by the Regimental Staff. One room was sufficient since there were only a few messengers and an ordnance officer to accomodate. There was no command organization, forward artillery observer, radio or teletype units, clerk and so on.

"You have enough experience at the front to know what lies ahead of you", explained the Rgt. Commander to me following the briefing. "I will do what I can to help you. But you must realize that I have no more reserves available."

The enemy continued his offensive at daybreak, opening with a one to two hour long preparatory barrage. Mercilessly the massed Soviet artillery thundered, countless mortar barrels spat, bombs from low flying aircraft bored into the sandy ground and H.E. shells from the Sherman tanks in front of us shattered the trunks and crowns of the pines. Certainly this event was no different than many others. I thought of the Sowjose Tawrowka near Walki, of the following battles of August and September 1943, of the actions north of Stanislawowo in August 1944. Would the men stand this? Must it simply be too much for them? Who would and who could help us? But how often in this war have we asked ourselves similar questions!

As expected, as the fire abated the enemy's infantry attack had begun, which already was under fire from our own artillery. The forward artillery officer I had been promised had not turned up. Amazing that our artillery could operate effectively without observed fire. But for this, the enemy attacks would not have been halted at the rail embankment or broken up in individual actions.

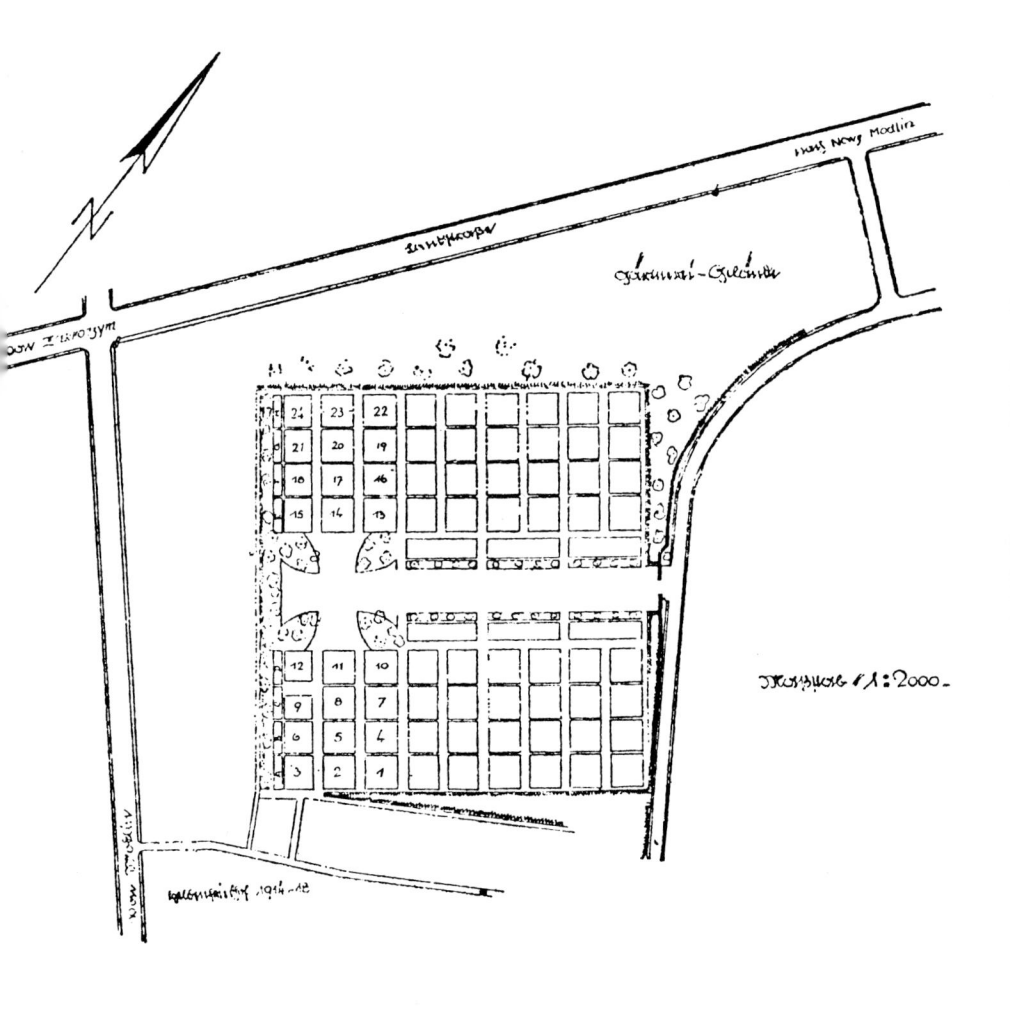

IV. SS-Pz.Korps cemetery at Modlin.

Very soon the Alert-Battalion's main line of resistance had been smashed, the coherence of the defence crumbled and the provisional unit disintegrated. Through the fighting spirit of the officers detailed as Company Commanders, all three of whom were inexperienced in combat, and thanks to the steadfastness of the few NCO's and men, it was possible to avoid the understandable panic, create some breathing room through local counterattacks and finally to hold the positions around the Battalion command post.

Again and again the enemy barrages fell on the Letniska forest, enemy aircraft repeated their attacks and the Soviets attempted to help their soldiers forward with concentrated fire from their heavy weapons. Individual units were probably able to win ground in the rear of the remaining positions of the Alert Battalion; he neither succeeded nor even attempted to advance into the centre.

A serious worry for me was the many severely wounded who filled the other rooms of the cellar and who received only very basic treatment from a first-aid man. They did not only have to deal with their severe pain, but also with the mental stress which was caused by the long futile wait for transport out of this inferno.

The enemy barred the way to the rear with his artillery fire so that supply was impossible, ambulances could not drive in, the forward artillery officer was forced to turn back and contact patrols could not reach us. The lines to Regiment were naturally broken immediately, with no possibility of restoration. An attempt to establish radio contact using the equipment in my SPW was unsuccessful. To the left and right existed only occasional contact. Once or twice a contact patrol from our neighbour to the left reached me—according to my memory, from I./ WESTLAND. It fought desperately for possession of the cemetary which stretched north to the Letniska forest. In these days the cemetary changed hands several times.

South of the forest II./WESTLAND under the command of SS-Stubaf. Walter Schmidt defended using the fortress works of Michalow. It was supported effectively by Panzer V's of II. Battalion Pz.Rgt. 5, whose actions also had a relieving effect on the fighting by the Alert Battalion. A special contribution to the defensive success of his battalion was made by the brave chief of 5. Company WESTLAND Rgt., Ostuf. Lotze. He destroyed 2 enemy tanks in close combat and distinguished himself in leading a counterattack in which he was killed.

By the evening, the combat forces in the Letniska forest had been worn down from approximately 400 men to something like 40 stalwarts. These defended in a hedgehog position around the command post.

Enemy in the rear! No contact with the rear and without support to the right and left! It will have to be handled on our own! So I decided to give up the position and try to find the way back to our own forces, in addition without issuing a warning order or hinting as to my plan. The Soviets had suffered heavy losses and were obviously not in the position to advance past our strongpoint during the night. So we could wait until about an hour before dawn before beginning the withdrawal. But first the severely wounded had to be transported out. In doing so a route of no more than 3-4 kilometres was covered when the Regimental command post was still located in its previous position. The transport was carried out by my SPW alone, which, thank God, was still operational. The unfortunate wounded had to be crammed into this. The plucky driver in fact succeeded in making three or four trips, and in spite of the dark night and fortunately undisturbed by the enemy, brought his comrades to the ambulance loading post. A splendid accomplishment!

Soon afterward the situation changed unexpectedly. The Regimental Commander appeared in the door of our cellar room. He was the first to make contact with us, while a large counterattack was in progress which had been launched with concentrated forces to win back the rail embankment. Until the morning of the following day the defence was reorganized in the old positions. Supporting the Battalion were Sturmgeschütze of I. Battalion Pz.Rgt. 5 under Ostuf. Wertz and an Untersturmführer with his radioman as Art.Rgt. 5's forward artillery observer.

As was to be expected, the Soviets continued their attack in unwavering uniformity, which they always prepared with concentrated artillery and mortar fire and mostly also with attacks by tactical aircraft in an effort to pave a way for the exhausted infantry. However, the Alert battalion was able to hold its barricading position in the Letniska forest for two further days. Decisive for this success was the mobile and effective action of the artillery. With help from the forward observer it always succeeded in placing its fire on the right place at the right time and through short barrages often smashed enemy attacks as they began.

The forest was totally unsuitable for the operation of Panzers. Here however, they provided the defence with powerful support. They destroyed Sherman tanks when they attempted to drive into the forest lanes, provided support with H.E. when lost positions had to be retaken or quite simply inspired fear and terror in the enemy.

On the third night of the action, the rest of the Alert Battalion was relieved by Hauptsturmführer Pleiner's II./*GERMANIA*, whereby the situation again stabilized. During the previous weeks this battalion had been employed in a comparatively quiet sector on the Narew north of Zegrze. Franz Pleiner had understood that his purpose there was to once again make his unit combat capable.

Taking into consideration the considerable shortcomings in respect to personnel and material, the "lost crowd", who were called the "Alert Battalion of the *WIKING* Division", had achieved a notable success. According to the writings of the Ic, in the period of 13.-15. October 1944, two enemy divisions supported by 24 tanks had attempted in vain to force a breakthrough in the Letniska forest sector.

I could now take a breather and finally got the opportunity to concern myself with my own Battalion. But how it looked! SS- Obersturmführer Julius Weck's 2. Company had been forced to suffer heavy losses near Nieporet-Wieliszew: nearly 20 dead, including Ustuf. Köpke, and approximately 50 wounded. As the Division's last reserve, 3. (armoured) Company had also been sent into action. At least now all companies had been relieved and once again reformed as a battalion.

Only two days later I was called again. I had to take command of II./*GERMANIA* in the Letniska forest since SS- Hauptsturmführer Pleiner had been wounded during a night counterattack. The Battalion had been severely weakened and had lost three company commanders in a short time. As ordered, on the following night I switched over to the second position which had been built in the Lajsk hills. With the Sturmgeschütze of SS- Ostuf. Chemnitz' Panzerjäger-Abt. 5, I left in the advance guard the Letniska forest which had been the scene of such bloody fighting.

The Soviets did not slacken their efforts, however, to yet force a breakthrough in the direction of Modlin. Again and again they went to the attack and always with heavy preparatory artillery fire which, nevertheless, was limited in duration and scope compared to the first day of the defensive battle. Only with the help of the well directed fire of the artillery and mortar batteries and the support of a company of II./Pz.Rgt. 5 was it possible to repulse these attacks or to clear up local penetrations. However, the fighting power of the battalion was reduced to such an extent that there was scarcely any infantry resistance to speak of. After the last company commander, the chief of 8. (heavy) Company, also fell out, there were no more officers on the field with the exception of an Oberjunker who was performing the duties of adjutant. Only a few NCO's had survived the last ten day's fighting. The comparatively large numbers of Luftwaffe replacements brought in by night brought little relief in this situation. They were untrained for infantry combat and naturally were not up to the psychological stresses of the ground war.

So the Regimental Commander decided to relieve the Battalion with I./ WESTLAND which had only just begun refitting. For its part, II./GERMANIA by no means received the opportunity to restore its fighting power. For the next few weeks it was employed in a comparatively quiet sector north of the Marem. There I was relieved once more."

The commander of Volksgrenadier-Rgt. 1,077, Major Kopp, who took over this unit on 12. 10. 1944, moved into a counterattack sector forward of Nassielsk against the Russian bridgehead at Serock. He remembers those days and weeks: "My neighbour to the right near Wola-Smolana was a regiment of the SS--WIKING. Although our heavy weapons were intact my infantry strength in the trenches was weak. The Russians continuously felt out the defences. In this situation, without great formality or calling on a higher service authority, my neighbour to the right handed over a Panzer company to strengthen the line. For Regiment 1,077 this meant that although the trenches were fully manned, it had only to occupy several strongpoints and thus after the long nights its men once again had the opportunity to sleep their fill.

Generally the defensive tactics used by WIKING at that time were very unconventional compared to those of a "classic" defence. The effect, however, was successful thus logical and by today's standards almost modern. Making use of favourable terrain, they occupied powerful strongpoints with mixed weapons, destroyed villages using available cellars and rear-sloping wooded areas. From these they carried out, with fire and movement, a very effective and mobile defence, which the Russians, who were at that time still unused to such tactics, could do little to oppose."[1]

In conclusion follows the description by the commander of the Heavy Flak Battery, Heinrich Grabner, of the action by his forces in the third defensive battle for Warsaw in October 1944:[2]

"In spite of previous heavy action, I received orders to secure the road to Modlin against Russian tank attack at a boundary position between two divisions in the area east of Modlin. In order to be able to carry out this assignment the battery was strengthened through the addition of a self-propelled light gun and two additional 8.8 cm. guns. The resulting Kampfgruppe possessed a total strength of five 8.8 cm. guns, three 2 cm. guns and three self-propelled 3.7 cm. guns. Together with the Battery Officer and the leader of the Light Flak Platoon, I reconnoitred the positions that night by moonlight since they had to be occupied before daylight. The heavy guns were set up on the eastern edge of Carolino and dug in as well as time allowed. Infantry protection for the heavy guns was provided by part of an infantry regiment from a Wehrmacht division. An attack by powerful Russian infantry and tank forces was expected for the next day. Shortly after dawn, the Russians began preparing for their attack with heavy artillery fire. Bombers and fighter-bombers were also employed. This preparatory bombardment, which we had to endure in our dugouts for about two hours, transformed the village into a burning, smoking heap of ruins. The first Soviet tanks appeared, accompanied by Russian infantry some of whom were riding in horse drawn *panje* wagons. Their appearance was a relief for us all because now the unbearable tension disappeared, which was necessary for everyone as we so often faced numerical superiority when holding our position. The Russian attack rolled slowly toward our positions. We made out approximately 30 to 35 T-34 and T-41 type tanks escorted by billowing dust clouds as they pressed forward across a flat field beside the road echeloned to the sides and rear. This iron colussus which approached us irresistably on a front of nearly a kilometre, and which with fire from individual tanks again and again forced us to take cover, had something of a steel irresistability about it which threatened to crush everything in its path. I had enjoined all gun commanders not to open fire until the tanks had reached the most favourable firing range of about 300 metres, because only through a surprise barrage from all guns could we hope to defend against a numerical superiority on this scale. The battle-tested men also stood this last test of nerves and almost on one command we opened fire. The surprise was complete. The first shots achieved hits and moments later several tanks were burning in front of us. The attack faltered and now a short artillery duel began between our dug-in heavy guns and the enemy tanks. The air was filled with the crack of our guns firing, the detonations of the impacting Russian H.E. rounds, crashing fountains of earth, whizzing shell fragments, fire commands and the shouts of joy from the men which broke out every time a Russian tank was hit. All the while hammered the 2 cm. guns, which had taken the Russian infantry as their target. Suddenly there was movement in the Russian tank formation and through the dust, smoke and powder smoke we observed that the still undamaged Russian tanks were withdrawing to the rear. A sigh of relief went through our ranks, because we had done it! A breakthrough by enemy tanks had been averted.

But the real difficulty had just begun because now Russian infantry launched attacks on our positions without regard for their losses. At the same time we once again came under massive artillery fire. But the situation first became critical when we discovered that our comrades of the infantry who were supposed to protect us from Soviet infantry attack had pulled back under the pressure of the Russian tank assault and were no longer to be seen. We thus had to depend on ourselves and now had to attempt to fight off the Russian infantry attack with our gun crews. The situation was further aggravated because the Russians had worked their way toward us along the ditches at the side of the road, so that we had to anticipate a break into our positions at any moment. In this situation, which could have spelled the end for us all, an Oberscharführer who commanded the two light Flak guns distinguished himself through particular bravery. Under Russian rifle and machine gun fire he successfully moved both guns from cover metre by metre until they could reach the concealed ditches and streets. After a few bursts, his guns had driven the Russians from their cover and forced them to retreat. In doing so he had prevented a Russian penetration of our positions which would have led to the destruction of our heavy guns. This accomplishment was carried out by Oscha. Schmalz and his gun crews in an examplary display of devotion to duty. Oscha. Schmalz himself was wounded several times. Through the magnificent bravery of both gun crews was brought about a decisive turn in our defensive battle. The Russian infantry was left standing beyond our positions outside the range of our light guns while their tanks bypassed us on the left in a wide arc. As twilight fell, under the protective fire of our own artillery, we successfully pulled our guns out of their positions under the eyes of the Russians with the help of the so-called

"Scheunentore" (barn doors—12 ton tractors). I first learned on arriving at the Division command post that the HKL already lay eight kilometres behind our positions and that they had considered all guns as lost. Through the bravery of every man we had successfully carried out our assignment and kept the road to Modlin open. In doing so we had prevented a Russian breakthrough at the sensitive boundary position but we had also kept open the route for the withdrawal of our own units who were still fighting in front of our sector and saved the lives of many of our comrades. The best news was that we had suffered only light losses. Here the old front line maxim that "sweat saves blood!" had been proven correct once again. Because our guns had been well dug-in, they offered a poor target to the attacking tanks. Recognition for this difficult action was not long in coming. General Gille himself expressed his personal thanks and appreciation. Uscha. and gun commander Alois Schnaubelt from Silesia, who had destroyed 15 enemy tanks from point blank range during the tanks versus guns duel on 20. October, was awarded the Knight's Cross as recognition for his outstanding bravery."

The efforts of the men of the Luftwaffe and Navy, with limited infantry training and no experience in ground warfare, who were transferred to the Waffen-SS in those weeks must be appreciated. These reinforcements had to be used by the Division as a result of personnel shortages and they fought bravely while suffering heavy losses.

Thus the third defensive battle for Warsaw came to an end. Measured against the facts that the Soviets had deployed 21 divisions and various support units against the Corps' sector and succeeded in pushing the HKL back only a few kilometres, the battle may be seen as a complete success for the German forces.

XIII. BATTLE IN HUNGARY

Christmas night 1944. Following the hard and costly defensive battles northeast of Warsaw and in the "wet triangle" the Division lay in positions near Modlin. Exhausted, the men allowed themselves a few days rest. The replacements, primarily members of the Luftwaffe, were taken into the units and trained. Weapons and material were overhauled, the positions made more comfortable. This was how the Division, with the exception of Kampfgruppe Dorr which was the Armee reserve, spent Christmas. Everyone enjoyed this breather before the next action as only veteran front line soldiers could.

"Dorpmüllern to the Julischka"

Christmas peace also reigned at the Division command post. Then at approximately 21.00 hours on Christmas night the telephone rang. The O 1, Obersturmführer Jahnke, answered. "Obersturmführer, you are wanted by Corps". The Chief of Staff is already on the line. "Schönfelder here, is the Division Commander not present?"—"No Obersturmbannführer, the Oberführer has gone forward to spend Christmas with the men in the positions."—"Very well, I'm handing you over to the Obergruppenführer!" The last trace of the peaceful atmosphere abruptly disappeared. The speculation over the meaning of the call was quickly ended. "I hear that Ullrich isn't there", spoke "Isegrim", "so pay attention." The O 1 was all ears and ready to soak up the information like a dry sponge. "We Dorpmüllern to the Julischka..." Short pause. "Have you got that?" And you can bet that Jahnke had got it, because that could only mean that the WIKING Division as part of IV. SS-Pz.Korps was to be transferred by rail to Hungary.[1] Courageously, the O 1 asked the question: "When, Obergruppenführer?" And right away came the answer: "Immediately! Dorr this evening, you tomorrow morning!" Then Gille hung up.

At approximately 18.00 hours, the momentous teletype had arrived at the Corps Headquarters from the FHQ in Rastenburg. The teletype ordered transport by rail of the Staff of IV. SS- Pz.Korps and its cadre divisions TOTENKOPF and WIKING to the Komarom area of Hungary in order to begin at the earliest possible target date (1. 1. 1945) the relief of IX. SS-Geb.Korps under the command of SS-Gruppenführer and Generalleutnant der Waffen-SS von Pfeffer-Wildenbruch which was surrounded in Budapest. The encircled Gebirgskorps consisted of numerous Hungarian units, two SS-Cavalry divisions, as well as 13. Pz.Div. and the FELDHERRNHALLE Division. At that time the Corps would come under the command of 2. Armee under its Commander in Chief Generaloberst Weiß which was once again part of Heeresgruppe Mitte under its Commander in Chief Generaloberst Reinhardt.

After the TOTENKOPF Division had been pulled out of the old sector of the front, the WIKING Division also expected to be transferred. Despite the serious situation, WIKING was relieved sector by sector by its neighbour to the right which had to extend itself to the north. All initiates were surprised at the time when this sector of the front, recognized as a focal point, was stripped of all Panzer divisions and the remaining Army divisions in this already too thinly-held sector were extended further. The relief was executed smoothly, undisturbed by the enemy. The loading of the Division at about fifty (!) stations in the Modlin-Nasielks area also proceeded smoothly. Secrecy was strictly maintained and no one discovered the route, time enroute or destination.

In his "Memories of a Soldier", Gen.Oberst Guderian wrote[2]: "On 25. December, the first day of the Christmas holiday, I travelled back to Zossen by train. During the trip Hitler ordered behind my back the transport of SS-Korps Gille with its two SS-Divisions from the area north of Warsaw, where it was assembled behind the front as Heeresgruppe Reinhardt's reserve, to Budapest to relieve this city from its encirclement." The retired Generaloberst had erred on two counts: The order to transfer WIKING arrived on 24. December between 17.00 and 20.00 hours. Besides, the Division was not in reserve, but in action. A little later Guderian wrote: "On New Year's morning I went once more to see Hitler in order to report to him that the SS-Korps WIKING under the command of Armee Balck would begin the attack to relieve Budapest on the evening of 1. January. Hitler looked forward to this attack with great expectations. I was sceptical, because the preparation time had been very short and the troops as well as the command no longer possessed the energy that they had before. Despite initial success, the attack did not get through."[3] These remarks by Generaloberst Guderian, always highly respected by the Waffen-SS, do not appear to do justice to the troops, who in the action for the relief of Budapest once again met with great success.

The Encirclement of Budapest

The situation in Hungary had long been more than precarious. The chaos in Rumania had reached Hungary. A lightning-quick action by the SIEBENBÜRGEN Gruppe, which consisted of elements of 8. SS-Kavallerie-Division FLORIAN GEYER, had cost the life of SS-Obergruppenführer Phleps. He was well-known to his comrades in the WIKING Division as the Commander of the WESTLAND Regiment during 1941/42 and was respected by all. At that time the German-Hungarian front extended for nearly a thousand kilometres. Generaloberst Hans Frießner had completely insufficient forces at his disposal to carry out the defence of this long front. Certainly, the combined German-Hungarian forces had succeeded on 5. September 1944 in throwing the Russians and the Rumanian units fighting under Russian control back behind the Maros sector and in doing so preventing for the time being a Russian penetration through the Iron Gate into the heart of Hungary. However, the Soviet's 2nd Ukrainian Front had assembled approximately twenty five rifle divisions and four fast corps for a new assault against Hungary.

The political about-face by the Reich Administrator, Admiral Horthy, contributed to the intensity of the situation. While a Hungarian delegation negotiated in Moscow, the 2nd Hungarian Army withdrew from Klausenburg. The German 8. Armee, still fighting in the north of the Szekler point, thus lost its connections to the right and left. On 6. October, into the midst of this tense situation in Hungary, rolled the Red Army's great offensive. The Soviets pressed forward in three assault groups, consisting mostly of tank, motorized and cavalry units. The first blow, on the right wing with five fast corps, fell on the German 76. Inf.Division under General Abraham which was defending vital Großwardein. In the centre, the Red Army attacked the German 1. and 13. Panzer divisions defending the Schnellen Kreisch with seventeen rifle divisions. The 4th Hungarian Infantry Division was overrun in the first storm, and facing only the desperately defending 23. Pz.Division, the Soviets succeeded in crossing the Schnelle Kreisch near Komady.

At that time, the sneaking betrayal had long since worked its way down from the commanding staff to the troops of the Honvéd fighting at the front. On the night of

7./8. October 1944, the Hungarian forces in the Gyula-Arad area deserted almost to a man to the Red Army. A Kampfgruppe from 8. SS-Kavallerie-Division *FLORIAN GEYER* under SS-Hauptsturmführer Anton Vandieken, which had been employed as support for the Hungarians, appeared to be lost. The onrushing Red Army flowed past the SS- Cavalrymen on the left and right. In spite of the hopeless situation, Vandieken kept his head and fought back bravely with his men despite heavy losses until he could again make contact with the newly-created defensive front. On 10. October, despite everything, the German forces successfully cut off the three Soviet spearheads from their rearward contact. Near Debrecen it came down to a heavy tank battle. However, the Klausenburg bridgehead fell and the Hungarians finally evacuated Szegedin. While the Honvéd troops fought bravely, their High Command appeared hesitant.

"While the Russians pushed farther to the west and German units continued to throw themselves against them, a sinister quiet brooded in Budapest. If the allied bomber squadrons had not flown over Budapest daily to drop their deadly greetings from the west, one could have thought that it was peacetime. In the streets of the city sauntered elegant Hungarian officers with even more elegant women. From the bars rang the fiddles of gypsy bands and a gaiety prevailed which was indescribable. Only a few knew that at that hour, in which the flood of the Red Army pressed ever closer to the city of the Crown of the Holy Stephan, two groups were in a life-and-death struggle: on one side the Germans and the Hungarian nationalists, on the other side Horthy, the Lakatos government and the High Command of the Honvéd army. Quietly, Sturmbannführer Otto Skorzeny had moved several units of the SS-Jagdverband Mitte to Budapest, paratroops arrived, and shortly thereafter, General Walther Wenck, who in the event serious fighting broke out was to take command of the German forces in Budapest."[1]—With the new Szalsi government the situation at first stabilized. In the Budapest bridgehead at the beginning of December were the 8. and 22. SS-cavalry Divisions, 13. Pz.Div., Pz.Gren.Div. *FELDHERRNHALLE* and 357.Inf.Division. On 5. December, SS-Obergruppenführer von Pfeffer-Wildenbruch had taken command of the battle for Budapest. At that time the defence line still ran far to the east and the Russians stood in a wide arc, which led from Kerepes, Pécel, Pest, Erzsébet, Vecsés to Soroksar. Although the Russians had reached the city suburbs they had not been able to penetrate the city proper.

To the west of Budapest, Stuhlweißenburg, Polgardy and Balatonfökajar fell to the Russians. While a bitter battle was being fought south of the city, in the north the Red Army turned and attacked Budapest with powerful forces. Despite determined resistance, the suburbs of Alag and Kisalag were lost on 11. 12. 1944. At the same time, the units of the Red Army which had reached the Danube pushed on into the Vertes mountains and took Tata.

With a Kampfgruppe of German police under the Oberst of Municipal Police Dörner, 25,000 German soldiers found themselves in the besieged city. In addition, there were 45,000 Hungarian soldiers under the command of Ivan von Hindy, recently promoted to Generaloberst and who was to remain loyal to the Germans until the last. They formed the 1st Hungarian Korps with the rest of the 10th and 12th Hungarian Infantry Divisions under the brave Oberst Vertassy. Also remaining in the city were 800,000 Hungarian civilians who still had to be fed.

The First Relief Attempt

On 28. December, the first elements of the *TOTENKOPF* Division arrived in Armeegruppe Balck's area at the unloading stations of Raab and Komarom. At 09.00 hours on 1. 1. 1945, the Staff of the *WIKING* Division reached Raab station. Following, during the course of the afternoon, were further parts of the Division which were immediately led to assembly areas just west of Tata where they found Kampfgruppe Dorr.

By 17.00 hours, the Signals Battalion finally had all of the units again on the telephone line, so that the attack at 18.00 hours on that same day could begin as ordered. While the Panzergruppe under SS-Ostubaf. and Commander of the Pz.Rgt. Darges attacked along the Tata—Felsögalla road, II./*GERMANIA* struck out to the south, attempting to take the village of Agostian. The attack was supported by I. and III./*GERMANIA*. The HKL was crossed at about midday and by approximately 04.00 hours the attack's objective was reached.

Already during the morning of 31. 12. 1944, General der Panzertruppen Balck had been forced to set the diversionary maneuvre near Ösi in motion prematurely, since the units planned for the attack were arriving so irregularly. 711. Inf.Div., for example, which came from Holland, first reached the unloading station at Komarom as the attack was already underway.

General Balck had decided on the northern solution, which foresaw an operation from the area southeast of Komarom toward the southeast. Because of the fighting still going on, it offered a good prospect for surprise and had a secure north flank thanks to the Danube and LVII. Panzerkorps which was staggered along the river's northern bank. This meant that an attack could be carried out with limited forces since its flank was secured by the Danube. Balck hoped to be able to minimize the disadvantage, that the operation led through the north of the Vértes mountains and was less favourable for Panzers, by quickly taking possession of the southern Danube roads. From there, they were offered the possibility of advancing as far as Gran and with a thrust to the south, of outflanking the enemy in the Vértes mountains.

IV. SS-Pz.Korps, which had been moved by rail from the area north of Warsaw, was strengthened by the addition of 96. Inf.Div. under Generalmajor Harrendorf and 711. Inf.Div. under Gen.Leutnant Reichert. "The Pape Gruppe (Commander and Staff of *FELDHERRNHALLE*) joined the attack with its Kampfgruppe Philipp (reinforced Pz.Rgt. 11) on the right wing of the Panzerkorps."[1] The bulk of the Corps launched the main attack from the area of Naszaly—Tata—Felsögalla on 1. January 1945 at 22.30 hours. In order to increase the surprise, artillery preparation was avoided as the attack began. The Panzers rolled over the first Soviet positions and while the Divisions *WIKING* and *TOTENKOPF* attacked left via Tata in the direction of Tarjan and Bickse, 96. Inf.Div. advanced to the northern bank of the Danube, crossed the river near Nyergesujfalu in approximately 100 assault boats and took the village and locality of Süttö by storm. Within a short time the Division had forced a breakthrough into the area of the Soviet 31st Guards Rifle Corps (belonging to 4th Guards Army) which, for the Soviets, could not have been more dangerous.

For the first time following a steady three month retreat, a large German force had gone over to the offensive and at a time when the Commanders in Chief of both Ukrainian Fronts believed that Heeresgruppe Süd (Army Group South), following the blows suffered in December, was no longer capable of mounting offensive operations. Although the transfer from Poland to Hungary of the IV. SS-Pz.Korps had not remained hidden from Marshall Tolbuchin, the location of its assembly area, which was actually quite small, had not been discovered. The tight radio silence and well-camouflaged concentrations of the German attack forces succeeded so completely, that the High Command of the 4th Guards Army first became aware of the offensive by the SS-Pz.Korps (3. SS *TOTENKOPF*, 5. SS *WIKING* and 2 Wehrmacht divisions) from the area south of Komarom, at midday on 2. 1. 1945.[2]

With the taking of the first objective, Agostian, by the *GERMANIA* Rgt. and the rest of II./Pz.Rgt. 5, they also succeeded in freeing nearly one thousand German and Hungarian prisoners. However, they also witnessed a horrible sight: soldiers of the Army and Waffen-SS who had broken out of Budapest were found murdered along the side of the road. But the attack toward the southeast continued, however the going became increasingly difficult. The Panzers could only move along the roads, which the Soviets attempted to block with barricades of up to 20 heavy antitank guns. Still more difficult was the operation of artillery in this hilly and complex terrain. In this heavily wooded terrain the enemy now repeatedly attacked the German flanks in groups up to battalion strength. The rapid advance had come to an end. The troops now laboriously fought their way forward a hundred metres at a time.

On 3. January, the Commanding General and those of the Army promptly appeared at the Division's headquarters. But after seeing the terrain firsthand they declared themselves satisfied with the Division's progress. Still, on this day the armoured spearhead reached Vertes-Tolna which had already been occupied by II./*GERMANIA* under Hstuf. Pleiner. At approximately 17.00 hours, the Division Staff arrived in Torjan while fighting was still going on in the south of the town. In action in this battle was the Ground Support Geschwader "*Immelmann*" of *Oberst* Rudel, who had just received Germany's highest decoration for bravery in the Führer Headquarters. The following account from his memoirs is significant in regard to the description of this situation: ..."The Führer took me to the map table and told me that the briefing just given concerned the situation at Budapest; I had come from that sector. He repeated once again the reasons which had been reported to him for the less than favourable progress of the forces in the area of Budapest, which had not yet linked up with the surrounded city. Weather, transport and other difficulties were mentioned but not the mistakes, which we saw daily on our missions; the splitting up of the Panzer divisions and the unfavourable terrain chosen for the operations of the Panzers and infantry. I voiced my opinion, based on years of Eastern Front experience and on the fact that during this campaign I spent up to eight hours a day flying over this sector, mostly at low level. Everyone listened quietly. After a brief pause the Führer said with a glance at those around him, "You see, that is how I am lied to—who knows for how long?" He reproached no one, although he now knew the true circumstances, but one could tell that it had hit him hard. With his hands on the map he indicated that he would like to regroup in order to try once again to relieve Budapest. He asked me where there would be favourable terrain for the Panzer attack. I gave my opinion. This operation was later successful and the attack group reached the spearhead of the defenders of Budapest who were attacking outward from the city."[3] It must be mentioned at this point, that this quote is not intended to prove that "the Führer would have won the war, if he had not been continually lied to". However,

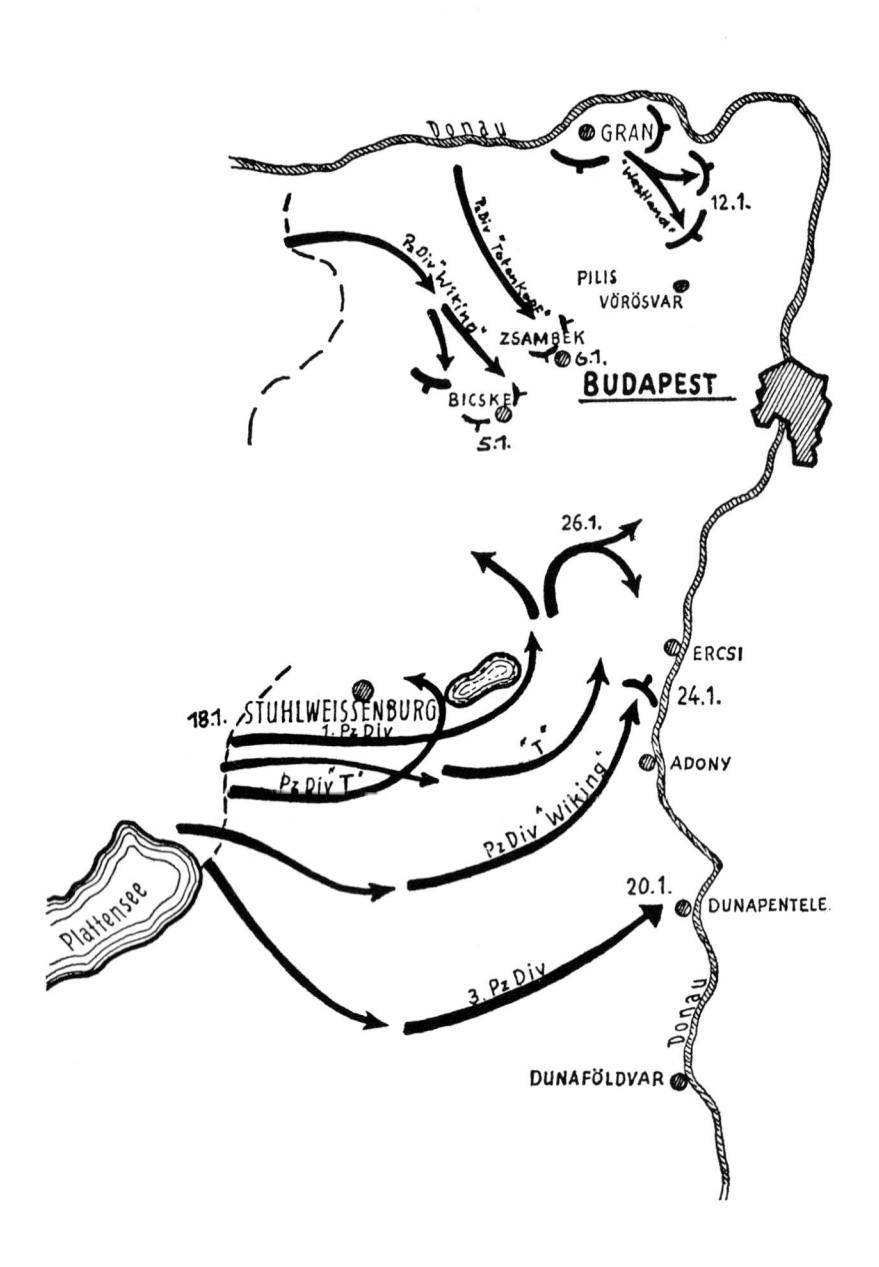

The relief advance on Budapest 1945

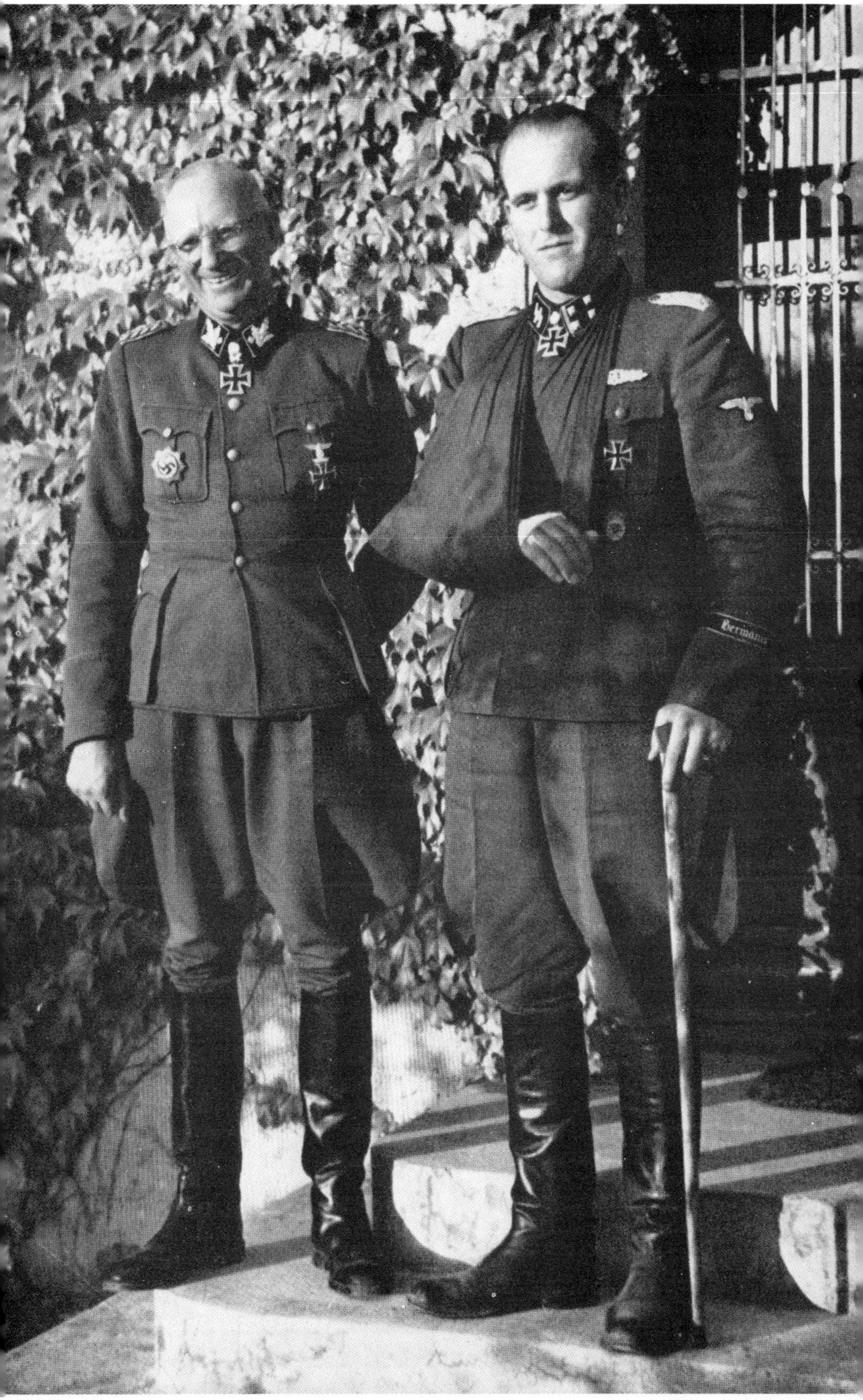

Dutch SS-Untersturmführer of the *GERMANIA* Regiment during hand grenade training.

Member of a machine gun team.

◄ SS-Obergruppenführer and Gen.d.Waffen-SS Gille with the commander of the *GERMANIA* Regiment Ostubaf. Dorr.

At the old Czarist fort on the bend in the Narew Autumn 1944.

An 8.8 cm Flak
is towed into position.

The Iron Cross IInd Class
for the gunner of a Flak 88
in position as
an antitank weapon.

The gun section
of 7. Battery
on a muddy
Russian road.

Early 1944:
Position on the edge of Kovel-South.

Exhausted! Overtaxed infantry
in the "wet triangle"—autumn 1944.

No rest from the lice!

Changing position

18. January 1945—Obersturmbannführer Dorr in his command vehicle.

Obersturmbannführer Schönfelder,
Division Ia and later Chief of Staff
of IV. SS-Pz.-Korps.

March 1945
in the streets of Stuhlweißenburg.

1945
Last defence in Hungary.

March 1945:
Vescprem/Hungary

SS-Obergruppenführer Gille in discussion with SS-Standartenführer Mühlenkamp and Major i.G. Kleine (Ia) October 1944 near Skrezeszew.

The commanding general of IV. SS-Pz.Korps, Gille, in discussion with *WIKING*'s last commander, Ullrich. Left: commander of SS-Pz.Art.Rgt. 5, Ostubaf. Bünning; right: commander of IV./SS-Pz.Art.Rgt. 5, Stubaf. Wittich.

In a mortar position.

Radio operators are always in action.

13. January 1945: SS-Standartenführer Ullrich awards the Iron Cross Ist Class to a Company Chief southwest of Estergom/Hungary.

Rudel's report is of significance, especially since it indicates that the operations of the Panzers and infantry were poorly led.

But things had not yet reached that point. When the first reports of deep penetrations reached Army General Zacharow of the Soviet 31st Guards Riflecorps, all reserves, consisting of the 5th Guards Cavalry Corps, the 7th Mechanized Corps, the 18th Tank Corps and the 2nd Guards Mechanized Corps, were thrown into the fighting but were unable to change the situation. "The attack by IV. SS-Pz.Korps hit them with full force, threw them back and at first frustrated all attempts to prevent a further advance. Felsögalla, Bajna and Tarjan were taken and while 96. Inf.Div. drove in the direction of Gran—Dorog, the Panzers of the WIKING and TOTENKOPF Divisions rolled further to the southeast toward the road junction at Bickse."[4]

That reads well, however, in reality the attack moved laboriously forward. It went no better with the Division's neighbours, indeed they even lagged behind, and that is why they could not take care of securing the flanks of the advance. As a result, WIKING and TOTENKOPF were forced to continually detach combat units to guard their flanks. To the WIKING Division's right was 6. Pz.Div. and to its right Kampfgruppe Pape. To TOTENKOPF's left was 96. Inf.Div. and its neighbour to the left was once again 711. Inf.Division.

On 4. January, the GERMANIA Regiment only advanced roughly five kilometres. But the terrain was now more open and level. The enemy concentrated his air attacks in this area and losses were heavy. On Friday morning, the Division attacked with both regiments, GERMANIA and WESTLAND, with heavy artillery support. Despite continually stiffening Soviet resistance, they succeeded in crossing the rail line and advancing to just outside Bicske. At first light on 6. January, Pz.Rgt. 5 under Obersturmführer Darges linked up with the NORGE Gren.Btl. under SS-Hstuf. Fritz Vogt. During the night the Panzers had crossed extremely difficult and above all steep terrain—the Panzers were sometimes towed up the hills by tractors! However, they were unsuccessful in their attempt to take Bicske. Instead, the Panzer men and infantry moved into an old Hungarian castle which quickly became the target for concentrated Soviet artillery, tank fire and enemy bombers. The drama which was played out in the Hegyiks farmyard in the following several hours was described by a PK-Reporter of the KURT EGGERS Regiment[5]:

"Next to the road, surrounded by an old wall, rose a Hungarian castle in the Hegyks farmyard. It became the core of the Gruppe's hedgehog position. The Grenadiere placed their security positions outside the wall. Behind the wall, only sixty metres from it, Ostubaf. Darges set up his command post. The enemy had spotted the movements of the German troops. He began to fire...An enemy reconnaissance party was reported at the south of the wall: it was shot up by several of our men. Shortly afterward 20 Soviet tanks attacked. They ran into the waiting Panthers. A short combat, the closest T-34 lost its turret, the rest turn away. Before darkness fell, Hauptsturmführer Fritz Vogt made the necessary infantry preparations. In the darkness the Panzers can see little, therefore, the burden of the fighting will fall on the shoulders of the Grenadiere. The exposed MG posts are brought back within the wall. The Panzers are so placed that they can provide artillery support for the Grenadiere's defensive battle. The first attack on the castle began shortly before midnight. After a heavy preparatory artillery barrage, enemy infantry simultaneously stormed the wall from two sides. At the wall there was wild hand to hand fighting and hand grenade duels.

A flickering Hindenburg lamp lit the commander's ice-cold command post. He emerged from the dimness with an overtired serious face. Hands buried in their pockets, shivering slightly in the cold, the commanders and chiefs squatted around the Obersturmbannführer. The Regimental commander had a difficult decision to make, a life and death decision for the men surrounded within the castle wall. All inquiries to Division had gone unanswered. The Panzers had no more fuel and were down to their last three H.E. shells. The battalion was also short of ammunition. They could still fight off an assault troop but then they would have only their empty weapons left. And outside the walls circled 20 Soviet tanks.

Something must happen, that is clear to every officer. Soon the enemy will launch another attack, which the defences will no longer be able to cope with. Then the Division can strike the surrounded troops from its list. The only way out seems to be offered by a withdrawal to the edge of the forest if there is sufficient fuel. The Obersturmbannführer stands. He says a few words. The withdrawal is justified although it will mean giving up a hard-won success and abandoning an important key point for the later attack on Budapest.

The commander disappears into the darkness with one of his Regiment's battalion commanders. Then he again stands before his officers. He says only three words: We stay here.

The basis for this extraordinary decision is his firm conviction that the Division will not abandon its armoured group and that the enemy will surely assemble stronger forces before he attacks the castle again. Should the rest of the ammunition be exhausted, the commander will fire a whistling signal flare. That will be the signal for the surrounded men to retreat. The Obersturmbannführer's faith in the arrival of help was not misplaced. Several hours after midnight, a Panzer-escorted convoy brought ammunition, fuel and rations..." The courageous garrison held out for several more days until complete contact was reestablished with the Division.

On 7. January 1945, the Commanding General of IV. SS-Pz.Korps issued the following order:

"On the occasion of the visit by the Chief of the Army General Staff, Generaloberst Guderian, on 6. January 1945, I emphasized to him explicitly the decisive importance of IV. SS-Pz.Korps' thrust into the area of Budapest. Next to the military necessities, namely relieving the garrison and winning back the Budapest area, enter the political, because Budapest is Hungary. In addition, this operation, if completely successful, could bring about a change in the area of Hungary and possibly influence decisively the conduct of the war on the entire Eastern Front. The Führer has given this task to IV. SS-Panzer-Korps and expects of his divisions that they be imbued to the last man with a tremendous, unstoppable impetus and the iron necessity to reach under all circumstances the goal assigned to them. The first goal of the battle, to push through the forest area, is nearly reached. The proud booty is evidence of the severity of the fighting and the heavy enemy losses. We will push on to the final goal, because it must and will be reached. The courageous, hard fighting garrison of Budapest looks to us!"

It hardly required the determined attack by the *WIKING* and *TOTENKOPF* Divisions on the morning of 8. January to establish that the German forces were too weak. Certainly the Panzer units succeeded in pushing forward as far as the Bicske churchyard, but by midday, due to heavy German losses, the attack had to be seen as a failure. At the same time this meant that the first attempt to relieve Budapest had also failed. The attempt had cost IV. Korps (less 711. Inf.Div.) the loss of 2,938 men from 1.- 7. January 1945. In the period 1. to 4. January 1945, IV. Korps destroyed or captured 79 tanks, 160 guns and 107 antitank guns.[6]

The Second Relief Attempt

On the night of 8./9. January 1945, the Division was relieved and received new orders. Preparations for the second attempt to relieve Budapest began with the transfer into the Estergom area. Misty winter weather and isolated snow showers permitted the transfer to take place by day. Under periodic observation by the enemy, in the late hours of the afternoon the Division moved along icy field roads just behind the front. During the course of the eve of 10. January, *WIKING* encamped in its assigned assembly areas in 711. Inf.Division's sector.

With the *GERMANIA* Regiment to the right and *WESTLAND* to the left, the Division awaited the commencement of the attack to be launched at daybreak. However, at roughly 01.00 hours, Armee cancelled the attack ostensibly on the Führer's orders. On the other hand the Division pressed for a quick attack. Were their comrades in Budapest not expecting to be relieved? Finally, at noon, they received the go-ahead. The Division set out at 20.30 hours. As expected, the enemy was taken completely by surprise. Nevertheless, the terrain made the going difficult. But the attack went forward.

"The attack also made progress on 11. January. The Russians fell back steadily. The morale of the troops was indescribable. Now it had to succeed! We knew that there were ten thousand German and ten thousand Hungarian comrades in Budapest. There were two thousand German Wehrmacht female auxiliaries and aid personnel alone within the encircled city! On 12. January, Philisszentkereszt was taken by the *WESTLAND* Regiment against weak opposition. Numerous prisoners and a rich booty in captured equipment was brought in by the beaming Waffen-SS men.

Budapest was still twenty one kilometres away! Twenty one kilometres and the Russians running before the German attack, running as only they could!...Everyone now believed that the Budapest pocket could be opened. One more day and *WIKING* would be in Budapest!" Thus did Erich Kern[1] describe the situation. His experiences were typical of the men of the *WIKING* Division at that time.

In spite of haze and smoke, the men could already recognize clearly the church spires of the encircled city. More and more the enemy's resistance weakened and the morale of the fighting "Wikinger" grew. There was no doubt, this time they would succeed!

Then the incomprehensible happened: at approximately 20.00 hours, orders arrived to break off the attack. General Gille implored the Heeresgruppe to withdraw the order but the attempts were fruitless. Heeresgruppe insisted. This measure was completely unintelligible to everyone, especially since there lay before the Division a weaker, outgunned enemy. Add to that, that flanking attacks in this terrain were scarcely possible since the advance on Budapest followed two valleys. For the same reason there was no fear of enemy tank attack. Most important, however, was the fact that the enemy was still reeling from surprise. Could such an operation have started under more favourable omens?

But it did no good. The Division had to shift to the Vesprem area. Once again everyone drove to the health spa at Dobogekö in order once more to see the spires of Budapest with their own eyes...

The Third Relief Attempt

On Monday, the 14th of January, the Division shifted in a motorized march via Komarom—Raab—Papa to Vesprem in the area north of Lake Balaton (Germ. Platensee). Assembled with it within IV. SS-Pz.Korps in the area west of Stuhlweißenburg (Székesfehéváf) was the TOTENKOPF Dvision under General Thunert and 3. Panzerdivision under General Söth. A new, third attempt to break the encircling ring around Budapest was to be undertaken from here. The attack's first objective was the Danube south of Budapest. 3. Panzerdivision made up the right wing, 1. Panzerdivision the left, while the two Waffen-SS Divisions were to break through in the centre. The decision, whereby the so-called "northern solution" was replaced by the "southern solution", was said to have been reached by Hitler on 9. January.[2]

"On 18. January at 05.00 hours, the attack by the reinforced IV. SS-Pz.Korps against the Soviet positions began after a brief barrage. The fighting strength of the attacking forces was relatively high; its advance was effectively supported by 135 aircraft of Luftflotte 4. The first day's fighting led to a considerable success. On the second day of the attack the breakthrough was enlarged to a depth of 65 kilometres, during the course of which the WIKING Division crossed the canal near Kaloz on 19. January and the right wing (3. Pz.Div.) reached the Danube near Dunapentele on 20. January."[3]

In fact, at the beginning the attack made little progress at all. The enemy defended his main line of resistance desperately, which was not only heavily mined, but for the first time featured electrically charged wires. General Gille appeared at the Division command post with the Army Chief of Staff, General Gaedtke, who was highly annoyed. The Division Commander, SS- Oberführer Ullrich, decided to immediately commit the armoured Dorr Gruppe which was not supposed to go into action until the HKL was broken. With the assistance of this armoured Gruppe, the strongly fortified HKL was broken through in the evening. Behind the HKL the German forces found only light enemy resistance. At 03.00 hours on 19. January, Gruppe Dorr and the following Division combat echelon reached the town of Kislang south of Stuhlweißenburg approximately 40 kilometres east of the HKL. After crossing the canal at noon, the attack rushed onward again. On this day the remaining divisions were lagging somewhat behind onrushing WIKING Division. On the following day, TOTENKOPF and 1. Panzerdivision reached the canal, the latter with the assignment to veer off toward Stuhlweißenburg.

The enemy's attacks had already increased on 20. January and on Sunday the 21st, they concentrated their efforts toward Sarosd. As a result, the Division's spearhead was cut off and Sarosd temporarily occupied by the enemy. The situation was cleared up by 14.00 hours; Sarosd was again in German hands and contact had been reestablished with the advance forces. However, this was to be a black day in the Division's history; a direct hit by an antitank shell killed several officers who had arrived for a briefing at GERMANIA's command post. Wounded in the incident was the longtime regimental commander, SS- Obersturmbannführer Hans Dorr. This was the sixteenth time that Dorr had been wounded and he would later die in Vienna as a result of the wounds which he sustained on this day. His name is inseparably associated with the history of the GERMANIA Regiment and the WIKING Division.

The Soviets were also encountering difficulties at this time. Peter Gosztony describes these as outlined in the work of Soviet historian M. M. Malachow[3]:

"At the same time, the Soviet command endeavoured to seal off the enemy penetration to the south. In complete overestimation of the German attack forces, Marshall Tolbuchin, who since 19. January had taken over command of the defence from Army General Zacharow, feared that the German forces which had reached the Danube would catch the 57th Guards Army and the 1st Bulgarian Army in a pincer movement with the German 2. Panzer Armee and destroy them. In this state, Tolbuchin advised the commander in chief of the 57th Guards Army, General Scharochin, that the danger existed that the entire 57th Army would be surrounded. Would it not be better to begin an immediate retreat and pull the army back behind the Danube? Scharochin rejected this. He decided, rather, not to give up his positions...

The Soviet crisis culminated on 21. January. They were short of everything: on reinforcements and a greater shortage of munitions...The final decision depended on the direction of the German advance. On the following day, when the fall of Stuhlweißenburg as well as the appearance of both SS-Pz. Divisions on the northern edge of Lake Velencze became known and the German advance continued toward the south, Marshall Tolbuchin decided to continue the battle in the South-Transdanube.

The capture by night of Stuhlweißenburg, the rich haul of captured Soviet equipment as well as the offensive's previous successes gave wings to the German troops. Although the hard fight for the city had demanded heavy casualties, especially of the Hungarian volunteer Kampfgruppe Ney, the area of west Hungary was the only sector on the entire Eastern Front in which the German Army was conducting offensive operations. The password was "on to Budapest!" While the area around Stuhlweißenburg was cleared by 1. Pz.Div., on 22. January the -WIKING Division advanced far to the northeast. Following was the TOTENKOPF Division whose spearheads likewise reached the Danube on 23. January. The splitting of the 3rd Ukrainian Front was thus accomplished."

On 23. January, when WIKING's spearheads reached the Danube near Adony, the Division regrouped for the new assault to the north. On the following day, GERMANIA attacked on the right of the bank of the Danube, WESTLAND on the left. Stiffening enemy resistance, but also adverse weather conditions made the attack more difficult. On 25. January, the attack had to be halted completely, especially since the Division's western neighbour could not keep pace. "During the night of 24./25. January 1945, Pz.Gren.Rgt. 1 was involved in fighting for Pettend between the Pz.Pioniere and Kampfgruppe Marcks supported on the left wing by SS-Pz.Gren.Btl NORGE (SS-WIKING). The fighting here was unbelievably bitter, since the Grenadiere had been witnesses to the cruelty inflicted by the Russians on German and Hungarian wounded."[4] Until 28. January, the Division was forced to fight off increasingly heavy attacks from the south.

Concerning the events of 29. January 1945, the historian wrote laconically, "On 29. January, the situation also came to a head in the north, where both SS-Pz. Divisions were forced onto the defensive. The result was a several hour long tank battle near Pettend which cost both sides heavy losses. A continuation of the German attack did not take place: the units were bled and as a result of their dispersal were no longer capable of a successful defence. In view of the heavy pressure from the Soviets, during the night the front was pulled back from the northern edge of Lake Velencze to the Baracska—Petend hills. This was the beginning of the German retreat."[5]

The Soviet historian's view is underlined by the diary entry of the 1. Ordonnanzoffizier of 5. SS-Pz. Division *WIKING* for 29. January 1945:

The attack on Budapest was launched at roughly 07.00 hours. According to information from the Armee Ic, the enemy before *WESTLAND* consisted of only a battered Cavalry Division. We were to push through to Budapest in train. Due to fog the attack was put back to 08.00 and then 09.00 hours.

Shortly before the last appointed start time the Russians attacked on all fronts with very heavy air support. The focal point was in our left flank near the *NORGE* Battalion under Stubaf. Vogt. There the Russians had committed a recently arrived tank corps with 180 tanks. Only heroic action by the *NORGE* Battalion prevented the Division from being rolled up from the west. Vogt himself destroyed 6 tanks with *Panzerfaust*...With the help of all reserves, including the A.A. which had been held back as long as possible as a reserve for the anticipated attack on Budapest, it was possible to seal off all enemy penetrations by the evening and straighten out the situation during the night..."[6]

The assault by *Panzerkampfgruppe PHILIPP*, with which the Division had contact on 10. January, was also broken off on orders from above on 26. January when only about 16 km. west of the encircling ring around Budapest[7]. At the time there was talk of betrayal.

Irresistable Retreat

On 30. January, Gen. Maj. Gaedcke, the Chief of the General Staff of *Armeegruppe Balck*, reported to the Chief of Staff of the *Heeresgruppe* that the strength of the Panzer divisions had sunk considerably. In the report, the Panzer strength of the *TOTENKOPF* Division was given as 9 and *WIKING* as 14. The failure of the third attempt, the difficult defensive fighting and the beginning of the retreat had cost heavy losses in men and material. On 1. 2. 1945, the Division was forced to leave the Danube and withdraw to the west. It was clear down to the last man that the relief of Budapest had ultimately been a failure. The hopes which the surrounded garrison had placed in the IV. SS-Pz.Korps are described by Dr. Hübner of the *FELDHERRNHALLE* Division:

"New "Kessel Latrinen" (soldier's jargon for rumours) concerning the approach of General Gille circulated hourly. A telegram from the Führer and even a call to hold out from Himmler reached us. But it was clear to everyone that we could hold out only for a few short days, perhaps even hours!"[1] W. Jester added: "The news of General Gille seeped through to the last foxhole. At any minute he must open the pocket. His name was mentioned everywhere, everywhere he was the anchor of our morale. For hours everyone forgot the terrible privation, resigned themselves to the sickening conditions in the cellars. Our rescue was getting nearer!"[2]

Radio reports, picked up on 1. February, revealed the growing disillusionment of the surrounded troops. Just as disheartened were the men of the *WIKING* Division, who for the first time had been unable to fulfill the high expectations placed in them. "We have no guilt!", so wrote the O 1 on this day on his pocket calendar. This view may be unreservedly supported. However, it changed little the fate of their surrounded comrades and less the general dejection of the troops, who perhaps had also begun to suspect that the war was coming to an unhappy end.

Nevertheless, no one could imagine that the war was ending, much less that it was lost. The password which motivated the men was "We will win, because we must win!" That they maintained their fighting spirit is at best comparable to the greatest achievements in the Division's history. Still, nothing helped. Fighting a delaying action and suffering heavy casualties, the Division moved back toward Stuhlweißenburg. Such a sentence is easily written. But what the end result was, especially for the infantryman, is conveyed by the experiences of Dieter Kuhlmann, who still remembers clearly that Sunday of 18. February:

18. February 1945. The last snow lies gray and dirty in the roadside ditches of the fields of northern Hungary. The roads and fields are dotted with large puddles which reflect the low-hanging clouds.

The whole night we have marched, marched, marched...And the winegrower's hut, lying at the foot of a gently climbing vineyard, is shelter for only a few hours. From without comes now and then the crack of a shot through the twilight, the roar of a shell heading our way. From far away we can hear the grinding of tank tracks.

Then suddenly there is movement at the entrance. Excited whispers, maps are unfolded, a low voice quietly and firmly gives orders. Immediately a command spreads from man to man to the farthest corner of the hut into the dark cellar where stands a lost ancient wine press.

The first group is already leaving our shelter. Others follow. Outside it is still dusk; wearily we shuffle along through the puddles, leave the worn-down road and trudge across a wet field. Ahead of us and behind us, the widely spaced company. Man after man. And no one knows to where. Ahead a Russian machine gun begins to stutter nervously. The point stops the length of a heartbeat and then the company pushes slowly on toward the Ivans.

Suddenly the veil of mist raises before us. It provides a clear view of a vintners' village which appears to be uninhabited. To the left is a vineyard. Far ahead a long hill cuts diagonally across the direction of our attack.

Quickly the company goes to ground. Up front at the point kneels our "old man", observing the terrain through his field glasses. Then we hear him speak a command, listen as it is passed from man to man and at the same time we perceive a rattling ahead of us: tanks! Then the command reaches us: "Panzerschreck forward!"

Mechanically we reach for our launcher, the ammunition, the Panzerfäuste. Hurrying forward, we move past the long row of the company to the right toward the first hut. Between the huts turn the T-34 and Russian self-propelled guns as if it were important to plow everything round about...

With flying hands we load and secure. The loader takes cover. A flash of fire, a dull crack. Already the first is burning! Over there the second T-34 comes to a halt with a jolt. Smoke pours from every opening. Our platoon leader stands on the third, raises the hatch and jumps off. It too is disabled. The crew of a self-propelled gun surrenders, pale and shaking they stumble to the rear. A light tank sits at the corner of a house and fires like mad with its machine gun. It soon meets its fate as well. Then, from the left, two sharp pistol shots. There! A Russian tank commander attempted to save his life by climbing out and fleeing. However, the third man of my crew was quicker.

As quickly as the show had begun, it was over. How long it lasted and exactly what happened in detail was observed differently by everyone. Six, seven, eight burning tank wrecks between the huts are all that remain.

Exhausted, we assemble in the shadow of a hut and take count. Thank God! No one is missing. Someone passes out cigarettes. His hand, dirty and damp with sweat, still shakes a bit. Greedily, we suck the smoke into our exhausted lungs.

We have not noticed that in the meantime the company had attacked and pushed through the village. Past us march the battalion's other companies. Jokes pass back and forth but we are too tired to laugh. From the right a group of field grey figures approach across the open field. Then we recognize the commander. Our platoon leader gets up to make his report. The "old man" gestures for him to sit. He throws a look around and nods appreciatively. Fiddling with his uniform, he takes down his Iron Cross, First Class and pins it on our platoon leader. His face beams, he can't hold it in. We congratulate and celebrate with him. Then we pick up our weapons and equipment again, form up and plod wearily on.

We leave behind an empty village, some burned-out wrecks and several dead..."

The Division's difficult fighting retreat in the first half of February led through Hippolitpuszta and Seregelyes, which the Division only left on explicit orders from the Armee, to Falubattian. Since 2. February, it had been under the command of III. A.K.. On 6. February, it was showing serious signs of exhaustion. Nevertheless, it carried out its attack; however, the enemy succeeded in penetrating the so-called "Margarethen position" in the Seregelyesz—Velencze—See sector. These penetrations were cleared up with the help of 1. Pz.Division. On that day, at the command post of III. Pz.Korps, General der Waffen-SS Gille presented the commander of 1. Pz.Division, Gen.Major Thunert, with the Knight's Cross. Since 7. February, the Division had been counterattacking with 1. Pz.Division. Advancing slowly against enemy opposition, they captured and held Hills 129 and 130. Hurried improvements to the defensive positions provided the troops with little rest.

On 12. February, the Division was regrouped and given a new defence sector. At the same time it relieved the *TOTENKOPF* Division but had to stretch its lines as far as the southern edge of Stuhlweißenburg. The Division command post was moved to Sarpentele, 8 km. southwest of Stuhlweißenburg. The Division was once again under the command of IV. Armee Korps.

At this hour the fate of the Hungarian capital and its courageous defenders was decided. SS-Obergruppenführer and General of Police and the Waffen-SS Pfeffer-Wildenbruch fell into Soviet hands, the commander of 8. SS-Kav.Division, SS- Brigadeführer and Generalmajor der Waffen-SS Rumohr was killed in action and the severely wounded *SS-Brigadeführer* and Generalmajor der Waffen-SS Zehender of 22. SS-Kav.Division took his own life rather than be captured by the Russians. Only 785 men, including a third of the *FELDHERRNHALLE* Division, under the command of Oberstleutnant Wolff, succeeded in reaching the German lines on 13. February. They alone had succeeded in breaking out of the city. The rest were captured by the Russians or were killed attempting to break out. The firing stopped in Budapest. The Hungarian capital was lost in the Red flood.

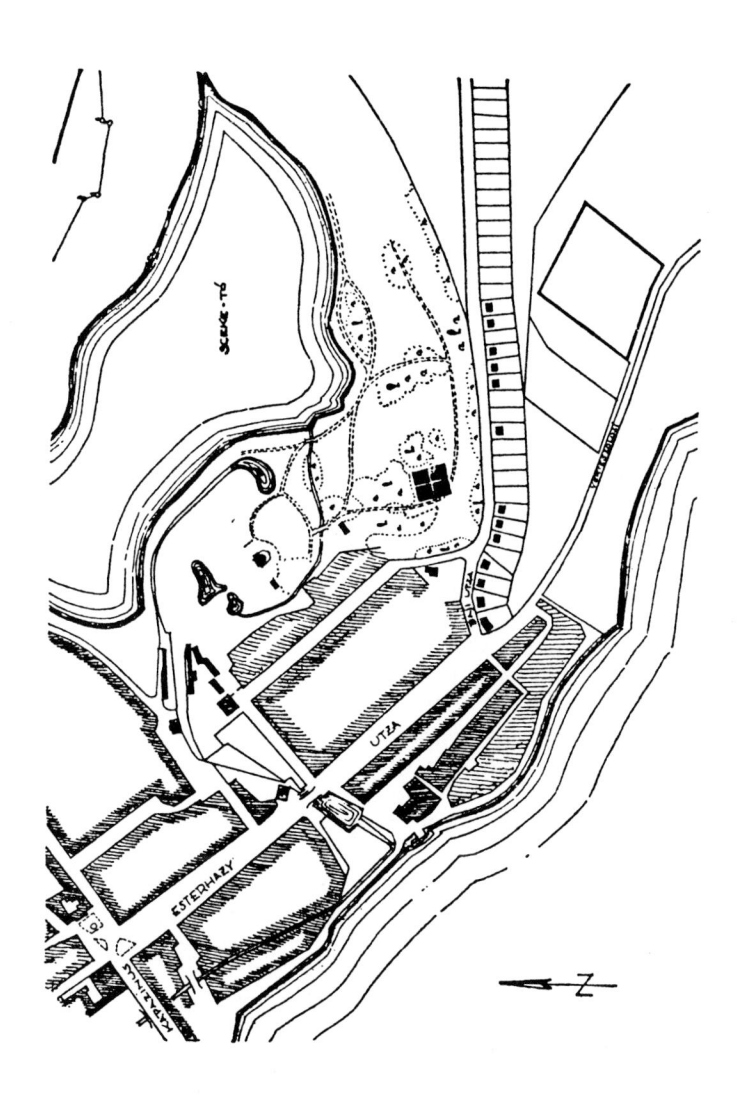

The Waffen-SS cemetery at Tata Tavoros/Hungary

The Arrival of 6. SS-Panzer-Armee

From the end of February to the middle of March, 6. SS- Pz.Armee commanded by Oberstgruppenführer and Generaloberst der Waffen-SS Sepp Dietrich arrived. The Armee comprised I. and II. SS-Pz.Korps with the SS-Divisions *LEIBSTANDARTE, HITLERJUGEND, DAS REICH* and *HOHENSTAUFEN*. This was an unusually large concentration and gave rise to great speculation and hope. However, there were also dissenting voices stating that ground and weather conditions were unsuitable for a massed attack by the Panzer divisions. Besides, what was the use of all the secrecy, when already since the middle of February, elements of I. SS-Pz.Korps had to be employed in 8. Armee's sector to reduce the Soviet Gran bridgehead?

The planned offensive foresaw three main efforts:
1. consisting of 6. Armee (Balck) and 6. SS-Pz.Armee (Dietrich), breaking out of the area between the Plattensee and Lake Velencze and reaching the Danube near Dunaföldvàr;
2. consisting of 2. Pz.Armee, attacking south of the Plattensee between Drau and Plattensee and advancing eastward to the Danube. The Armee's 16. SS-Pz.Gren.Div. RF-SS would advance from the area of Nagy Kanisza via Kaposvàr:
3. consisting of Heeresgruppe E (Balkan), moving between Esseg and Miholijac across the Drau and pushing northeastward to Mohàc on the Drau.

Of course, nearly all the requirements for this operation were lacking, but orders remained orders...

Still, on 24. February, 12. SS-Pz.Div. *HITLERJUGEND* succeeded in completely eliminating the Gran bridgehead. "It was the Division's last successful large attack operation. Several units had suffered severe losses. Once again the losses among NCO's were disproportionately high."[1]

Until the middle of March, the situation on the *WIKING* Division's front remained relatively calm. Then, however, large enemy troop movements were observed and enemy patrol activity increased noticeably. On 16. February, a tremendous barrage of all calibres fell on the entire sector. Continuous Soviet attacks were beaten off from the defensive positions which had been improved and extended during the lull. The central thrust of the Soviet attack had not yet become apparent.

The Evacuation of Stuhlweißenburg

In a rapid advance, the Soviets succeeded in surrounding the city of Stuhlweißenburg and its defenders, who were left with but a single road linking them with the south. The corridor in which *WIKING* and part of 1. Pz.Div. found themselves was approximately 15 kilometres long and only 3 to 5 kilometres wide. When the report arrived that the enemy spearheads were said to have already reached Papa, the resulting confusion was great. At midday on 21. February, radio contact was finally reestablished. But it brought only the categoric order from the Führer: "Stuhlweißenburg will hold under all circumstances!" All military considerations spoke against the fulfillment of this order. And it would have been the certain end of the *WIKING* Division, since a relief operation in the face of the enemy streaming irresistably westward was no longer thinkable. Therefore, the commander of 5. SS-Pz.Div. WIKING, Oberführer Ullrich, decided to order the evacuation of Stuhlweißenburg and consequently to act contrary to an order from the Führer. It was a decision which could not have been pleasant for a soldier like Ullrich.

The Division gathered its forces in the Urhida area so as to commence the breakout toward the west-southwest at dawn on the 22nd in as concentrated a mass as possible. In doing so, it was not clear where the linkup with the German front would take place.

In the dawn twilight, the Division moved in two Kampfgruppen in the general direction of the northern edge of the Plattensee. The WESTLAND Regiment under Hack screened to the north against Nadasladany, while the main group with all of the armoured forces were to attempt to force a breakthrough. Despite powerful enemy assaults from the south, the Division succeeded in winning ground to the southwest. However, the armoured units—Panzers, Sturmgeschütze and SPW, as well as II./A.R. 5 (self- propelled artillery)—were lost in running battles with new enemy units which continually appeared. The units forced their way through fighting now more as assault troops. When, roughly at midday, more troops were sighted fleeing toward the west, it became clear that the Southern Front had collapsed. The value of a disciplined unit was proven once again in this disastrous confusion. Only thus did the WIKING succeed in frustrating the enemy's intention to finally destroy the Division.

It must be noted here that 9. SS-Pz.Div. HOHENSTAUFEN under its commander, SS-Brigadeführer and Generalmajor der Waffen-SS Sylvester Stadler, played a decisive role in the successful breakthrough by the WIKING Division. Contrary to orders, Stadler had shifted his front as far as possible to the northern part of the Plattensee in order to hold that sector open for WIKING. At roughly 16.00 hours, the Division operations staff arrived at HOHENSTAUFEN's divisional command post in Papkesi. Two hours later, all elements of the WIKING Division had assembled behind HOHENSTAUFEN's front.

Afterward, Oberführer Gille was anxious to reestablish contact with III. Armeekorps. In Balatonfökajar he was greeted warmly by General Breith and congratulated on the Division's successful breakout. However, on the following day, 23. March, Ullrich, whose Division was once again under the command of IV. SS-Pz.Korps, received new orders.

During this week the enemy was extremely active in the air. Naturally the Soviets had not been able to create such an airforce from the ground up on their own. However, myth gave rise to the contention that the Soviets were dependent in this area on the lend-lease deliveries from their American allies.

The situation was anything but gratifying: the enemy was rapidly advancing to the west north of Vesprem, already in Russian hands. The Division was in positions on both sides of the Vesprem—Tapolca road and had once again settled down somewhat. Contact was established to the right, however, there were apparently no German forces to the left.

On 24.3.1945 at approximately 18.00 hours, the enemy attacked on both sides of the road with powerful motorized forces. The remaining combat ready troops, mainly infantry, gathered around the few SPW, including that of the Division Commander, which formed the loose defensive front built in the form of strongpoints. But they were no longer a match for the overwhelming Soviet forces.

What was left of the once so proud Division? When the commander of II./A.R. 5, Sturmbannführer Bühler, hurried forward on 25. March to take the place of the severely wounded Sturmbannführer Müller of the GERMANIA Regiment, he found the SPW of a battalion commander, the Division Radio Section's SPW and that of the Division Fe.Truppe! The situation was similar with the WESTLAND Regiment. The losses of the last days had been heavy and resulted from the constant retreat and frequent defensive actions. Only the Aufklärungsabteilung, which had been granted a few days of rest in Kopolcz, had been able to once again become a relatively complete unit under its new commander, SS-Sturmbannführer Fritz Vogt. Now it was deployed to cover literally an entire division's sector! However, despite enemy attacks, it succeeded in holding the defensive positions it had taken over throughout the entire day of 26. March. Not until the evening did it withdraw to the new line as ordered.

In retrospect it can be said that in those days and hours the officers, NCO's and above all the men accomplished great individual achievements. Everyone fought bitterly against the overwhelming superiority of the enemy. Alexander Werth, a German immigrant who experienced the war in the Soviet Union, wrote in his book "Russia in the War":[2] "Now as before, there were excellent German soldiers—above all in the Waffen-SS—who were ready to fight to the end, and who would sooner commit suicide than surrender."

The Division's situation was so desperate—the commander had been cut off for a time—, that many of the men believed they were leaderless. But the "Reichsrottenführer", experienced in war and peace, instinctively fought their way with their companies or platoons back to the Division. That should say a great deal, when the Division O 1 himself had reached the conclusion at that time that the entire front had disintegrated.

Again and again, the Division's withdrawals, which now were happening in longer jumps, were too late. Often the Soviets got there before them. The Division landed in the Vasvar bridgehead on 29. 3. 1945. However, the Soviets had already pushed north and south of it far to the west.

What followed, happened very quickly: on 29. March, the tank spearheads of the 3rd Ukrainian Front reached the border of the Reich near Guns, northwest of Steinmanger, and entered Austria. At the same time, the 2nd Ukrainian Front was likewise advancing rapidly westward north of the Danube. On 4. April, the Slovakian capital, Preßburg, fell and twenty four hours later, Malinowski's spearheads entered Vienna.[3]

On 30. March, the Division command post was transferred into the southern part of the Vasvar bridgehead near the single bridge over the Raab.

The units received orders to assemble in the Division's supply area in Fürstenfeld and to place all men and weapons in the Division's sector in the "Reich defence position". Everyone who followed this order had to cross the border of the Reich. Even the streaming sunshine could not change the serious expressions on the hardened faces of the men...

From there on all roads were jammed. On the highway to Fürstenfeld there were two to three columns of trucks. The efforts of numerous staff officers and military police could scarcely alter the confused situation.

As if scorning the name of this rear position, the enemy had already entered before the Division had fully reached the line. In numerous small counterattacks it had to attempt to throw the enemy back and in this it succeeded. A difficult test was Hill 385 in the Fürstenfeld area around which the battle raged from 9.-13. April. During this defensive fighting, an infantry battalion under Hstuf. Schneider, which comprised the remnants of the once proud SS-Pz.Rgt. 5, distinguished itself. The battalion's weapons, with which it was able to repel day-long enemy attacks sometimes in four to five waves, consisted solely of infantry small arms and a limited supply of ammunition.

And the sacrifice was still not at an end. Such outstanding leaders and comrades as Stubaf. Vogt, commander of SS-A.A. 5 and wearer of the Oak Leaves, who was severely wounded by strafing aircraft on 2. April and died a day later, or Hauptscharführer Ballschuß who was killed with two others during the attack on Jennersdorf, had to give their lives at the last moment. Their names are representative of many other comrades whose fulfillment of duty meant more to them than their own lives.

XIV. SURRENDER AND IMPRISONMENT

Late on the evening of 7. April, Generaloberst Lothar Rendulic arrived from the Kurland in St. Leonhard west of St. Pölten to take the place of Gen.d.Inf. Otto Wöhler as Commander in Chief of Heeresgruppe Süd. United with Sepp Dietrich, the native Austrian was concerned mainly with holding Vienna, a task contrary to the orders of Hitler. However, in the middle of March, the spotlight which had been on the events in Hungary, Slovakia and eastern Austria for the past three months shifted. The southeast became a secondary theatre, because raising itself again for the last time in the war was the Soviet danger on the Oder; the assault on the Reich capital and the Elbe was beginning. The men of the *WIKING* Division also received the last Order of the Day from the Supreme Commander of 16. April 1945 in which among other things he said: "If every soldier on the Eastern Front does his duty in these coming days and weeks, the last assault from Asia will be broken, exactly as the invasion by our enemy in the west will fail in the end in spite of everything. Berlin remains German, Vienna will be German again and Europe will never be Russian." Who should blame these soldiers therefore when, faithfull to their oath, they continued to fight bitterly until the end of the war?

This end was long anticipated. But honestly, who at that time could already imagine it? Numerous replacements were still arriving. Intensive training was carried out at the end of April, instruction in hand to hand combat etc.. Discipline was outstanding. Replacements likewise reached the artillery regiment from its replacement garrison as well as new guns and tractors! An additional battery was to be established, which in fact took place just northeast of Graz. The German war machinery appeared simply inexhaustible...On 5. May, all of the Division's Ia and IIa were ordered to the Commander of the Armee to which the Division was attached in the Graz area. He told them of the capitulation of the German Wehrmacht in Italy and the general situation which indicated that the end would soon come. This bad news spread like lightning. Certainly it hit the foreign and *Volksdeutsche* volunteers, whose countries had been overrun, the hardest. In those days the bond of comradeship once again grew all the stronger and gave comfort and confidence during the most difficult hours.

As strange as it may seem, the units were now showered with food of the highest quality. On one hand this was proof of the efficiency and foresight in stockpiling of the German war economy, on the other, proof of the morbid adherence to their beloved hoards of supplies. In any case that must have been the way the soldiers saw it.

Although the front around Walkersdorf was firm—several days before, another successful local attack had been carried out—a Divisional order reached SS-Pionier-Btl. 5 at noon on 7. May, ordering that the front be abandoned since the surrender was only hours away.

On this 7th of May, the preliminary orders were rushed through and a command briefing fixed for 13.30 hours. As a result, preparations were to be made for a withdrawal to the west. The commanders were advised to remain together, so as to be able to receive new orders, as the Division commander had been ordered to the Armee at 16.00 hours. This briefing took place at 17.00 hours: the surrender was expected within hours. The commander, SS-Oberführer Karl Ullrich, returned from Corps during the night of 7./8. May. When he advised that the Division was to disengage from the enemy from 12.00 hours on the following day and must withdraw over 200 kilometres to the north behind the American demarcation line, everyone reacted almost automatically. The last act was to be carried out...

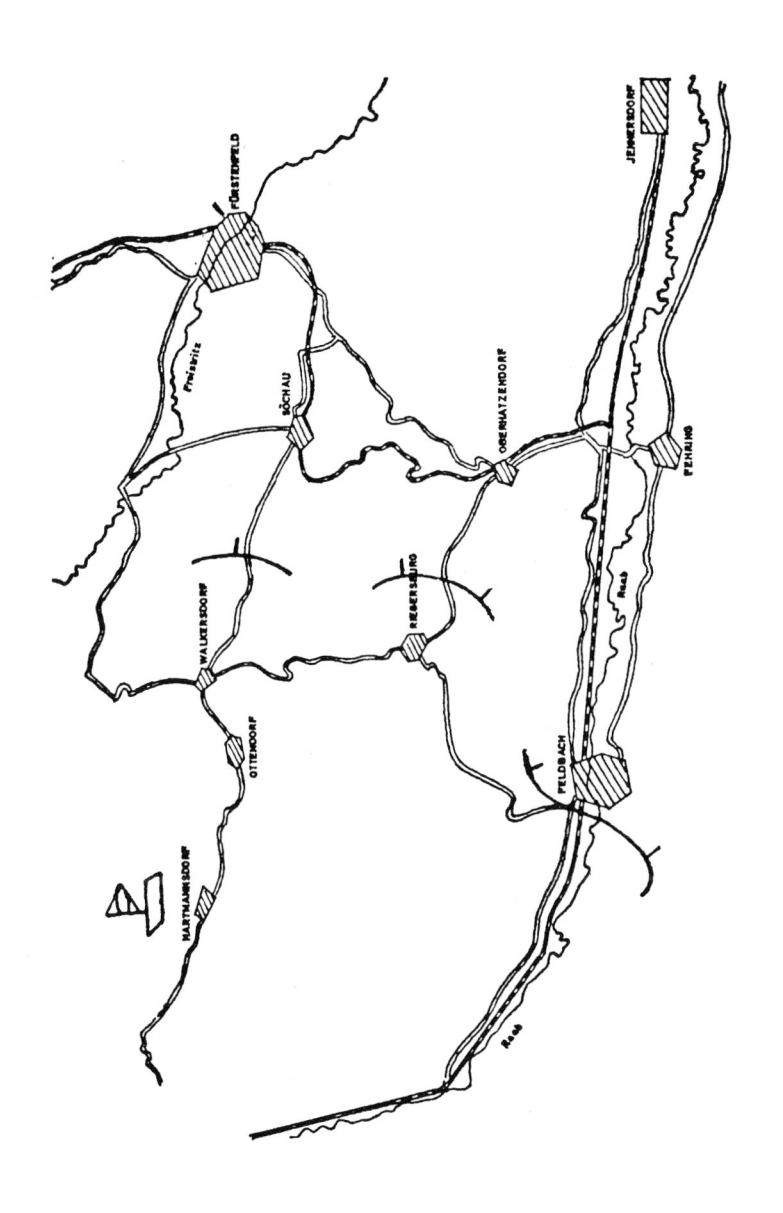

Positions on 8. May 1945

The information declared that the withdrawal to the west would follow three code words in three phases. Not until the third code word had been given would the command authority of the Army expire. Since no one wished to be taken prisoner by the Soviets, it was ordered that all trucks were to be used only for the transportation of troops.

While the infantry had to carry out one last attack on the morning of 8. May 1945, in order to enable the planned withdrawal to go ahead, the Army had already issued the last code word, "Funkstille" (radio silence), at 03.00 hours. As a result, the "general surrender" was to follow at 12.00 hours. As a consequence of an early pull out by its neighbour to the left, the Division suffered unnecessary casualties. The Russians moved forward into the vacated area and WESTLAND was forced to fight its way out. Nevertheless, everyone succeeded in reaching Graz after all written documents, surplus vehicles and material had been destroyed.

Part of the population had evacuated to the caves here in the face of bombing attacks and there was a great deal of sickness among the children. Resistance appeared here and there, allied with former concentration camp inmates. The released Russian prisoners of war on the other hand, asked to be taken along toward the west. A request, which due to a shortage of transportation space, could not,unfortunately, be granted. They were also dominated by fear of their own countrymen and the commissars. Now red and white Austrian flags appeared here and there. The confusion is barely describable. While, for example, the Field Training Battalion marched in faultless order singing through Graz, the populace lining the streets displayed no animosity. Cries like "come again!" and "Auf Wiedersehen!" rang through the streets and alleys.

Once again the commander took the marchpast of several of his units. It was a moving and unforgettable scene for all participants as these men, unbroken and disciplined, filed singing past their last commander. What home did they have now, except with the "old crowd"?

The Division members passing Graz somewhat later had it more difficult. They were fired on and reached the bridge on the Mur only with difficulty where they were surprised by Soviet cavalry and T-34 tanks. Half of the Pionier platoon of the former Pz.Rgt. 5 came through to Tamsweg and at first became prisoners of the British. However, the majority "took off" during the first night and met the Americans near Radstadt. Nearly everyone experienced the day of surrender differently.

On the day of surrender there were long march delays through the mountains. Rumours, orders and requests buzzed through the confusion. Many wanted to reach the mountains. Supplies, weapons and equipment were brought into the "Alpine fortress". Many prepared for a long stay. Everyone was left to his own discretion. But the old discipline and unequivocal orders allowed the masses to be held together as before. At roughly 18.00 hours, followed a further march to Mauterndorf, where in the night hours of 8. May, the first American advance guards were encountered. However, they paid little notice to the German column. They were attempting to move east as quickly as possible to, as they said, to halt the Soviets as far to the east as possible.

Near Wagrain, just before the demarcation line, the commander once again assembled his officers. Oberführer Ullrich released the commanders and officers from their oath and left them free to go into an uncertain imprisonment with the troops or to strike out into the mountains and attempt to reach their homes. He himself, he explained, preferred to remain with his men in order to fulfill their trust in the difficult times ahead. All of the assembled officers shared the view of their commander and went into American captivity as a complete unit, which was to prove to be an immeasurable advantage.[1]

Slowly and haltingly the long line of vehicles wound its way up the Tauern pass. The pass was cleared on 12. May and from there on things moved faster. The troops appeared to be in good spirits.

On the eve of 13. May, the Division's command section reached the American barricades. All weapons had to be surrendered, only the officers being permitted to retain their pistols. Still, they were fortunate to have escaped the Russians. Then they moved via Radstadt and Wagrain into the valley of the Little Arl where the rest of the Division camped from 14. to 31. May 1945. Only an American barricade at the entrance to the valley indicated to a casual passerby that they were prisoners.

Still everything was bearable. Certainly the horses of the mounted police platoon had already been slaughtered and many non- essentials had been bartered for food. However, no one was in need or felt themselves hard-pressed. The residents helped the men wherever they could. Reports and bits of news for which everyone was eager were received via salvaged radio receivers or from the first news sheets from the "Armee De Angelis". But what was contained therein to read was difficult to understand for the men who in those days indulged in the sun, the deceptive peace and the view of their beloved mountains.

The history of the *WIKING* Division would not be complete without mention of the astonishing drive "home into the Reich" unescorted by foreign soldiers. Those responsible had two aims in mind in their dealings with the Americans: first, no handing over to the Soviets but rather passage directly into the Reich; second, transport only in their units' own vehicles. In fact the Americans agreed to these terms and ensured that the necesary vehicles were serviced. By 31. May 1945 all was ready for departure. In a large convoy in an almost peacetime fashion and with a minimum of overseeing, the rest of the Division was brought up from Wagrain on 1. June, destination the "old Reich". The drive proceeded via Markt Pongau, Bischofshofen, Golling, Hallein, Salzburg, Freilassing, Traunstein, Rosenheim, Bad Aibling and Bad Tölz to Eberfing. Here and there their march was like one of triumph, as in passing through Bad Tölz where the people, especially the women, lined the streets and showered the column of vehicles with cigarettes, flowers and food although American Negro soldiers were posted at the street corners. Enroute, on the open road, the column was overtaken by a high-ranking American officer in a jeep, who stood up in his vehicle, saluted and clapped his hands while yelling incessantly, "Bravo, *WIKING* Division!" Officers, NCO's and men looked on in amazement. One could have thought that it was they who had won the war.

But the illusion was all too soon to be shattered. The provisional stay in Eberfing lasted from 2. June until 26. June, when they were transferred to a camp on the Riegsee in Upper Bavaria. Although they now gradually began to feel the pangs of hunger, the men were relatively free and enjoyed the magnificent summer weather, the mountain scenery and as often as possible a refreshing bath. And yet—they were prisoners in their own country! When the camp on the Riegsee was disbanded at the beginning of September, the ultimate and irrevocable end of the Division had come. For many of the *Kameraden*, in particular for the European volunteers, there now began a lonely road of distress, terror and despair which these men did not deserve. That so many of them successfully withstood their test of fate and today are still proud to profess their former comradeship does honour to the Division and to the Regiments, Battalions and Sections in which they fought during the Second World War.

XV. DOCUMENT APPENDIX

Document Appendix No. 1

SS-Führungshauptamt Berlin-Wilmersdorf, 28. 3. 1941
Ia/Tgb. Nr. 76/41 geh.Kdos. 95 Copies
G./Keu. Copy No. 8

Secret Military Document!

Re: Assignment of the SS-Division WIKING

Distribution:				
SS-Div. WIKING	10	Amt VI	3
RF SS	4	Amt VII	3
FHA	6	Amt VIII	10
Amt I	10	HA SS-Court	1
Amt II	10	HA Budgeting and	
Amt III	1	Structures	1
Amt IV	10	RuS HA	1
Amt V	10		

It is ordered with the agreement of the OKH:

Effective **1. 4. 1941**, the SS-Div. (mot) WIKING is integrated into the Army and placed under the command of Heeresgruppe O.

The authority of the Reichsführer-SS in the area of ideological training, the filling of officer positions as well as the reporting of replacements, remains hereby untouched. In **these** areas direct communication will take place between the Reichsführer-SS and the SS-Div. (mot) WIKING. Accordingly the Reichsführer-SS retains the right in agreement with the responsible superior officers to assist in the service of the SS-Div. (mot) WIKING.

For rendering and settlement of accounts the SS-Div. (mot) WIKING is allocated to the Superintendant of Accounts of H.V. VII in Munich. Army Post Finance Office Munich is responsible for all voucher accounts belonging to the Division's units.

The Chief of Staff
signed Jüttner
SS-Brigadeführer

Document Appendix No. 2

SS-Division WIKING

Division Headquarters
2. 7. 1941

Divisional Order

SS-Standartenführer Wäckerle, the commander of the WESTLAND Regiment, was killed in action on 2. July.

After building up the Regiment under the most difficult conditions, imbuing it with the best soldierly spirit and training it thoroughly, on 1. 7. 1941 he led the Regiment in an auspicious and successful combat which resulted in victory and witnessed the proud confirmation of his tireless efforts. On the following day, he died a hero's death as one of the first of his Regiment.

A soldier's life, whose content was the service of Germany, has been extinguished. His death is a symbol for the young Regiment. He not only lived as example for the Regiment, but was also an example in death.

The Regiment and every volunteer owes him the highest thanks. This will be paid through every success and the Regiment will never forget its founder and first commander. Today the Division and the WESTLAND Regiment salute their dead regimental commander for the last time.

signed Steiner

Document Appendix No. 3

SS-Division *WIKING*   Div. Headquarters, 12. 7. 41
II a

Men of the SS-Division *WIKING!*

During the past days the Division has been put to a hard test. You have stood that test.

The *GERMANIA* Rgt. has defeated superior enemy forces in three hard battles, the *WESTLAND* Rgt. has passed its test of fire brilliantly in the past three days of fighting, the *NORDLAND* Rgt. has overcome powerful enemy infantry and tank forces. The achievements of A.R. 5 have been beyond all praise.

The Reconnaissance Battalion, Panzer-Jäger Battalion and Flak Battalion have been fully proven, as have the Pionier Battalion, the Signals Battalion and the Medical Battalion.

The supply services have performed excellently under the most difficult conditions. Especially prominent have been the tireless efforts of the Quartermaster Section of the Divisional Headquarters. I am filled with confidence in the Division and I go into the coming decisive battles at its head, confident that the *WIKING* Division will further distinguish itself and add to its glory. I thank all members of the Division for your loyalty and courage. The sacrifices you have made have not been in vain. They serve to overcome all of the destructive elements and to bring about the rise of a new peaceful Europe.

                                                                        signed Steiner

Document Appendix No. 4

SS-Division *WIKING*   Div. Headquarters, 20. July 1941
I a

Divisional order for the defence on 20./21. 1941

1. **Powerful enemy forces** have today attacked in several places, mainly Kirdany and Kriwa. They were repulsed. It is reckoned that reinforced the enemy will carry out further attacks on 21. July.

2. **On 20./21. July, the Division will arrange the defence and defend in the present positions which are:**

    (a) **Gefechtsgruppe Stolz**

    Units:
    Rgt. H.Q. WESTLAND
    Rgt. Units WESTLAND
    reinf. II./WESTLAND Rgt.
    reinf. III./GERMANIA Rgt.
    II./A.R. 5
    one hvy.Battery 602
    one Company Pz.Jg. 5
    two Flak platoons Flak 5

    in the line Hf. Nawesseliza
    —group of houses south of Taraschtscha echeloned to the southeast.
    Reconnaissance: to the southeast of Lukjanowka and towards the forest southwest of Taraschtscha.

    (b) **Gefechtsgruppe Joerchel**
    Units:
    reinf. II./GERMANIA Rgt.
    (less 7./GERMANIA Rgt.)
    7./WESTLAND Rgt.

    on the south and southeast edge of Taraschtscha

    (c) **Gefechtsgruppe v. Reitzenstein**
    Units:
    A.A. 5
    reinf. 7./GERMANIA Rgt.
    2./WESTLAND Rgt.
    1./Pz.Jg.Abt. 5

    the north road Taraschtscha —Kirdany including hills due east of Kriwa.

    (d) **Gefechtsgruppe von Oberkamp**
    Units:
    reinf. I./GERMANIA Rgt.
    reinf. 15./GERMANIA Rgt.
    reinf. III./WESTLAND Rgt.
    1./Pi.Btl. 5
    H.Q. and 2./Pz.Jg. 5

    in the hill sector due north of Kriwa—hill east of Ssalika—west part of Ssinjawa factory south bank of the Ross to Ostroff and 1 km. northeastward on the route to Pugatschowka.

(e) **Gefechtsgruppe Klein**
 Units:
 Pi.Btl. 5   in the sector 1 km.
 (less 1./Pi. 5)   southeast of Pugatschowka
   —Koshanka strongpoint
   both sides of Pugatschowka.

3. **Boundaries**

   (a) **between Gefechtsgruppe Stolz and Joerchel** road fork 1.5 km. west of Taraschtscha—road fork 800 metres southeast of Taraschtscha—"W" from Wissokij.

   (b) **between Gefechtsgruppe Joerchel and v. Reitzenstein** northeast corner of Tschernin—road fork on the northern exit from Taraschtscha—Taraschtscha road—Bolkun (this for Gef.Gruppe v. Reitzenstein).

   (c) **between Gefechtsgruppe v. Reitzenstein and von Oberkamp** north edge of Tschernin—northwest edge Kriwa.

   (d) **between Gefechtsgruppe v. Oberkamp and Klein** northwest edge—Nastaschka—northwest edge Ostroff.

4. **Artillery organization:**

   (a) **Art.Kampfgruppe Richter** (II./A.R. 5 and a heavy battery 602) under the command of Gefechtsgruppe Stolz.

   (b) **Art.Kampfgruppe Paul** (heavy Art.Abt. 602 [less one battery] 12./A.R. 5, 3./A.R. 5) assigned to work in conjunction with Gefechtsgruppen Joerchel and v. Reitzenstein in the area northeast of Uleschowka.

   (c) **Art.Kampfgruppe Fick** (I./A.R. 5 [less 3. Battery] assigned to work in conjunction with reinf. I./GERMANIA Rgt. in position in the area south of Ssalinka.

   (d) **Art.Kampfgruppe Brasack** (IV./A.R. 5 [less 12. Battery]) assigned to work in conjunction with III./WESTLAND Rgt. in position around area 207.

Fire concentrations east of Taraschtscha, west of Kirdany, eastern part of Ssinjawa, southern edge of Rokitno.

Barrage fire areas determined by Art.Commander. Part of Flak 5 integrated into the fireplan by A.R. 5. Barrage fire in front of Gefechtsgruppe Klein will be given by Art. 9. Pz.. AV command to individual Kampfgruppen and battalions respectively.

5. **Div. Reserve**
   Reinf. I./WESTLAND Rgt. (less one company) in the woods south of the road fork southwest of Ssaliska.

6. **Reconnaissance:** During the night intensive battle reconnaissance will be conducted ahead of the front.

7. **Liason** between the individual Gefechtsgruppen will be established and carefully maintained to the left and right.

8. **Signal communications:**
   Wire to Gefechtsgruppe Stolz, Joerchel, v. Reitzenstein and Artillery C.O. 5 v. Oberkamp.
   Radio by heterodyne (less Gefechtsgruppe Joerchel) to Kampfgruppe Klein over radio line Ib.

9. **Light signals:** white: front line
   green: request for barrage fire

10. **Medical clearing station:** Road fork 1 km. north of Ulaschowka.

11. **Div.Command Post:** Road fork 3 km. north of Ulaschewskaja Odaja.
    F. d. R   Signed in draft:
    signed Ecke   Steiner

Document Appendix No. 5

SS-Division *WIKING*   Div. Headquarters, 21. July 1941
I a

Divisional Order for 22. July 1941

1. **Before the Division's front** in the Taraschtscha Pugatschjowka sector, renewed enemy concentrations, new batteries and movements have been recognized.

   Enemy attacks from the direction of Kirdany and the northwest are expected tomorrow. It is presumed that the enemy thrusts will take place southwest of Rokitno with limited objectives and increased artillery activity.

   Opposite Gefechtsgruppe Stolz the enemy has in the course of the afternoon of 21. 7. brought up new forces respectively shifted from the eastern front and apparently a cavalry brigade has occupied the hills near Beresjanka and to the west. The enemy has gone over to the defensive on the edge of the forests east and north of Ssedlezkaja Sloboda as well as near Lukjanowka.

2. **XIV. A.K.** will attack tomorrow morning first with the Pz.Rgt. of 9. Pz.Div. from the direction of Juschow Rog—Stanischowka toward Luka to the southeast toward Swenigorodka.

   The WIKING Division will follow with South Group (Gef.Gruppe Stolz) the attack by 9. Pz.Div.'s Pz.Rgt. and attacking to the Pz.Rgt.'s left, advance through the forest southwest of Taraschtscha, push through Lukjanowka with the right wing in order to first win the line-south edge Wyssokij Lipnjak—wooded hill 2.5 km. to the west-and open the Taraschtscha—Luka road, at the same time defending with Gef.Gruppen Joerchel, von Reitzenstein, von Oberkamp and Klein in a northwesterly direction against the enemy forces standing near Taraschtscha on the Ross.

3. In addition, **Gefechtsgruppe Stolz** will be in readiness by 07.30 hours to attack with Kampfgruppe Schönfelder from west of Naweszeliza with the right wing toward the southern edge of Lukjanowka and advance along the brook northeast of Lukjanowka as far as Wyssokij Lipnjak.

   The mass of Gef.Gruppe Stolz will be in readiness northwest of Kampfgruppe Schönfelder to advance with the right wing toward the road fork 1 km. northwest of Lukjanowka and then northeast along the forest road winning the forest clearing west of Wyssokij Lipnjak.

   Kampfgruppe von Hadeln is to follow behind the left wing and toward Taraschtscha.

4. All depends on screening the preparations for the attack to the northeast from the enemy near Beresjanka until 15. Comp. of Kampfgruppe von Hadeln in the rear is in readiness to protect the flank and prevent an attack by the enemy into the flanks of the attack group from the direction of Beresjanka until Pz.Rgt. 33's attack takes place.

5. Supporting the attack:

   (a) Art.Gruppe Richter   in the morning will move up to
                                 new firing position east of Potoki.

   (b) Art.Gruppe Paul   northwest of Taraschtscha

   Command of the artillery through Arfü 5. Cooperation between Kampfgruppe Schönfelder and Stoffers and individual batteries in particular to be arranged through Arfü 5.

   Assignments:
   With the crossing of the Welikaja Wolnjanka—Lissowitschi field road by the spearhead of Pz.Rgt. 33, concentrated fire by Gruppe Richter on the forest edge opposite Kampfgruppe Stoffers (2 km. east of Lissowitschi), then with the advance by Pz.Rgt. 33's spearhead across the Beresjanka—Lissowitschi road shift fire onto the wood 1,500 metres west of Lukjanowka, then project forward onto Lukjanowka and the forest to the west in order to pave the way into the enemy for Kampfgruppen Stoffers and Schönfelder advancing into the forest.

   Gruppe Paul is to be called in from the northwest to provide fire on the forest southwest of Taraschtscha.

6. **STUKA attacks** on Lukjanowka and the wooded areas southwest of Taraschtscha will precede the attack.

7. **Conduct of battle**
   Heavy infantry high angle weapons and antitank are placed under the command of the attack battalions and rear battalions are to be provided with sufficient antitank companies as well as assault Infanterie Pioniere placed under the command of the attack companies, as well a detachment from Pi.Btl 5 each with a flamethrower to Kampfgruppe Schönfelder and Stoffers as well as Kampfgruppe von Hadeln.

   Supply by Pi.Btl 5 until 05.30 hours to Potocki.

8. Kampfgruppen Joerchel, von Reitzenstein, von Oberkamp and Klein retain their assignments from 21. 7. and defend against enemy attack from the east into the Korps' flank. **Artillery support** is to be controlled by Arfü 5 in such a manner, that cover to the northeast is guaranteed without weakening the artillery support ahead of the attack Gruppe Stolz.

9. **Flak Abt. 5** will place a light 2 cm. platoon from the Division defence group under the command of Gefechtsgruppe Stolz and provide this to Gef.Gruppe Stolz by 06.00 hours.

10. **Signal communication:** To Gefechtsgruppe Stolz, Arfü 5 by wire, as for the rest, as before.

11. **Forward aid station** is to be set up by the Div. medical officer in Potocki.

12. **Division command post** as of 07.00 hours north of Potocki.

F. d. R
signed Ecke   signed Steiner

Document Appendix No. 6

SS-Division *WIKING* Div.Headquarters, 29. 7. 1941
Commander

Divisional Order of the day

I express my highest appreciation to the elements of the Division involved in the decisive defensive battles around Taraschtscha, 7./SS-Rgt. *GERMANIA*, 2./SS-A.A.5, the Bartols Pz.Jg. Platoon and the Pionier Platoon of 4./SS-A.A.5, for their outstanding bravery and exemplary conduct in the critical moments.

During this fighting the following have especially distinguished themselves:

SS-Hstuf. Walther	7./SS-Rgt. GERMANIA
SS-Ostuf. Schlei	2./SS-A.A. 5
SS-Istuf. Bartols	1./SS-Pz.Jg.Abt. 5
SS-Oscha. Jörg	4./SS-A.A. 5
SS-Uscha. Schneider	7./SS-Rgt. GERMANIA
SS-Uscha. Schreiber	7./SS-Rgt. GERMANIA
SS-Schütze Barth	2./SS-A.A. 5

It is thanks to the unshakeable steadfastness of all of the remaining elements of the Division, that the heavy attack by five enemy divisions collapsed before the Division's front, thus making a decisive contribution so that Panzergruppe 1 was able to swing to the south and the encirclement of the enemy could follow.

The artillery has performed excellently under the reliable leadership of the Artillery Commanders.

In these days the Division has stood its greatest test. I am grateful to all members of the Division for this achievement and look forward with complete trust and inner confidence to the future.

Sieg Heil to the Division and its courageous Regiments.

signed Steiner

Document Appendix No. 7

SS-Division *WIKING* Div.Headquarters, 7. 9. 1941

Divisional Order of the Day

Today in the combat near Smela, next to many loyal SS-Men and soldiers, fell.

The Division's 1. General Staff officer, SS-Sturmbannführer Güther Ecke, holder of the Iron Cross 1st and 2nd Class.

The Division, which owes this outstanding officer a great debt, stands full of grief and sorrow at the grave of its 1. General Staff Officer.

His memory is inseparably linked with the history of the Division.

His life, his work and soldier's death will always be remembered in the Division.

We salute him for the last time.

signed Steiner
SS-Brigadeführer
Generalmajor and Div. Commander

Document Appendix No. 8

SS-Division *WIKING* Div.Headquarters, 7. 9. 1941
I a

Divisional Order
for
Enlarging of the Bridgehead and the Attack on Kamenka

1. **Enemy** in front of the bridgehead approx. 2—3 divisions. Powerful enemy attacks were repulsed everywhere in the last days. In Kamenka one enemy division.

   See enclosure for enemy disposition.

2. **The Division** will go to the attack at 07.00 hours on 8. 9. from the reconnoitred assembly areas, throw back the enemy near Kamenka and take possession of this town.

   Later assignments: Defence to the north and northwest.

3. In addition, move into assembly areas in the night of 7./8. 9. and attack on the morning of 8. 9.:

   (a) **Gef.Gr. Stolz** right from the northwest part of 60 I.D.(mot)'s position due north of the boundary between I.R. 92 and 120.

   Committing at 07.00 hours, the Rgt. will first advance northwest and take possession of the ridge northeast of Kamenka, cover itself to the northeast, and after occupying the designated ridge, veer with a rear Kampfgruppe to Kamenka, bypassing the forward enemy positions.

   Then turn against enemy forces on the northeast edge and drive through the northeast edge of Kamenka to the northwest.

   Objective . . .
   Echelon in depth in the town.

   (b) **Gef.Gr. v. Oberkamp** left from the southern part of I.R. 120's positions.

   The Rgt. will advance at approx. 09.00 hours, coordinated to follow Gef.Gr. Stolz' penetration into Kamenka, with an assault group north of the enemy barracks installation south of the town's main street, follow with a further group advancing south of the barracks in the sandy terrain and bring its reserves from the left Kampfgruppe to cover to the south. First attack objective is the barracks camp and area to the north.

4. **Formation** of the attacking units in assault groups in accordance with verbal briefing. Allotment of heavy infantry weapons, flamethrowers and assault engineers as per special order.

5. **Boundaries** between Gef.Gr. Stolz and v. Oberkamp the town's main street, which is to be bypassed by both Gef.Gr.

6. **Artillery:** Commander Arko 3 Generalmajor v. Roman
   (a) **Formation:**
   Right Ikagruppe SS A.R. 5 (commander Oberst Gille) Assigned to collaborate with Gef.Gr. Stolz.
   Left Ikagruppe Reinf. Artl.Rgt. 13 (commander C.O. A.R. 13), I/SS-A.R. 5 (with Gef.Gr. v. Oberkamp)
   Main effort Gruppe A.R. 160, Nebel-Lehr.Rgt. Artillery suppression Gruppe: reinf. A.R. 511 in addition: Corps Artillery Rgt. Italian Exp. Corps and two 8.8 cm. batteries.

   (b) From 06.25 all artillery will engage all recognized enemy targets.

   1. In particular, the following are to be engaged with heavy destructive fire:

      Enemy occupied positions on the edge of Kamenka and strongpoints and trenches in the northern and southern parts of the town, that is:

Right Ikagruppe	on the section of town around the eastern point in the sector of Gruppe Stolz
Left Ikagruppe	on south and southeast sections of Kamenka in the sector of Gruppe v. Oberkamp
Corps Artl.Rgt. Ital. Exp.Corps	on the south and southwest edge of Kamenka. Neutralize the enemy forces occupying the southern edge of Kamenka.

   2. **from 07.00 hours** engage and put out of action all recognized enemy batteries in and northwest of Kamenka.

Ikagruppe Gille	Concentrated fire in front of Gef.Gr. Stolz attack sector, hold down the enemy.
Ikagruppe Waentscher	Continuation of harassing fire on designated targets and target areas.
Corps Artl.Rgt. Ital. Exp.Corps	Engage enemy batteries with flanking fire. Fire on the southwest edge of Kamenka.

3. **Further developments** with the committing of the infantry to Kamenka. (Time will be determined with Arko following report to Division by Gef.Gr. Stolz.) Concentrated fire by all Ikagruppen on sections of the town and enemy occupations in the designated target areas for a duration of 5 minutes (committing of Gef.Gr. Stolz and v. Oberkamp and penetration into the town) Increased effect of fire by Ital. Exp.Corps on enemy batteries, holding down of enemy occupations in the southwest part of Kamenka.

Concentrated fire by **Nebel-Lehr.Rgt.** on central Kamenka, lay down fire with explosive-smoke ammunition and explosive on the west section of the town from north to south (no interference with our own artl. observation!) With the penetration of the infantry into Kamenka: Fire on further pockets of enemy resistance.

(c) **Artillery Suppression Abt.** engage and put out of action with the earliest observation opportunities. Assignments through Arko. 3. Especially important is the total neutralization of the heavy enemy battery on the northwest edge of Kamenka and somewhat north of Kamenka and, with the assistance of artillery spotter aircraft, silencing of the flanking batteries, especially in and southwest of Podgorodnoje.

(d) **The 8.8 cm. Battery** will engage recognized enemy batteries in the area around Kamenka from its firing positions with direct fire.

7. (a) **Kradschützen Battalion 60 I.D.** from 09.00 hours tie down the enemy opposite its front with intensive fire and after von Oberkamp's forward Kampfgruppe's penetration into Kamenka, follow the attack staggered to the left rear protecting this against enemy action from the sections of the town on the Dnjepr.

(b) I.R. 120 will clear the mines laid in Gruppe v. Oberkamp's attack sector, I.R. 92 those in Gruppe Stolz' attack sector so that the attack can be safely carried forward.

(c) 60 I.D. is requested to stagger its reserves behind the left wing of I.R. 92 so that a threat of attack from the north can be blocked by reserves.

8. **Medical Battalion 5.** will set up forward dressing station with 1. Company on the north bank (of the Dnepr). Main dressing station in Dnepropetrovsk with 2. Company. Ambulance loading station at the ferry station. Field hospital 5 ready to admit in Krinitschki, 8 km. northwest of Newossolka.

9. **Signals communication** to gef.Gr. Stolz and v. Oberkamp as well as Art. Commander by wire, backup by wireless.

10. **Division reserve** A.A. 5 and parts of Pi.Btl. 5 and a Company of SS-Pz.Jg. 5 in the area around Dijewka.
11. **Div. Headquarters** Dijewka

signed Steiner

Special Distributor

ANNEX 1
to SS-Division WIKING
Ia from 7. 9. 1941

Enemy forces in Kamenka
The statements of a deserter (messenger of II./982nd IR) from Kamenka, who deserted on the evening of 5. 9., revealed the following enemy forces present in Kamenka:

The 275th Rifle (Infantry) Division with the 980th, 982nd and 984th Rifle (Infantry) Regiments. Location of the regiments on 5. 9.: somewhat southeast of the tip of Lake Sinikowka—southeast corner of Kamenka—along the south edge of Kamenka to the west to about the southern tip of Lake Schpakowo respectively Regiments 980, 982, 984.

The Division Headquarters of the 275th Rifle Division is in the southeast part of the town.

In addition:
2 light batteries (cal. 7.62—10 cm.)   1 battery each in the
1 heavy battery (cal. 15—18 cm.)   centre of the town and 1
(in the area of the NW corner of   battery in the area of
Kamenka—Nikolajewka)   the NW tip of Lake Sinikowka
1 Battalion of workers and Young Communists, approx. 1,200 men
4 heavy tanks
2 armoured scout cars (2 MG each)
1 mortar platoon per battalion
antitank

Armament:
majority automatic weapons
4 snipers per platoon
2 light MG per platoon
2 heavy MG per company
sufficient ammunition on hand

Training status: 50% not trained

Personnel status: Units received full complement of
                                        replacements up to beginning of Sept.
                                        Officer and commissar positions filled.
(Company commander—Lieutenant,
Battalion commander—Captain,
Regiment commander—Major or Lt.Colonel)

Document Appendix No. 9

The Commander in Chief Gr.Headquarters, 12. IX. 41
of Panzergruppe 1

Order of the day

The Panzergruppe is approaching a new assignment. III. Korps must at first remain behind in its bridgehead. That is not easy.

Therefore, I wish at this moment to express to III. Korps with its three courageous bridgehead divisions and its plucky Pioniere my thanks and appreciation for its efforts.

While the other Panzer and motorized divisions lay in their refitting areas or were on the watch on the Dnepr, III. A.K. was involved in the heaviest fighting which demanded the employment of everyone. And the battle for the bridgehead is still not over. The previously shown bravery and resolute support of the Pioniere guarantees that you will remain victorious in the battle for the bridgehead.

I hope that soon you will again roll against the enemy with the other two Korps of the Panzergruppe and will be able to go over to the pursuit.

Until then you must hold out in your position, tie down further strong enemy forces and continue to beat off all attacks. You have already performed a great service for the Heeresgruppe and eased the crossing of the Dnepr for the infantry divisions.

R. d. A signed von Kleist
signed Rohrer
Ltn. and Ord. Officer

Document Appendix No. 10

The Commander in Chief	Gr.Headquarters, 24. 9. 1941
of Panzergruppe 1

The battle of encirclement east of Kiev has ended for the Panzergruppe. On 12. 9. Panzergruppe 1 broke out of the Kremenchug bridgehead, made contact with Panzergruppe 2 in the shortest time and then repulsed in heavy fighting all attempts by the numerically far superior enemy to break out. In the fighting powerful enemy units were destroyed and huge quantities of prisoners and captured material brought in. Up to the evening of 23. 9. the count was:

        over   200,000 prisoners
                         100 tanks
                         698 guns
                         106 antitank guns
                         116 Flak
                     13,862 motor vehicles

The Panzergruppe now approaches a new assignment. A Korps with 3 divisions is leaving the units of Panzergruppe 1 after three months in the Gruppe and is joining Panzergruppe 2. An important new assignment lies ahead for the other two Korps. The end of the campaign in this sector is also an opportunity for me to express my deep thanks and appreciation to my Korps and its brave divisions for their great success. The Panzergruppe can be proud that it has achieved such tremendous success in a short time.

I am firmly convinced that all future assignments will be carried out just as quickly, resolutely and thoroughly. Forward then to the final battle!

To the departing XXXXVIII. A.K., 9. Pz.Div., 16. I.D. (mot) and 25. I.D. (mot) my warm farewell and continued success!

Heil to our Führer!   signed von Kleist

Document Appendix No. 11

The Commanding General
of III. Armeekorps

Korps Headquarters, 29. Sept. 1941

Korps Order of the Day

The difficult days of fighting in the Dnepropetrovsk bridgehead have been brought to a successful conclusion. During this time not one drop of blood was shed in vain. We now know that our bridgehead, won on 25. 8. in a daring leap across the Dnjepr, deceived the Russian Army Command concerning the true main direction of the thrust into the rear of the 4 enemy armies fighting for possession of Kiev. It thus contributed to a success for German arms unique in the history of the world in the battle for Kiev with its 2/3 of a million prisoners. This deception would have become futile had the brave and courageous divisions of III. Armeekorps not repulsed the enemy attacks launched again and again at the bridgehead. Therefore every foot of ground had to be fought for, and it was fought for.

The deception was such a complete success because the divisions continued to advance and gain ground. Not even the persistent concentrated fire of the enemy could prevent it. We can all look back on this hard week with pride and inner satisfaction. The troops in the fighting for the bridgehead have proved that the German soldier is made of steel and iron not only as a hammer but as the anvil as well.

I am particularly pleased that my old reliable 13. Panzerdivision which for its part made the jump across the Dnepr, played a decisive role in yesterday's final opening of the bridgehead. I express my thanks and appreciation to all officers and men. All arms have contributed to the final result. I would particularly like to think of the Pioniere who gave their best in the battle with the river and despite enemy fire always maintained contact with the bridgehead.

After today the 60. Inf.Div. (mot) and 198. Inf.Div. leave my area of command. It is only with sadness that I see both divisions leave. The 60. Inf.Div., under my command since the fighting for Fastow, took part brilliantly in the pursuit operations to the Dnepr, both divisions stood in the bridgehead, their men's conduct exemplary, likewise side by side with them the SS Div. *WIKING*. To them, with their commanders at their head, I wish continued luck and victory.

Heil to the Führer!

signed Mackensen
Cavalry General

Document Appendix No. 12

Kampfgruppe Maack   O.U., 10. 10. 1941

Kampfgruppen Order

1. **The Division** is again placed under the command of XIV. A.K., in the advance to the east with the limited objective for today up to the line Kolonie Kirschwald—Nowaja Karakuba—Nowyi Krementschik and the organization of crossings for the following XIV. A.K.

2. **Kampfgruppe Maack:** has the assignment observe,
   Units: recoinnoitre and secure the sector
   III./SS-NORDLAND   Ljubokut to the road due south of
   3./SS Pz.Jg.Abt. 5   of 71.2—Bogodar until relieved by
   + one platoon GERMANIA   Italian troops.
   2./SS Pz.Jg.Abt. 5   Because of the weak troop strength
   reinf. 15./SS "G"   occupying this sector, everything
   reinf. 15./SS "N"   depends on deceiving the enemy,
   + two platoons WESTLAND through brisk patrolling and motorized
                                                 liason activity, into believing the sector
                                                 is more heavily occupied. The bulk of the
                                                 forces in this sector are being held back
                                                 as reserves.

3. In addition the following detailed orders:

   (a) **III./SS NORDLAND**, with Ljubokut as boundary to the right, secure with a company each southwest of Fjodorowka, Marfopolje and Guljaj Polje, the bulk at the Guljaj Polje railroad station.

   (b) **reinf. 15./SS GERMANIA** secure following III./SS "N" with the north edge of Guljaj Polje as right boundary and the left boundary 70.5 (excl.) each with two Gruppen which will make contact with their neighbouring Gruppen at regular intervals in the morning and afternoon. The bulk of the Company will be held at the Gajtschur station as mobile reserve. Likewise "2./SS Pz.Jg.Abt. 5

   (c) **reinf. 3./SS Pz.Jg.Abt. 5** secure following 15./SS "G" and situate bulk of forces HF.BRA. 1.5 km southeast of BF Gajtschur.

   (d) **reinf. 15./SS NORDLAND** with right boundary 67.5 and left boundary the road due south of 71.2—Bogudar secure the sector and situate bulk of forces in Chutor Chamrajka. Contact is to be maintained with the Italion Division.

4. **Forward edge of the line of security:** Road which runs parallel in front of Gajschur river from Petro Pawlowka to Nikolajewka, to the left of it the high ground in front of Gajschur river.

5. **Communications** with 15./SS "G" and 15./SS "N". Radio. Radio link to III./SS NORDLAND is being prepared. Messenger to 2./ and 3./SS Pz.Jg.Abt. 5, in addition the units in radio contact will detach messengers.

6. The units will report particular incidents by 19.30 and 02.30 daily.

7. **Kampfgruppe Headquarters:** BF. Gajtschur. Transfer forward to Guljar Polje expected tomorrow morning, notice will be given.

F. d. R. (signed) Maack
signed Rohrer Major and Commander
Leutnant and O.O.

Document Appendix No. 13

Copy!

The Commander in Chief Headquarters, 10. 10. 1941
Heeresgruppe Süd

Order of the Day

Through exemplary cooperation and supported by Luftflotte 4, as always at the highest combat readiness, 11. Armee and 1. Pz.Armee have destroyed large parts of two Soviet armies and driven the rest in flight toward the east. Units of our Italian, Rumanian and Slovakian allies have played an important part in this battle in which the troops have once again achieved great success in obstinate defence and daring attacks. The troops have proven that despite the heaviest fighting and greatest exertions their power is undiminished, while the enemy, here as on the entire front, evidently faces collapse. I express once again my thanks and complete appreciation to the troops of the Allied and German units.

It is important now, despite the difficulties with the roads, the weather and supply, to smash the enemy wherever he still stands, to wipe out the rest of his armies in tireless pursuit and reap the fruits of our victory.

The order of the hour reads:

"Forward regardless!"

F.d.R.d.A. signed von Rundstedt
signed Rohrer
Leutnant and Adjutant

Document Appendix No. 14

SS-Division WIKING Div.Headquarters, 26. Nov. 1941
Commanding Officer

Wikinger,

Now that the fighting in the area of Rostov can be considered on the whole as concluded, it is an opportunity for me to thank you all for your great bravery and loyalty which you have proven in the past days of heavy fighting. Shoulder to shoulder with 16. Pz.Div., the Division has victoriously repulsed the thrust against Rostov's flank by the entire enemy 37th Army.

The Division's North Group under the command of Oberst von Scholz was attacked by the Red Army's 51st, 295th, 96th and 253rd Divisions, the 56th Cavalry Division and the 11th Tank Brigade.

In the closest comradeship, the NORDLAND Rgt., SS-Pionier Btl. 5, I. and II./ GERMANIA, its artillery, the Panzerjäger-Abt. and SS-Flak-Abt. 5 victoriously repulsed the Red assault in three days of heavy fighting and inflicted heavy losses on the enemy.

You have accomplished many heroic deeds, prominent among which are the battle for Ljubinaja, the action by Oberstleutnant Brassack, the daring feat of arms by Oberleutnant Faulhaber and his men and the assault on Balabanoff led personally by Oberst von Scholz.

Meanwhile, the WESTLAND SS-Rgt. under Oberst Stolz, shoulder to shoulder with III./SS-GERMANIA, I./SS A.R. 5, Panzerjäger.Abt. 5 and 2./Flak-Abt. 5, successfully repulsed an attack by the Soviet 150th Rifle Division, 66th Cavalry Division and a tank brigade. After the victorious battle, the Division and 16. Pz.Div. were able easily to disengage from the enemy and behind the strong Tusloff sector to parry every further threat. You carried out this difficult operation with the best discipline and order. Confident of your superior training, your martial spirit and your morality, you continue to demonstrate to the enemy daily your fighting composure and superiority.

When I thank you today for your bravery and confidence in my command, I do so from the depth of my heart and close comradeship with you.

Hail to you, Wikinger! signed Steiner

Document Appendix No. 15

SS-Division WIKING   Div.Headquarters, 1. 12. 1941
I a

Divisional Order of the Day

1. This evening, **XIV. Pz.Korps** will withdraw from its present positions for operational reasons and pull back into the positions behind the Mius sector. To the right of SS- Division WIKING, 16. Pz.Div. Left Slovakian Division.

   boundary right: Southern edge of Stara Rotowka—mouth of the Mius—Krynka inclusive—grid line 78.

   boundary left: This for the withdrawal and occupation of the new positions: Grid lines 92—234 inclusive.

   boundary between WESTLAND and NORDLAND Regiments: intersection of grid lines 96—76—intersection of grid line 90—Mius—northern edge of Awilofederowka.

   between NORDLAND and GERMANIA: grid line 84—north edge 351.

2. **HKL:**

   Southern edge Aleksandrowka—southern edge Aleksejewka—hill due north Nw. Nadjeschda—hill in the bend of the Mius 2 km. west 357—eastern edge Kutscherowo—hill 2 km. west 355—eastern edge Petropolje—heights on the Mius to bend in the Mius 500 metres south of Russkoje—eastern edge Russkoje—eastern edge Derestowo—hill 1.5 km. to the northwest.

3. **The WIKING Division** less those elements still under 16. Pz.Div.'s command for the withdrawal will disengage from the enemy in the course of the night and move back into its combat sector in the Mius position.

4. Withdraw as follows:
   (a) **Artillery** vacate its gun positions at 17.00 hours.
   Route for IV. Battalion:
   Rawnopol—Golodajewka—Bachmutskij into gun position south Bachmutskij.
   Route for III. Battalion:
   via Nikolajewka—Nw. Jasinowskij, bridge site near Jasinowskij into gun position north Gustavfeld.
   Route for II. Battalion:
   Nw. Marjewka—Bol. Kirsanowka into gun position north Nw. Nadjechda.

One half of a battery will remain in the old gun position in every combat sector in order to cover the withdrawal of the infantry if necessary.

These half batteries are to follow their combat batteries at 21.00 hours on the ordered routes and bridges. Half 8. Battery, rear guard battery. This half battery's gun position will remain occupied until 01.00 hours. By firing it will deceive the enemy as to the existing artillery strength.

Withdraw via Nikolajewka—Jasinowskij.

(b) **Infantry**
The infantry will leave its positions at 23.30 hours, leaving behind one platoon per battalion, assemble near Rawnopol Nowikowka—Nikolajewskij—Reschetowskij and withdraw by vehicle.

Kampfgr. Jörchel via Pisarewka—bridge site north edge Russkoje.

Kampfgruppe Dieckmann Nowikowka—Rawnopol—south bridge site Russkoje.

Kampfgruppe Schönfelder Nw. Spasowka—Nw. Jasinowskij—bridge site Jasinowskij.

Kampfgruppe v. Reitzenstein via Nw. Marjewka—bridge site near Jasinowskij—route Nw. Kirsanowka—Bol. Kirsanowka.
Crossing point there is held for Gef. Gr. Stolz and may not be used.

(c) All trains and headquarters laying west of the line Nowowosselij—Nw. Spasowka—Nowikowka—Rawnopol will withdraw during the course of the day into areas which will be specified verbally.

Flakartl. is to be withdrawn behind the Mius sector from 15.30 hours.

5. The Kampfgruppen are responsible that the withdrawal routes and bridge sites, as well as the new combat positions are reconnoitred during the course of the day (Infantry only in large platoons).

Bridge sites will be occupied by officers, who will control traffic.

6. **Rearguards**
Each Kampfgr. one reinf. platoon with reliable vehicles to remain in position on both sides of the main withdrawal road in their combat sector until 02.00 hours and at 03.00 hours withdraw to an intermediate rearguard position near Nikolajewskij—Nw. Spasowka—Nowikowka—Rawnopol.

Leave these positions at 06.30 hours and withdraw via the bridge sites at Jasinowskij—Russkoje South and North behind the Mius.

Combat patrols remain in contact with the enemy until 05.45 hours, simulating through fire and light signals the occupation of the old positions until 05.45 hours and then pull back toward the rearguard.

7. **Bridge sites** near Bol. Kirsanowka, Jasinowskij, Russkoje South and North are to be prepared for demolition by Pi. Btl. 5. Demolition squad with light MG to remain at the bridges and detonate as soon as the last combat patrols are completed. Combat patrols will withdraw later across the available fords or ice.

8. **The Regimental command posts** will be occupied from 15.00 hours by advance headquarters, wire lines to be laid to the fixed command posts from that time onwards.

9. All units report immediately by radio

    (a) crossing of the Mius by main body,

    (b) passing the rearguard and the crossing of the Mius by the rearguard, as well as taking up positions on the west bank of the Mius to Division by telephone.

10. Order to blow the bridges is to be transmitted by the commander of the Gef. Gr. to the demolition squad by the Ord. Off. The bridges may first be blown, when it proves necessary as a result of close enemy pursuit.

11. Panzerarmee has reserved issuing the order to withdraw to the Mius to itself. Pz.Armee order arrives this afternoon. Withdrawal of the infantry then by radioed orders from Division.

12. Div.Headquarters from 16.00 hours Kalinowo. Advance headquarters Sardy.

signed Steiner

Document Appendix No. 16

SS Division WIKING Div.Headquarters, 29. 12. 1941

Divisional Order of the Day

The Reichsführer-SS visited the Division on the afternoon of 26. and morning of 27. Dec. and has asked me to convey to all members of the Division his greetings and his thanks for the Division's accomplishments. At the same time he brought the greetings of the Führer and Supreme Commander.

During his twelve-hour stay, the Reichsführer-SS was witness to the fighting on the Mius by the Division. He instructed me to convey his special appreciation to II./SS-GERMANIA and its commander, 5./SS Rgt. GERMANIA and its commander, Oberleutnant Juchem, 3./SS A.R. 5, Oberstleutnant Brasack and IV./SS A.R. 5 for their fighting performances.

The performances of these units in these past few days have been particularly mentioned in the Army report.

Special Distributor signed Steiner

Document Appendix No. 17

SS Panzer Jäger Abteilung 5 Abt.St.Qu., 1. 1. 1942
Commander

SS Men, Comrades

Our Battalion was established within the space of one year.

Veteran frontline officers, NCO's and men provided the backbone of the young battalion, young recruits filled the companies.

We were animated by a will to make the companies ready for action. The stay on the Heuberg training grounds provided the finishing touches. On 1. April the Battalion could be reported as ready for use in the field.—

The hour of its test of fire is now long behind the Battalion. The companies have, in uninterrupted action—usually parcelled out by platoon or gun, often alone without infantry support—fulfilled their duty in the front lines.

The Battalion has thus passed a crucial test and found complete acceptance.

The names of the Panzerjägern are mentioned in every Divisional order of the day.

Until today, 22 members of the Battalion have been awarded the E.K. 1, 190 the E.K. 2 and 23 the Kr.V.Kr.(*). The Battalion has been able to capture or destroy 33 tanks, while 15 were damaged through direct hits and forced to retire. In action as escorting weapons for the infantry, the Battalion's crews and their guns have made themselves indispensable; in the attack and in defence they have often created room to breathe for the infantry through exemplary cooperation and comradeship. Panzerjäger were everywhere that the situation demanded.

The Battalion's losses have been hard; many brave and courageous comrades have fallen in the face of the enemy. Their example stands before us reminding and binding us to fight on in their spirit. There are none in our ranks who will shirk from this charge.

Rather, I know you so well, that I know that each of you, whether officer, NCO or soldier, wishes to achieve still more—and of course as Panzer-**Jäger**, who deservedly carry this name.

Our wish for the new year, therefore, is to receive new antitank weapons so that we may be deployed together as the Division's central antitank weapon in the attack.

My comrades, I thank you for your readiness for action, for your composure and your courage. I am certain that I can depend on you implicitly in good and bad days.

Long live our homeland, for which no sacrifice is too great!

Long live the Führer!
signed Maack

(*) Kr.V.Kr.—Kriegsverdienst-Kreuz (War Service Cross)

Document Appendix No. 18

SS Division WIKING   Div.Headquarters, 22. 1. 1942
Commander

Subject: Education of the men and training in war.

More than all other units the Division must be careful, that the command of the troops by their superiors is handled in the correct manner.

Mistakes made with the Division's multifarious replacements, who gradually can grow together into a firm comradeship, have a greater effect than with a unit composed solely of Reichsdeutsche.

The most important consideration for a reasonable human command is the **tireless and continuing care of the superior for his subordinates**. He must reach the state where all of his subordinates have complete trust in him and know for certain that he is always their best comrade.

Accordingly, it is fair, correct and kind treatment which in principal the superior must provide to his subordinates. The men should love him. Every superior must therefore be firmly bound up with his troops. In particular, platoon and company commanders must always be around their men. They must be their men's model and example, have their confidence in all manners and never allow them to be strangers.

The more sensible, superior and warmhearted the leadership of a unit, the greater is its unity and fighting value. In regard to our Nordic volunteers this humane command of troops appears to me to be of quite decisive meaning.

I ask all superiors that they attempt patiently and with all seriousness to create such a human atmosphere within their units. In doing so, the Division's work will be eased decisively and will be more happily carried out by every superior **and** subordinate.

                                                              signed Steiner

Document Appendix No. 19

Source: US National Archives
Microfilm Publications
Microcopy T-175
Roll 107 Frame 2630548

Copy

SS-High Command Berlin-Wilmersdorf, 20. 9. 1941
Abt.Org./Tgb. Nr. 3989/41 geh. Kaiserallee 188
Ma.

SECRET

Subject: Formation of a Sturmgeschütz Battery (mot) for the SS-Division WIKING
Plan: 1 only for SS-Mot.Veh.Repl.Abt.
Distributor Special distributor.

1. A Sturmgeschütz Battery (mot) is formed for the SS-Division WIKING.
2. **Day of formation:** 25. 9. 1941
3. **Formation position:** Berlin-Lichterfelde, LSSAH barracks.
4. **Structure and equipment:** 1 StuGesch. Battery (mot) KSt. and KAN 446 of 18. 4. 1941 Beh.
5. During formation, the Sturmgeschütz Battery will be under the command of SS-Mot.Veh.Repl.Abt. disciplinarily and economically.
6. **Personnel:**
   Battery Commander: SS-Ostuf. Lange, SS-Div. WIKING
   Battery Officers: SS-Ustuf. Frhr. von Poleberg, SS-Art.Ers.Rgt.
   SS-St. O. J. Grachwitz, SS-J.Sch. Tölz SS-St.
   O. J. Wagner, Willi, SS-J.Sch. Tölz
   SS-Oscha. FA. Wild, Ludwig, SS-Kraftf.Ers.Abt.
   NCO's and men will be assigned to the Sturmgeschütz Battery by SS-FHA, Command Office of the Waffen-SS, Abt. I E and IIb.

(Page two missing)

Document Appendix No. 20.

SS Panzerjäger-Battalion 5   Btl. Command Post, 5. 3. 1942

Battalion Order

On 28. 2. 1942

SS Hauptsturmführer Karl Böhmer
Chief of the Sturmgeschütz Battery of the SS Division WIKING was killed in action while heroically defending against a powerful Russian attack. There are none among us who will not receive this report with the greatest pain.

SS Hauptsturmführer Böhmer, former Chief of 2. SS Panzer Jäger Abteilung 5, is for us all an ideal, for every young soldier of the Battalion an example in his straightforwardness, steadiness and his sincere spirit.

Working tirelessly, SS Hauptsturmführer Böhmer formed a company in the winter of 1940/41 which in action proved itself to be steady and reliable in every situation. In all modesty, this proud accomplishment is and remains Hauptsturmführer Böhmer's.

In recognition of his accomplishments he was given the opportunity to command the Sturmgeschütz Battery of the SS- Division WIKING. His first action with this Battery demanded of him his last sacrifice.

SS Hauptsturmführer Böhmer will live on in our ranks. He has fulfilled the words of Walter Flex, according to which, dying as an example is part of living as an example.

                                            signed Maack
                                         SS Obersturmführer
                                         and Commander

Document Appendix No. 21

SS Division WIKING Div.Headquarters, 10. 2. 1942
Ia

Divisional Order

On 27. 1. 1942, I. Battalion of the SS Rgt. WESTLAND was attacked by superior enemy forces.

Owing to snowdrifts, the enemy was able to settle in with units on the edge of Berestowo.

A counterattack led by the Chief of 2. Company threw the enemy back across the Mius with bloody losses.

This dashing success by 2. Company received special mention in the Army's report.

I express now my appreciation to 2. Company and the remaining elements of the battalion involved in this success after determining that in the opening phase of the battle the attacking enemy ran into an alert and defensively ready company.

F.d.R.d.A.: (signed) Steiner
signed Rohrer
Oberleutnant and Btl. Adjutant

Document Appendix No. 22

I./SS Artillery Regiment 5   Btl. Headquarters, 9. 9. 1942

Copy

SS Artillery regiment 5   Rgt. Headquarters, 27. 8. 1942

Special Regimental Order

On 21. 7. 1942 the Regiment set out on a new attack from the winter position on the Mius.

The assault on Rostov, the crossing of the Don, Kuban and Laba and the taking of the oil region at Muk-Chadyshenskaja are milestones on our Division's new victorious path, in whose successes our Regiment has played a leading part.

In all of these battles the Regiment has proved itself brilliantly, and I express my appreciation and thanks to every member of the Regiment and above all to the forward observers and artillery liason units who moved up behind the Panzer spearhead in armoured vehicles.

Deserving special recognition is SS-Sturmmann Langjahr of 2. Battery for his courageous conduct; he came to the advanced observation post as a trouble shooter and discovered the 2. V.B. and his radio operator dead. Alone, without training in artillery firing and under enemy pressure, he immediately took over direction of fire for the battery. Through this courageous, independent decision, an enemy attack was halted.

In the name of the Führer, I have presented SS-Sturmmann Langjahr the Iron Cross 2nd Class and on his leaving for the Junkerschule the Sturmabzeichen.

At this time we think with proud respect of our fallen comrades. Their deaths shall be an example and an obligation for us in the coming battles!
The Regiment stands firm in the belief in our Führer and in victory and awaits further orders!

F.d.R.d.A.   Heil to our Führer!
signed Jahnke   signed Gille
SS-Untersturmführer   SS-Oberführer and
and Adjutant   Regimental Commander

Document Appendix No. 23

SS-Panzer-Grenadier-Division　　　　　　　　　Div.Headquarters, 15. 2. 1943
WIKING
Ic

Interrogation Result

From the prisoner Lieutenant P. . ., 9th Independent Guards Tank Brigade.

Tank destroyed, taken prisoner by WESTLAND SS-Rgt. on 13. 2. near Ssachalin.

22 years old, technical student, from Dnepropershinsk, nationality: Russian.

9th Independent Guards Tank Brigade had been formed from the remnants of 17th Tank Brigade in mid-December 1942 in Wladimir (17th Tank Brigade had been sent into action near Rshew and suffered heavy losses there).

After four weeks of rest, on 17. 1. the 9th Independent Guards Tank Brigade entrained and was transported by rail to Kalatsch via Moscow, Reihenburg and Mitschurinsk. Disembarked there on 3. 2. and then ordered from there into this area by land march. March route: Kalatsch — Sawin — Kolesniko — Archenowskij — Werchnij — Schwecchaiko — Kaschari — Dektewa — Kudinowka — Nowo Silowka — Belowodog — Nowo Archangelskoje — Starobelsk — Nowo Astrachan — Kremenoje — Krassnij Liman — Kramatorskaja. Arrival there on 9. 2.

Composition:
    2 Tank Battalions
    1 Rifle Battalion
    1 Antitank Battalion
    1 Flak Battalion with 12 guns

Composition of a Tank Battalion:
    2 Companies each with 10 T-34　　= f　　20 tanks
    1 Company with 12 T-70　　　　　=　　12 tanks
    total brigade strength　　　　　　=　　64 tanks

Composition of a Rifle battalion
    1 Rifle Company with 120
    1 M Assault Engineer Company with
    1 heavy machine gun platoon
    1 antitank rifle

Assignment:　　　　　　　　　　　　　　(original incomplete, damaged)

March in southerly direction and . . .

Assignment of prisoner's company: on the morning of 13. 2. from east edge of Grischino with 6 tanks to occupy Rudina and Ssachalia.

Operation under command of Captain Mutjanow who was killed in action. After occupying Krassnoarmeijskoje the brigade was to hold until a stronger force arrived under the command of Lieutenant General Remisow or General Rakasowskij (earlier of the Stalingrad front). A breakthrough to Dnjepropetrowsk or Stalino was to follow.

Taking part in the same operation were elements of the 14th and 66th Tank Brigades, the IVth Guards Tank Corps and the 11th Independent Guards Tank Brigade. The prisoner had learned of these from his own observations in the Kramatorskaja area.

Strength of the Other Units: Unknown to the prisoner.

11th Independent Guards Tank Brigade should be as strong as the 9th and of similar composition. Whether all of these units have reached Krassnoarmeiskoje on time is also unknown to the prisoner.

Losses: On 12. and 13. 2. the 9th Brigade lost 9 T-34 and 8 T-70 as well as heavy losses among the crews. This combat was the Brigade's first action.

Special Observations: In Krassnoarmeiskoje: A group of 17 German prisoners were seen in the town who were marched off. 10 dead German soldiers were seen lying dead at a crossroads in the western part of the town.

Supply: Regular and secure, of late motorized sleds have been used.

Replacement Situation: The IVth Tank Corps regularly carries along a replacement company with 17 T-43 which is usually 50 km. behind the front. (original incomplete, damaged)

March Procedures: The 9th Brigade's overland march from Kalatsch to Kramatorskaja was carried out by day. Camouflage against view from the air was guaranteed by the use of white netting over tanks and vehicles.

The new KV Tank: Since the prisoner as a technician has a great interest in tanks, he already has knowledge of the KV tank type which is still under test. He had the following to say on the subject:
    Heavy armour, consisting of a new alloy
    Weight ca. 40—45 tons
    Cross sountry speed 50 km.
    Motor 750 H.P.
    Armament: 1 long barreled 76 mm.
             3 super heavy MG, of which 2 are coupled
             in the turret, 1 forward in radio operator
             position.
             1 flamethrower
    Crew: 5 men

In addition there is said to be provision for installation of rocket launchers on the rear decking of the tank.

Inventor of the tank is Kostjubkow, who likewise is said to have invented a Flak gun using the same principle as the automatic cannon.

Condition of the Russian armaments industry: Armaments works in the Urals area

Nishni Tagil:	Construction of 35-40 T-34 daily in addition aircraft factories for production of IL fighters
Tschel Jabinsk:	Production of 25—30 T-34 and 40 of a new type **daily** besides
Slatoust:	Aircraft works
Siberia: Omsk	N
Nowo Sibirsk:	(original incomplete, damaged)
Groki, Kirow:	

Railway lines from the Urals

I. Moscow—Orechowo—Sujew—Gorki—Kirov—Molotov—Nsihni—Tagil.

II. Moscow—Arsamas—Kassan—Sarapul—Tschel Jakiask.

Every quarter of an hour a train loaded with materials and troops leaves for the front.

F.d.R.
signed signature
SS-Obersturmführer

Document Appendix No. 24

SS-Panzer-Grenadier-Division
WIKING
Ia, Tgb.Nr. 72/43 secret

Div.Headquarters, 19. 2. 1943
Secret!

U.
Copy for your information.
The proclamation of the Führer and Supreme Commander is to be made known to the companies immediately.

For the Divisional Command
The First General Staff Officer
signed Schönfelder

Distributor C

Copy

Soldiers of Army Group South and Luftflotte 4!

The results of a battle of worldwide importance rest with you. The fate of present and future Germany will be decided a thousand kilometres from the borders of the Reich. You must bear the main burden of this battle.

At the beginning of the winter, wide gaps had developed at the front. The reasons why this could happen are known to you. Through these alone the enemy, who you had defeated in so many battles, was able to temporarily set out against you with superior forces. Nevertheless, you my soldiers, together with your comrades of Army Groups A and Centre, led by selfless officers and motivated by your courage against these Bolshevist masses have despite the unfavourable winter weather achieved the unthinkable. The German people follow your battles. All their thoughts are with you, because they know that you are their only protection. I myself know the difficulty of your struggle, the magnitude of your sacrifice. I feel with you, and I am endeavouring through my work to give practical expression to your heroism. The entire German nation is therefore mobilized. To the last man and last woman everything will be placed at the service of your battle. Youth in the Flak arm is protecting the German cities and workplaces. New divisions are continuously being formed. Previously unknown, unique weapons are on the way to your front.

I know that I make very difficult demands of you, but you must defend every square meter of earth bitterly in order to give me time to bring into action these units and new weapons. If today the Russian is still advancing, the moment will come, as it did in the previous winter, when in the dirt and mud, far from his supplies, his advance will inevitably flag. Therefore I have flown to you in order to exhaust all means to ease your defensive battle and in the end transform it into a victory.

If each of you helps me, with the help of the Allmighty we will still succeed as before. Therefore I entrust to your bravery, your stamina in the face of the enemy and your sense of responsibility the fate of our true homeland and our people.

signed Adolph Hitler

Document Appendix No. 25

Copy

3. Panzer Division   Div.Headquarters, 7. Oct. 1943
Commander
F.P.Nr. 29 985

To the Commander of SS-Panzer-Grenadier-Division WIKING Herr Generalmajor der Waffen-SS Gille

I./GERMANIA with its remaining 34 men participated in the attack by 3. Panzer-Division against the bridgehead near Silischtsche. In spite of its weakened condition thanks to the pluck of its men it made a considerable contribution to reducing the bridgehead against an enemy superiority in infantry of 10 to 15 to one. Particularly well-deserving is the indestructible Hauptsturmführer Dorr, who through his courageous and circumspect conduct in leading his men provided valuable support. While I wish the courageous SS-Panzer-Grenadier-Division WIKING success and good luck in the future, I remain

F.d.R.d.A.   Heil Hitler!
signed Westphal   yours respectfully,
                                                                   signed Westhoven

Document Appendix No. 26

NATIONAL COMMITTEE
FREE GERMANY
LEAGUE OF GERMAN OFFICERS

Officers and soldiers
of 72. I.D., 57. I.D., 389. I.D., SS-Division WIKING
and attached units!

You are surrounded and are facing destruction. You can no longer expect help. The tragedy of Stalingrad repeats itself. Then 200,000 of your comrades were killed on Hitler's orders. You are threatened with the same fate. Hitler will also forbid you to accept every offer to surrender by the Red Army.

Take you fate into your own hands!

There exists in Russia a powerful German freedom movement, which has taken as its task, the freeing of Germany from the tyranny of Hitler and the opening of peace negotiations. Also marching in this "Free Germany" movement is the League of German officers under the command of Artillery General Walther von Seydlitz. The undersigned are empowered as members of the League of German Officers opposite your sector to make contact with you. We have gone through the hell of Stalingrad and therefore know your misery.

Come to us and take protection under the League of German Officers. Make contact with us. Send emissaries to us to whom we can give exact instructions. Each emissary should make himself recognizable at the front with a white cloth and demand to speak with one of the undersigned officers. We guarantee every emissary an unhindered return to his unit. The Red Army staff have appropriate instructions.

Comrades! Act before it is too late! Do not sacrifice yourself for Hitler. Germany needs you to rebuild. Come and fight with us for peace and for a free and independent Germany!

In the field, 4. February 1944

Steidle
Oberst and Rgt. C.O. of
Gren. Rgt. 767, 376 I.D.

Büchler
Major and C.O. I./Flak Rgt. 241

Röckl
Oblt. and Battery Chief
II./s.A.R. 46 (mot)

Document Appendix No. 27[1]

"To the Commander of the SS-Division WIKING
Gruppenführer Gille

Herr Gille!

I am writing to you, the Commander of the SS-Division WIKING, in the name of General Seydlitz and at the same time in the name of the League of German Officers as a German who is concerned with all my heart to conserve the lives of my German comrades... Your desperate hope, that a breakout with help from the relief attack by the German forces from the southwest will succeed, is delusive...

Probably, the second reason why you continue to fight may be the concern for the future fate of your officers and SS-men and the fear that on the Russian side charges will be raised against your Division.

General von Seydlitz gives you the assurance that the National Committee "Free Germany" and the League of German Officers are in the position to have all proceedings against you and your troops struck down. Of course this is on the condition that you and your troops voluntarily lay down your weapons and join the National Committee in its fight.

In the interests of protecting the lives of your soldiers, it is your duty to agree to General von Seydlitz' suggestion. I would add that today many officers and soldiers of the Waffen-SS are already fighting in our ranks...

While I hope that this letter contributes to ending the hopeless battle and the senseless deaths of our comrades, I salute you across the front.

                                                              signed Korfes
                                                              Generalmajor"

Document Appendix No. 28

ULTIMATUM

to the Commander of 42. Armeekorps,
to the Commander of 11. Armeekorps,
to the commanders of 112., 88., 82.,72.,
167., 168., 57., and 332. Infantry Divisions,
the 213. Security Division, the SS-Panzerdivision
WIKING, the WALLONIEN mot. Brigade
and the entire officer corps of the German units
surrounded in the Korsun—Schewtschenkowsky area.

The 42. and 11. Armeekorps of the German Wehrmacht are completely surrounded.

The units of the Red Army have enclosed this Heeresgruppe in a firm ring. The encircling ring will be drawn ever tighter. All of your hopes of salvation are in vain. The German 3., 11., 13., 16., 17. and 24. Panzerdivisions which were rushing to your aid, were smashed during the attempt and their remnants encircled and wiped out.

The attempt to supply you with munitions and fuel by aircraft has failed. In two days alone, on 3. and 4. February, land units and the Airforce of the Red Army shot down over 100 JU-52 aircraft. You, as commander, and all officers in the pocket know very well that you have no real chance of breaking through the encircling ring.

Your situation is hopeless and further resistance senseless. It will only lead to a collossal sacrifice of German officers and soldiers.

To avoid unnecessary bloodshed we suggest that you accept the following terms of surrender:

1. All surrounded German troops, led by you and your staff, immediately cease combat operations.

2. You surrender to us the complete complement of personnel, weapons, all combat equipment, transport and all the Army's goods in an undamaged condition.

We guarantee all officers and soldiers who cease resistance life and security and following the war a return to Germany or a country of choice for the prisoners of war.

All personnel of the surrendered units will be permitted to retain uniforms, badges of rank, decorations, personal property and valuables and the officer corps its swords.

All wounded and sick will receive medical attention.

Your answer will be expected on 9. February 1944 at 11.00 hours in written form from your representative who will take the Korsun—Schewtschenkowsky road through Steblew to Chirowka in a staff car with white flags.

Your representative will be met by a fully empowered Russian officer at the east end of Chirowka on 9. February at 11.00 hours Moscow time.

Should you reject our suggestion to lay down your weapons, the units of the Red Army and its air forces will begin operations to destroy the surrounded German forces, but you will bear the responsibility for their destruction.

THE REPRESENTATIVE OF THE SUPREME COMMANDER
MARSHALL OF THE SOVIET UNION
ZHUKOV

THE COMMANDER OF TROOPS
OF THE FIRST UKRAINIAN FRONT
ARMY GENERAL
WATUTIN

THE COMMANDER OF TROOPS
OF THE SECOND UKRAINIAN FRONT
ARMY GENERAL
KONIEV

Document Appendix No. 29

NATIONAL COMMITTEE
FREE GERMANY
LEAGUE OF GERMAN OFFICERS

By all means accept the ultimatum!

Officers and soldiers in the pocket!

On behalf of Artillery General Walther von Seydlitz, President of the League of German Officers, we call on you most forcefully to under all circumstances accept the ultimatum of the Red Army and immediately cease all resistance. Time is running out! Your situation is hopeless!

The Red Army's ultimatum is absolutely honourable since any further resistance has nothing to do with soldierly fighting. Or do you wish to throw away your life senselessly for Hitler, who has written you off long ago?

We fighters of Stalingrad know from our own experience what it means to reject a Russian ultimatum. Only as a result of rejecting such an ultimatum, which also followed Hitler's order, an additional 120,000 men died at Stalingrad!

Don't risk it! Then a true hell will stand before you!

Once again: Accept the ultimatum immediately!

Nothing will happen to you in Russian captivity.

Grenadiers, fusiliers, canoniers, men of the SS—everyone in the pocket—cease resistance!

Lay down your weapons!

Immediately after you are taken prisoner you will meet representatives of the "Free Germany" movement or we ourselves will make contact with you.

Steidle
Oberst and Rgt. C.O. of
Gren.Rgt. 767, 376 I.D.
Vice-President of the League
of German Officers

Röckl Oblt and Battery Chief II./s.A.R. 46 (mot) Member of the managing board League of German Officers	Büchler Major and C.O. I./Flak-Rgt. 241 Member of the managing board League of German Officers

Document Appendix No. 30

SS-Panzer-Aufklärungs-Abteilung 5   O.U., 7. 3. 1944
I a

Combat Report
for the Abteilung's breakout on 16. 2. 1944

1. **Situation:**
   Our powerful forces surrounded and pressed into a narrow pocket in the Sawadski—Schanderowka—Chilki—Novo-Buda area intended to break through the enemy barricading positions on the night of 16./17. 2. 1944 in order to meet the Panzer forces which were beginning the relief attempt in the Lissjanka—Oktjabr area.

2. **Assignment:**
   The reinforced SS Panz.-Recon.-Abt. 5, as the spearhead of SS Panzer Div. WIKING's attack, had the assignment to assemble in the area west of Chilki near 213.1 and with the beginning of the attack at 23.00 hours to push through toward 239.0 setting out by way of the lake south of Chilki—west edge of the forest southeast of Dshurshenzy, in order to make contact with our Panzer forces.

3. **Units:**
   SS Panzer Aufklärungs-Abteilung 5 (3 companies employed as infantry) 1 company SS Panzer-Jäger-Abteilung 5 (employed as infantry) 2 batteries Wespen SS-Panzer-Artillerie- Regiment 5

4. **Formation:**
   in the assembly area and at beginning of the attack. Forward right: 3./SS Panz.-Aufkl.-Abt. 5 Forward left: 2./SS Panz.-Aufkl.-Abt. 5 1./SS Panz.-Aufkl.-Abt. 5 positioned behind 3. and 2./SS Panz.-Aufkl.-Abt. 5 Wespen batteries: Panzer-Jäger company assigned as infantry cover.

5. **The attack:**
   The Abteilung went to the attack at 23.00 hours. Contact existed to the right with 72. I.D.. The open left flank was watched over by a platoon from 1./SS Panz.-Aufkl.-Abteilung 5. Our forces moved out as quietly as possible. The line of hills due south of Chilki was not occupied by the enemy and could be passed unhindered. The Wespen had to drive around the lake south of Chilki and pass by a bridge farther south. Thus direct coordination between the Abteilung and the Wespen was no longer guaranteed. Stopping the Abteilung to pick up the Wespen was not possible as the entire attack would have come to a standstill leading to a major delay. After a rapid advance the Abteilung encountered the first weak enemy outposts on the hills due south of point E—Petrowskoje which were overcome after a short firefight. The attack was carried farther forward through Br. to the southwest and encountered stronger enemy positions (2 antitank—4 light MG) on the ridge

of hills southwest of Br.. Beneath the hill an assembly area was occupied briefly and the companies reformed. A short time later the Abteilung launched the attack and took the hill by storm within a few minutes. Destroyed were two 7.62 cm. antitank guns and two tractors. After the hill was taken heavy mortar fire began from the Balka to the southwest as well as from the forest south of it. The Abteilung suffered heavy losses here. The attack was immediately carried further into the Balka and the mortar positions overrun. 1./SS Panz.-Aufkl.-Abteilung 5 went into position on the southern edge of the Balka while the Abteilung regrouped. Several Wespen which had meanwhile arrived on the already captured hill likewise secured toward the forest. After the Abteilung had regrouped the attack was carried on from Dshurshenzy across the ridge south of Y and the east—west running Balka south of Dshurshenzy reached without enemy interference. The hill which climbed steeply south of the Balka was recognized as occupied by the enemy, likewise the southeast edge of Dshurshenzy.

Following brief preparations the attack was carried forward with great energy against the hill south of the Balka. Also participating in this attack was a company from II./SS WESTLAND which had been requested as reinforcements as our own forces were exhausted and the losses suffered had made themselves noticeable. The Panzer-Jäger company under the Abteilung's command could no longer be concentrated and employed as ordered as the company commander could not be located and the company was scattered. The hill was taken following a short combat during which the flank was threatened from the right (southeastern edge of Dshurshenzy), from where an antitank gun and several machine guns hindered a further advance. At 04.30 hours the Balka north of 239.0 was reached, from where it was discovered that there were strong enemy positions near 239.9 as well as on the road which led to the north. Several tanks were spotted. After brief preparations the attack was launched against 239.0. If possible, the enemy was to be overrun before daybreak. Just before that point the attack collapsed in the face of heavy tank, antitank and machine gun fire. The following elements gradually backed up and it became day. A combined command was no longer possible since the enemy hindered our regrouping from all sides. The forces still remaining on hand were led back to the east into the woods west of Oktjabr from where the brook was then reached.

signed Debus
SS-Obersturmführer and
representative of the Abteilung Commander

Document Appendix No. 31

Pass

for surrendering prisoners

Every German soldier and officer, as well as every group of German soldiers and officers, will on presentation of this pass be taken immediately to the nearest Red Army headquarters for transport onward to a prisoner of war camp.

The Soviet government complies strictly with all international conventions concerning the treatment of prisoners of war. All prisoners of war without exception are guaranteed: life, good treatment, accomodations, food, work in the hinterland and return home following the war or entry into any other country as the prisoner wishes.

Deserters will be granted privileges in food and choice of work. Names of prisoners of war will not be published without their consent.

The Command of the Red Army

Document Appendix No. 32

—A—   —1—

Berlin: (DNB—Radio Intercept)

Sender Moscow: **"The liquidation of the German-fascist units surrounded in the Korsun—Schewtschenkowskij area."** Under this heading the Information Bureau released the following **Special Bulletin**:

In the course of the offensive at the beginning of February from the area north of Kirowograd in a westerly direction and from the area southeast of Belaja-Zerkow in an easterly direction, the troops of the Second Ukrainian Front and the First Ukrainian Front broke through the strongly manned German defensive zone and in daring and skillful maneuvres encircled a large group of German-fascist troops north of the line Swenigorodka—Schpola.

As a result of this operation our troops have surrounded: the German 11. Army Corps under Generalleutnant Stemmermann and the German 42. Army Corps under General der Infanterie Mattenkloth.

The surrounded German Corps include: the 112. Infantry Division of Generalmajor Lieb, Oberst Bärman's 88. Infantry Division, Generalmajor Heine's 82. Infantry Division, Oberst Honn's 72. Infantry Division, Generalleutnant Traunberg's 167. Infantry Division, Generalmajor Schmidt-Hommer's 168. Infantry Division, Generalmajor Darlitz' 57. Infantry Division, Generalleutnant Geschen's 332. Infantry Division, the SS-Panzer-Division WIKING under Brigadeführer Gille and the SS-Motorized Brigade WALLONIEN under Major Lippert. The strength of the surrounded units is 70—80,000 soldiers.

The Soviet high command represented by the deputy of the Supreme Commander of the Red Army, Marshall of the Soviet Union Zhukov, the Commander of the Second Ukrainian Front, Army General Koniev, and the Commander of the First Ukrainian Front, Army General Watutin, presented an ultimatum to the command and the entire officer corps of the surrounded German troops in the Korsun—Schewtschenkowskij   area   on   8.   February   1944, demanding that they cease resistance in order to avoid senseless bloodshed and the destruction of the German forces.

The ultimatum stated:

In order to avoid unnecessary bloodshed we suggest that you accept the following terms of surrender:

1.   Led by their headquarters all surrounded German troops will immediately cease combat operations.

2.   You will surrender to us all personnel, weapons and all combat equipment, all means of transport and all war material in an undamaged condition.

We guarantee to all officers and soldiers who cease resistance, life and security and a return to Germany or any other country after the war according to the prisoner's wishes.

The personnel who surrender will be permitted to retain all personal possessions: uniforms, badges of rank and decorations, all personal effects and valuables. The senior members of the officer corps will be permitted to retain their swords. All sick and wounded will be granted medical attention. All surrendering officers, noncommissioned officers and men will be guaranteed immediate rations.

Your answer will be expected at 11.00 hours on 9. 2. 1944, Moscow time, in written form by your personal representative who must drive in a staff car with white flags to Chirowka on the road which leads from Korsun—Schewtschenkowskij via Steblew. Your representative will be received by a fully empowered Russian officer in the area of the eastern periphery of Chirowka on 9. 2. 1944 at 11.00 hours Moscow time.

If you reject our suggestion to lay down your weapons, then the forces of the Red Army and the Airforce will begin combat operations to destroy your surrounded forces and you will bear the responsibility for their destruction.

Among the commanders of the surrounded German troops there were generals and officers who saw the hopelessness of the German forces surrounded by Soviet forces and facing death who wished to accept the offer of the Soviet High Command and surrender. But the commanders and men of the surrounded German forces were duped by Hitler, who demanded in an order to the surrounded officers and men that they hold at any price and assured them that measures were being taken by the German Army's High Command which would guarantee rescue of the German troops in the "Kessel".

After one such order from Hitler the command of the surrounded German-fascist troops rejected the Soviet High Command's ultimatum. In view of the ultimatum's rejection, our forces began a general attack on the surrounded enemy divisions and set in motion decisive combat operations in order to quickly destroy the enemy forces.

In the course of the fighting to destroy the surrounded enemy group of forces our troops took the important fortified strongpoints of Korsun, Schewtschenkowskij, Olschana, Sawadowka, Drenkowez, Tagantscha, Petropawlowka, Olowez, Gorodischtsche, Werbowka, Goljaki, Janowka, Steblew and Schanderowka as well as the rail stations at Waljawa, Sawadowka, Tagantscha and Sotniki.

The rest of the surrounded German troops, totalling 3—4,000 men, made the attempt, since they no longer had any towns in their possession, to save their lives in the ravines and small woods south of Chanderowka. But they were destroyed there by our fighters.

The surrounded German units left 52,000 dead on the battlefield. 11,000 men surrendered. The Germans succeeded in removing scarcely more than 2—3,000 officers from the number of surrounded German troops.

Beginning on 5. February, the German High Command launched attacks from south of Swenigorodka in a desperate attempt to break through to the surrounded German forces and lead them out. Eight Panzer Divisions from various sectors were concentrated in the area west and southwest of Swenigorodka equipped mainly with "Tiger" and "Panther" type tanks and "Ferdinand" assault guns as well as several infantry divisions which were further reinforced by considerable forces from the High Command's reserve. Concentrated in the battle area were more than 600 bomber, fighter and transport aircraft.

Suffering enormous losses, the enemy succeeded in driving meaningless wedges into our combat forces south of Swenigorodka. But after encountering determined resistance and being bled white and exhausted in the fighting, the Germans were unable to bring help to the surrounded group.

In this fighting from 5.- 18. February, the German-fascist forces lost 20,000 officers and men killed in their unsuccessful attempt to break through to the surrounded group.

During the same period 329 German aircraft, including 179 three- engined JU-52 transport aircraft, more than 600 tanks and 374 guns were destroyed. Our troops captured 256 tanks and 134 guns from the enemy.

As stated by captured officers from the surrounded units, following the failure of the attempted relief of the German forces who were in the "sack", Hitler gave another order demanding that the surrounded officers and men sacrifice themselves in order to hold up the Russian divisions for some time, since this was ostensibly necessary in the interests of the German front. The mentioned order of Hitler's contained a direct order for the surrounded German officers and soldiers to commit suicide if their situation became hopeless. In addition the captured Germans stated that during the last 3—4 days plenty of suicides were observed. On orders from German commanders wounded officers and men were killed and burned. During the occupation of the villages of Steblew and Schanderowka for example, our troops discovered a large number of burned out trucks which were filled with the corpses of German soldiers and officers.

The operation to liquidate the surrounded German units was conducted by Army General Koniev.

Document Appendix No. 33

SS-Panzer-Regiment 5 Kovel, Easter 1944
Commander

Order of the Day

On 5. April 1944, the Regiment's II. Battalion with 6. and 7. Companies in cooperation with units of 4. Pz.Div. broke through the powerful encircling ring around Kovel and in doing so opened an exit for the garrison which had been encircled for 19 days. Through the initiative of its veteran commander, SS- Obersturmführer Nicolussi-Leck, 8. Company had already succeeded in breaking into Kovel in a daring operation. The Company formed the backbone of the surrounded garrison. Cut-off elements of 8. Company under Hauptsturmführer Faas defended themselves in an exemplary fashion.

5. Company, which was deployed in another sector, supported the heavy attack by its neighbouring division. Spurred on by the concern for the men of Kovel who were defending magnificently under our Div. C.O., SS-Gruppenführer and Generalleutnant Gille, but were in the greatest danger, each and every man of the Regiment risked everything.

Thus the Regiment's II. Battalion under the most difficult conditions has struck decisively in its first action and followed worthily the traditions of our I. Battalion.

The Regiment's fallen comrades are due our highest thanks. The enemy has suffered heavy losses in men and equipment in the several days of fighting.

With confidence in our magnificent Panzer arm and belief in our fatherland we hold ourselves ready.

Long live our Führer!
signed Mühlenkamp
SS-Obersturmbannführer
and Regimental Commander

Document Appendix No. 34

SS-Headquarters
Amt II Org.Abt.Ia/II
Tgb.Nr. 1665/44 g.Kdos.

Berlin-Wilmersdorf
Kaiserallee 188

SECRET MILITARY DOCUMENT

Subj: Rest and refitting of SS-Panz.Div. WIKING
Refer: FS-Order RF-SS, Tgb.Nr. 662/44 g.Kdos. v. 1. 6. 44
Distributor: Special Distributor   70 Copies
                                     12th Copy

1. **5. SS-Panz.-Div. WIKING** (less armoured Kampfgruppe) is withdrawn on the order of the Führer and refitted and rested at the SS-Troop Training Grounds "Heidelager". Elements of the Division will be reformed at the SS-Troop Training Grounds "Böhmen".

2. **An armoured Kampfgruppe** (SPW Battalion and Pz. V Battalion) under 1 Rgt. H.Q. placed under the command of II. SS-Pz.Korps.

3. In the course of the refitting 5. SS-Panz.Div. WIKING is to be reorganized according to the SS-FHA Order, Org.Abt. Ia, Tgb.Nr. 1491/44 g.Kdos. of 2. 6. 44 on "independent formation".

4. **Personnel:** (a) All personnel still with the Division are called in for rest. Allocation of officers, NCO's and men by SS-FHA will follow, numbers as determined at conference in SS-FHA on 13. 5. 1944. (b) The personnel of the Stu.Gesch.Abt. still with 5. SS- Panz.Div. WIKING will be used mainly in refitting and integrating the Pz. IV Abt.

5. **Equipment:**

   Special order OKH/Gen.St.d.H./Org.Abt. states that in all respects relating to material refitting 5. SS-Panz.Div. WIKING is under the control of Heeresgruppe Mitte. Allocation of weapons, equipment and vehicles published in special order by SS-FHA, Org.Abt. Ib joint allocation Gen./Qu.

6. **New Formations:**

   Independent of the establishment the following units will be newly formed for 5. SS-Panz.Div. WIKING:
   (a) SS-Panz.Aufkl.Abt. 5 and III./SS-Panz.Gren.Rgt. WESTLAND at the "Böhmen" troop training grounds.
   (b) SS-Panz.Jäg.Abt. 5 at the "Heidelager" troop training grounds.
   (c) 2. Med.Company/5. SS-Panz.Div. WIKING (responsible to SS-FHA Amtsgr.) Formation of men and material is to be carried out in direct agreement by 5. SS-Panz.Div. WIKING.

(d) As a replacement for the Railroad Maintenance Company released to SS-FHA, a completely equipped Maintenance Company will be made available by SS-FHA, Dept. X, up to 15. 7. 44.
Assignment of personnel for the newly formed units by 5. SS- Panz.Div. WIKING will follow within the scope of the personnel allocated by SS-FHA. Material refitting will be carried out according to the weapons and equipment units allocated by Gen./Qu.

7. Responsible for the refitting and new formations is 5. SS- Panz.Div. WIKING.

8. Refitting is to be carried out so that it is completed by 31. 7. 1944.

9. Status reports are to be submitted at the times ordered according to SS-FHA, Dept. II, Org.Abt. Ia, Tgb.Nr. II/5929/44 secret of 20. 4. 44.

signed Jüttner

F.d.R.
SS-Hauptsturmführer

Document Appendix No. 35

Copy

General Command IV. SS-Pz.-Corps　　　　Corps Headquarters, 12. 8. 44
The Commanding General

Special Corps Order

The Führer has charged me with the command of the SS- Panzerkorps effective 20. 7. 1944.

With pride and full faith and belief in the power and victory of our arms I have taken over this responsible position.

Only with difficulty do I leave my old, faithful WIKING Division. Deserving of my special thanks today are all officers, noncommissioned officers and men who in untiring fulfilment of duty and readiness for action, in the heaviest fighting and in the most difficult situations, have always stood brave and true to our flag and done their duty. The order of the Reichsführer-SS fills me with particular joy since it states that 5. SS-Pz.Div. WIKING will remain as the cadre Division of IV. SS-Panzerkorps and thus we will remain together in the future.

The Führer has charged

SS-Standartenführer **Mühlenkamp**
with the command of 5. SS-Panzer-Division WIKING.

With this SS-Leader a deserving, proven, old WIKINGER has been placed at the head of the Division. I expect that all Division members will fulfil their duty with the same loyalty and devotion under their new commander as they did under my command.

In addition, the IV. SS-Pz.Korps has been allocated 3. SS-Pz.Div. TOTENKOPF. I salute all officers, noncommissioned officers and men of this Division and I am particularly pleased that this veteran, battle-tested, experienced eastern Division has been united with the WIKING Division in an SS-Panzerkorps. I am certain that 3. SS-Pz.Div. TOTENKOPF under its new commander, SS- Oberführer **Becker**, will strike with the same courage and reliability as it always has in the past.

The IV. SS-Pz.-Korps with both SS-Divisions

TOTENKOPF and WIKING

must become in a short time a symbol of terror for the enemy. We wish not only to be iron hard and fanatical in defence, but also a sharp weapon in attack which stands ready to strike hard and quickly at any time.

I expect, therefore, of every SS-man in the coming decisive times full and restless action so as to earn the Führer's praise.

Long live the Führer!
signed Gille

F.d.R.d.A.
signed Wolf
SS-Obersturmführer and
Regimental Adjutant

Document Appendix No. 36

SS-Panzer-Regiment 5　　　　　　　　　　Rgt. Headquarters, 7. 9. 1944
Commander

Special Regimental Order

During the fighting in the period 29. 3. 1944 to 7. 9. 1944, SS- Panzer-Regiment 5 has achieved its

500th Tank Kill

In the same period were destroyed or captured:

4	armoured cars
71	antitank rifles
787	heavy antitank guns
363	light antitank guns
34	antitank-antiaircraft guns
38	infantry guns
10	heavy mortars
44	8.5 cm. antiaircraft guns
3	2 cm. antiaircraft guns
6	gun carriages
3	17.2 cm. artillery pieces
11	guns with ammunition
15	heavy machine guns
14	light machine guns
4	aircraft
26,735	enemy dead
125	trucks
1	tractor
1	SP.

The Regiment is proud of this unique success. It has spurred us on so that we may soon report our 1,000th tank kill.

　　　　　　　　　　　　　　　　　　　　signed Darges
　　　　　　　　　　　　　　SS-Obersturmbannführer and
　　　　　　　　　　　　　　　　　Regimental Commander

XVI. *WIKING* DIVISION COMMANDERS

Commanders and Officers of *5. SS-Panzer-Division WIKING*

The Divisional Headquarters

	Commander	Ia	Ib	Ic
1940	Steiner	Ecke	Reichel	Paetsch
1941	Steiner	Ecke/Reichel	Reichel/Sporn Kille/Büthe	Paetsch
1942	Steiner deputy C.O. Gille	Reichel	Schönfelder Büthe	Paetsch Dr. Falz Prof. Jankuhn
1943	Gille	Schönfelder	Büthe Scharf	Jankuhn
1944	Gille Mühlenkamp Ullrich	Schönfelder Kleine	Scharf Dr. Fischer	Jankuhn Glanert
1945	Ullrich	Braun Klose	Dr. Fischer	Glanert

The GERMANIA Regiment

	Commander	I. Btl.	II. Btl.	III. Btl.
1940	v. Oberkamp	Dieckmann	Joerchel	Braun
1941	v. Oberkamp	Dieckmann	Joerchel	Braun Schönfelder
1942	v. Oberkamp Wagner	Dieckmann Krocza	May Scheibe	Schönfelder Hack
1943	Wagner Ehrath	Krocza Dorr	Juchem Schröder	Hack Kümmel
1944	Ehrath Dorr	Dorr Müller Kruse	Amberg Pleiner	Murr
1945	Dorr Müller Bühler	Kruse	Pleiner Amberg	

The WESTLAND Regiment

	Commander	I. Btl.	II. Btl.	III. Btl.
1940	Wäckerle	Dr. v. Hadeln	Kummer	Steinert
1941	Wäckerle Diebitsch Phleps	Dr. v. Hadeln	Koeller	Steinert
1942	Phleps Maack Geißler	Dr. v. Hadeln	Koeller Steinert	
1943	Polewacz Reichel	Dr. v. Hadeln Sitter	Ziemssen Schmidt	
1944	Marsell Hack	Sitter Gerres	Schmidt Heindl	Oeck Silberleitner
1945	Nedderhof Hack	Sacher	Heindl	Nedderhof Schlupp

The Volunteer Pz.Gren.Btl. NARWA

	Commander
1941	Eberhardt
1942	Eberhardt
1943	Eberhardt Koop Grafhorst

as of March 1944 "Narwa" became III./WESTLAND

The *NORDLAND* Regiment

	Commander	I. Btl.	II. Btl.	III. Btl.
1940	v. Scholz	Polewacz	Fortenbacher	Plöw
1941	v. Scholz	Polewacz	Stoffers	Plöw
1942	v. Scholz	Polewacz Lohmann	Krügel	Plöw
1943	v. Scholz Joerchel	Lohmann	Krügel	Collani
1944	The Regiment left the Division as of May 1944			

Finnish Volunteer Battalion

	Commander
1942	Collani from 1943 became III./*NORDLAND*

Pz.Gren. Battalion *NORGE*

	Commander
1944	Vogt
1945	Vogt

Pz.Gren. Battalion *DANMARK*

| 1944 | Im Masche |
| 1945 | Im Masche |

Sturmbrigade *WALLONIEN*

	Commander
1943	Lippert, Degrelle
1944	Degrelle

275

Feld-Ersatz. Btl 5

	Commander
1942	Nedderhof
1943	Müller
1944	Nedderhof, Kruse

Pz. Art. Rgt. 5

	Commander	I. Btl.	II. Btl.	III. Btl.	IV. Btl.
1940	Gille	Wiehle Brasack	Richter	Schlamelcher	Heldmann
1941	Gille	Fick Kausch	Richter	Schlamelcher	Heldmann Brasack
1942	Gille	Kausch Bünning	Richter Gattinger	Schlamelcher Bühler	Brasack
1943	Gille Richter	Bünning	Gattinger	Bühler Bernau	Richter Wittich
1944	Richter Bünning	Bünning Bernau	Gattinger Huber Pauck Bernau Bühler	Bühler Pleiner Pintscher	Wittich
1945	Bünning	Bernau	Bühler	Pintscher Janhorst	Wittich

Note: From April 1945 the remnants of the Regiment were concentrated under the commander of I. Battalion.

Pz.Rgt. 5

	Commander	I. Btl.	II. Btl.
1942	Mühlenkamp		
1943	Mühlenkamp	Mühlenkamp Köller	Scheibe
1944	Mühlenkamp	Köller Kümmel Säumenicht	Scheibe Klapdor Paetsch Reichert Darges
1945	Darges	Hein Nicolussi-Leck	Flügel Berndt Lichte

Pz.Pi.Btl. 5

Commander				
1940	1941	1942	1943	1944	1945
Klein	Klein Albert Schäfer	Schäfer	Schäfer Eichhorn Stieglitz	Braune Heder	Heder

Pz.A.A. 5

Commander				
1940	1941	1942	1943	1944	1945
von Reitzenstein	von Reitzenstein	von Reitzenstein Paetsch	Saalbach Füting	Debus Hack	Wagner Vogt Oeck

Pz.Jgr.Abt. 5

Commander

1940	1941	1942	1943	1944	1945
Maack	Maack	Köller	Oeck	Oeck	Korff

Flak Abt. 5

Commander

1940	1941	1942	1943	1944	1945
	Stoffers	Diebitsch Braun Kurz	Kurz Stoige	Stoige Winkelmann	Winkelmann Eberhard

Pz.Nachr.Abt. 5

Commander

1940	1941	1942	1943	1944	1945
Kemper	Kemper	Kemper Elmenreich	Weitzdörfer Hüppe	Hüppe	Hüppe Schmeißer

San.Abt. 5

Commander

1940	1941	1942	1943	1944	1945
Dr. Unbehaun	Dr. Unbehaun	Dr. Schmück	Dr. Wille	Dr. Thon	Dr. Thon

Div.Nachsch.Tr.

Commander					
1940	1941	1942	1943	1944	1945
		Eggersdorf	Wolfsreder	Honsell	Honsell

Wi-Btl. 5

Commander					
1940	1941	1942	1943	1944	1945
Meier	Meier	Meier	Derda	Dr. Herdach	Dr. Herdach

Inst.Abt. 5

Commander					
1940	1941	1942	1943	1944	1945
Sporn	Sporn	Sporn	Endress	Bretterbauer	Bretterbauer

XVII. DECORATIONS

BUNDESARCHIV
Central Records Office
I 5—344/66 5. SS-Pz.Div. "WIKING"

Name	Rank and Position	Unit	Awarded on:
	Knight's Cross of the Iron Cross with Oak Leaves, Swords and Diamonds		
Gille, Herbert	SS-Gruf. and Gen.Lt. W-SS Commander		19. 4. 44 as 12th soldier
	Knight's Cross of the Iron Cross with Oak Leaves and Swords		
Dieckmann, August	SS-Ostubaf. Commander	SS-Pz. GR WESTLAND	10. 10. 1943 as 39th soldier K.I.A. 10. 10. 43
Gille, Herbert	SS-Gruf. and Gen.Lt. W-SS Commander		20. 2. 1944 as 47th soldier
Dorr, Hans	SS-Stubaf. Commander	SS-Pz. GR 9	9. 7. 1944 as 77th soldier
	Knight's Cross of the Iron Cross with Oak Leaves		
Steiner, Felix	SS-Gruf. and Gen.Lt. W-SS Commander		23. 12. 1942 as 159th soldier
Dieckmann, August	SS-Stubaf. Commander	SS-Pz. GR WESTLAND	16. 4. 1943 as 233rd soldier
Gille, Herbert	SS-Brif. and General Maj. W-SS Commander	1. 11. 1943	as 315th soldier
Dorr, Hans	SS-Hstuf. Commander	I./SS-Pz GR GERMANIA	13. 11. 1943 as 327th soldier
Schmidt, Walter	SS-Hstuf. Commander	III./SS-Pz GR WESTLAND	14. 5. 1944 as 479th soldier
Mühlenkamp, Rudolph	SS-Staf. Commander		21. 9. 1944 as 596th soldier
	Knight's Cross of the Iron Cross		
von Scholz, Fritz	SS-Oberf. Commander	SS-Rgt. NORDLAND	18. 1. 1942 died of wounds 28. 7. 44
Pförtner, Helmut	SS-Ustuf. Platoon Leader	2/SS-R GERMANIA	18. 1. 1942 K.I.A. 28. 2. 43
Schlamelcher, Karl	SS-Hstuf, Leader	III/SS-A.R. 5	1. 3. 1942
Dieckmann, August	SS-Stubaf. Commander	I./SS-R GERMANIA	23. 4. 1942 K.I.A. 10. 10. 43
Mühlenkamp, Rudolph	SS-Stubaf. Commander	SS-Pz A 5	3. 9. 1942
Dorr, Hans	SS-Hstuf. Chief	4/SS-JR GERMANIA	27. 9. 1942
Gille, Herbert	SS-Oberf. Commander	SS-AR 5	8. 10. 1942

Name	Rank and Position	Unit	Awarded on:
Polewacz, Harry	SS-Stubaf. Commander	SS-JR NORDLAND	23. 12. 1942 K.I.A. 12. 1. 43
Faulhaber, Markus	SS-Ostuf.	3/SS-R GERMANIA	25. 12. 1942
Eichhorn, Hugo	SS-Hstuf.	SS-Pi B 5	15. 1. 1943
Schäfer, Max	SS-Stubaf.	SS-Pi B 5	12. 2. 1943
Reichel, Erwin	SS-Stubaf. Commander	SS-PZ GR WESTLAND	28. 2. 1943 died of wounds 28. 2. 1943
Eßlinger, Willi	SS-Hscha.	3/SS-Pz JA 5	19. 6. 1943
Wagner, Jürgen	SS-Oberf. Commander	SS-Pz GR GERMANIA	24. 7. 1943
Eberhardt, Georg	SS-Stubaf.	SS-Pz GB NARWA	4. 8. 1943
Schmidt, Walter	SS-Hstuf. Commander	III/SS-Pz GR WESTLAND	4. 8. 1943
Müller, Albert	SS Hscha. Platoon leader	4/SS Pz GR WESTLAND	4. 8. 1943
Sitter, Günther	SS-Hstuf. Commander	I/SS-Pz GR WESTLAND	12. 9. 1943
Juchem, Hans	SS-Hstuf. Commander	II/SS-Pz GR GERMANIA	12. 9. 1943 K.I.A. 13. 8. 43
Bauer, Helmut	SS-Oscha. Platoon leader	3/SS-Pz R 5	12. 9. 1943
Drexel, Hans	SS-Ostuf. acting Cdr.	2/SS-Pz GR WESTLAND	14. 10. 1943
Trabandt, Paul	SS-Hscha.	2/SS-Pz JA 5	14. 10. 1943
Hinz, Bruno	SS-Ustuf.	2/SS-Pz GR WESTLAND	2. 12. 1943
Zepper, Erich	SS-Hscha.	2/SS-Pz GR WESTLAND	2. 12. 1943 M.I.A.
Schreiber, Gustav	SS-Hscha.	7/SS-Pz GR GERMANIA	2. 12. 1943
Schönfelder, Manfred	SS-Ostubaf. Div. Ia		23. 2. 1944
Ehrath, Fritz	SS-Ostubaf. Commander	SS-Pz GR GERMANIA	23. 2. 1944
Richter, Joachim	SS-Ostubaf. Commander	SS-AR 5	23. 2. 1944
Nicolussi-Leck, Karl	SS-Ostuf. Chief	8/SS-Pz R 5	9. 4. 1944
Debus, Heinrich	SS-Ostuf. acting Commander	SS-Pz A A 5	4. 5. 1944
Meyer, Werner	SS-Ostuf. Commander	1/SS-Pz GR GERMANIA	4. 5. 1944
Schneider, Otto	SS-Ostuf.	7/SS-Pz R 5	4. 5. 1944

Name	Rank and Position	Unit	Awarded on:
Hein, Willi	SS-Ostuf. Company Cdr.	I/SS-Pz R 5	4. 5. 1944
Schumacher, Kurt	SS-Ustuf. Company Cdr.	I/SS-Pz R 5	4. 5. 1944
Fischer, Gerhard	SS-Uscha. Platoon Leader	3/SS Pz JA 5	4. 5. 1944
Hack, Franz	SS-Stubaf. Commander	III/SS-Pz GR GERMANIA	14. 5. 1944
Biegi, Fritz	SS-Oscha. Platoon Leader	5/SS-Pz GR 9	16. 6. 1944
Großrock, Alfred	SS-Ustuf. Platoon Leader	6/SS-Pz R 5	12. 8. 1944
Murr, Heinz	SS-Hstuf. Commander	III/SS-Pz GR 9	21. 9. 1944
Flügel, Hans	SS-Hstuf. Commander	II/SS-Pz R 5	16. 10. 1944
Ruf, Hugo	SS-Oscha. Platoon Leader	3/SS-Pz R 5	16. 10. 1944
Franz, Egon	SS-Uscha. Platoon Leader	3/SS-Pz R 5	16. 10. 1944
Schnaubelt, Alois	SS-Uscha. Gun Commander	3/SS-Flak A 5	16. 11. 1944
Heder, Eberhardt	SS-Hstuf. Commander	SS-Pz Pi B 5	18. 11. 1944
Senghas, Paul	SS-Ostuf. Company Cdr.	I/SS-Pz R 5	11. 12. 1944
Lotze, Gerhard	SS-Ostuf. Company Chief	II/SS-Pz GR 10	1. 2. 1945
Kam, Sören	SS-Ustuf. Commander	1/SS-Pz GR 9	7. 2. 1945
Darges, Fritz	SS-Ostubaf. Commander	SS-Pz R 5	5. 4. 1945
Styr, Josef	SS-Hscha. Platoon Leader	10/SS-Pz GR 9	5. 4. 1945
Sigmung, Hans	SS-Oscha. Platoon Leader	11/SS-Pz GR 9	5. 4. 1945
Picus, Karl	SS-Ostuf.		17. 4. 1945
Draxenberger, Sepp	SS-Hscha. Pi Platoon Leader	HQ Company Pz.Rgt. 5	17. 4. 1945 K.I.A. 22. 3. 45 southwest of Stuhlweißenburg

Name	Rank	Unit	Date and Loc	Cited on

Named in the Honour Roll of the German Army were:
(Wearers of the Honour Roll clasp)

Name	Rank	Unit	Date and Loc	Cited on
Harbich, Adolf	SS-Uscha.	14/SS-R GERMANIA	28. 2. 1942 near Chadyshenskaja	
Laßmann, Fritz	SS-Scha.m.s.Gr.	5/SS-JR GERMANIA	16. 8. 1942 near Chadyshenskaja	
Fechner, Heinz	SS-Ustuf. Platoon Leader	7/SS-JR NORDLAND	10. 11. 1942	26. 2. 43
Mühlinghaus, August	SS-Ostuf. Commander	11(Finn) SS-JR NORDLAND	15.—17. 10. 1942 near Malgobek	18. 4. 43
Könönen, Kallevo	SS-Rottfhr.	III/(Finn) SS-JR NORDLAND	7. 12. 1942 near Tschikola	27. 8. 43
Pyyhtiä, Yrjo	SS-Schtz.	III/(Finn) SS-JR NORDLAND	7. 12. 1942 near Tschikola	27. 8. 43
Hein, Willi	SS-Ustuf. Commander	2/SS-Pz R 5	31. 8. 1943 near Kharkov	7. 11. 43
Klein, Otto	SS-Ostuf. Commander	3/SS-Pz GR GERMANIA	12. 2. 1944 near Schanderowka	27. 4. 44
Styr, Josef	SS-Oscha. Platoon Ldr.	10/SS-Pz GR 9	30./31. 3. 1944 near Starykosary	7. 6. 44
Genz, Herbert	SS-Uscha.	Pz. Cdr. Staff Comp. II/SS-Pz R 5	18. 8. 1944 near Tluszcz	7. 12. 44
Velde, Johann	SS-Ostuf. Adjutant	SS-Pz GR 9 GERMANIA	17. 2. 1944 near Chilky	17. 12. 44
Kruse, Martin	SS-Hstuf.	I/SS-Pz GR 9	20. 10. 1944 near Zageroby	5. 2. 45
Selle, Siegfried	SS-Hstuf.	14/SS-Pz GR 9	22. 10. 1944 near Serock	5. 2. 45
Pleiner, Franz	SS-Hstuf.	II/SS-Pz GR 9	1./2. 1. 1945 near Agostian	15. 3. 45

—Decided on by OKH-PA: "EB"—Not Published

Name	Rank	Unit	Date and Loc	Cited on
Zäh, Fritz	SS-Hstuf.	5/SS-Pz AR 5	20. 1. 1945 near Sarosd	—
Vincx, Jan Pieter	SS-Ustuf.	4/SS-Pz AR 5	22. 1. 1945 near Pusztazabolcs-Ercsi	—
Solty, Karl	SS-Ustuf.	6/SS-Pz R 5	1. 2. 1945 near Adony	—

Name	Rank	Unit	Date and Loc.	Awarded On:
Certificate of Recognition from the Commander in Chief of the Army				
Bühler, Karl-Heinz	SS-Stubaf. Commander	II/SS-Pz AR 5	17. 2. 1944 near Chilky	
Bünning,	SS-Ostubaf. Commander	SS-Pz AR 5	17. 2. 1944 near Chilky	
Zäh, Fritz	SS-Hstuf. Chief	5/SS-Pz AR 5	17. 2. 1944 near Chilky	
Knight's Cross of the War Service Cross with Swords				
Weise, Erich	SS-Ustuf.	SS-Pz R 5	—	16. 11. 1943
The German Cross in Silver				
Dr. Schopper, Hubert	SS-Hstuf. Doctor	I/SS-Pz AR 5	—	10. 2. 1945
Muster,	SS-Stubaf.	IV/SS-Pz AR 5	—	10. 2. 1945

Name	Rank	Unit	Awarded On:
The German Cross in Gold			
von Scholz	SS-Staf., Cdr.	SS-R NORDLAND	22. 11. 1941
Koller	SS-Hscha. Platoon Ldr.	11/SS-NORDLAND	22. 11. 1941
Pförtner	SS-Ustuf. Platoon Ldr.	2/SS-R GERMANIA	22. 11. 1941
Stoffers	SS-Hstuf. Commander	II/SS-R NORDLAND	15. 12. 1941
Walther	SS-Hstuf. Chief	7/SS-R GERMANIA	15. 12. 1941
Polewacz	SS-Stubaf. Commander	I/SS NORDLAND	19. 12. 1941
Dorr	SS-Ostuf. Commander	1/SS-GERMANIA	19. 12. 1941
Dr. v. Hadeln	SS-Hstuf. Commander	I/SS-WESTLAND	19. 12. 1941
Bartols	Leutnant Platoon Ldr.	1/SS-Pz.Jg. A 5	2. 1. 1942
Kepplinger	SS-Ostuf. Commander	10/SS-R WESTLAND	28. 2. 1942
Gille	SS-Oberf. Commander	SS-AR 5	28. 2. 1942
Dieckmann	SS-Stubaf. Commander	I/SS-R GERMANIA	28. 2. 1942
Joerchel	SS-Stubaf. Commander	II/SS-R GERMANIA	28. 2. 1942
Gattinger	SS-Hstuf. Chief	10/SS-AR 5	28. 2. 1942
Rosenbusch	SS-Hstuf. Chief	9/SS-R NORDLAND	28. 2. 1942
Steiner	Gen.-Maj. Waffen-SS Commander	SS-Div. WIKING	22. 4. 1942
Hämel	SS-Hscha.	5/SS-R GERMANIA	11. 6. 1942
Schönfelder	SS-Hstuf. Commander	III/SS-R GERMANIA	11. 6. 1942
Scheibe	SS-Hstuf. Chief	11/SS-R GERMANIA	14. 6. 1942
Haus	SS-Ostuf. Commander	I/SS-JR GERMANIA	29. 8. 1942
May	SS-Hstuf. Chief	7/SS-JR GERMANIA	19. 9. 1942
Körbel	SS-Hstuf. Chief	8/SS-JR WESTLAND	19. 9. 1942
Juchem	SS-Ostuf. Commander	5/SS-JR GERMANIA	19. 9. 1942
Klose	SS-Hstuf. Commander	1/SS-JR GERMANIA	27. 10. 1942

Name	Rank	Unit	Awarded On:
Rothofer	SS-Hscha.	7/SS-AR 5	5. 11. 1942
Flügel	SS-Ostuf. Company Cdr.	SS-Pz. A 5	8. 12. 1942
Wagner	SS-Staf. Commander	SS-JR GERMANIA	8. 12. 1942
Bünning	SS-Hstuf. Commander	I/SS-AR 5	8. 12. 1942
Steinert	SS-Stubaf. Commander	II/SS-JR WESTLAND	8. 12. 1942
Laug	SS-Oscha.	11/SS-AR 5	13. 12. 1942
Stender	SS-Oscha.	11/SS-JR GERMANIA	19. 12. 1942
Hack	SS-Hstuf. Commander	III/SS-JR GERMANIA	8. 1. 1943
Fischer	SS-Hstuf. Chief	1/SS-AR 5	8. 1. 1943
Müller	SS-Hstuf. Chief	5/SS-AR 5	8. 1. 1943
Schreiber	SS-Uscha.	7/SS-JR GERMANIA	8. 1. 1943
Albers	SS-Oscha.	3/SS-JR GERMANIA	8. 1. 1943
Oeck	SS-Hstuf. Chief	3/SS-Pz.Jg. A 5	10. 1. 1943
Krügel	SS-Hstuf. Chief	6/SS-JR NORDLAND	10. 1. 1943
Bäurle	SS-Hstuf. Chief	1/SS-JR WESTLAND	20. 1. 1943
Horstmann	SS-Ostuf. Commander	7/SS-JR WESTLAND	14. 2. 43
Mellinghaus	SS-Ostuf. Commander	7/JR NORDLAND	14. 2. 1943
Wanhöfer	SS-Ostuf. Commander	1/SS-Pi B 5	11. 3. 1943
Gruben	SS-Ustuf. Commander	3/SS-SR WESTLAND	11. 3. 1943
Lieb	SS-Ustuf.	1/SS-SR WESTLAND	11. 3. 1943
Lohmann	SS-Hstuf. Commander	I/SS-JR NORDLAND	11. 3. 1943
Heder	SS-Ostuf. Commander	3/SS Pi B 5	11. 3. 1943
Schreier	SS-Hscha.	4/SS-SR WESTLAND	14. 3. 1943
Hauschild	SS-Ostuf.	8/SS-SR WESTLAND	29. 3. 1943
Meier	SS-Ustuf.	2/SS-JR NORDLAND	29. 3. 1943
Wagner	SS-Hstuf.	2/SS-JR NORDLAND	29. 3 1943
Gotthardt	SS-Hscha.	6/SS-SR WESTLAND	29. 3. 1943
Hopfenmüller	SS-Hscha.	1/SS-SR WESTLAND	29. 3. 1943
Spörle	SS-Ostuf. Commander	1/SS-Pz.GR NORDLAND	2. 4. 1943
Schmidt	SS-Hstuf. Commander	II/SS-Pz GR WESTLAND	9. 4. 1943

Name	Rank	Unit	Awarded on:
Porsch	SS-Ostuf. Commander	10/Finn. SS-JR NORDLAND	14. 4. 1943
Hinz	SS-Ustuf. Commander	2/SS-Pz. GR WESTLAND	17. 4. 1943
Paetsch	SS-Stubaf. Commander	SS-AA 5	24. 4. 1943
Schust	SS-Ostuf.	2/SS-AA 5	24. 4. 1943
Lotze	SS-Ustuf. Commander	8/SS-Pz GR WESTLAND	24. 4. 1943
Mühlinghaus	SS-Ostuf. Commander	11/Finn. SS-JR NORDLAND	30. 4. 1943
Senghas	SS-Hscha.	1/SS-Pz R 5	9. 6. 1943
Großrock	SS-Oscha.	1/SS-Pz R 5	9. 6. 1943
Weißschuh	SS-Oscha.	2/SS-Pz R 5	9. 6. 1943
Casper	SS-Hscha.	7/SS-Pz GR GERMANIA	6. 7. 1943
Iden	SS-Ostuf. Commander	1/SS-Pz GR GERMANIA	6. 7. 1943
André	SS-Ostuf. Commander	8/SS-Pz GR GERMANIA	10. 7. 1943
Drexel	SS-Ostuf.	10/SS-Pz GR GERMANIA	3. 8. 1943
Gutowski	SS-Ostuf.	7/SS-Pz GR GERMANIA	3. 8. 1943
Hess	SS-Oscha.	1/SS-AA 5	3. 8. 1943
Siewert	SS-Oscha.	6/SS-Pz GR GERMANIA	3. 8. 1943
Nimtz	SS-Hscha.	3/SS-Pz GR GERMANIA	3. 8. 1943
Klingenschmid	SS-Oscha.	6/SS-Pz GR WESTLAND	2. 10. 1943
Gerres	SS-Hstuf. Chief	6/SS-Pz GR WESTLAND	2. 10. 1943
Gunkel	SS-Ostuf. Commander	1/SS Pz GR WESTLAND	2. 10. 1943
Bernau	SS-Hstuf. Chief	7/SS-AR 5	1. 11. 1943
Köller	SS-Stubaf. Commander	I/SS-Pz R 5	8. 11. 1943
Barten	SS-Ustuf.	2/SS-Pz GR GERMANIA	8. 11. 1943
Richter	SS-Ostubaf. Commander	SS-AR 5	17. 11. 1943
Multhoff	SS-Ostuf. Commander	I/SS-Pz R 5	17. 11. 1943
Murthum	SS-Hstuf. Chief	10/SS-AR 5	17. 11. 1943
Wolters Commander	SS-Ustuf.	1/SS-Pz GR GERMANIA	17. 11. 1943
Kempcke	SS-Ustuf. Adjutant	I/SS-Pz GR GERMANIA	17. 11. 1943
Zäh	SS-Ostuf. Chief	9/AR 5	21. 11. 1943

Name	Rank	Unit	Awarded on:
Schraps	SS-Ostuf. Commander	2/Pi B 5	21. 11. 1943
Velde	SS-Ostuf. Commander	3/Pz GR GERMANIA	21. 11. 1943
Meyer	SS-Ustuf.	1/SS-Pz GR GERMANIA	21. 11. 1943
Jessen	SS-Ostuf. Commander	I/SS-Pz R 5	15. 12. 1943
Leisterer	SS-Hscha.	5/SS-Pz GR WESTLAND	15. 12. 1943
Ludwigs	SS-Oscha.	5/SS-Pz GR WESTLAND	17. 12. 1943
Jäck	SS-Oscha.	6/SS-Pz GR WESTLAND	17. 12. 1943
Jungnickel	SS-Uscha.	7/SS-Pz GR WESTLAND	22. 12. 1943
Schweiß	SS-Uscha.	2/SS-Pz R 5	30. 12. 1943
Schumacher	SS-Ustuf. Commander	3/SS-Pz R 5	30. 12. 1943
Hein	SS-Ustuf. Commander	2/SS-Pz R 5	30. 12. 1943
Jira	SS-Ostuf. Commander	3/SS-AA 5	30. 12. 1943
Huber	SS-Ustuf.	II/SS-Ar 5	6. 1. 1944
Foditsch	SS-Uscha.	1/SS-Pz GR WESTLAND	6. 1. 1944
Lebkücher	SS-Hscha.	1/SS-AA 5	6. 1. 1944
Marquardt	SS-Oscha.	1/SS-Pz GR WESTLAND	6. 1. 1944
Debus	SS-Ustuf. Commander	1/SS-AA 5	23. 1. 1944
Klein	SS-Ostuf. Commander	3/SS-Pz GR GERMANIA	31. 1. 1944
Schneider	SS-Hstuf. Commander	I/SS-Pz R 5	28. 4. 1944
Homolka	SS-Uscha. Platoon Ldr.	1/Pz GR GERMANIA	1. 6. 1944
Wittich	SS-Stubaf. Commander	IV/SS-Pz AR 5	1. 6. 1944
Kruse	SS-Hstuf. Chief	2/SS-Pz GR GERMANIA	1. 6. 1944
Wolf	SS-Ostuf. Commander	8/SS-Pz AR 5	1. 6. 1944
Weck	SS-Ostuf. Commander	SS-Pz. Pi B 5	4. 6. 1944
Mahn	SS-Ustuf. Platoon Ldr.	11/SS Pz GR GERMANIA	4. 6. 1944
Balduff	SS-Hscha. Dpty. Btl. Cdr.	15/SS-pz AR 5	4. 6. 1944
Süchting	SS-Uscha.	7/SS-Pz AR 5	4. 6. 1944
Harbort	SS-Uscha.	3/SS-Pz GR 9 GERMANIA	4. 6. 1944
Pianka	SS-Oscha. Platoon Ldr.	6/SS-Pz GR 9	9. 10. 1944
Theismann	SS-Oscha Tr. Ldr.	7/SS-pz GR 9	9. 10. 1944

Name	Rank	Unit	Awarded on:
Hannes	SS-Hstuf. Commander	12/SS-Pz GR 9	9. 10. 1944
Swatosch	SS-Uscha.	6/SS-Pz R 5	9. 10. 1944
Schmits	SS-Hscha.	9/SS-Pz GR 9	10. 10. 1944
Martin	SS-Ostuf. Commander	6/SS-Pz. R 5	10. 10. 1944
Gütt	SS-Ustuf.	IV/SS-Pz AR 5	18. 12. 1944
Eidens	SS-ustuf.	II/SS-Pz GR 10	18. 12. 1944
Wolf	SS-Oscha.	7/SS-pz R 5	18. 12. 1944
Dr. v. Kulesca	SS-Hstuf. Rgt. Med. Off.	I/SS-Pz GR 10 WESTLAND	18. 12. 1944
Barthel	SS-Ustuf. Commander	3/SS-Pz GR 9 GERMANIA	18. 12. 1944
Wolf	SS-Ostuf. Adjutant	SS-Pz R 5	18. 12. 1944
Jauss	SS-Oscha.	8/SS-pz R 5	18. 12. 1944
Locker	SS-Oscha.	3/SS Pz GR 10 WESTLAND	18. 12. 1944
Adolph	SS-Ustuf. Commander	8/SS-Pz GR 10 WESTLAND	18. 12. 1944
Dr. Fecke	SS-Stubaf.	1/SS-San. A 5	30. 12. 1944
Dr. Thon	SS-Stubaf. Commander	SS-San. A 5	30. 12. 1944
Westphal	SS-Hstuf. Division O 1		30. 12. 1944
Köhle	SS-Uscha.	1/SS-Pz AR 5	30. 12. 1944
Schulze	SS-Stubaf. Div. Adjutant		30. 12. 1944
Hüppe	SS-Stubaf. Commander	SS-Pz Nachr A 5	30. 12. 1944
Albrecht	SS-Ostuf. Commander	4/SS-Pz AR 5	30. 12. 1944
Kometer	SS-Uscha.	2/SS-Pz AR 5	30. 12. 1944
Faas	SS-Hscha.	8/SS-Pz R 5	30. 12. 1944
Rammelkamp	SS-Ostuf. Chief	2/SS-Pz AR 5	30. 12. 1944
Rutzen	SS-Ustuf.	HQ Comp./SS-Pz GR 9	30. 12. 1944
Weber	SS-Uscha.	5/SS-Pz AR 5	6. 1. 1945
Pleiner	SS-Hstuf. Commander	II/SS-Pz GR 9	6. 1. 1945
Laible	S-Ostuf. Chief	1/SS-Flak A 5	6. 1. 1945
Mozisch	SS-Oscha.	2/SS-pz AR 5	6. 1. 1945
Jahnke	SS-Ostuf.	HQ/SS-Pz Div. WIKING	8. 2. 1945
Bock	SS-Oscha.	2/SS-Pz R 5	8. 2. 1945
Mittelbacher	SS-Ostuf.	I/SS-Pz R 5	8. 2. 1945

Name	Rank	Unit	Awarded on:
Brieger	SS-Oscha.	9/SS-Pz AR 5	8. 2. 1945
Fischer	SS-Hstuf. Chief	3/SS-Pz AR 5	8. 2. 1945
Richert	SS-Oscha.	1/SS-Pz AR 5	8. 2. 1945
Weerts	SS-Ostuf. Commander	4/SS-Pz R 5	8. 2. 1945
Kammer	SS-Hscha.	9/SS-Pz GR 9 GERMANIA	8. 2. 1945
Sigmund	SS-Oscha. GERMANIA	11/SS-Pz GR 9	8. 2. 1945
Stürtzenbaum	SS-Hstuf.	I/SS-Pz GR 9 GERMANIA	8. 2. 1945
Hermann	SS-Oscha. Commander	5/SS-Pz GR 9 GERMANIA	8. 2. 1945
Loibl	SS-Hscha.	2/SS-Pz Pi B 5	28. 2. 1945
Fietz	SS-Hscha.	12/SS-Pz GR GERMANIA	28. 2. 1945
Olin	SS-Ostuf.	7/SS-Pz R 5	28. 2. 1945
Fischer	SS-oscha.	2/SS-Pz R 5	28. 2. 1945
Styr	SS-Oscha.	10/SS-Pz GR 9 GERMANIA	28. 2. 1945
Stichnoth	SS-Ostuf. Commander	HQ Comp/SS-Pz AA 5	10. 3. 1945
Nielkamp	SS-Ostuf. Chief	2/SS-Pz AA 5	10. 3. 1945
Scholven	SS-Hstuf. Commander	10/SS-Pz GR 9	10. 3. 1945
Kaufmann	SS-Ostuf. Commander	1/SS-Pz AA 5	10. 3. 1945
Nicolussi-Leck	SS-Ostuf. Commander	8/SS-Pz R 5	10. 3. 1945
Krausch	SS-Oscha.	3/SS-Pz GR 10 WESTLAND	10. 3. 1945
Neswadba	SS-Oscha.	5/SS-Pz GR 10 WESTLAND	22. 3. 1945
Rappl	SS-Hscha.	SS-Pz Pi B 5	22. 3. 1945
Gerdes	SS-Ustuf. Adjutant	II/SS-Pz GR 10	15. 4. 1945
Bruder	SS-Oscha.	3/SS-Pi R 5	15. 4. 1945
Schlupp	SS-Hstuf. Commander	III/SS-Pz GR 10	15. 4. 1945
Heindl	SS-Hstuf. Commander	II/SS-Pz Gr 10	15. 4. 1945
Meinköhn	SS-Ostuf. Commander	12/SS-Pz GR 9	15. 4. 1945
Geiger Kornelimünster 29. 8. 1966	SS-Uscha.	7/SS-AR 5	27. 4. 1945

Addenda

Name	Rank—Position	Unit
	Knight's Cross of the Iron Cross	
Bühler, Karl-Heinz	SS-Ostubaf. Rgt. Cdr.	SS-Pz GR 9
Lichte, Karl Heinz	SS-Hstuf. Btl. Cdr.	II/SS-Pz R 5
	German Army Honour Roll Clasp	
Bernau, Hans-Günter	SS-Stubaf. Btl. Cdr.	I/SS-Pz AR 5
	German Cross in Gold	
Lüers, Hans-Helmut	SS-Hstuf. Battery Chief	7/SS-Pz AR 5
Solleder, Gerd	SS-Hstuf. Battery Chief	6/SS-Pz AR 5
Pintscher, Rudolf	SS-Hstuf. Btl. Cdr.	III/SS-Pz AR 5

XVIII. *WIKING* DIVISION STRENGTH REPORTS

The following information on the strength of the SS-Division WIKING was taken from the Waffen-SS strength reports compiled by Senior Government Councillor Dr. Kochen of the "RF-SS Institute for Scientific Statistics".

30. 6. 1941			total	19,377
31. 12. 1942	521 officers	15,407 NCO's and men	total	15,928
31. 12. 1943	383 officers	2,490 NCO's / 10,054 men	total	12,927
SS-Pz.Rgt. 5	47 officers	259 NCO's / 1,415 men	total	1,720
	430 officers	2,748 NCO's 11,469 men	total	14,647
30. 6. 1944	435 officers	3,066 NCO's 13,847 men	total	17,348
20. 9. 1944	614 officers	3,923 NCO's 13,260 men	total	17,797
(10. 9.)	454 officers	3,097 NCO's 14,465 men	total	18,016

(included in personnel strength are 305 volunteer auxiliaries)

A letter from the RF-SS Headquarters Section (Ia/3530/44 from 7. 9. 1944) shows a strength report from the *SS-Division WIKING* with a complement of:

1. 9. 1944   449 officers   3,054 NCO's   13,964 men   total   17,467

According to the contents of SS-FHA Arms-Inspection, Diary No. 104/40 from 14. 1. 1941, the SS-Division *WIKING* was allocated the following replacements from its position as of 31. 12. 1940:[1]

Div. Units	54 officers	3,788 NCO's and men	total	3,842
WESTLAND Rgt.	29 officers	1,885 NCO's and men	total	1,914
NORDLAND Rgt.	25 officers	1,509 NCO's and men	total	1,534
	108 officers	7,182 NCO's and men	total	7,290

A memo completed after the formation of III. (Germ.) Pz.Korps, whose date may lay between July/August 1943, broke down the SS-Division's strength by nationality:[2]

German nationals:	8,892	Norwegian:	47			
Volksdeutsche:	715	Swedes:	5			
Dutch:	130	Estonians:	664			
Danes:	177	Finns:	1			
Flemish:	619	Other:	4			
	10,533		721	Total	11,254

A strength report by the *WIKING* Division's Abt. IIb from 18. 8. 1941 shows a total of 1,142 Germanic volunteers from the Division's state on 22. June 1941 as follows:[3]

621 Dutch
294 Norwegian
216 Danes
1 Swede   At this time 421 Finns were members of
1 Swiss   the Division.

As of 19. 9. 1941, 1,416 Germanic volunteers were members of the Division including 821 Dutch, 291 Norwegians, 251 Danes, 45 Flemish and 8 Swedes.[4]

Since the formation of the Germanic volunteers gives no information concerning the Finnish volunteers the following supplementary information is provided:

According to SS-FHA, Abt.Org., Tgb.Nr. 2413/41 of 19. 6. 1941 orders were given to set up the SS-Vol.Btl. *NORDOST (Finn)*. Date of formation: 15. 6. 1941, location: Vienna. Composition was foreseen as 3 rifle companies and 1 MG company. Commander was SS-Hauptsturmführer Collani. The *WIKING* Division received the first shipment of 116 Finnish volunteers on 6. 5. 1941 and a second of 257 men on 15. 5.. Included among these were 10 active officers, 66 reserve officers and 29 active NCO's of the Finnish army. These first two contingents received their training in Heuberg, were divided among practically all of the Division's units and took part in operations from the first day of the Eastern Campaign. Three further batches of volunteers — 326 men on 23. 5. 1941, 289 men on 2. 6. 1941 and 219 men on 5. 6. 1941 — were ordered to Vienna and there formed the actual Finnish Volunteer Battalion which received its flag and was sworn in on 15. 10. 1941. Following completion of training the Battalion was transferred to the troop training grounds at Groß-Born and incorporated into the *NORDLAND* Regiment as III. Battalion. The volunteers, who carried the Finnish national coat of arms on their lower left sleeves, did not wear the "Finn. Vol. Btl. Waffen-SS" sleeve band but that of the *WIKING* Division.

From the beginning the Battalion included army chaplains. SS-Ustuf. Ensio Pihkala first held this position and following his death SS-Hstuf. (later Ostubaf.) Kalervo Kurkiala served his countrymen. The designated ministers carried the designation "Liason Officers". On 16. 9. 1942 a 200 man strong replacement battalion arrived from Finland. After training in Vienna the replacement company under SS-Ostuf. Schröder was divided among the existing companies on 7. 12. 1942. On 28. 5. 1943 the Finnish volunteers began their return to Finland.

A total of 255 Finns were killed in action on the Eastern Front while others died in Finland as a result of their wounds.

XIX. OFFICIAL LIST OF ENGAGEMENTS
Official Battle and Engagement Designations*

1. XII.	1940 — 21. VI.	1941	employment on the home front
22. VI.	1941 — 28. VI.	1941	assembly for the Eastern Campaign

1941

29. VI.	1941 — 12. VII.	1941	frontier battles in Galicia
29. VI.	1941 — 1. VII.	1941	1st advance toward Tarnopol
2. VII.	1941 — 10. VII.	1941	battles for Tarnopol and penetration toward Proskurov and Starakonstantinow
14. VII.	1941 — 28. VII.	1941	battles in the area southeast of Shitomir
14. VII.	1941 — 16. VII.	1941	(a) advance via Shitomir toward Bialacerkiew
17. VII.	1941 — 28. VII.	1941	(b) battles in the Taraschtscha—Boguslaw area
28. VII.	1941 — 25. VII.	1941	battle of pursuit to Dnepropetrovsk
26. VII.	1941 — 28. IX.	1941	defensive fighting in the bridgehead at Dnepropetrovsk
29. IX.	1941 — 10. X.	1941	battle on the Sea of Azov
12. X.	1941 — 21. XI.	1941	battles of pursuit toward the Donez
12. X.	1941 — 20. X.	1941	1. pursuit battles toward Rostov in the east Ukraine
21. X.	1941 — 21. XI.	1941	2. fighting in the Don basin
22. XI.	1941 — 21. VII.	1942	defensive battles in the Donez region
21. XI.	1941 — 1. XII.	1941	1st defensive battle east of the Mius
1. XII.	1941 — 21. VII.	1942	2nd defence in the Mius position

For the members of the SS who remained behind in Lublin, the following was entered in their *Wehrpaß* from 22. VI. 1941 until their return to their units: employed in the Army's rear areas.

1942

21. VII.	1942 — 18. XI.	1942	offensive to the east
21. VII.	1942 — 25. VII.	1942	battle for Rostov and Bataisk
26. VII.	1942 — 18. VII.	1942	advance across the Kuban into the Maikop region
19. VIII.	1942 — 14. IX.	1942	battles in the Caucasus mountain region and West Caucasus
15. XI.	1942 — 18. XI.	1942	battles in the Terek region
19. XI.	1942 — 30. XII.	1942	battles in the Terek region

1943

31. XII.	1942 — 5. II.	1943	attack and defensive battle east and south of the lower Don and on the Manytsch
6. II.	1943 — 4. III.	1943	defensive battle in the Donez region
5. III.	1943 — 31. III.	1943	defensive fighting in the Donez and Mius positions
1. IV.	1943 — 12. VII.	1943	defensive battles on the central Don
13. VII.	1943 — 16. VII.	1943	defensive battle for Kharkov
17. VII.	1943 — 23. VII.	1943	defensive battle near Isjum
24. VII.	1943 — 10. VIII.	1943	defensive battle for Kharkov
11. VIII.	1943 — 14. IX.	1943	defensive battles in the area west of Kharkov
15. IX.	1943 — 27. IX.	1943	defensive battles east of Kiev
28. IX.	1943 — 12. XI.	1943	defensive battles on the Dnepr
13. XI.	1943 — 13. XII.	1943	defensive battles near Cherkassy
14. XII.	1943 — 17. II.	1944	defensive battles and breakout from Cherkassy pocket

1944

18. II.	1944 — 17. III.	1944	transfer and reestablishment in the Lublin area
18. III.	1944 — 17. III.	1944	battle for Kovel
11. V.	1944 — 18. VII.	1944	end of reestablishment — Army Group reserve in Lublin area — to SS-Troop Training Grounds Heidelager — into area of Sokal and east of Cholm

19. VII.	1944 — 27. VII.	1944	defensive battles in the area Wysokie — Mitewskie
28. VII.	1944 — 12. VIII.	1944	counterattacks in areas of Stanislow and Radzymin
13. VIII.	1944 — 30. VIII.	1944	1st defensive battle for Warsaw east of Radzymin
31. VIII.	1944 — 9. X.	1944	2nd defensive battle for Warsaw near Zergce
10. X.	1944 — 28. X.	1944	3rd defensive battle for Warsaw near Nieporet Serock
29. X.	1944 — 25. XII.	1944	defensive battles east of Modlin
26. XII.	1944 — 31. XII.	1944	transfer to Hungary into the Satz area

1945

1. I.	1945 — 13. I.	1945	1st attack for relief of Budapest—Bicske and Pilis mountains
14. I.	1945 — 27. I.	1945	transfer into Vészprém area and 2nd attack for relief of Budapest with advance to the Danube
28. I.	1945 — 22. II.	1945	defensive battles south of Stuhlweißenburg
23. II.	1945 — 15. III.	1945	defensive battles in the area of Stuhlweißenburg
16. III.	1945 — 21. III.	1945	battle for Stuhlweißenburg
22. III.	1945 — 30. III.	1945	fighting retreat to the Reich Defence position—Heiligenkreuz
31. III.	1945 — 8. V.	1945	defensive battles in the Reich Defence position and south of Fürstenfeld
8. V.		1945	German Army surrenders * Dr. K. G. Klietmann. The Waffen-SS — A Documentation".

XX. WEHRMACHT BULLETINS

Wehrmacht Bulletins which mentioned actions by the WIKING Division
(Karl Cerff. Waffen-SS in Wehrmacht Bulletins. Osnabrück. 1971)

24. 7. 1942	As reported in a special bulletin, troops of the Army, the Waffen-SS and Slovakian units, supported by the Luftwaffe, have broken through Rostov's strongly-manned and built defensive positions along the entire front and after hard fighting have taken this city which is important as a traffic and port centre.
4. 8. 1942	In a daring advance, fast units of the Army and Waffen-SS have reached the Kuban river in several places.
5. 8. 1942	On the Kuban the important rail junction point Krapotkin was taken by storm by a unit of the Waffen-SS after heavy fighting.
9. 8. 1942	Fast units of the Army and the Waffen-SS have crossed the Laba and are attacking westward in the direction of Maikop.
7. 10. 1942	Despite unfavourable weather and terrain, south of the Terek units of the Army and the Waffen-SS have taken the important oil region city of **Malgobek** following bitter close-in fighting.
28. 12. 1942	The **SS-Division WIKING**, comprising Danish, German, Finnish, Flemish, Dutch and Norwegian volunteers, has once again distinguished itself in battle.
6. 12. 1943	Near **Cherkassy** units of the **SS-Panzerdivision WIKING** have especially distinguished themselves through their exemplary conduct in fighting during the day-long seesaw battles.
18. 2. 1944	Further to the reported freeing of the German Kampfgruppe encircled west of **Cherkassy**, the Wehrmacht High Command reports: the reception of the units which fought their way free is completed. The forces of the Army and Waffen-SS which have been cut off in this sector under the command of Artillery General Stemmermann and Generalleutnant Lieb since 28. January, have resisted heroically the attacks by far superior enemy forces and in bitter fighting have broken through the enemy's encircling ring. In doing so, the commanders and troops have added a further glowing example of heroic perseverance, daring spirit of attack and self-sacrificing comradeship to the history of German soldiery.
3. 4. 1944	During the fighting in the **Kovel** area during recent days, **SS-Obersturmführer Nicolussilek, Company Commander in an SS-Panzerregiment**, has especially distinguished himself.
6. 4. 1944	The garrison of the city of **Kovel**, encircled since 17. March, has resisted weeklong attacks by far superior enemy forces with exemplary bravery under the command of **SS-Gruppenführer and Generalleutnant der Waffen-SS Gille**.
11. 7. 1944	In the **Kovel** area units of the Army and Waffen-SS have in four days of hard defensive fighting repulsed the advance of ten Soviet rifle divisions, a tank corps and two tank brigades causing the enemy considerable losses in men and material. During this fighting, the cooperation of all arms at the front and in the rear

resulted in the destruction of 295 enemy tanks. The 342. Inf. Division from the Rhine-Mosel area commanded by Generalmajor Nickel, the 26. Inf. Division from Rhine-Westphalia under the command of Oberst Frommberger and **a Kampfgruppe of 5. SS-Pz.Div. WIKING commanded by SS-Standartenführer Mühlenkamp** have distinguished themselves through their exemplary steadfastness.

2. 8. 1944   North of **Warsaw**, units of the Army and Waffen-SS, supported by close support aircraft, threw back the Bolsheviks in a counterattack.

25. 8. 1944   During the successful defensive fighting on the Vistula and northeast of Warsaw, **IV. SS-Panzerkorps** has destroyed 98 enemy tanks between 18. and 22. August.

2. 9. 1944   During the successful defensive battles northeast of **Warsaw**, the **IV. SS-Panzerkorps under the command of SS-Gruppenführer and Generalleutnant der Waffen-SS Gille** with the SS-Panzerdivisions WIKING and TOTENKOPF and the Army units under its command has distinguished itself through unshakeable steadfastness and courageous counterblows.

20. 1. 1945   In **Hungary** units of the Army and Waffen-SS have broken through the strongly-built Bolshevik positions east of the **Platensee** and have advanced as far as the Danube.

8. 4. 1945   At the **German-Hungarian frontier** units of the Army and Waffen-SS have brought the enemy's assault in the direction of Graz to a halt in day long attack and defensive battles and closed the gaps in the front.

XXI. TABLE OF FIELD POST NUMBERS

Status as of 26. May 1941

Division Headquarters with motorcycle messenger platoon 16 284
SS-Inf.Regiment GERMANIA

    H.Q. with signals platoon, motorcycle messenger platoon 30 003
    and band platoon.

I. Battalion	33 576	14. Company	37 705
II. Battalion	30 629	15. Company	37 705
III. Battalion	34 002	16. Company	37 705
13. Company	37 705	17. Company	09 335

SS-Inf.Regiment WESTLAND

    H.Q. with signals platoon, motorcycle messenger platoon 25 854
    and band platoon.

I. Battalion	26 907	14. Company	30 377
II. Battalion	27 026	15. Company	31 465
III. Battalion	28 109	16. Company	32 517
13. Company	29 238	17. Company	09 998

SS-Inf.Regiment NORDLAND

    H.Q. with signals platoon, motorcycle messenger platoon 17 038
    and band platoon.

I. Battalion	18 149	14. Company	22 540
II. Battalion	19 272	15. Company	13 648
III. Battalion	20 361	16. Company	24 735
13. Company	21 497	17. Company	10 230

SS-Art.Regiment 5

    H.Q. with signals platoon, met. unit, printing troop 20 060
    and music corps.

I. Battalion	21 432	III. Battalion	23 604
II. Battalion	22 855	IV. Battalion	24 976

SS-Survey Battery 25 328

SS-Signals Battalion 5

    H.Q. 33 631
    1. Company 35 883
    2. Company 34 759

SS-Reconnaissance Battalion 5

H.Q.			39 688
1. Company	40 546	3. Company	35 883
2. Company	41 487	4. Company	42 213

SS-Pionier Battalion 5

H.Q.	44 189	3. Company	47 118
1. Company	45 054	Bridging Column	46 899
2. Company	46 029	1st Pi-Column	47 926

SS-Panzerjäger-Abt. 5

H.Q.	45 750	2. Company	43 578
1. Company	44 615	3. Company	42 439

SS-Flak-MG-Battalion

H.Q.	41 386	2. Company	43 128
1. Company	40 249	3. Company	44 467

Status as of Summer 1944

Division H.Q.
SS-Panzer-Grenadier-Rgt. 10
SS-Panzer-Grenadier-Rgt. 9
SS-Panzer-Grenadier-Btl. NARWA
SS-Aufklärungs-Abt. 5   48 314

SS-Panzer-Regiment   56 601

H.Q.	58 040	II. Battalion	57 084
I. Battalion	08 158	5. Company	58 753
1. Company	09 274	6. Company	57 062
2. Company	10 927	7. Company	59 907
3. Company	11 031	8. Company	56 834
4. Company	48 968	Pionier Company	56 305

SS-Panzerjäger-Abt. 5
SS-Sturmgeschütz-Abt. 5   02 131
SS-Sturmgeschütz-Battery   27 203
SS-Art.Regiment 5

SS-Flak-Abt. 5

H.Q.					40 017
1. Company	41 432		3. Company		43 187
2. Company	42 640		4. Company		25 596

SS-Pionier-Battalion 5
SS-Nachrichten-Abt. 5
SS-Feldersatz-Battalion 5   19 637

XXII. WAFFEN-SS SERVICE RANKS

SS-Rank	Wehrmacht
SS-Schütze	Schütze
SS-Sturmmann	Gefreiter
SS-Rottenführer	Obergefreiter
SS-Unterscharführer	Unteroffizier
SS-Scharführer	Unterfeldwebel
SS-Oberscharführer	Feldwebel
SS-Hauptscharführer	Oberfeldwebel
SS-Sturmführer	Hauptfeldwebel
SS-Standarten-Oberjunker	Fähnrich
SS-Untersturmführer	Leutnant
SS-Obersturmführer	Oberleutnant
SS-Hauptsturmführer	Hauptmann
SS-Sturmbannführer	Major
SS-Obersturmführer	Oberstleutnant
SS-Standartenführer	Oberst
SS-Oberführer	—
SS-Brigadeführer and Generalmajor der Waffen-SS	Generalmajor
SS-Gruppenführer and Generalleutnant der Waffen-SS	Generalleutnant
SS-Obergruppenführer and General der Waffen-SS	General
SS-Oberstgruppenführer and Generaloberst der Waffen-SS	Generaloberst Generalfeldmarschall also Feldmarschall

XXIII. EXPLANATION OF GERMAN TERMS AND ABBREVIATIONS

Aufklärungs-Abteilung (A.A.) — Reconnaissance battalion
Abteilung (Abt.) — Usually a battalion also a section or detachment
Adjutant beim Stabe (IIa) — Staff adjutant
Armee-Korps (A. K.) — Army Corps
Artillerieführer (Arfü) — Division artillery commander
Artillerie-Regiment (A.R.) — Artillery regiment
Armee-Oberkommando (AOK) — Army high command, headquarters
Artilleriekommandeur (Arko) — Artillery commander
Aufschlag-Zünder (A.Z.) — Impact fuse
Balka — Russian. A gorge or ravine
Beiwagen-Kraftrad (B-Krad) — Sidecar motorcycle
Beobachtungs-Offizier (B-Offz.) — Artillery observation post officer
Beobachtungsstelle (B-Stelle) — Observation post
Bund Deutscher Offizier (BDO) — League of German Officers. A group formed from captured German officers sympathetic to the Soviets

Division Nachschub Führer — Chief of supply services (Div.)
Divisionsarzt — Division surgeon
Einsatzort (E.O.) — Area where units are to be sent into action
Eisernes Kreuz (E.K.) — Iron Cross
Erkennungsmarke (Erk.Marke) — Identification disk, "dog tag"
Ersatzabteilung (E-Abt.) — Replacement training battalion
Fernsprechtrupp (Fe Trupp) — Telephone section
Flak-Abteilung (FlakAbt) — Antiaircraft battalion
Fliegerkorps — Air corps, subordinate to a Luftflotte
Flugabwehr-Kanone (Flak) — Antiaircraft gun
Freikorps — Post WW-I military formation of ex-Army members
Führerhauptquartier (FHQ) — Hitler's field headquarters
Führungshauptamt (FHA) — Administrative headquarters
Funkstaffel — Radio detachment
Gebirgs-Division (Geb.Div.) — Mountain infantry division
Gebirgsjäger (Geb.Jg.) — Mountain infantryman
Gefechtsgruppe (Gef.Gr.) — A combat group which could be comprised of elements of units. Not a permanent formation as a Division but intended to perform a specified function for a period of time.

Gefechtsstand (Gef.Std.) — Command post
geheim (geh.) — secret
geheime Kommandosache (geh.Kdos.) — Secret military document
General der Artillerie (Gen.d.Art.) — General of the Artillery
General der Gebirgstruppen (Gen.d.Geb.Tr.) — General of Mountain Troops
General der Kavallerie (Gen.d.Kav.) — General of the Cavalry

General der Panzertruppe (Gen.d.Pz.Tr.)	General of Panzer Troops
Generalkommando (Gen.Kdo.)	Corps Headquarters
1. Generalstabsoffizier (Führung) (Ia)	1st General Staff Officer (Command)
2. Generalstabsoffizier (Versorgung) (Ib)	2nd General Staff Officer (Supply)
3. Generalstabsoffizier (Ic) (Feindnachrichten/ Sicherheit)	3rd General Staff Officer (Intelligence on the enemy/ security)
GPU	Abbreviation for Soviet Secret Police
Hauptamt (HA.)	Headquarters
Heeresgruppe (H.Gr.)	Group of armies
Hauptkampflinie (HKL)	Main line of resistance
Infanteriedivision (I.D. or Inf.Div.)	Infantry division
Infanteriegeschütz (IG)	Infantry gun, howitzer. A light piece which travelled with the infantry.
Infanteriepionier Infantry combat engineer	Ikagruppe Infantry combat group
Infanterie-Regiment (Inf.Rgt.)	Infantry regiment
Jägerdivision, Regiment	Light infantry division or regiment
Kavallerie-Division (Kav.Div.)	Cavalry division
Kessel	Literally "cauldron" equivalent to a pocket—refers to encircled forces
Kolkhoze	Russian. Soviet collective farm
Kraftrad (Krad)	Motorcycle
Kommandeur (Kdr.)	Commander, commanding officer
Kommandierender General (Komm.Gen.)	Commanding General
Kompanie (Kp.)	Company
Kradmelder	Motorcycle messenger
Kriegstagebuch (KTB)	War diary
Lastkraftwagen (LKW)	Lorry, truck
Maschinengewehr (MG)	Machine gun
Mörser	Howitzer calibre 210 mm or larger
motorisiert (mot.)	Motorized
Maschinenpistole (MPi.)	Submachine gun
Nachrichtenabteilung (Nachr.Abt.)	Signals battalion
Nachschubtruppen (Nachsch.Tr.)	Supply troops, units
Oberbefehlshaber (OB)	Commander in Chief
Oberkommando des Heeres (OKH)	Army High Command
Oberkommando der Luftwaffe (OKL)	Airforce High Command
Oberkommando der Wehrmacht (OKW)	Command of the Armed Forces
Ordonnanzoffizier (OO)	Special missions staff officer
O1/O2/O3	1st, 2nd and 3rd special missions staff officers
Orts Unterkunft (O.U.)	Billets
Pakfront	Antitank position
Panje	Russian. Horse drawn cart common in the Soviet Union

Panzerabwehr-Kanone (Pak)	Antitank gun
Panzerfaust	Hand held antitank weapon
Panzergrenadier-Regiment (Pz.Gren.Rgt.)	Motorized infantry regiment
Panzerjäger (Pz.Jg.)	Member of an antitank unit
Panzerjägerabteilung (Pz.Jg.Abt)	Antitank battalion
Panzerkraftwagen (PKW)	Armoured car
Panzerkorps (Pz.Korps)	Armoured corps
Panzerschreck	Antitank weapon similar to American "bazooka"
Panzerspähwagen	Armoured scout car
Personalabteilung (IIb)	Personnel section
Personenkraftwagen (PKW)	Personnel carrier, motor car
Pionier-Bataillon (Pi.Btl.)	Engineer battalion
Reichsarbeitdienst (RAD)	Reich Labour Service
Reichswehr	German army following WW-I
Ritterkreuz (RK)	Knight's Cross
Sanitäts-Abteilung (San.Abt.)	Medical battalion
Schützen-Division (Schtz.Div.)	Rifle division
Schützenpanzerwagen (SPW)	Armoured personnel carrier
Schwimmwagen	Swim capable version of VW-Kubelwagen
Schützenpanzerwagen (SPW)	Armoured personnel carrier
Sturzkampfbomber (Stuka)	Dive bomber
SS-Verfügungstruppe (VT)	SS-Reserve unit
Storch (Fl-156)	STOL aircraft built by Fieseler often used as communications and liason aircraft
Sturmgeschütz (StuG)	Assault gun
Tagebuch-Nummer (Tgb. Nr.)	Log book number
Truppenkameradschaft WIKING (Tr.Kdschft WIKING)	WIKING members association
Versorgungsdienst	Supply service
verstärkt (verst.)	Reinforced
Vierlingsflak	Quadruple barrelled 20 mm antiaircraft gun
Volksdeutsche	People of German descent living in a country other than Germany
Vorausabteilung (VA)	Advance detachment
Vorgeschobener Beobachter (VB)	Forward (artillery) observer
Zugkraftwagen (Zkw)	Prime mover, half track carrier
Zwillingsflak	Twin barrelled 20 mm antiaircraft gun

XXIV. FOOTNOTES

Introduction

1. In the case of the Danish volunteers, of whom approx. 11,000 served in the German combat forces and about 30% were killed in action, they were guaranteed explicitly that they would be entitled to their previous positions within the Danish Armed Forces on their return. (Aide-mémoire from Udenrig Minister concerning *Freikorps DANMARK*) Following the war, however, the Danish government, acting on a suggestion from the Danish resistance movement, passed a law on 1. 6. 1945 which not only abolished these guarantees but imposed severe penalties, loss of assets and loss of political and other rights for having served in the German armed forces. All this took place even though all of the Danish career officers were in possession of a Royal authorization which permitted them to serve with German combat forces and was signed by the War Minister.
2. *"Die Freiwilligen—Idee und Opfergang"*, Göttingen, 1958
3. *"Soldaten wie andere auch—Der Weg der Waffen-SS "* (Soldiers like the Others—The Path of the Waffen-SS), Paul Hausser, Osnabrück, 1966, pages 43—47

I. Establishment and deployment

The Division's Origins

1. From Dr. K. G. Klietmann, *"Die Waffen-SS—eine Dokumentation"*, Osnabrück, 1965, page 133
2. SS-FHA Ia diary No. 184/40 from 3. 12. 1940
3. From Dr. K. G. Klietmann, *"Die Deutsche Wehrmacht—Uniform und Ausrüstung 1934—45"*, page 164. This states that the corresponding order of the *RF-SS* was published in the *Waffen-SS* Orders Paper, third year, No. 17, page 71, No. 303 on 1. Sept. 1942. Dr. Klietmann further points out that according to an explanation by Gen. Gille, the sleeve bands were likely already given out to the troops in early 1941.
4. See the *Waffen-SS* Orders Paper, Third Year, Berlin, 1. 12. 1942, No. 23, Page 103, No. 428

The Commanders

1. *"Die SS—Tragödie einer deutschen Epoche"*, Munich, 1956, page 91
2. *"Geschichte der Waffen-SS"*, Düsseldorf, 1967, page 263

Experiences with the European Volunteers

1. From Egon Alois Bartetzko, "Military Collaboration in the Germanic Countries 1940—45", chapter "The Formation of the Wiking Division", University of California, Los Angeles, USA, 1966, Thesis for Degree of Master of Arts in History
2. Leader of the Nationaal Socialistische Beweging (NSB) Holland (Dutch National Socialist Movement)

Drill and Training Grounds
1. See Document Appendix No. 1

II. Action in the East
Lemberg—Tarnopol—Proskurow—Shitomir
1. *"Geschichte des Zweiten Weltkriegs"*, Bonn 1951
2. *"Der Hitler-Stalin-Pakt"*, Darmstadt, 1962
3. *"Verlorene Siege"*, Godesberg, 1955
4. W. Görlitz, *"Keitel—Verbrecher oder Offizier"*, Göttingen, 1961
5. J. von Ribbentrop, *"Zwischen London und Moskau"*, Leoni, 1961 and A. von Ribbentrop, *"Deutsche-englische Geheimverbindungen"*, Tüblingen, 1966

First Test against the Enemy
1. Combat report in possession of the WIKING Tr.Kdschft. archive
2. Compare also H. Lanz *"Gebirgsjäger—Die 1. Geb. Div. 1935—1945"*, Bad Nauheim, 1954, page 139
3. See Document Appendix No. 2
4. Testimony before the International Military Tribunal in Nuremberg in July 1946

Tarnopol—Satanow—Husyatin—Proskurow
1. From H. Lanz *"Gebirgsjäger—Die 1. Geb. Div. 1935—1945"*, pages 139/40
2. as 1.
3. See Document Appendix No. 3

The *NORDLAND* Rgt. Stops a Soviet Army Corps
1. Enemy signals summary No. 40 PzA.O.K.1—Ic/AO No. 4627/41 secr.

The *GERMANIA* Regiment's Defensive Success
1. See Document Appendix No. 4

Combat in the Battle for Uman
1. See Document Appendix No. 5
2. See Document Appendix No. 6

III. Through Smela—Korsun to the Dnjepr

The Battle near Smela
1. See Document Appendix No. 7
2. Compare also v. Mackensen, *"Vom Bug zum Kaukasus"*, Neckargemünd, 1967

Crossing the Dnjepr—Establishing the Bridgehead
1. Compare also G. Werdorf, *Standartenoberjunker Normann* ", Siegburg, 1962, page 113
2. Report by W. Tieke in possession of the WIKING Tr.Kdschft. archive
3. See Document Appendix No. 8

The Capture of Kamenka and Enlarging the Bridgehead
1. From *"Die Freiwilligen"*, Steiner, Göttingen, 1958, pages 104/105

Krementschug—Opening the Dnjepropetrowsk Bridgehead
1. See Document Appendix No. 9
2. See Document Appendix No. 10
3. See Document Appendix No. 11

A Destructive Battle of Encirclement
1. See Document Appendix No. 12
2. See Document Appendix No. 13

IV. The Winter Battle for Rostov
1. From Eberhard von Mackensen, *"Vom Bug zum Kaukasus "*, Neckargemünd, 1967

Advance Despite Stiffening Resistance
1. From Hans Steets, *"Gebirgsjäger zwischen Dnjepr und Don"*, Heidelberg, 1957, pages 52/53

In Combat with Superior Enemy Forces
1. From Hans Steets, *"Gebirgsjäger zwischen Dnjepr und Don"*, Heidelberg, 1957, pages 70/71
2. From Wolfgang Werthen, *"Geschichte der 16. Pz.Div. 1939—1945"*, 1958, pages 75/76

First Retreat
1. See Document Appendix No. 14
2. from Hans Steets, *"Gebirgsjäger zwischen Dnjepr und Don"* (Mountain Troops between the Dnjepr and Don) page 107

In the Winter Position on the Mius
1. Compare Hans Steets, *"Gebirgsjager zwischen Dnjepr and Don"* page 107
2. See Document Appendix No. 15
3. See Document Appendix No. 16

A High Ranking Visitor from Finland
1. See *WIKING* Division strength reports (XVIII.)
2. Compare also *"Der Schicksalsweg der norwegischen Freiwilligen-Div. der Waffen-SS"*, Osnabrück, vol. 12, issue 4 from April 1966, page 11

Turn of the Year 1941/42
1. See Document Appendix No. 17
2. See Document Appendix No. 18
3. See Document Appendix No. 19
4. See Document Appendix No. 20
5. Compare Leon Degrelle, **"Die verlorene Legion**", Stuttgart, page 54

With *I./WESTLAND* in the *"Felsennest"*
1. See Document Appendix No. 21
2. See Document Appendix No. 21

Bringing Men and Material up to Strength
1. Written statement provided to the author
2. One of the former K.U.K. officer's favorite methods of address

Attack on Rostov
1. Ziegler was later transferred to the *Waffen-SS*, named Chief of the General Staff of *III. (germ.) SS-Pz.Korps* and following his promotion to the rank of *SS-Brigadeführer und Generalmajor der Waffen-SS* in 1944 became Commander of *11. SS-Pz.Gren.Div. NORDLAND* following the death of *SS-Gruppenführer und Generalleutnant der Waffen-SS* Fritz von Scholz. In that post he fell during the defence of Berlin.
2. From Johannes Mühlenkamp, the capture of Rostov in *"Der Freiwillige"*, volume 23, issues 5 and 6 from May/June 1977

V. Forward to the Caucasus!
1. From Paul Carell, *"Unternehmen Barbarossa"*, Frankfurt/M., 1963, pages 488/489

The battle for Krapotkin
1. See appendix, "Official List of Engagements"
2. In *Tr.Kdschft. WIKING* archive
3. See appendix, "Wehrmacht Bulletins"

The Laba Sector and Belaja
1. From Paul Carell, *"Unternehmen Barbarossa"*, page 495

Conquest of the Maikop Oil Region
1. See Document Appendix No. 22

VI. Battle in the Caucasus

Transition to Defence

1. From the notes of Max Stöckle, in possession of the *Tr.Kdschft.* WIKING archive

A Difficult Operation

1. From A. S. Sawjalow—T. J. Kaljadin, *"Die Schlacht um den Kaukasus 1942—1943"* (The Battle for the Caucasus 1942—1943), East Berlin, page 65
2. From *"Die Freiwilligen—Idee und Opfergang"*, (Ideal and Sacrifice) Felix Steiner, Göttingen, 1958, page 169
3. From the notes of Max Stöckle, in possession of the *Tr.Kdschft.* WIKING archive *The Capture of Malgobek*
1. From *"Del Caucaso A Leningrado"* (From the Caucasus to Leningrad), v. Argent, Mil. Verein, Buenos Aires, 1958, volume II, pages 67/68
2. From the notes of Max Stöckle, in possession of the *Tr.Kdschft.* WIKING archive

Defence between Fiagdon and Alagir

1. From the personal records of Felix Steiner
2. From *"Kampf im Gebirge"* (Battle in the Mountains), Munich, 1957, pages 196/202
3. From *"Die Schlacht um den Kaukasus"* (The Battle for the Caucasus 1942—1943), page 117

VII. Return to the Donez

1. From *"Verlorene Siege"* (Lost Victories), v. Manstein, Godesberg, 1957, page 376

Departure from the Caucasus

1. Neckargemünd, 1962, pages 94/95

Turn of the Year 1942/43—the Race to Rostov

1. Report in possession of the *Tr.Kdschft.* WIKING archive
2. Document in possession of the *Tr.Kdschft.* WIKING archive
3. Note in *Tr.Kdschft.* WIKING archive
4. Steiner, *"Die Freiwilligen"*, pages 189/191

In Combat with Tank Group Popoff

1. Text as recalled by General Steiner in his records
2. v. Tippelskirch, *"Geschichte des 2. Weltkrieges"* (History of the Second World War), Bonn, 1951, page 282

3. Text from Felix Steiner's records
4. See Document Appendix No. 23

The End of Tank group Popoff
1. See Document Appendix No. 24
2. v. Manstein, *"Verlorene Siege"*, Bonn, 1955, page 449
3. In possession of *Tr.Kdschft. WIKING* archive

In the Suchoj-Torez Sector
1. Original in the *Tr.Kdschft. WIKING* archive

Departure of the *NORDLAND* Regiment and the Finnish Battalion
1. Mauno Jokipii, *"Suomalaisen SS-pataljoonan hajoittaminen v. 1943"* (The Disbanding of the Finnish SS-Battalion in the Year 1943), *Historiallinen Aikakauskirja Nr. 2/1960, Helsinki, pages 251/252*
2. as 1.

Arrival of the Estonian Battalion
1. From *"Die deutsche Wehrmacht 1934—45"*, Dr. K. G. Klietmann, volume 19, *"Finnisches Frw. Bataillon der Waffen-SS"*
2. From *"Die Waffen-SS"*, Dr. K. G. Klietmann, Osnabrück, 1965, page 134
3. Bonn, 1955, page 501

VIII. Defensive Battle for Kharkov and Isjum

The Estonians' Baptism of Fire
1. Wolf Schneider, *"Mit der I./SS-Pz.Abt. 5 im Osten"*, manuscript in *Tr.Kdschft. WIKING* archive
2. The Defensive battle for Kharkov and the Dnjepr

The Defensive battle for Kharkov and the Dnjepr
1. According to Eggers the *Waffen-SS* frontline reporter unit was later named *Standarte Kurt Eggers*
2. Copy of the manuscript of the PK report in the *Tr.Kdschft. WIKING* archive

In Combat with Partisans and Enemy Paratroops
1. From Gen.d.Pz.Tr. a.D. Walther K. Nehring, *Der Einsatz russischer Fallschirmverbände in Kampfraum des XXIV. Panzerkorps"* (The Operations of Russian Paratroop units in the Combat Zone of XXIV. Panzer Corps), *Deutsches Soldaten-Jahrbuch 1963 (German Soldiers Yearbook)*, Munich, pages 208/215
2. Condensed from history of 57. I.D. from May 1963 in manuscript, pages 15/16

IX. Defensive Battle on the Dnjepr

1. In possession of the *Tr.Kdschft. WIKING* archive
2. See Document Appendix No. 25

Sturmbrigade *WALLONIEN* Reaches *WIKING*

1. Degrelle, *"Die Verlorene Legion", page 176*
2. K. G. Klietmann, *"Die Waffen-SS—eine Dokumantation "*, Osnabrück, 1965, page 94

Battle at the Irdyn Marsh

1. Members of the "Organization of the communist youth of Russia"

X. The Tscherkassy Pocket

The Pocket Wanders to the West

1. From, *"Der Kessel von Tscherkassy"*, by the *Tr.Kdschft. WIKING*, Hannover, 1963

The Wait for Relief

1. See illustration on page—
2. From *"Sie kämpften für Deutschland"* (They Fought for Germany), East Berlin, 1959
3. See Document Appendix No. 26
4. From, *"Verräter—Das Nationalkomitee "Freies Deutschland" as Keimzelle der sog. DDR"* (Traitor—The National Committee "Free Germany" as germ cell of the so-called DDR) (DDR ® the German Democratic Republic—East Germany), Munich, 1960, page 258
5. Rolf Stoves, *"Die 1. Pz.Div. 1935—1945"*, Bad Nauheim 1961, page 506
6. From, *"Der Kessel v. Tscherkassy"*
7. As 7.

The Last Act

1. See Document Appendix No. 28
2. See Document Appendix No. 29
3. Degrelle, *"Die Verlorene Legion"*, page 294
4. N. von Normann, *"Tscherkassy"*, Heidelberg, 1954, page 116
5. as 4. pages 302/303
6. as 4. page 24
7. as 4. page 526

Breakout to Freedom

1. E. G. Krätschmer, *"Die Ritterkreuzträger der Waffen-SS"*, Göttingen, 1955, page 286
2. See Document Appendix No. 30
3. War diary in possession of the *Tr.Kdschft. WIKING*
4. as 3. page 314
5. Paul Carell, *"Verbrannte Erde"*, Frankfurt Main, 1966, page 380
6. See Document Appendix No. 31
7. See reproduction on page—and Document Appendix No. 32
8. Report in possession of *Tr.Kdschft. WIKING* archive
9. Degrelle, *"Die Verlorene Legion"*, pages 327/328

XI. "Fortress" Kovel

Ostuf. Nicolussi Leck's Success

1. In addition compare the Kovel report of Dr. M. Renz in the magazine *Der Freiwillige*, Osnabrück, volume 12, issues 9-12/1966

The Freeing of Kovel

1. See Document Appendix No. 33

The Tank Battle of Maciejow

1. See also Dr. M. Renz, *"Die Panzerschlacht von Maciejow"*, *"Der Freiwillige"*, Volume 12, issue 3/1966, Osnabrück, page 10
2. See Document Appendix No. 34

XII. From Bialystok to Warsaw

The Division's "Toughest Assignment"

1. Report in possession of the *Tr.Kdschft. WIKING* archive
2. Outflanking the enemy so as not to be seen

Formation of IV. SS-Panzerkorps

1. See Document Appendix No. 35

The Second Defensive Battle

1. See Document Appendix No. 36
2. Ploetz, History of the Second World War, Bielefeld, 1951, page 48

The Third Defensive battle

1. report in possession of the *Tr.Kdschft. WIKING* archive
2. Appendix XIX.

3. In infantryman's jargon "Stalin Organ"
4. According to a report on the Third Defensive battle for Warsaw written following the war by General Gille. Volume with 30 handwritten pages in possession of the *Tr.Kdschft.* WIKING archive

The Battles in the "Wet Triangle"
1. Notes in possession of the *Tr.Kdschft.* WIKING archive
2. Walter Kopp, Oberst in the Bundeswehr, since deceased
3. Report in possession of the 6602Tr.Kdschft. WIKING archive

XIII. Battle in Hungary

Dorpmüllern to Julischka
1. refers to Dr. Julius Dorpmüller, Reich Minister of Transport from 2. 2. 1937 responsible at that time for rail transport
2. Heinz Guderian, *"Erinnerungen eines Soldaten"* (Memories of a Soldier), Heidelberg, 1951, page 349
3. as 2.

The Encirclment of Budapest
1. From Erich Kern, *"Die letzte Schlacht—Ungarn 1944—1945"* (The Last Battle—Hungary 1944—45), Göttingen, 1960, page 53

The First Relief Attempt
1. Stoves, pages 709/710
2. From Peter Gosztony, *"Kampf und Ende der Stadt Budapest"* (The Battle and End of the City of Budapest), Hungarian Institute, Munich, 1964, page 43
3. Hans-Ulrich Rudel, *"Trotzdem"*, Zurich, 1950, pages 212/213
4. as 2. page 43
5. From *"Das Schwarze Korps"*, 1. 2. 1945 *"Das Fort der Unbeugsam* (The Black Corps—The Fort of the Uncomprimising)
6. From *Heeresgruppe Süd* war diary

The Second Relief Attempt
1. Erich Kern, *"Die letzte Schlacht—Ungarn 1944—45"*, page 152

The Third Relief Attempt
1. From Gosztony, *"Kampf und Ende der Stadt Budapest"*, page 50
2. as 1., page 53
3. *Ot Balatona do Veny"* (From Lake Balaton to Vienna), M. M. Malakov, Moscow, 1959, pages 55/56
4. From *"Die 1. SS-pz.Div. 1939—1945"*, Stoves, page 726

5. as 3., pages 58/59
6. Diary of *Ostuf.6601 Jahnke in Tr.Kdschft.* WIKING archive

Irresistable Retreat
1. From *"Die 1. SS-pz.Div. 1939—1945"*, Stoves, page 731
2. Personal notes of Dr. Hübner, History of the *Panzer* units employed in Hungary, Mil.Archives, Koblenz, H. 91-7/1
3. From W. Jester, *"Im Todessturm von Budapest 1945"*, Neckargemünd, 1960, page 126

The 6. *SS-Panzer-Armee* Arrives
1. Kurt Meyer, *"Grenadiere"*, Munich, 1956, page 339
2. Pocketbook release, Munich 1967, page 560
3. From Otto Merk, *Deutscher Kreuzweg 1945—Chronik der letzten 130 Kriegstage"* (German Crossroads—Chronicle of the last 130 Days of the war), special edition of the *"Münchner Merkur"*, February to March 1955, page 14

XIV. Surrender and Imprisonment
1. From the memoirs of R. Pintscher, *"Aus—vorbei?"*, notes in possession of Tr.Kdschft. WIKING

SOURCES

War Diaries, Chronicles
War Diary *heeresgruppe Süd*
War Diary *SS-Pz.Rgt. 5* from 26. 3.—30. 11. 1944
Excerpt from War Diary *III./GERMANIA* from 17. 3. 1944—17. 5. 1944
Chronicle of *2./SS-Panzer-Pionier-Bataillon 5*
War Diary *I./SS-Pz.Rgt. 5,* No. 1, from 9. 2. 1944—30. 11. 1944

Diaries, notes and manuscripts

Bartetzko, Alois Egon Los Angeles	"Military Collaboration in the Germanic Countries 1940—1945". Thesis for a Masters Degree of Arts in History, University of California,
Dr. Hübner	History of the *Panzer* units employed in Hungary. Mil.Archives, Koblenz, H.91-7/1
Gille, Herbert O.	Notes on the Defensive Battles for Warsaw, *Tr.Kdschft. WIKING* Archive
Jahnke, Günther	Diary Dec. 1944—4. 8. 1945. *Tr.Kdschft. WIKING* Archive
Klapdor, Ewald	Study of the outbreak of war between Germany and Russia, manuscript.
Pintscher, R.	"Aus—vorbei?", manuscript
Schneider, Wolf	"*Mit der I./SS-Pz.Abt. 5 im Osten*" Manuscript.
Steiner, Felix	"*Mehrvölker Division WIKING*", Manuscript.
Div. History 57. Inf. Div.	Manuscript, May 1963
Phleps, Arthur	Personal diary
Dorr, Hans	Personal diary

Literature

Buchner, Alex	"*Kampf im Gebirge*", Munich 1957
Carell, Paul	*Unternehmen Barbarossa*", Frankf./M 1963
Carell, Paul	*Verbrannte Erde*", Frankf./M, 1966
Fabry, Philipp W.	*Der Hitler-Stalin Pakt*", Darmstadt, 1962
Görlitz, Walter	*Keitel—Verbrecher oder Offizier*", Göttingen, 1961
Gosztony, Peter	*Kampf und Ende der Stadt Budapest*", Munich, 1964
Guderian, Heinz	"*Erinnerungen eines Soldaten*", Heidelberg, 1951
Hausser, Paul	"*Soldaten wie andere auch—Der Weg der Waffen-SS*", Osnabrück, 1966
Hausser, Paul	"*Waffen-SS im Einsatz*", Göttingen 1953
Kalinov, Kyrill	"*Sowjet Marschälle haben das Wort*", Hamburg, 1950
Kern, Erich	"*Die letzte Schlacht—Ungarn 1944*", Göttingen, 1960
Kern, Erich	"*Der Große Rausch*", 2nd edition, Göttingen, 1961
Klatt, P.	"*Geschichte der 3. Geb.Div. 1939—1945* ", Bad Nauheim, 1958
Klietmann, K. G.	"*Die Waffen-SS—eine Dokumentation*", Osnabrück, 1965
Klietmann, K. G.	"*Die Deutsche Wehrmacht 1934—1945*", Volume 29: "*Ärmelstreifen der Waffen-SS I: 5 SS-Pz.Div. WIKING*", Berlin, 1964
Krätschmer, E. G.	"*Ritterkreuzträger der Waffen-SS*", Göttingen, 1955
Lanz, Hubert	"*Gebirgsjäger—Die 1. Gebirgsdivision 1935—1945*", Bad Nauheim, 1954
v. Mackensen, Eberhard	"*Vom Bug zum Kaukasus*", Neckargemünd 1967
Malakov, M. M.	"*Ot balatona do Veny*", Moscow, 1951
v. Manstein, Erich	"*Verlorene Siege*", Godesberg, 1955
v. Manteuffel	"*Die 7. Pz.Division im Zweiten Weltkrieg—Einsatz und Kampf der* "*Gespenster-Division" 1939—1945*", 1965
Marini, A.	"*Del Caucaso A Leningrado*", hrsg. v. Arg. Militärverein, Buenos Aires, 1958, 2nd vol.
Panzermeyer	"*Grenadiere*", Munich 1956
Ploetz	"*Geschichte des Zweiten Weltkrieges*" Bielefeld 1951
Rebentisch, E.	"*Zum Kaukasus und zu den Tauern, die Geschichte der 23. Pz.Div. 1941—1945*", 1963

Reitlinger, Gerard	"Die SS—Tragödie einer deutsche Epoche". Munich 1956
Reitlinger, Gerard	"Ein Haus auf Sand gebaut, Hitlers Gewaltpolitik in Rußland, 1941—1944". Hamburg 1962
Ribbentrop, Annelies v.	"Deutsch-englische Geheimverbindungen" Tübingen 1966
Ribbentrop, Joachim v.	"Zwischen London und Moskau", Leoni 1961
Rudel, Hans-Ulrich	"Trotzdem", Zurich 1950
Savyalov, A. S. and Kalyadin, T. J.	"Die Schlacht um den Kaukasus 1942—43" East Berlin
	"Sie Kämpften für Deutschland", East Berlin 1959
Dr. Schwarz, Andreas	Chronik des Inf.Rgts. 248, Vol II,Füth Bavaria, 1977
Steets, Hans	"Gebirgsjäer zwischen Dnjepr und Don ", Heidelberg 1957
Stein, George H.	"Geschichte der Waffen-SS, Düsseldorf, 1967
Stoves, Rolf	"1. Panzerdivision 1935—1945", Bad Nauheim 1961
Straßner, Peter	"Verräter—Das "Nationalkomitee" "Freies Deutschland" als Keimzelle der sog. DDR", Munich 1960
v. Tippelskirch, Kurt	"Geschichte des Zweiten Weltkrieges", Bonn 1951
v. Vormann, N.	"Tscherkassy", Heidelberg 1954 "Waffen-SS im Bild", Göttingen 1957
Wanhöfer, Günter	"Pioniere nach Vorne", Neckargemünd, 1962
Werdorf, G.	"Standartenoberjunker Normann", Siegburg 1962
Werth, Alexander	"Rußland im Krieg 1941—1945", Munich 1965
Werthen, Wolfgang	"Geschichte der 16.Pz.Division 1939—1945", Bad Nauheim 1958
Wich, Rudolph	"Baden-Württemb. Divisionen im Zweiten Weltkrieg—23. Pz.Div. ", "Zwei Weltkriege im Buch", Milit. Schriftweiser, Vol. 2, 3. Neckargemünd 1966 "Der Kessel von Tscherkassy", Tr.Kdschft. WIKING", Hannover 1963

Literature and Publications Concerning the *Waffen-SS* European Volunteers

Degrelle, Leon	"Die Verlorene Legion", Stuttgart
Herzog, Robert	"Die Volksdeutschen in der Waffen-SS", Tübingen 1955
Klietmann, K. G.	"Die Deutsche Wehrmacht—Uniform und Ausrüstung 1934—1945" Vol. 19 "Finnisches Freiw. Bataillon der Waffen-SS", Berlin 1960
Lappi-Seppälä,	"Haudat Dnjeprin varrella. SS-miehen Sakari päiväkirjan lehtiä", Helsinki 1945
Lauttamus, Niilo	"Vieraan kypärän alla" Novel by a former volunteer, 1957, 4th edition
Lauttamus, Niilo	"Rautasaappaat", 1965
Parvilahti, Unto	"Terekille ja takaisin. Suomalaisen vapaaehtoisjoukon vaiheita Saksan itärintamalla 1941—1943", Helsinki 1959
Tyrkkö, Jukka	"Suomalaisen suurodassa. SS-vapaaehtoisten vaiheita jääkäreiden jäljillä 1941—43", Helsinki 1960
Jokipii, Mauno	"Suomalaisen SS-pataljoonan hajoittaminen v. 1943", Helsinki 1960
Jokipii, Mauno	"Himmlerin Suomen-matka v. 1942", helsinki 1960
Jokipii, Mauno	"Panttipataljoona", Helsinki 1968